Islamabad and the Politics of International Development in Pakistan

This is a highly original account of the design and development of Pakistan's capital city: one of the most iconic and ambitious urban reconstruction projects of the twentieth century. Balancing archival research with fresh, theoretical insights, Markus Daechsel surveys the successes and failures of Greek urbanist Constantinos A. Doxiadis's most ambitious endeavour, Islamabad, analysing how the project not only changed the international order, but also the way in which the Pakistani state operated in the 1950s and 1960s. In dissecting Doxiadis's fraught relationship with Pakistani policy makers, bureaucrats and ordinary citizens, the book offers an unprecedented account of Islamabad's place in post-war international development. Daechsel provides new insights into this period and explores the history of development as a charged, transnational encounter between foreign consultants and donors on the one side, and the post-colonial nation state on the other.

MARKUS DAECHSEL is Senior Lecturer in Modern South Asian History at Royal Holloway, University of London.

Islamabad and the Politics of International Development in Pakistan

Markus Daechsel

CAMBRIDGE
UNIVERSITY PRESS

CAMBRIDGE
UNIVERSITY PRESS

University Printing House, Cambridge CB2 8BS, United Kingdom

Cambridge University Press is part of the University of Cambridge.

It furthers the University's mission by disseminating knowledge in the pursuit of education, learning and research at the highest international levels of excellence.

www.cambridge.org
Information on this title: www.cambridge.org/9781107057173

© Markus Daechsel 2015

First published 2015

Printed in the United Kingdom by Clays, St Ives plc

A catalogue record for this publication is available from the British Library

Library of Congress Cataloguing in Publication data
Daechsel, Markus.
Islamabad and the politics of international development in Pakistan / Markus Daechsel.
    pages   cm. – (Studies in international planning history)
Includes bibliographical references.
ISBN 978-1-107-05717-3 (Hardback)
1. City planning–Political aspects–Pakistan–Islamabad.   2. Economic development–Political aspects–Pakistan.   3. Economic assistance–Political aspects–Pakistan.   4. Islamabad (Pakistan)–History–20th century.-   I. Title.
HT169.P32I8153   2015
307.1′21609549149–dc23   2014039490

ISBN 978-1-107-05717-3 Hardback

Contents

Figures

Acknowledgements

This book has been long in the making, and it is impossible to mention everybody who has helped to make it possible either in a professional or personal capacity.

However, I would like to record my specific thanks to the following:

Alexandros Kyrtsis, who started it all when out of the blue he invited me to speak at the C. A. Doxiadis conference in Athens in December 2006, and opened my way into the Doxiadis Archive, not to mention offering me his hospitality and expert advice on numerous matters relating to this book. A very big 'thank you' also to Giota Pavlidou, librarian and archivist at the Doxiadis Archive, who in her capacity has quite simply been the best professional help any historian could ever hope for.

In Pakistan, Fatima Kaniz Yusuf, Rafay Alam, Sayid Qazi and family, Kamil Khan Mumtaz (and many others) for sharing their expertise with me. Likewise the staff of the National Documentation Centre and CDA Library, Islamabad, for their unfailing professionalism.

Everyone who was available for an oral history interview (see list in Bibliography). Gustav Papanek, Doxiadis's contemporary in Pakistan in the 1950s, for responding to an e-mail enquiry about Doxiadis.

Academic colleagues past and present: Crispin Bates, Paul Nugent, Gajendra Singh, Ashok Malhotra in Edinburgh; Sarah and Humayun Ansari, Dan Haines, Elisabeth Leake, Ali Usman Qasmi, Sandra Halperin at Royal Holloway; elsewhere and through many workshops and conferences: Stephen Legg, Matthew Hull, Stephan Miescher, Will Gould, Ravi Ahuja, Henrike Donner, David Arnold, David Hardiman, Prashant Kidambi, Projit Mukherjee, Jahnavi Phalkey and many others for comments and inspiration along the way. Francis Robinson, Florian Schui and Julia Gallagher for reading parts of the draft.

The Carnegie Endowment for Scottish Universities and the British Academy for awarding me for this project funding as part of the Small Research Grant scheme.

The anonymous readers of the manuscript (as well as of the associated articles listed in the Bibliography). Marigold Acland, Lucy Rhymer and

Amanda George at Cambridge University Press who kept their faith in me despite long delays.

Finally, three children have accompanied this book: Adam – born almost simultaneously with the start of the project and veteran companion on research travels around the world at a very young age, Leo – keeping me company during the writing-up phase, and Amira – recent reminder that it was now really time to finish. To them – and to Yasmin for her never failing patience and love throughout those years – do I dedicate this book.

Note on spelling: In order to avoid anachronisms, the spelling of place names used in the book reflects the usage of the 1950s and 1960s and ignores recent indigenization, e.g. 'Calcutta' instead of 'Kolkata', 'Bombay' instead of 'Mumbai', 'Dacca' instead of 'Dhaka'.

Introduction

The early 1960s brought Pakistan worldwide fame for some of the most ambitious urban reconstruction projects ever attempted: comprehensive slum clearance measures, vast new suburbs, modernist university campuses and, as the crowning achievement of it all, the creation of a new capital city for the nation – Islamabad.[1] These projects were as integral to the dream of 'development' – that great venture of transformation that gripped the world in the second half of the twentieth century – as the jute and cotton mills, hydroelectric dams, green technologies and five-year plans more readily associated with the period. Around the world, from Tema to Brasilia, and from Chandigarh to Ciudad Guyana, new cities and administrative centres were designed from scratch to control the process of urbanization that rapid modernization was expected to unleash.[2] These new departures in urban planning had an immediate

[1] The scholarly literature dedicated to Islamabad as a city and development project is still small. The only monograph in print was written by a leading participant in the project: Yakas, O. (2001), *Islamabad, the birth of a capital*, Karachi, Oxford University Press. Although containing some useful information it is entirely based on the 'official' story of Islamabad from the point of view of the consultancy firm Doxiadis Associates. The most extensive discussion from an architectural point of view is Mahsud, A. Z. K. (2008), *Constantinos A. Doxiadis's plan for Islamabad: the making of a city of the future, 1959–1963*, PhD, Katholieke Universiteit Leuven. For an anthropological take on present-day Islamabad with some useful historical analysis, see Hull, M. S. (2012), *Government of paper: the materiality of bureaucracy in urban Pakistan*, Berkeley, University of California Press. For a historical evaluation that formulates some of the ideas of this book, see Daechsel, M. (2013), 'Misplaced Ekistics: Islamabad and the politics of urban development in Pakistan', *South Asian History and Culture* 4(1): 87–106.

[2] See Arnau, F. (1960), *Brasilia: Phantasie und Wirklichkeit*, Munich, Prestel-Verlag; Evenson, N. (1966), *Chandigarh*, Berkeley, University of California Press; Nilsson, S. (1973), *New capitals of India, Pakistan and Bangladesh*, Lund, Studentlitteratur; Sarin, M. (1982), *Urban planning in the Third World: the Chandigarh experience*, London, Mansell; Holston, J. (1989), *The modernist city: an anthropological critique of Brasilia*, University of Chicago Press; Prakash, V. E. (1997), *Theatres of decolonization: architecture, agency, urbanism*, Seattle, University of Washington Press; Kalia, R. (1999), *Chandigarh: the making of an Indian city*, New Delhi; Oxford, Oxford University Press; Prakash, V. (2002), *Chandigarh's Le Corbusier: the struggle for modernity in postcolonial India*, Seattle, University of Washington Press; Gordon, D. L. A. (2006), *Planning twentieth century*

and lasting impact on the lives of millions, and possessed unique symbolic power to represent what 'development' was all about. Nothing was a more tangible example of 'backwardness' than the unsanitary squalor and chaotic mingling of crowds in Pakistan's historic inner cities, or the fading grandeur of colonial public structures in its cantonments and civil lines; and nothing encapsulated the future better than multitudes settled in row after row of functional mass housing units, new high-rise buildings of concrete and steel, or free-flowing motor traffic on gridiron road patterns. Above all, the optimism of the time demanded a sense of getting things done, and there was no better place to see it in action than a gigantic building site with its newly imported pieces of machinery and armies of workers, and the spectacle of a landscape being gradually transformed by human hand.

Like other advances in development, many of these projects were closely associated with the coming to power of Pakistan's first military regime. Urban reconstruction was one of General Ayub Khan's foremost priorities. Within weeks after the *coup d'état* in October 1958, he had it announced that by summer of the following year, the administration would clear the metropolis Karachi of hundreds of thousands of slum-dwellers and resettle them in the satellite town of Korangi, yet to be designed and built.[3] No Pakistan government before or since has ever attempted such an ambitious display of executive power; and even if not everything turned out to be quite so solid in its success as it first appeared, projects like this earned Ayub a privileged place in history. The 1960s are still commonly remembered as Pakistan's 'golden age', despite such glaring failures as the fruitless 1965 war with India, or the escalation of political discontent in East Pakistan towards secession.

---

capital cities, London, Routledge; Gautherot, M., K. Frampton, S. Burgi and S. Titan (2010), *Building Brasilia*, London, Thames & Hudson. The 'hero' of this book, Constantinos A. Doxiadis, played a major role in several of these landmark projects and was one of the most influential figures to elaborate the connection between development and physical planning at a global scale. But he was hardly unique. Albert Mayer, American architect and urbanist, was a crucial figure in India's first development initiatives, working in the fields of rural reconstruction (the Etawah Pilot Project) as well as city planning (in Bombay and in Chandigarh) and large architectural projects (Gujarat University, Allahabad Agricultural Institute). See Mayer, A. (1967), *The urgent future: people, housing, city, region* [with illustrations], New York, McGraw-Hill Book Co.; Mayer, A. (1958), *Pilot project, India: the story of rural development at Etawah, Uttar Pradesh, by Albert Mayer and associates, in collaboration with McKim Marriott and Richard L. Park. With a foreword by Govind Ballabh Pant*, Berkeley, University of California Press.

[3] This project is discussed extensively in Chapter 4. For an overview see Ansari, S. (2005), *Life after Partition: migration, community and strife in Sindh 1947–1962*, Karachi, Oxford University Press, 181–191; Daechsel, M. (2011b), 'Sovereignty, governmentality and development in Ayub's Pakistan: the case of Korangi Township', *Modern Asian Studies* 45(1): 131–157.

Especially when contrasted with the troubles of more recent decades, the era of development was also the period when for many Pakistanis the Islamic element in the nation's identity did not seem to clash with aspirations of 'modernity', when a growing number of people began to feel 'middle class', and when consumer goods that had been hard to obtain over much of the 1950s became ubiquitous in the market place. More than anything else, Pakistan felt respected in the world. The national airline clothed its flight attendants in uniforms designed by Pierre Cardin, and bureaucrats from South Korea would come to learn from their Pakistani counterparts how economic 'take-off' was achieved.[4]

Pakistan's emergence as a poster child for global development – while it lasted – was not simply the result of domestic political changes. It was a transnational project that involved a whole range of figures and institutions that had not played any major historical role before. There was a new breed of development agencies from the United States and other countries of the rich North, establishing new webs of influence far closer to the ground than conventional diplomatic missions. International organizations like the United Nations and the Colombo Plan set up their own representatives and agencies, as did private philanthropic foundations with global ambitions. They all contributed to the emergence of a footloose and cosmopolitan community of development consultants, ranging from the celebrity expert staying only in five-star hotels and conferring directly with prime ministers and presidents, to humble craftsmen, doctors and engineers sent out on long-term assignments in far flung locations. The Korangi project – Ayub's first flagship development scheme – was an excellent example for the new modus operandi. It involved the Ford Foundation and the United States International Cooperation Administration (the forerunner of USAID) as sources of finance, and was planned and overseen by Constantinos A. Doxiadis, an architect and urbanist from Greece. When the new satellite town was complete, it immediately attracted scores of international visitors. Two American presidents came, as well as other heads of state and royalty from around the world; and with an eye on how such achievements could be replicated in their own countries, also hundreds of development

---

[4] Interview with Shaikh Abdul Rashid (Lahore, 31 October 2007). Samuel P. Huntington regarded Ayub Khan as the 'Lycurgus' of the Third World, Huntington, S. P. (1968), *Political order in changing societies*, New Haven, CT, Yale University Press, p.251. See also Haq, M. u. (1966), *The strategy of economic planning: a case study of Pakistan*, Karachi, Pakistan Branch; Gauhar, A. (1996), *Ayub Khan, Pakistan's first military ruler*, Oxford; New York, Oxford University Press; with more scepticism Talbot, I. (2012), *Pakistan: a modern history*, London, C. Hurst & Co. Publishers Ltd, pp.164–172.

functionaries from Iraq to Indonesia.[5] Korangi, and for that matter most of the other mega-projects of the period, were not only Pakistani achievements, they were milestones for global development as a shared enterprise.

'Development' had the power to change the very nature of the Pakistani state. It not only enmeshed it in a web of international connections but also extended into areas of activity that had not previously been seen as the state's remit. New structural links emerged that tied even the poorest and least educated of Pakistani city dwellers, via local development agencies both inside and outside the official bureaucracy, their foreign consultants and sponsors, to the corridors of power in the rich North. A whole range of otherwise unconnected sites of struggle were brought to influence each other. Battles between the Ford Foundation and right-wing members of Congress in Washington D.C., for instance, began to have a bearing on commercial competition between British and Greek firms of architects, and on institutional rivalries within Pakistani government departments, down to ethnic and family tensions between individual civil servants. Even sectarian clashes between Sunni and Shi^ca Pakistanis in new residential neighbourhoods were now located within a global reference frame.

Nobody personified the international character of development more than Doxiadis, the Greek architect of the Korangi Township, who for a few years at least, became the general's most favoured consultant. The company he had founded in the early 1950s also worked in more than twenty other countries across four continents, and collaborated with colleagues from Egypt, France, the United States and a host of other nationalities.[6] Doxiadis owed much of his global success to the fact that he was seen as America's man by influential circles in Washington D.C., while not being American himself, or, for that matter, of another nationality with a problematic colonial legacy. He had robust anti-communist credentials but otherwise was flexible enough to do business in any kind of political environment across the global South. Customers included not only military autocrats and Middle Eastern petroleum royalty but also charismatic anti-colonial nationalists like the Ghanaian independence leader Kwame Nkrumah. Doxiadis's acquaintance with Pakistan had been long-standing even before he entered the services of the military regime. Between 1954 and 1958, he had been involved with the national

---

[5] See discussion in Chapter 4, pp.170–174.

[6] Bromley, R. (2003), 'Towards global human settlements: Constantinos Doxiadis as entrepreneur, coalition-builder and visionary', *Urbanism: imported or exported?* J. Nasr and M. Volait (eds.), New York, Wiley: 316–340. For a detailed and fully referenced account of Doxiadis's life and career see Chapter 1, pp.34–40.

Planning Commission, helping to draw up the ultimately unsuccessful First Five Year Plan. Later under Ayub, Doxiadis was employed on a dozen or so high-profile commissions across the country, making him one of the most influential practitioners of developmental urbanism of the twentieth century.

While Doxiadis's role in Korangi is often forgotten today, just as the satellite town itself has become yet another part of Greater Karachi, his flagship project is still known to every Pakistani and around the world. It was Islamabad, the new capital. The Greek architect provided the original master plan, which is still followed today, and his company went on to construct the first residential neighbourhoods. Even if it took several more decades to settle and populate the area to give it a real urban feel, by which time Doxiadis was no longer involved with the project, and although most of the monumental buildings in the city were designed by other foreign architects,[7] it is entirely appropriate to refer to him as the 'father' of the city. With its orientation towards future growth and its unusual axial design, Islamabad was a space of development par excellence. It exemplified both a new way of making sense of the world, and new possibilities of governance. Doxiadis's vision was meticulous, intrusive and self-consciously altruistic. At least on paper, no aspect of urban life had been overlooked and nothing had been left to chance, from how a prospective resident slept or cooked to the precise width of a sewerage outlet. In fact, far more emphasis was placed on everyday urban functions than on the usual requirement to symbolize national aspirations. This marked a reversal of established priorities. New capitals had been founded by South Asian rulers many times in the past to give an architectural shape to their power and political ideals – for example Emperor Akbar's Fatehpur Sikri, Maharaja Jai Singh's Jaipur, New Delhi under the British, and closest in time to Islamabad itself, Nehru's Chandigarh.[8] But as a sign of changing times, Doxiadis's

---

[7] CDA publicity material published in 1979 includes Gio Ponti, Edward Stone and G. W. Brigden among others. Wasti, S. A. T. (1979), *Islamabad ... the city of peace*, Islamabad, Directorate of Public Relations, Capital Development Authority. Kenzo Tange's botched Pakistan Supreme Court Building of the 1980s was the latest notable addition designed by international celebrity architects. Husain, H. (2005), 'Kenzo Tange – obituary', *Archi Times*, May, p.19.

[8] See Rizvi, S. A. A. (1972), *Fatehpur Sikri*, New Delhi, Director General, Archaeological Survey of India (1992 [printing]); Nilsson, S. (1973), *New capitals of India, Pakistan and Bangladesh*, Lund, Studentlitteratur; Metcalf, T. R. (1989), *An imperial vision*, Berkeley, University of California Press; Kalia, R. (1999), *Chandigarh: the making of an Indian city*, New Delhi; Oxford, Oxford University Press; Sachdev, V. and G. H. R. Tillotson (2002), *Building Jaipur: the making of an Indian city*, London, Reaktion; Legg, S. (2007), *Spaces of colonialism: Delhi's urban governmentalities*, Oxford, Blackwell.

vision was different to these precedents, even the most recent.[9] In his creation the state no longer appeared primarily as a majestic wielder of great sovereign power that needed to be represented to its subjects; it was now a more or less centreless network of services designed to meet the scientifically ascertained needs of a population.

A small but highly symbolic choice within the remit of the project sums up perfectly what the new vision was all about: when it came to designing a logo for the project that could be displayed on manhole covers and bus shelters, Doxiadis proposed a motif from the Indus Valley civilization that had existed in the area of West Pakistan between 3000 and 2000 BC.[10] Not only did this choice bypass any reference to Pakistan's most obvious marker of identity – Muslim culture and history – it also uniquely represented the ethos of the post-World War II order. Indus Valley civilization had been impressively urban and, what is more, in a strikingly 'developmental' fashion. The excavation of Mohenjo Daro and Harappa revealed some of the most sophisticated municipal water supply and sewerage systems of the ancient world, but (discounting the separate 'citadel') no clear reference to any seat of sovereign power, no palaces of kings. As far as one could tell from such evidence, Indus Valley civilization was a civilization of community-minded 'citizens' in the original sense of the world. However, Islamabad never became the latter-day Mohenjo Daro its 'father' had envisioned it to be. Doxiadis's reference to the civic ideals of the Indus Valley civilization was not adopted by the Capital Development Authority (CDA). Instead and very revealingly, the organization came to use a faintly horticultural and conservative logo combining calligraphy and floral motifs, more a reference to the Mughal past than to developmental ambitions, and more self-assumed stately sovereignty than a sense of service or functionality.

Even in its most successful days, international development was never wholly compatible with Pakistan's distinctive post-colonial politics. The new transnational reality of development did not sit easily with the other great ideological venture of the period: post-colonial nationalism. The latter had at its very centre the burning desire to defend the sovereignty of the nation state and to celebrate its majesty, rather than to make it disappear in a globalized web of functional connections. The very demand for independence was a demand to 'box off' the state from

[9] The important difference between Chandigarh and Islamabad is discussed in Chapter 5.
[10] CADA: Pakistan Volume 194, Correspondence July–December 1963, File C-PI 5424. This is not the only reference to Mohenjo Daro in Doxiadis's Islamabad project. He poignantly included a map of the ancient settlement in the article that was meant to introduce Islamabad to the professional public. Doxiadis, C. A. (1965), 'Islamabad: the creation of a new capital', *The Town Planning Review* **36**(1): 1–28, p.10.

international connections and to clearly define its boundary lines, both with regard to its own citizens and with even greater urgency in its relationship to the outside world. This desire was particularly acute in Pakistan. The Partition of India had been won with great loss of life and against the force of established social, economic and geographic realities.[11] Ever since the national flag was first hoisted, the Pakistani state elite had been obsessed with the possibility that the creation of their country may yet be undone by nefarious acts of foreign subversion, and propagated this fear at every opportunity to the wider public.[12] For all its international glamour, there was a deep sense of distrust at the very heart of the venture to develop Pakistan. It would come to the fore whenever results turned out to be either too successful and gave too much credit to foreign contributions, or not successful enough and brought the Pakistani state into the firing line of criticism. The international connections of development consultancy, even the religious backgrounds of some consultants, would be seen as a direct threat to national survival.[13] 'Development' had as much potential to threaten the Pakistani state, as it could endow it with the warm glow of internationally recognized achievement.

Despite best intentions, development was by and large unable to turn the people of Pakistan from 'subjects to citizens', to use the title of a recent intervention in the literature on the early post-independence state in South Asia.[14] As this book will seek to demonstrate, this was never only the result of a moral failing on behalf of Pakistan's political leadership. It is not the purpose of this case study of urban reconstruction in the 1950s and 1960s to offer yet another debunking of the 'Ayub Khan myth', suggesting that contrary to popular memories and histories inspired by regime propaganda, he was not really a hero of development,

---

[11] This view is now universally accepted in the non-nationalist literature about the formation of Pakistan, first emphasized in a detailed historical study in Jalal, A. (1985), *The sole spokesman: Jinnah, the Muslim League and the demand for Pakistan*, Cambridge University Press. See also Footnotes 36 and 37 in this Introduction.

[12] As often noted by Western diplomats, e.g. NARA: State Department Central Files, Pakistan 1945–49 M1448, File 845F.00/9–148, Despatch 390 Karachi, 1 September 1948; Despatch 439 Karachi, 5 October 1948; File 845 F.00/6–2149 Despatch Karachi 219, 21 June 1949; RG 59, File 790D.00/12–3151, Despatch 120 Lahore, 31 December 1951.

[13] The Jewish origin of several members of the Harvard Advisory Group was used to discredit the mission in the late 1960s. Rosen, G. (1985), *Western economists and Eastern societies: agents of change in South Asia*, 1950–1970, Baltimore, Johns Hopkins University Press, p.192.

[14] Sherman, T. C., W. Gould and S. Ansari (2011), *From subjects to citizens: society and the everyday state in India and Pakistan, 1947–1970*, Cambridge University Press.

but only a cynical manipulator preoccupied with his self-preservation in power.[15] This is no doubt what a disgruntled Constantinos Doxiadis and others like him would have insinuated after they found their influence waning, but it does not do justice to the complexity of the situation; and like most arguments predicated on the failings of individual human beings will never suffice as historical analysis. It is the contention of this book that the grafting of a transnational venture of development onto a very differently conceived and constructed state in the global South led to structural incompatibilities that stood beyond problems of 'plan' and 'execution' or of 'intention' and 'outcome'. This line of argument challenges some of the received wisdom about the relationship between state and development in the post-World War II era, particularly the easy assumption that – at least in theory and as an aspiration – the post-colonial state *ought* to be a developmental state. Why such a conflation has occurred so often and so easily, and how it may be challenged is the subject of much of what follows in this Introduction.

The consultant's archive

This book approaches development history from a somewhat unusual angle: it places centre stage the experience of a prominent international consultant and seeks to understand the politics of development in 1950s and 1960s Pakistan through his eyes. This breaks new ground in several ways. As far as Pakistan is concerned, there is still a dearth of development history of any kind.[16] A substantial body of work on areas associated with development – economics, education, public health, women's advancement, green technology and so on – does of course exist,[17] but it

---

[15] For a classic account along those lines see La Porte, R. (1976), *Power and privilege: influence and decision-making in Pakistan*, Berkeley; London, University of California Press.

[16] A recent exception is Haines, T. D. (2013), *Building the empire, building the nation: development, legitimacy, and hydro-politics in Sind, 1919–1969*, Karachi, Oxford University Press Pakistan. Aspects of development history are, of course, often mentioned in passing in other histories written by social scientists – the political economy of the Ayub, Bhutto and Zia regimes, for instance, the emergence of separatist nationalism in East Pakistan or, more generally, the economic history of Pakistan, for example Noman, O. (1988), *The political economy of Pakistan 1947–85*, London, KPI; Noman, O. (1990), *Pakistan: a political and economic history since 1947*, London, Kegan Paul International; Burki, S. J. (1980), *Pakistan under Bhutto, 1971–1977*, London, Macmillan; Burki, S. J. (1986), *Pakistan: a nation in the making*, Boulder, CO, Westview Press; Pakistan, Oxford University Press.

[17] Key examples in the field of urban reconstruction and economics include: Haq, M. u. (1966), *The strategy of economic planning: a case study of Pakistan*, Karachi, Pakistan Branch; Papanek, G. F. (1967), *Pakistan's development: social goals and private incentives*. [S.l.], Cambridge, MA, Harvard University Press; Hasan, A. (2006), *The scale and causes of urban change in Pakistan*, Karachi, Ushba Publishing International;

is written for a different purpose and with an altogether different sensibility for methodology, causality and detail. As far as this book is concerned, this material constitutes a primary source – evidence of how development practitioners in the past have sought policy solutions in their respective fields – rather than a set of secondary sources that require historiographical engagement. In the few instances when the past is examined at length and with due attention to the micropolitics of development – for instance in Samia Waheed Altaf's wonderfully vivid account of the 1990s Social Action Programme in Pakistan[18] – it is still with a view to learn from mistakes to make future development better. As will be pointed out in greater detail later, such expectations decisively skew the analysis and are irreconcilable with the greater sense of historical detachment that this book as a work of history seeks to bring to its subject matter.

The current lack of development histories is part and parcel of a more general malaise in historical research about Pakistan's post-1947 past. While there have been a number of landmark accounts of Pakistan's progress by social scientists and journalists over the years, work by professional historians has only begun to pick up relatively recently.[19] It remains illustrative of the current state of scholarship that Ayesha

Hasan, A. and Shehersaaz (2009), Planning and development options for Karachi, Islamabad, Shehersaaz; Hasan, A. (2010), *Participatory development: the story of the Orangi Pilot Project Research and Training Institute and the Urban Resource Centre, Karachi, Pakistan*, Karachi, Oxford University Press; Sarmad, K. (1984), *A review of Pakistan's development experience (1945–50 to 1979–80)*, Islamabad, Pakistan Institute of Development Economics (PIDE); Qadeer, M. A. (1983), *Lahore: urban development in the Third World*, Lahore, Vanguard. For literature on other aspects of development from the 1960s to 1980s, see David Taylor, *Pakistan: a Bibliography*, World Bibliographical Series, pp.102–192.

[18] Altaf, S. W. (2011), *So much aid, so little development: stories from Pakistan*, Baltimore, Johns Hopkins University Press.

[19] The history department of Government College University, Lahore, under the leadership of Tahir Kamran (and later of Muhammad Ibrahim) has produced a number of regional histories that bridge the colonial/post-colonial divide. Notable examples in print are Niaz, I. (2010), *The culture of power and governance of Pakistan, 1947–2008*, Karachi, Oxford University Press; Qasmi, A. U. (2014), *The Ahmadis and the politics of religious exclusion in Pakistan*, New York, Anthem Press. Notable histories of Pakistan by non-historians include Sayeed, K. B. (1980), *Politics in Pakistan: the nature and direction of change*, New York, Praeger; Munir, M. (1980), *From Jinnah to Zia*, Lahore, Vanguard Books; Ali, T. (1983), *Can Pakistan survive? The death of a state*, Harmondsworth, Penguin; Burki, S. J. (1986), *Pakistan: a nation in the making*, Boulder, CO, Westview Press; Pakistan, Oxford University Press; Cohen, S. P. (2004), *The idea of Pakistan*, Washington, D.C., Brookings Institution [Bristol: University Presses Marketing, distributor]. For a landmark achievement in Urdu see the multivolume Cauhdrī, Z. h. and H. a. J. Zaidī (1989), *Pākistān kī siyāsī tārīkh*. Lāhaur, Idārah-yi Muṭāla'ah-yi Tārīkh.

Jalal's famous account of the rise of the martial state in 1950s Pakistan still stands unrivalled more than twenty years after its first publication, as does Ian Talbot's path-breaking *History of Pakistan*, the first to be written by an academic historian with full mastery of his craft.[20] Leaving aside the complex political pathologies that have led to the marginalization of historical awareness in Pakistani public life,[21] a substantial problem for aspiring historians of Pakistan has been the availability of sources. While some efforts have been made over the last few years to make the Pakistani state's own records more easily available to scholars, there remain substantial problems with access and with the very preservation of key document series. As a result, many scholars (including Talbot and Jalal) have sought to write the history of Pakistan 'from the outside in', by relying on the diplomatic records of the US State Department and the British Foreign Office. This choice has had the advantage of capturing the all too real influence that Western foreign policy exercised over the construction of the Pakistani state, but it is hard to see how any area of historical research can live with such colossal problems of source authenticity for long.

It is before this background that the serendipitous discovery of Constantinos Doxiadis's work in Pakistan felt like an exciting breakthrough. The central figure of this book is not only a worthy topic of historical investigation because of his work and legacy, he also happens to have left an extensive and well-ordered *private* archive, which so far has been almost entirely untapped by historians of development. From it, we not only get to know the full extent of his plans for major projects like Islamabad, but also a great deal about what the policy environment in Pakistan was like in the 1950s and 1960s. Apart from an unrivalled collection of photographs, travel impressions and other data about the country and its cities, there is correspondence and accounts of meetings with prime ministers, generals and senior bureaucrats, as well as thousands of letters to minor civil servants, municipal officials and contractors. There are even documents of the Pakistani state not easily accessible in the country itself – minutes of meetings of local councils, for instance, as well as papers relating to the national Planning Commission. Through Doxiadis's files we learn details not to be found anywhere else, for instance, how much illegal income a middle-ranging civil servant

---

[20] Jalal, A. (1990), *The state of martial rule: the origins of Pakistan's political economy of defence*, Cambridge; New York, Cambridge University Press. Talbot, I. (2012), *Pakistan: a modern history*, London, C. Hurst & Co. Publishers Ltd.

[21] On the politics of history in Pakistan see Jalal, A. (1995), 'Conjuring Pakistan: history as official imagining', *International Journal of Middle East Studies* 27: 73–89; Aziz, K. K. (1993), *The murder of history: a critique of history textbooks used in Pakistan*, Lahore, Vanguard.

working in the housing field could expect to make in 1960s Pakistan; and we hear not only the voice of General Ayub Khan or that of his closest associates in power, but also that of much humbler people who experienced 'development' directly in their daily lives: that of Forest Ranger Mohammad Sadiq Altaf trying to record and preserve the religious significance of certain banyan trees on the Islamabad site, for instance; or of Shamsuddin, a Korangi resident threatened by eviction for non-payment of lease.

For its empirical richness alone, this collection of material is a historian's dream. But there is more at stake. Doxiadis's archive opens up development in a manner that is distinct from the conventional state-centric approach that has come to dominate the literature, especially the more historically informed analyses of development that in all other respects have greatly inspired the arguments of this book. Pioneer historians of development and critical voices within development studies alike[22] have been keen to dismiss older official histories of development that had stressed its international and cooperative character. Development was a new venture brought about by the onset of decolonization and the attempt to create a more equitable world order after World War II, these older voices had argued. Although they often conceded that some of the foundations of the great project could be dated to the late colonial period, they treated these instances as early departures *away* from colonialism, often associated with exceptional and enlightened individuals. The real

---

[22] Mitchell, T. (1988), *Colonising Egypt*, Cambridge; New York, Cambridge University Press; Cooper, F. and R. M. Packard (1997), *International development and the social sciences: essays on the history and politics of knowledge*, Berkeley, University of California Press; Scott, J. C. (1998), *Seeing like a state: how certain schemes to improve the human condition have failed*, New Haven, CT; London, Yale University Press; Mitchell, T. (2002), *Rule of experts: Egypt, techno-politics, modernity*, Berkeley, University of California Press; Cooper, F. (2005), *Colonialism in question: theory, knowledge, history*, Berkeley, University of California Press; Zachariah, B. (2005), *Developing India: an intellectual and social history, c. 1930–50*, New Delhi, Oxford University Press. Less overtly critical but no less careful in tracing colonial/post-colonial continuities are Harper, T. N. (1998), *The end of empire and the making of Malaya*, New York, Cambridge University Press; Amrith, S. S. (2006), *Decolonizing international health: India and Southeast Asia, 1930–65*, Basingstoke; New York, Palgrave Macmillan; Harper, T. N. and S. S. Amrith (2014), *Histories of health in Southeast Asia: perspectives on the long twentieth century*, Bloomington, Indiana University Press. Similarly most contributions to Bayly, C. A., University of Manchester Brooks World Poverty Institute and World Bank Development Research Group (2011), *History, historians and development policy: a necessary dialogue*, Manchester; New York, Manchester University Press: distributed exclusively in the USA by Palgrave Macmillan. From the critical 'development studies side' see Kothari, U. (2005), *A radical history of development studies: individuals, institutions and ideologies*, London; New York, Zed Books; Hettne, B. r. (2009), *Thinking about development*, London; New York, Zed Books; Nederveen Pieterse, J. (2010), *Development theory: deconstructions/reconstructions*, London, SAGE.

starting point for development remained later moments such as the foundation of the United Nations, the Bretton Woods agreement or Truman's Point Four address.[23] For the new generation of critical historians such notions of a new beginning were little more than propaganda. Not only did development's intellectual genealogy reach much further back than World War II, there was also a long and intrinsic connection between the will to better the world and unwholesome ideas of Western superiority. In short, 'development' was not colonialism's redeemer but its continuation, with ideologies, personnel and even concrete projects easily crossing the colonial to post-colonial divide.

The close association of development with colonialism had consequences for what really mattered about development in historical analysis, both for the colonialists themselves and for those recent voices who have sought to criticize development because of its association with colonialism. Both privileged the sense of historical agency that development bestowed on its protagonists, and both then identified this agency very closely with a single institution: the state. State agency had always been the lynchpin of colonial self-justification. The people of the non-West were seen as Europe's legitimate prey precisely because they had lacked a *state* (in a modern sense, not counting oriental 'despotisms'), which was considered to go hand in hand with a general lack of historical agency.[24] Development thus defined what the colonial presence could and indeed should do to reshape its definitive 'other': (indigenous) 'society'; what having power 'over the natives' was ultimately all about. Unsurprisingly it was the recovery of precisely this agency and its institutional embodiment, 'the state', for the 'native' that stood at the centre of anti-colonial nationalism.

The easy identification of development with state agency was strengthened by archival structures, through how the 'sources' of development history were originally produced and later interpreted by historians. The colonial state itself had ensured that its own voice would be heard first, by collecting a substantial body of material for the history of development in the most accessible sections of its official archive. For historians about to start their research, 'development' began with great plans and projects, as they were formulated in enquiry commission

[23] Packenham, R. A. (1973), *Liberal America and the Third World: political development ideas in foreign aid and social science*, Princeton University Press; Arndt, H. W. (1987), *Economic development: the history of an idea*, University of Chicago Press; Meier, G. M. (ed.) (1994b), *From classical economics to development economics*, London, Macmillan.

[24] See Inden, R. B. (1990), *Imagining India*, Oxford; Cambridge, MA, Basil Blackwell, pp.51–74. More generally Young, R. (1990), *White mythologies: writing history and the West*, London; New York, Routledge.

reports, regional plans, development schemes, debates on economic policy and so on. These all belonged to a kind of discourse that highlighted the colonialists' sense of being in charge, of standing at the helm of historical change. Other voices, like 'resistances' from those affected by actual development schemes, may not have disappeared from this story altogether, but they remained confined in a binary framework that pitted the foreign-controlled state against 'local' societies, and bifurcated the story of development between plan and implementation. This methodological bias continued when historians went on to follow the paper trail further as it crossed into the post-decolonization period. Not only the archive at the heart of most research remained the same, but even some files, which had been opened by the late colonial regime and were simply continued by the new post-colonial bureaucracies.[25]

What is still largely missing in accounts exclusively derived from archives of this kind is the *trans*national character of development practice highlighted earlier, and the dispersal of agency along a far-reaching network of connections involving state as well as non-state actors, rather than its concentration in a single institutional structure. It is striking, for instance, how little historians of India writing about the 1950s and 1960s have had to say about what scores of international development consultants have contributed to the country's history, emphasizing instead how the new nationalist elite became obsessed with Soviet-style planning that may or may not have 'failed'.[26] Thanks to its archival hegemony inherited from the colonial past, the Nehruvian state has clearly managed to inscribe itself as the sole location of development agency into the history books. Even in a project like Chandigarh where foreign celebrity architects played a formative role, and where ample evidence exists of a complex and at time troubled relationship with Indian planners, workers and bureaucrats, it is from the voluminous correspondence of the ever-present Jawaharlal Nehru that historians most frequently quote to make sense of what happened.[27]

Even though continuities between the colonial and the post-colonial remain important – and are addressed many times in this book – there

---

[25] The Commerce and Industry Proceedings (B) at the National Archive of Bangladesh, for instance, are bundled for the years 1940–1953. Several post-independence projects like the Karnaphuli multi-purpose scheme documented therein were started by colonial administrators and then continued.

[26] E.g. Frankel, F. R. (1978), *India's political economy, 1947–1977: the gradual revolution*, Princeton University Press, pp.156–200; Khilnani, S. (1998), *The idea of India*, New York, Farrar Straus Giroux, pp.75–81.

[27] For instance Kalia, R. (1999), *Chandigarh: the making of an Indian city*, New Delhi; Oxford, Oxford University Press, esp. chapter 1–3.

has to be a more clearly decolonized reading of development, one that takes the difference between the old order and the new seriously. The purpose here is not to go back beyond critical histories of development and to somehow rehabilitate the pieties of post-war benevolence, but to offer a more differentiated reading of how development changed during the colonial/post-colonial transition. The question is how could development – a project that started off as an embodiment of the state's agency – also become the embodiment of something very different: a scientific rationality that so conspicuously tried to *hide* any clearly identifiable centre of power, represented so nicely in Doxiadis's reference to the sewers of Mohenjo Daro.

The relationship between state and development cannot be adequately grasped from within a world of documents that the state has produced about itself. In order to avoid the trap of automatically equating development with state agency, we need an alternative location of analysis, and it is the contention of this book that the consultant's archive is precisely such a location from where a new history of development can be written. It is useful here to emphasize two peculiarities that made the hero of this book stand out even from the crowd of other international experts operating at the same time, and which give his accumulated material added critical importance. First, the fact that he was a free-standing entrepreneur and not a straightforward representative of either a government or an international organization. Doxiadis's country of origin, Greece, has little or no impact on our story, what mattered was his ability to draw on boundary-transcending connections around the globe. He was not only an international but a truly *trans*national actor. Moreover, as an entrepreneur, Doxiadis was ultimately answerable not to political pressures of any state but to his company's balance sheet. Operating under his own name in many countries at the same time, he could not afford to downplay political tensions with his clients once they drew him into the firing line of criticism. To save his own reputation he would on occasion have to spill the beans on those who hired him. Through his eyes we are able to perceive contestations and fissures in the development encounter that are elsewhere all too easily hidden from the historian's view.

This tendency was heightened, secondly, by the fact that he was an architect and urbanist, and not, let us say, a development economist or malaria prevention expert. Focusing on development through the lens of urban reconstruction is about more than simply closing an important gap in the literature. Arguably it was in the field of urbanism that we get to see most clearly the conflict between development and state that is so important for our analysis. While this conflict also existed in other fields, it would never be as easily accessible through historical records. Other experts left official plans and reports, and occasionally a little oral history, but no independent documentary evidence of political conflict with their employers.[28] Their names are largely forgotten and also meant to be forgotten, as they saw themselves as minions of a larger impersonal venture. Nobody outside a very small circle of experts would remember the name of the person who designed the Aswan High Dam or the Rourkela steel works. The history books simply tell us that it was the state-representatives Nasser and Nehru, respectively, who 'built' these things. This is not the case with grand architectural projects, however; despite his omnipresence, it was not Nehru who 'built' the city of Chandigarh, for instance, but Le Corbusier, and not Ayub Khan (or later Ziaur Rahman) who 'built' the Parliament Complex in Dacca, but Louis Kahn.[29] These are the figures that Doxiadis had to compete with. Doxiadis aspired to be an international celebrity architect as well as a development expert. His authorial intentions and aesthetic visions had to remain visible as his own, unlike the ideas that influenced five-year plans or disease eradication campaigns. More than many other areas of history, architectural history idolizes great men protagonists and their personal papers.[30] This is the primary reason why there is a Doxiadis Archive, and why it is now appropriately housed in Greece's premier

---

[28] An exception with great relevance for this book is Rosen, G. (1985), *Western economists and Eastern societies: agents of change in South Asia, 1950–1970*, Baltimore, Johns Hopkins University Press. Rosen was a member of the Harvard Advisory Group for India while Doxiadis was on its counterpart in Pakistan. Apart from his own memories, Rosen draws extensively on oral history interviews with his Harvard colleagues that do address their relationship with key Pakistani and Indian bureaucrats and planners. In the case of Chandigarh in contrast, such matters are only hinted at in passing, for instance in Fry, M. (1977), 'Le Corbusier at Chandigarh', *The open hand: essays on Le Corbusier*, R. Walden (ed.), Cambridge, MA, MIT Press: 351–363, pp.353–357.

[29] On the meeting of two 'great men' – Nehru and Le Corbusier – see van Moos, S. (1977), 'The politics of the open hand: notes on Le Corbusier and Nehru at Chandigarh', *The open hand: essays on Le Corbusier*, R. Walden (ed.), Cambridge, MA, MIT Press: 413–457. Le Corbusier consistently stressed his role as 'great artist' and 'spiritual director' when working on the Chandigarh project. Sarin, M. (1977), 'Chandigarh as a place to live in', *The open hand: essays on Le Corbusier*, R. Walden (ed.), Cambridge, MA, MIT Press: 374–410, p.399. On Kahn's work in Dacca see Goldhagen, S. W. and L. I. Kahn (2001), *Louis Kahn's situated modernism*, New Haven, CT, Yale University Press, pp.162–198. As so often in architectural history there is hardly any discussion of Kahn's relationship with Pakistani or Bangladeshi power holders.

[30] It is striking, for instance, that Albert Mayer, planner of Chandigarh before Le Corbusier's arrival and Doxiadis's contemporary and rival, is one of the few development experts in Nehruvian India to receive sustained attention from historians. Leaving aside his personal acquaintance with Nehru, his luck was that he was not only a planner but also an architect, and that his papers were subsequently archived by the University of Chicago.

modern art museum.[31] It is this sense of historical agency that has the power to decentre the agency of the developmental state.

Challenging the developmental state

This book calls for a shift from state archive to private archive, and from a reading of development as a statement of state policy (and its 'implementation') to development as a more conflicted and transnational political process. This methodology challenges customary expectations that a post-colonial state must necessarily and by implication also act as a developmental state, and that where it fails to do so, this somehow marks some kind of historical failure or malignancy. Instead, it is assumed that what defined 'development' and 'the post-colonial nation state', respectively, are two very different attributes and characteristics, and that these were more likely to contradict each other than to work in tandem. In short, what needs to be explained is not why a nation state fails to act as a developmental state, but rather under what specific circumstances and within what limitations it ever could. This reversal of standard expectations is grounded in a radical re-evaluation of what constitutes the paradigmatic historical example for the post-colonial state. This book proposes to use *Pakistan* as an analytically more useful historical paradigm than the often invoked cases of Nehru's India, Mao's China or Nasser's Egypt. What justifies such a reversal is neither Pakistan's size nor its particularly successful or inspiring historical trajectory – it falls well short on both accounts when compared to its larger neighbour – but the fact that Pakistan's sense of statehood was based on a clearer, more radical reading of what it meant to be a post-colonial nation.

Let us consider what defined the Pakistani nation state when it emerged first as an idea and then as a reality over the course of the 1940s. Unlike in Nehru's India,[32] Pakistan's right to self-determination was never seen to be 'earned' through good economic behaviour, or for that matter, by anything else. Its only indisputable foundation was the fact that a growing number of Muslims believed in its existence. Even if there

---

[31] Benaki Museum, Pireas Street Annex.
[32] Congress nationalism was deeply rooted in the 'economic nationalism' of the late nineteenth and early twentieth centuries, e.g. Dutt, R. C. (1916), *The economic history of India under early British rule, from the rise of the British power in 1757 to the accession of Queen Victoria in 1837*, London, K. Paul, Trench. See Zachariah, B. (2005), *Developing India: an intellectual and social history, c. 1930–50*, New Delhi, Oxford University Press, pp.211–290; Khilnani, S. (1998), *The idea of India*, New York, Farrar Straus Giroux, pp.61–106.

were countless attempts to argue for Pakistan in an 'objective' manner –
on the basis of territory, history, even economics – none of these arguments really stood up to the criticism by its many political enemies at the
time and since.[33] As several historians from Ayesha Jalal to Yasmin Khan
and Farzana Shaikh have pointed out, no definition could ever be found
that really captured what the new nation was all about or who was
included (and excluded) within it.[34] If Pakistan had a clear meaning that
was understood by adherents and detractors alike, it was 'Muslim Raj',
a sense that Muslims were now in charge, and that this fact alone would
lead to a whole range of improvements from feeling better to living
better.[35] Self-determination produced a state of 'ease' (*chain*) as a nationalist poem put it.[36] Economic and social considerations were certainly
present in nationalist discourse but they never acquired the same primacy
in defining the new nation as they had across the border. Put very starkly,
the creation of the country would have been justified, even if it did not
make economic sense. Defending the will to self-determination of the
Muslim people was irreducible, even in its relationship with what defined
the nation. In the words of nationalist politician Mumtaz Daultana, to
wrest Muslim Kashmir from Hindu control was worth the sacrifice of
Islam itself.[37]

A collective will to power stood at the heart of Pakistani nationalism
as it emerged in confrontation with the more developmentally argued
nationalism of Nehru's Congress. This sense gives us an access point to
an alternative way of thinking about the post-colonial state. Nationalist

---

[33] Economic motivations played a certain role in why certain social constituencies ended
up supporting the demand for Pakistan, but they never amounted to a coherent
economic policy and were at any rate entirely subsumed in religious identity politics.
Talbot, I. (1994), 'Planning for Pakistan: the Planning Committee of the All-India
Muslim League', *Modern Asian Studies* **28**(4): 875–889; Hashmi, T. u.-I. (1992), *Pakistan
as a peasant utopia: the communalization of class politics in East Bengal, 1920–1947*, Boulder,
CO, Westview Press. For more recent attempts to interpret the Pakistani demand as one
based on objective geographic or economic realities see Ahsan, A. (1996), *The Indus saga
and the making of Pakistan*, Karachi, Oxford University Press; Talha, N. (2000), *Economic
factors in the making of Pakistan (1921–1947)*, Oxford; New York, Oxford University Press.

[34] Jalal, A. (1995), 'Conjuring Pakistan: history as official imagining', *International Journal
of Middle East Studies* **27**: 73–89; Khan, Y. (2007), *The great Partition: the making of India
and Pakistan*, New Haven, CT; London, Yale University Press; Shaikh, F. (2009),
Making sense of Pakistan, New York, Columbia University Press, pp.14–45.

[35] Daechsel, M. (2006), *The politics of self-expression: the Urdu middle-class milieu in mid-
twentieth century India and Pakistan*, London; New York, Routledge, pp.101–109,
262–267.

[36] Institute for Historical and Cultural Research library, Islamabad: 'Muslim', *Nāmghah-e-
Pākistān*, n.d. p.11.

[37] NARA: RG 59, Box 4146, File 790 D.00/10–752, Telegram 15, Lahore, 7 October 1952.

politics did not necessarily have to be 'developmentalist' or founded on an economic agenda, and neither did the states that they demanded and produced. In fact, there was something about the state that did not have to be argued or predicated on anything else at all; in its very essence the state came into existence through an act of self-assertion. It projected (a certain kind of) power, and therefore it was.

Redefining the grounds of argument in this way also addresses a political and moral problem. The conflation of development and state – which then ends in an attestation of 'failure' – has helped colonial rulers of the past and advocates of a neo-imperialist order today to question the very right of national self-determination. A state should only be free from violations or outright denial of its sovereignty, they argue, if it is able to show to the world that it can carry out 'development' successfully. If it does not – and this would apply to post-colonial nations around the world – foreign tutelage in one form or another remains justified. The implication is that because only the most advanced states of the rich North represent what every state should eventually become, they alone can also be truly sovereign. Everybody else, meanwhile, is permanently kept on notice, and in a state of not-quite statehood, not-quite sovereignty.[38] Although never entirely designated as an outright 'failure' like Somalia or Afghanistan, Pakistan has over the last decades emerged as one of the countries where such a line of argumentation has been invoked with particular frequency, leading to devastating consequences for its political culture.[39]

Using Foucault

Taking Pakistan as a new paradigm means to work on the assumption that the modalities of power associated with post-colonial state formation and with 'development', respectively, were distinct from each other, and

---

[38] E.g. Krasner, S. D. and C. Pascual (2005), 'Addressing state failure', *Foreign Affairs* **84** (4): 153–163; Mallaby, S. (2002), 'The reluctant imperialist: terrorism, failed states, and the case for American empire", ibid. **81**(2): 2–7. For a withering critique from a neo-liberal perspective see Easterly, W. (2006), *The white man's burden: why the West's efforts to aid the rest have done so much ill and so little good*, Oxford University Press, Chapter 8.

[39] Daechsel, M. (2009) 'An elite clings on to power: the idea that Pakistan is being "Talibanised" helps stifle dissent and protect privilege', *The Guardian – comment is free*, www.theguardian.com/commentisfree/belief/2009/mar/11/pakistan-islam-zardari [accessed 10/10/2013]. The idea of Pakistan descending into chaos has become a staple in Western media reports, often aided by the work of Pakistani journalists seeking a voice in the Western media arena, e.g. Moreau, R. (2007), 'Pakistan: the most dangerous?' *Newsweek*, 20 October; Rashid, A. (2008), *Descent into chaos: the US and the failure of nation building in Pakistan, Afghanistan, and Central Asia*, New York, Viking.

that their incongruence, even contradiction, was a constructive historical force rather than a pathological deviation from a global norm. 'Development' and 'state' did not stand in the simple relationship of a project and its primary agent but represented two very different ways of governing people and doing politics. For this kind of analysis important distinctions need to be made as to what power is, how it is deployed and how it affects those under its sway. We know such distinctions from the work of Michel Foucault, albeit derived from other historical periods or other fields of enquiry: the royal power of the executioner that targets the body of the condemned in a single act of ferocious violence is not the same as the continuous power of medicine or psychiatry, working to a large extent through self-policing by an individual; let alone the strikingly non-interventionist power of managerial styles of governance based on statistical probability determining the natural inclinations of a population.[40]

The use of Foucault for South Asian history is by no means new. From the late 1980s to the late 1990s a particular reading of Foucault all but dominated the critical historiography within Anglophone academia. Following in the footsteps of Edward Said, it combined French deconstructionism with a post-Marxist political sensibility and was exemplified by the work of David Arnold, Partha Chatterjee, Dipesh Chakrabarty and Gyan Prakash within the Subaltern Studies collective,[41] and in the wider field by gender and social historians like Ann Laura Stoler, Satadru Sen and Clare Anderson (among many others).[42] Without being ever

---

[40] The classic distinction between disciplinary and sovereign power was first proposed in Foucault, M. and J. Lagrange (2006), *Psychiatric power: lectures at the Collège de France, 1973–74*, Basingstoke; New York, Palgrave Macmillan, and then elaborated in the famous Foucault, M. (1977), *Discipline and punish: the birth of the prison*, New York, Pantheon Books. The broadening of this distinction into a three-fold system of sovereign, disciplinary and 'security' power was proposed in Foucault, M., M. Senellart, F. O. Ewald and A. Fontana (2007), *Security, territory, population: lectures at the Collège de France, 1977–78*, Basingstoke; New York, Palgrave Macmillan: République Française.

[41] For instance: Chakrabarty, D. (1989), *Rethinking working-class history: Bengal, 1890–1940*, Princeton University Press; Arnold, D. (1993), *Colonizing the body: state medicine and epidemic disease in nineteenth-century India*, Berkeley, University of California Press; Prakash, G. (1999), *Another reason: science and the imagination of modern India*, Princeton University Press; Chatterjee, P. (2004), *The politics of the governed: reflections on popular politics in most of the world*, New York, Columbia University Press.

[42] Stoler, A. L. (1995), *Race and the education of desire: Foucault's history of sexuality and the colonial order of things*, Durham, NC, Duke University Press; Sen, S. (2000), *Disciplining punishment: colonialism and convict society in the Andaman Islands*, New Delhi; Oxford; New York, Oxford University Press; Stoler, A. L. (2002), *Carnal knowledge and imperial power: race and the intimate in colonial rule*, Berkeley, University of California Press; Anderson, C. (2004), *Legible bodies: race, criminality, and colonialism in South Asia*, Oxford; New York, Berg; Sen, S. (2005), *Colonial childhoods: the juvenile periphery of India, 1850–1945*, London, Anthem Press; Sen, S. (2012), *Disciplined natives: race, freedom, and confinement in colonial India*, Delhi, Primus Books.

comprehensively rebutted or superseded, this trend has nevertheless lost much of its lustre over the last decade or so. Many scholars have returned to a new empiricism. But an interest in Foucault has lived on among South Asian historians, albeit often in a more diverse and sometimes idiosyncratic manner.[43] Its Foucault is no longer the same that dominated the earlier literature, in part because previously little known parts of his oeuvre are still entering the debate many years after their author's death, for instance the lecture cycles given to the College de France in the 1970s and 1980s that had not previously been edited and published.[44] It is this renewed and more open use of Foucault, one that seeks to think with and against him without wishing to slot into 1990s jargon and precedent, that this book has adopted as an inspiration.

Development as discourse

This book does not use the full potential of this 'later Foucault' straight away, however. Instead, it plots the unfolding of Doxiadis's encounter with the world of Pakistani politics against developments within Foucauldian theory itself, working its way from some more conventional readings proposed in the older literature to a more critical and dynamic view over the later chapters. To identify the starting point for this interpretative journey it is useful to remember once again Doxiadis's invocation of the Indus Civilization city of Mohenjo Daro as a symbolic representation of what 'development' meant in terms of a distinctive modality of governance. The underlying suggestion was that the power of development may not be located in any particular state institution – Mohenjo Daro was famously a city without recognizable palaces or other seats of government – but in a worldwide and centreless network, and

---

[43] Some of the UK-based contributors to this trend came together at the South Asian Governmentalities Workshop, The British Academy, 30 March 2012. Speakers included Shruti Kapila, Stephen Legg, Sarah Hodges, Srila Roy, Alex Tickell as well as the author of this monograph. Much of this work is still in progress but notable publications include Legg, S. (2007), *Spaces of colonialism: Delhi's urban governmentalities*, Oxford, Blackwell; Kapila, S. (2005), 'Masculinity and madness: princely personhood and colonial sciences of the mind in Western India', *Past and Present* **187**(1): 121–156; Kapila, S. (2007), 'Race matters: orientalism and religion, India and beyond c. 1770–1880,' *Modern Asian Studies* **41**(3): 471–513; Hodges, S. (2008), *Contraception, colonialism and commerce: birth control in South India, 1920–1940*, Aldershot; Burlington, VT, Ashgate.

[44] The publication of these lecture cycles is still ongoing. Most influential on the argument proposed in this book have been Foucault, M., M. Senellart, F. o. Ewald and A. Fontana (2007), *Security, territory, population: lectures at the Collège de France, 1977–78*, Basingstoke; New York, Palgrave Macmillan: République Française; Foucault, M., M. Senellart and Collège de France (2008), *The birth of biopolitics: lectures at the Collège de France, 1978–79*, Basingstoke; New York, Palgrave Macmillan.

that its peculiar mode of operation was not reducible to any intentional agency like the state. Such a vision of development seems to map on effortlessly to Michel Foucault's most famous insights from his 'classical' period: his well-worn concept of 'discourse'.

This was the analytical tool first used by a powerful strand of development scepticism of which the work of James Ferguson and Arturo Escobar are perhaps the best known examples.[45] It is worth examining their argument in some detail as they will often be used as a baseline throughout this book. These writers found Foucauldian theory attractive because it seemed to offer a radical way out of the impasse that had afflicted development both as an academic subject and as a political project in the 1990s. The practice of building new and better development paradigms on the rubble of the previous decade's policies had reached a dead end. All conceivable approaches from the neo-liberal worship of trade and markets to nationalist state capitalism, from big projects to local sustainability, from industrial 'take-off' to 'basic needs' had been tried and found wanting. There were no clear new options on the table and development studies splintered into an array of mutually irreconcilable positions.[46] For a small but vocal number of critics, this intellectual confusion, combined with mounting evidence of worsening economic and social misery around the world, meant that the project of development itself had become bankrupt.[47] This was an unprecedented step as even the most critical contributions to the development studies debate had never wanted to get rid of development altogether, only to replace a bad form of development with a better model.

Ferguson (and then Escobar) sought to transcend earlier debates by moving away from internal critiques of development that juxtaposed

[45] Ferguson, J. (1990), *The anti-politics machine: 'development,' depoliticization, and bureaucratic power in Lesotho*, Cambridge University Press; Escobar, A. (1995), *Encountering development: the making and unmaking of the Third World*, Princeton University Press. A first applications of Foucault's 'discourse analysis' (heavily influenced by Derrida) to development thought was Johnston, D. S. (1991), 'Constructing the periphery in modern global politics', *The new international political economy*, C. N. Murphy and R. Tooze (eds.), Boulder, CO, Lynne Rienner: 149–170. For the dissemination of Ferguson and Escobar's ideas see Grillo, R. D. and R. L. Stirrat (1997), *Discourses of development: anthropological perspectives*, Oxford; New York, Berg. For a critical dissection of development 'discourse' using non-Foucauldian linguistic analysis see Apthorpe, R. J. and D. Gasper (1996), *Arguing development policy: frames and discourses*, London; Portland, OR, Frank Cass in association with the European Association of Development Research and Training Institutes (EADI), Geneva.

[46] Leys, C. (1996), *Rise and fall of development theory*, Oxford, James Currey, pp.22–26.

[47] See contributions in two landmark anthologies: Sachs, W. (1992), *The development dictionary: a guide to knowledge as power*, London; Atlantic Highlands, NJ, Zed Books; Rahnema, M. and V. Bawtree (1997), *The post-development reader*, London, Zed Books.

good development intentions to bad policy formulation and implementation. Instead, they adopted an external position from where there was no longer good or bad development, but only development *effects* linked to a deeper level of analysis. In order to do so, the widely held idea that development was an easy-to-debunk smokescreen for Western economic interests had to be abandoned. It was not economics that really counted, but power in a harder to ascribe and more general sense. When studying international projects in Lesotho, Ferguson observed that few had any appreciable success according to the objectives for which they had been designed. They were also not particularly prone to making Lesotho easier to exploit by global capitalism, as dependency theorists would have argued. Development experts were bypassed and often ignored by the local Lesotho elite, and much of what they proposed existed on paper only. But even in its patent inability to deliver according to plan, development had a powerful effect. It acted as an 'anti-politics machine' by introducing a set of seemingly universal, scientific and non-political categories that produced a new managerial modality of control that could no longer account for local conflicts over power and interests. Even when it seemingly achieved nothing, global 'development' had diminished the possibility of questioning and contesting the power of the Lesotho elite.[48]

The theoretical tool that allowed this argument to be made was precisely the notion of 'discourse'. Foucault had come to it through the observation that the established 'order of things' in the post-Enlightenment world rested on deep epistemological foundations where both 'facts' and how these facts related to each other in arguments were always already constituted through relations of power.[49] A discursive formation not only constructed its own subjects, but also offered a scientific discipline to explain and validate their behaviour and a code of conduct that determined what constituted normality and how it could be monitored and enforced. This power was not conventionally 'political'. It was the power of doctors, psychiatrists, teachers or prison warders that could not be easily challenged even though they had the ability to closely regulate one's conduct, to detain, quarantine and physically violate a human being, even to define who and what one ultimately was.

---

[48] Ferguson, J. (1990), *The anti-politics machine: 'development,' depoliticization, and bureaucratic power in Lesotho*, Cambridge University Press, pp.16–18, 251–277.

[49] Foucault's fullest analysis of power/knowledge in his 'discourse' period is to be found in his magnum opus Foucault, M. (1970), *The order of things: an archaeology of the human sciences*, London, Tavistock Publications. For a standard discussion see Dreyfus, H. L. and P. Rabinow (1982), *Michel Foucault, beyond structuralism and hermeneutics*, University of Chicago Press, Part 1.

While the older powers of king and church had always been more or less transparent both in terms of where they were located, and in terms of what they could and could not control, discursive formations were deeply intrusive and transcended most recognized institutional boundaries. They were dispersed across the state, the legal system, academic science, the family and individuals themselves.[50] Conventional political analysis focused on a system of institutions or functional distinctions between different domains of human activity (the political, the economic, the religious, etc.) could not even fully perceive such power as a problem, let alone formulate ways to challenge it.

Arturo Escobar has offered the most well-known adoption of precisely this analysis to criticize 'development'. He pointed out that allegedly pre-ideological categories such as 'GDP per capita', 'farmer', 'village', 'illiteracy', 'the economy', 'hunger' or indeed 'poverty' were in fact all the products of development as a discursive formation.[51] This is to say, none of these categories was a simple reflection of 'reality out there' but rather the construction of certain ways of observing, measuring and acting that already constituted relations of power. Since most opposing strands of development theory – from Maoists to free-trade enthusiasts – used these categories, they were never able to challenge the essential power of development itself. Instead they embarked on a fruitless dance around secondary questions, for instance about economic policy or the role of the state. What is more, the creation of the basic categories on which 'development' is based always pushed non-Western people and countries into a subordinate position as a 'problem'. In so doing it automatically located a superior sense of agency in the hands of experts and bureaucrats who would discover and attest this backwardness through these very categories. A critique of development as 'discourse', Escobar and his supporters believed, would open up fresh possibilities of political debate; those affected by it would no longer have to accept their 'underdevelopment' as 'objective' facts; but could identify their own concerns as they arose directly from living conditions.[52]

The very fact that Foucauldian theory did away with the notion that power was held in particular locations and for particular purposes disabled

---

[50] See (among other references elsewhere in his work) Foucault's lectures to the Collège de France on 21 November, 28 November and 5 December 1973. Foucault, M. and J. Lagrange (2006), *Psychiatric power: lectures at the Collège de France, 1973–74*, Basingstoke; New York, Palgrave Macmillan, pp.39–122.

[51] Escobar, A. (1995), *Encountering development: the making and unmaking of the Third World*, Princeton University Press, esp. Chapters 2 and 4.

[52] Ibid. pp.212–226.

a far easier mode of attacking established and powerful ideas: 'ideological critique', a practice going back to Enlightenment thought and pushed to its limits in Marxist analysis.[53] It worked in a way that is relatively accessible – and therefore politically effective – by suggesting that any set of powerful ideas exists for somebody's benefit. Once we can identify who is behind an idea we can attack this somebody directly, while also dispelling the power of the idea itself in the process – be it fraudulent priests inventing religion to sexually exploit unsuspecting women, which critiques both priests and religion,[54] or the popular critique of development as a smokescreen for Western desires to exploit the people of the Third World. Foucault's dispersal of power removes the very possibility to locate a clear point of attack along such lines. Just as there was no way of demonstrating that psychiatry served the 'interests' of psychiatrists, or for that matter of 'the ruling class', there was no longer any way of arguing that 'development' was an ideological smokescreen protecting Western capitalism or cynical Cold War dictatorships. In Escobar and Ferguson's vision, development simply was – and had powerful political effects. One could no longer 'critique' it, in the established philosophical sense, only be against it.

The sense that 'development' was of such immense global power that only a total deconstruction would be able to tackle it, as it underlay many of the older Foucauldian accounts, was in itself historically conditioned. It emerged at a time when no matter what one thought about 'development', nobody could imagine a world without it. Historical investigation suggests that this was not the sense of the 1950s and only with qualifications that of the 1960s, no matter how strongly development discourse itself has attempted to portray itself as an inevitable historical force right from the start. Rather than to juxtapose Foucauldian analysis to earlier and less total forms of critique working with the notion of 'ideology' – which was the *raison d'être* of the arguments of Ferguson and Escobar – it may actually be possible to identify a single continuous spectrum of critique marking a historical progression. We can argue that while it was once possible, even easy, to dismiss development as the deliberate

---

[53] This tradition peaked in the seminal Mannheim, K. (1929), *Ideologie und Utopie*, Bonn, F. Cohen. After World War II, further developments in structural Marxism totalized ideological analysis to a point where it could meet Foucault's analysis of power/knowledge, esp. in Althusser, L. (1984), 'Ideology and ideological state apparatuses', *Essays on Ideology*, London, Verso: 1–60. For a general discussion of ideology in the Marxist tradition see Eagleton, T. (1994), *Ideology*, London; New York, Longman.

[54] A classic early case of this use of ideological critique was the idea of religion as a conscious clerical scam, popular among Enlightenment polemicists in eighteenth-century France. Sloterdijk, P. (1983), *Kritik der zynischen Vernunft*, Frankfurt am Main, Suhrkamp, Volume 1, pp.75–83.

misrepresentation of reality to somebody's advantage, this was no longer an easy or persuasive option later on, as development had itself changed its nature from an 'ideology' to a 'discourse'. In other words, the advance of development criticism was in itself part of the story of development. As the target of criticism grew in strength over time and acquired progressive immunity to attack, the critical momentum had to move to ever deeper and more general levels of analysis to locate and unmask its beneficiaries, until it reached the point when power appeared so absolute and so dispersed that such an unmasking was no longer possible.[55]

This reintegration of critique holds the potential to fine-tune the use of Foucault in an analysis of the developmental state. To counter the dangers of too consistent and rigorous an application of discourse analysis – generating totalized readings and overbearing power for the analyst – we can set into motion a deliberate play between later and earlier forms of critique, between 'ideology' and 'discourse', and between 'past' and 'present'. Transferences, resonances and analytical short-circuits of this kind are precisely what keeps historical methodology fertile and open. It is an unsettling presence that constantly reminds us of the central problem of development history itself: of how to account for a historical formation that, as this book will demonstrate, looks at times almost ridiculously flimsy and ill-conceived and at others so overwhelming and powerful; a formation that has inspired fervent belief and cynical manipulation simultaneously, and despite producing more self-described policy failures than successes, has somehow changed the world and appears inescapable.

Making development history

This book does not seek to improve how development is carried out in a country like Pakistan, not least because it does not share the still widely prevailing sense that 'development' is either a historically necessary or, indeed, an inherently beneficial pursuit. To be clear, this sense of development scepticism remains resolutely distinct from the yearning to protect and celebrate local cultural authenticity that has characterized other self-consciously development-critical or development-sceptical

---

[55] On the replacement of ideological critique by discourse analysis in development studies see Nederveen Pieterse, J. (2010), *Development theory: deconstructions/reconstructions*, London, SAGE, p.14. To read this replacement *as a historical progression*, follow Sloterdijk's 'eight moments of unmasking', connecting Renaissance scepticism via the discovery of ideology, psychoanalysis and structural Marxism to the crisis of Enlightenment critique of post-modernism: Sloterdijk, P. (1983), *Kritik der zynischen Vernunft*, Frankfurt am Main, Suhrkamp, Volume 1, Part 1.

interventions, for instance, the work of Ivan Illich, Wolfgang Sachs, Serge Latouche or Majid Rahnema.[56] A *historical* development scepticism as proposed here is not predicated on the idea that any kind of intervention to alleviate poverty or create jobs in industry are all wrong-footed or unnecessary, and that local people should go back to indigenous medicine or subsistence agriculture. What needs to be questioned is whether these efforts need to belong to a global venture called 'development'. This is not an innocent association but of major political importance; to call something part of development forestalls critical examination and political debate; it creates automatic positive connotations, unleashes a juggernaut of unquestionable international expertise and, most importantly, allows arguments of ends justifying the means. Once building a factory becomes part of 'development', the removal of local subsistence farmers from the land is no longer to be evaluated for its consequences in the here and now, but appears as a necessary sacrifice for (seemingly) inevitable gains in the future.[57]

Pakistan was not born as a developing nation, it became a developing nation only through its encounter with an army of experts and funding bodies, new international alliances and policy practices that all prescribed or facilitated a certain new way of making sense of the world. What made development 'development' is not a pre-existing state of severe social economic and political problems and the need to resolve them, it is a certain way of crafting an analysis of what needs to be done to a particular narrative framework. Pakistan faced many problems at the moment of decolonization – unclear borders and ethnic strife, millions of refugees, disrupted regional economies, destroyed infrastructures, famine, unbalanced rural economies – but this in itself did not make the country a 'developing' one. Despite degrees of deprivation and devastation that in many ways *surpassed* Pakistan's sorry state in 1947, nobody would have regarded Germany, France or Czechoslovakia as countries in need of 'development'. Instead, it was assumed that once the effects of war could be overcome through a massive effort of

---

[56] Illich, I. (1978), *Toward a history of needs*, New York, Pantheon Books; Sachs, W. (1992) *The development dictionary: a guide to knowledge as power*, London; Atlantic Highlands, NJ, Zed Books; Latouche, S. (1993), *In the wake of the affluent society: an exploration of post-development*, London; New York, Zed Books; Rahnema, M. and V. Bawtree (1997), *The post-development reader*, London, Zed Books.
[57] A recent example of how the rhetoric of development can be used to trump concerns of social justice and class politics in the here and now was the forcible eviction of small-scale cultivators in the West Bengal special economic zone of Nandigram to pave the way for industrial development. Sarkar, A. (2007), 'Nandigram and the deformations of the Indian left', *International Socialism*, www.isj.org.uk/index.php4?id=333&issue=115 [accessed 15/10/2008].

'rebuilding', these countries would be able to go back, more or less, to where they had been before. There were also people in Pakistan who looked at their problems in this way – as a particular legacy of British colonialism and the Partition process that required a specific and one-off solution.[58] Although they were later increasingly silenced – not least under the impact of consultants like Doxiadis – these voices proved once more that, at least in principle, one could be a post-colonial nationalist without necessarily also being 'developmentalist' – at least not in the usual sense.

Even if development appears to be such a catch-all, self-evidently right and inescapable project that its mere invocation can conjure up solutions to the most complex problems – from 'poverty' to 'Islamic terrorism' – there is no need for the historian to forget the basic fact that it was historically 'made' and that this process of 'making' was never smooth or inevitable, but instead riddled with contradictions, dead ends, inconsistencies. Much as this book has been inspired by the theoretical possibilities of Ferguson and Escobar and, of course, Foucault himself; it has been informed by works of history that have questioned any inherent consistency or essence behind the global venture of development. Detailed case histories of actual development policies or of discrete intellectual strands of development thought show that 'development' as a unified and powerful worldwide project was in itself a historical construction conjured up by its lead discourse looking back at its own success.[59] For development studies textbooks eager to provide a little historical context to new practitioners of their craft, development was a venture that started off in embryonic form, as it were, at some point after World War II – in moments like the foundation of the United Nations, the Marshall Plan or Truman's Point Four promise to share expertise with the underdeveloped countries around the world – only to seek its

---

[58] Mazhar Ali Khan, a leading left-wing journalist, for instance, regarded Pakistan's problem as one of 'reconstruction' rather than development, which did not require large-scale outside assistance beyond limited technical support, 'American aid', *Pakistan Times*, 3 July 1948. He reiterated a similar stance, but this time using terms such as 'backward country' and with an emphasis on the importance of planning in 1953, 'Pakistan's crisis', *Pakistan Times*, 22 July 1953, reprinted in Khan, M. A. (1996), *Pakistan, the first twelve years: the* Pakistan Times *editorials of Mazhar Ali Khan*, Karachi; New York, Oxford University Press, pp.441–443, 614–616.

[59] The contested and often incoherent nature of development policy in the 1950s and 1960s has been stressed by participants and historians alike: Rostow, W. W. (1985), *Eisenhower, Kennedy, and foreign aid*, Austin, University of Texas Press; Gilman, N. (2003), *Mandarins of the future: modernization theory in Cold War America*, Baltimore, Johns Hopkins University Press; Statler, K. C. and A. L. Johns (eds.) (2006), *The Eisenhower administration, the Third World, and the globalization of the Cold War*, Lanham, MD, Rowman & Littlefield.

destiny in a succession of policy paradigms stretching to the present.[60] But as critical development historians like Gilbert Rist have demonstrated, this 'development of development' is a myth produced by a spillover of development's own central metaphorical image: that of a mature plant developing out of a seed.[61]

As soon as we zoom in on the historical record in all its richness and without a sense of teleology, the narrative spine of development disappears. Rather, 'development' emerges as a bundle of ideological impulses, scientific ideas, policies, institutions and public images that, although never entirely internally coherent, congealed over the course of time to acquire a remarkable degree of resilience. The secret of its power lay in the fact that it worked at many levels simultaneously while providing a powerful narrative core that facilitates an easy transition between them. 'Development' has been an intermediary concept linking scientific discourse with popular aspirations and narrative identities. As such it is similar to other terms attached to mythological bundles of their own – 'the middle class', 'fundamentalism' or 'civil society', for instance – which have similarly survived in the cut and thrust of public debate long after significant sections of academics have questioned their very definability. Development survives because it has provided a semi-religious reassurance to a Western public that even after the catastrophes of World War II they still had a global mission to perform; it has conjured up the biblical image of charity and reaffirmed a politics of hope; it has given a name to the aspirations of people in the global South to live better, and an easy slogan for Southern elites to propose any number of policy initiatives from agrarian reform to rapid industrialization.[62]

This book is about how this venture of 'development' was introduced to Pakistan over the 1950s and 1960s, how it was transformed from a flimsy and always questionable ideology into a discourse with scientific

[60] Hettne, B. r. (1995), *Development theory and the three worlds: towards an international political economy of development*, Harlow; New York, Longman; Preston, P. W. (1996), *Development theory*, Oxford; Cambridge, MA, Blackwell Publishers.

[61] Rist, G. (1990), 'Development as part of the modern myth: the Western socio-economic dimension of "development"', *European Journal of Development Alternatives* 2(1): 10–21. See also Tucker, V. (1999), 'The myth of development: a critique of a Eurocentric discourse', *Critical development theory: contributions to a new paradigm*, R. Munck and D. O'Hearn (eds.), London; New York, Zed Books.

[62] This 'narrative' or 'mythical' character of development has first been stressed by Rist: Rist, G. (1997), *The history of development: from Western origins to global faith*, London; New York, Zed Books, Chapters 1 and 2. See also Sachs, W. (1992), *The development dictionary: a guide to knowledge as power*, London; Atlantic Highlands, NJ, Zed Books, pp.1–5. For a neo-liberal critique of development as the narrative giving a 'starring role' to Western policy makers see Easterly, W. (2006), *The white man's burden: why the West's efforts to aid the rest have done so much ill and so little good*, Oxford University Press, p.15.

truth value, and how it shattered again into a more complex interplay of powers that often saw the Pakistani state as an enemy rather than its ally. The career of Constantinos Doxiadis exemplified this larger story. It is narrated and interpreted in roughly chronological order over six chapters, beginning with his first journeys to Pakistan as part of the country's Planning Commission and ending with the winding down of his greatest projects of Islamabad and Korangi in the mid 1960s.

As a theoretician of urbanism starting out after World War II, Doxiadis used his work in Pakistan to construct one of the most sophisticated developmental worldviews of his time. In his readings, photographs, travel accounts and programmatic writings he created a model for what it meant to be a transnational consultant working in a newly decolonized nation state; one he hoped would be largely immune to direct criticism and operate as a new form of power that could easily trump the power of the Pakistani state and its elites (Chapters 1 and 2). But development was never only a discursive matter. It involved right from the start political elements in the established sense: the lobbying for contracts, the need to find a foothold in local and international power structures, the unthankful task of marrying byzantine funding arrangements to the pet interests of local potentates. While the discursive surface of 'development' became ever more glossy and hardened, its actual experience on the ground appeared ever more contested and contingent, as Chapters 3 and 4 will demonstrate with reference to Doxiadis's career shortly before and after General Ayub Khan's landmark *coup d'état* of 1958.

The architect's greatest triumph, the new city of Islamabad, was the product of both discourse and politics, an exemplary vision of a new global reality and a fractious response to the ideological needs of an embattled military regime. As discussed in detail in Chapter 5, 'development' and 'sovereignty', 'Islam' and 'modernity' never quite came together in the manner desired. Moreover, as houses were built and residents moved in, 'development' became a process in which various modalities of power interacted in ways that transcended any simple dichotomy between plan and implementation, 'development' and 'sovereignty', 'discourse' and 'politics'.

In Chapter 6 a new cast of actors moves centre stage: the junior engineers sent from Greece, their newly assertive counterparts from Pakistan, and above all, the 'subaltern' protagonists of development history: the labourers on the construction sites, the first residents, the 'basic democrats' appointed by the state to make the spaces of development governable. Their encounters marked the space where the power of development and the state was constructed and contested. The level richest in empirical detail, the often seemingly mundane exchanges of everyday life, is also the appropriate level for a final theoretical synthesis, proposing a new way of making sense of the post-colonial state of Pakistan and what it has to tell us about the wider question of development and its 'failure' around the world. Development, this book will argue in final conclusion, radically extended the areas of life that became subject to contestation by the Pakistani state, but in so doing it did *not* act as the kind of 'anti-politics machine' that Ferguson proposed many years ago. If anything the reverse was closer to the truth: development acted as a powerful 'politicization' machine, intensifying rather than suppressing conflict between the state and the governed.

1   Architect of development

The man who was to have a signature impact on Pakistan's most ambitious urban reconstruction projects first arrived in the country in October 1954. Constantinos A. Doxiadis, the charismatic Greek architect, was then on the cusp of becoming one of the foremost international development entrepreneurs of the post-war period. He had flown to the capital Karachi from his home base in Athens, via Cyprus and Beirut, and was about to embark on a month-long reconnaissance tour that was to take him first to Dacca, Chittagong, the Hill Tracts and Sylhet in the Eastern Wing of the country, and then starting again from Karachi on a journey north along the river Indus via Khairpur, Sukkur, Rahimyar Khan, Bahawalpur to Lahore, and on to Lyallpur (today's Faisalabad), Sargodha, Peshawar and the Khyber Pass. En route there were meetings with ministers and bureaucrats, town planners and architects, and a good deal of liaising with representatives of foreign funding organizations and other overseas experts. Of equal importance was his first attempt to survey and understand the country. Observations from walks around towns and villages intersected with more fleeting impressions gleaned through car, railway and plane windows, all more or less faithfully recorded on hundreds of photographs, and in hours of notes spoken onto a portable tape recorder.[1]

Doxiadis saw unfolding in front of him a tableau of 'colossal challenges' – to use one of his most favoured expressions: urban centres where the physical scars of the Partition of India were still visible; streets lined by burnt-out shops and derelict housing stock squatted in by poor refugees from across the new Indo-Pakistan border, whose numbers showed no sign of abating. In East Bengal settlements were washed away by floods every single year and lacked everything from drinking water to electricity supply and communication links. In northern Punjab, Doxiadis observed forlorn colony townships in the desert with roads so wide and facilities so poor as to leave their inhabitants exposed to dust storms and the extreme

---

[1] CADA: Pakistan Volume 2, Dox 20, Diary 12 October–23 November 1954.

heat. Some of the factories he visited possessed the latest production facilities recently imported from Europe, but dispatched their waste untreated into the surrounding patches of ground inhabited by the poorest of the poor.[2] Doxiadis's task was to turn this tableau of 'underdevelopment' into a field of 'action', where the foreign consultant could propose and realize his visions of a better future, and in the process also secure his own personal fortune.

Doxiadis was by no means the first international expert in the housing field to work in Pakistan. There had been others before him, sent either by one of the newly established development agencies of the United States Government or the United Nations, or working directly on the invitation of the Pakistani authorities. Some, like the Frenchman Michel Ecochard who redesigned Karachi University in the early 1950s, were men of world renown who were to make important contributions to Third World urbanism for decades to come; others like the Spaniard Jose Maria Muguruza – who will make a brief reappearance later in this book – left no international legacy to speak of. In contrast to most of these contemporaries, Doxiadis did not, and was not even asked to, build a single structure over the first five years of his involvement with Pakistan. His landmark projects like Islamabad or Korangi belonged to a later period in his life. At the beginning of his career stood an altogether more abstract assignment: he was chief consultant to the Pakistan Planning Commission, the body entrusted with the drafting of the country's First Five Year Plan. (Chapter 3 will cover the political twists and turns of this four-year period in greater detail.) Doxiadis was an architect of – and for – development: that great world historical venture. He was somebody who drew his projects on the same grand canvas as the macroeconomists or modernization theorists that rose to worldwide prominence over the 1950s.[3] He thought big and believed in an all-encompassing vision to perceive, explain and change the world around him, his objective being no less than salvation of human kind. Doxiadis was thus directly involved in the international effort that sought to bring Pakistan from the colonial past into a new post-war and post-colonial order.

It is easily forgotten today just how incomplete this transition towards a new way of making sense of the world still was in the early 1950s. At the time of Doxiadis's arrival in Karachi there was no universal agreement

[2] Ibid. pp.49–51, 182, 223, 268.
[3] Gilman, N. (2003), *Mandarins of the future: modernization theory in Cold War America*, Baltimore, Johns Hopkins University Press, pp.203–205.

over what 'development' meant, let alone how it was best achieved. The idea had yet to acquire that 'discursive' power – that (semi-)scientific truth value – that made 'development' such an inescapable fact of life in later decades. Western experts had only begun to speak about Pakistan as an 'underdeveloped country' for a few years, while Pakistani politicians and policy makers deployed the term with wilful imprecision. The discursive boundaries between international development as it was to become and 'development' as a somewhat 'underdeveloped' aspect of colonialism were still not clearly drawn. When formulating some of the earliest briefing papers on industrial policy for Prime Minister Liaquat Ali Khan's Cabinet, for instance, A. MacFarquhar, Pakistan's Secretary of Commerce, Industries and Works, could still wax lyrically about the possibilities of fruit-canning and other forms of agricultural processing, while proposing that further industrialization was to be discouraged because it was bound to create out-of-control cities and would upset stability in the countryside.[4] Sir Malcolm Darling, a British administrator and writer used in the historical literature as an exemplar of the 'colonial mindset', was still doing business well into Doxiadis's time, decades after he had first popularized the image of an India of 'sturdy peasants' and loyal village-folk to the British public.[5] In a striking image of the contemporaneity of past and future, a report on labour relations in Pakistan that he drew up for the International Labour Office found its place in the same archive folder as some of Doxiadis's earliest plans for a comprehensive housing and settlements plan.[6] Even the Americans, in many ways the original custodians of the new idea of development, were, as we shall see, still reticent to translate their stated policy ambitions into practice.

The purpose of this chapter is to capture some of the contested nature of 'development' as it existed in Pakistan at and shortly prior to Doxiadis's arrival. In juxtaposing this environment to an overview of Doxiadis's life and intellectual formation, the following pages establish a baseline for the argument of this book. We get a sense of what our central figure wanted to achieve, and how his work fitted in with the wider onward march and discursive consolidation of 'development' as a global venture; but the obstacles on his way emerge with equal clarity: contrary to the increasingly polished discursive surface of development – which

---

[4] NDC: File 213/CG/47 – Industrial Policy.
[5] For a classic discussion of Darling see Dewey, C. (1993), *Anglo-Indian attitudes: the mind of the Indian Civil Service*, London; Rio Grande, Hambledon Press. For Darling's own writings, Darling, M. (1930), *Rusticus loquitur; or, The old light and the new in the Punjab village*, London; New York, Oxford University Press; Darling, M. (1977), *The Punjab peasant in prosperity and debt*, New Delhi, Manohar Book Service.
[6] CADA: Pakistan Volume 8, File HS 77.

Doxiadis did so much to create as far as his own field of expertise was concerned – there was a good deal of instability and fractiousness lurking underneath, fuelled by misunderstandings, retracted commitments and political game-playing that would never disappear from Doxiadis's experience in Pakistan; indeed, one could argue, leading to his eventual defeat as a consultant and planner.

From Athens to the world

The fact that a Greek should play such a significant role in the development of post-colonial Pakistan is not as strange as it may first seem. The business of providing development assistance in the post-war period was always a strongly international endeavour, with experts from countries other than the old colonial powers or the new world hegemons United States and Soviet Union playing an increasingly important role. Besides, there was something about the recent historical experience of Greece that made it a significant role model for other parts of an emerging developing world. Before turning to Doxiadis's activities in Pakistan in more detail, it is important to first sketch the outlines of his global career, and provide an overview of his methodology and ideas.

Perhaps surprisingly for a man of his reputation – an article in *The New Yorker* once called him 'in terms of the number of human dwellings involved the greatest planner now at work in the world'[7] – there is still no comprehensive and critical account of Doxiadis's life and work. The one book-length biography in existence, Philip Deane's *Master Builder for Free Men* (1965), is, as the title suggests, a hagiography primarily aimed at shoring up Doxiadis's reputation among the general public. It portrays Doxiadis as a man who is 'always the boss', who touches children on his field trips as if he were a prophet, and whose sexy voice makes his secretaries swoon.[8] For several reasons (more about them below) such exuberance largely turned into silence after Doxiadis's death in 1975. It was only relatively recently that interest in the man has picked up again, culminating in a retrospective exhibition at one of Athens's premier museums in 2006.[9] Alexandros Kyrtsis's *Constantinos A. Doxiadis: texts, design drawings, settlements*, which appeared as a scholarly accompaniment to the exhibition, remains to date the best exploration of Doxiadis's life

---

[7] Rand, C. (1963), 'The Ekistics world', *The New Yorker*, 11 May, p.49.
[8] Deane, P. (1965), *Constantinos Doxiadis, master builder for free men*, Dobbs Ferry, NY, Oceana Publications, pp.8, 15, 17.
[9] 'Doxiadis: Ekistics and the architecture of Entopia', winter 2006/7. Benaki Museum, Athens.

and work. Although limited in circulation, it is based on archival sources and provides a reliable overview of the major developments of his life, his projects and intellectual trajectory.[10] Kyrtsis's Doxiadis remains an 'official' Doxiadis, however; he emerges from historical records that the man himself had in many ways prepared for 'public consumption' to eventually secure his legacy. They tell a compelling story of an enigmatic but self-mythologizing pioneer of development who perhaps more than his contemporaries remained a man of his time.

Constantinos A. Doxiadis was born in 1913, just before the outbreak of the Balkan Wars, in a Greek-dominated town in Eastern Rumelia (present-day Bulgaria). Soon after his birth, his family was forced to flee to the Kingdom of Greece in order to escape ethnic cleansing. His father, a paediatrician, got involved in refugee resettlement in Athens, and in 1922 became Minister of Relief in the government of Eleftherios Venizelos, the most prominent Greek prime minister of modern times. This was the moment when 1.5 million ethnic Greeks from the Eastern Aegean coast, Thrace, Anatolia and Pontus poured into Greece 'proper' after catastrophic defeat against Atatürk's Turkey. Their numbers increased the original population of Greece by almost one-third and led to severe problems of housing and economic integration, particularly in the greater Athens area where Constantinos Doxiadis was then entering his teenage years. His direct experience of urban reconstruction and refugee resettlement was to become one of the driving forces of his career as an urban planner, with particular resonance for some of his later landmark projects in Pakistan such as the Korangi scheme for destitute Partition refugees.

After studying architecture in Athens, Doxiadis went to Berlin for a doctorate and successfully defended a thesis on architectural space in ancient Greece in 1937.[11] The classical *polis* was to remain his point of reference throughout his life, even as his main field of work shifted from architecture to planning, and for the most time, had more to do with cutting-edge engineering than with history. Upon his return from Berlin, Doxiadis rose to leading positions in town planning in Athens and, after the outbreak of World War II, became involved in the Greek resistance against German occupation. It was then that he most likely made contact with British intelligence circles, which laid the foundations for his lifelong reputation as trustworthy stalwart of Western interests. As the war was ending, Doxiadis emerged on the international political scene as a

---

[10] See Kyrtsis, A.-A. (2006), *Constantinos A. Doxiadis: texts, design drawings, settlements*, Athens, Ikaros.
[11] Ibid. pp.337–339.

member of the Greek delegation to the very first session of the United Nations in San Francisco. Throughout the war, he had been collecting information about the impact of the conflict on economic life and the built environment in Greece. He now presented his findings in books, newspaper articles and international travelling exhibitions to influence ongoing debates on post-war reconstruction. Just before Marshall Plan funding began to pour into Greece, Doxiadis was put in charge of a newly formed Ministry of Reconstruction, which he served until 1950.[12] Although it is not entirely clear how successful his work in this role actually was, Doxiadis's involvement at a time of bloody and protracted civil war with communist rebels was to further enhance his reputation as a reliable Cold War warrior.

Economic and physical reconstruction in a country like Greece was very much in the spotlight of debates about economic development in the immediate post-war era. Some of the most important arguments in the emerging field of developing economics were first formulated with regard to the Southern European periphery; most notably Paul Rosenstein-Rodan's 'big push model' that argued for large-scale economic assistance to underdeveloped countries in order to overcome what his contemporary R. R. Nelson had called a 'low level equilibrium trap'. Greece (and southern Italy) thus emerged as test cases for the kind of development path that over the 1950s and 1960s was to be prescribed to countries around the world, including Pakistan.[13] A very significant objective of this discourse, which had already played a major role in the case of Greece itself, was to prevent the newly decolonized world from falling into communist hands. Greece and Turkey had in many ways been singled out as the test cases of US development aid policy, epitomized by the 'Truman Doctrine' of 1947 which predated the famous 'Point Four' promise of international technical assistance by two years.[14] As a Greek in government service, Doxiadis not only had significant input into how this early test case of 'development' turned out, he had also been in constant and direct contact with the major donor organizations through which aid was channelled. In consequence, Doxiadis could speak about development from something like a 'Southern' perspective and was well placed to deflect the distrust commonly felt against the

---

[12] Ibid. pp.346–351.

[13] Meier, G. M. (1994a), 'From colonial economics to development economics', *From classical economics to development economics*, G. M. Meier (ed.), London, Macmillan: 173–196; Rosenstein-Rodan, P. N. (1943), 'Problems of industrialisation of Eastern and South-Eastern Europe', *The Economic Journal* 53(210/211): 202–211.

[14] Packenham, R. A. (1973), *Liberal America and the Third World: political development ideas in foreign aid and social science*, Princeton University Press, pp.25–32.

proverbial out-of-touch and know-it-all development expert from the
United States, the Antipodes or Western Europe. His own country, after
all, had been a developing nation itself, and most of the knowledge that
he was to bring to bear as an advisor to other developing countries over
the 1950s and 60s was directly derived from local experience, rather than
from academic research in a metropolitan university.

Doxiadis was himself strongly aware of this position. In one of his
earliest reports in the field of international development he included the
following reflections about the time when he was not yet an expert
himself but rather at the receiving end of other people's expertise:

> [I]t was the greatest experience of my life to meet the foreign experts ... Some
> of them were outstanding people, with many ideas which could be applied in
> Greece, others capable experts who tried to handle the Greek problem as though
> it were a Western European or an African one, some were perhaps not of the level
> required by their important mission ... It was through these conflicts of ideas
> and personalities that we realised our faults and strengthened our convictions as
> to the rightness of some of our ideas ... Through dispute we arrive at truth.[15]

Doxiadis's emergence as a leading protagonist of Third World urban
development began around 1953, after an unsuccessful attempt to
become a tomato farmer in Australia. He had never been entirely out
of touch with the wider development debate. In 1952, for instance,
he had appeared on an NBC radio panel with the Arabist Gustave von
Grunebaum and sociologist Louis Wirth to discuss the application of the
Truman Doctrine to the Eastern Mediterranean.[16] His career-defining
moment, however, came when he was invited to the United Nations
conference on tropical housing in New Delhi in early 1954. As pointed
out by Alexandros Kyrtsis, Doxiadis made two crucial contacts at this
conference that were to sustain his rise to international stardom over the
next decade or so. He joined forces with the British planner Jaqueline
Tyrwhitt, who stood in the tradition of the early twentieth-century
visionary of regional planning, Patrick Geddes, and was instrumental
in preserving and communicating the latter's ideas, particularly in
South Asia.[17] Tyrwhitt became one of Doxiadis's closest intellectual
companions, helping to establish his trademark journal *Ekistics* as one
of the most significant voices in debates about Third World urbanism for
the next two decades. The other significant contact was Jacob L. Crane,
a leading American town planner and government advisor, who had

---

[15] CADA: India Volume 1, Dox 1, p.3.
[16] Kyrtsis, A.-A. (2006), *Constantinos A. Doxiadis: texts, design drawings, settlements*, Athens,
Ikaros, p.357.
[17] See Geddes, P. and J. Tyrwhitt (1947), *Patrick Geddes in India*, London, L. Humphries.

known Doxiadis from his work in post-war Greece, but had slipped out of touch until the two men met again in New Delhi.[18] As we shall see, Crane was highly effective at lobbying on Doxiadis's behalf in the United States, which allowed him to match up project ideas with corresponding development finance from government and private sources.

Doxiadis's trip to New Delhi never secured him any business in India itself but brought possibilities for involvement in several other countries. Before he came to Pakistan in autumn 1954, he had already visited Syria as part of an International Bank for Reconstruction and Development (IBRD, in popular parlance 'World Bank') mission and drawn up ambitious plans for urban reconstruction there.[19] Starting around the same time as his involvement with Pakistan, Doxiadis developed strong business interests in Iraq, which quickly turned into his first major international commissions. Between 1955 and the time the pro-Western Hashemite Monarchy fell in 1958, Doxiadis had assumed responsibility for resettling millions of Iraqis in new satellite towns around the big cities and in new rural centres. His third most important field of operations (after Iraq and Pakistan) was in Kwame Nkrumah's Ghana, where he designed the new city of Tema as part of the ambitious and ultimately ill-fated Akosombo Dam project.[20] Consultancies and building projects on a smaller scale took place in Lebanon, Jordan, Iran, Sudan, Libya, Ethiopia and several other countries in Africa and Latin America.[21] The high-water mark of Doxiadis's involvement in Third World development was reached at the end of the 1950s, at around the time when his involvement in Pakistan was also at its most intense. Later, in the 1960s, his main emphasis shifted to projects in the United States and Greece, and above all to theoretical work and blue-sky research about problems of global urbanism.[22]

Unlike many other Western development consultants of his time, Doxiadis made his career not as an expert on secondment from government or academic positions but as a free-standing development entrepreneur. His own personal involvement in projects around the world was backed up by a company, Doxiadis Associates (DA), which he had

---

[18] CADA: India, Volume 1, p.1. See also Kyrtsis, A.-A. (2006), *Constantinos A. Doxiadis: texts, design drawings, settlements*, Athens, Ikaros, pp.362–364.

[19] Ibid. pp.362–364.

[20] Miescher, S. (2012), 'Building the city of the future: visions and experiences of modernity in Ghana's Akosombo Township', *Journal of African History* 53(3): 367–390.

[21] Kyrtsis, A.-A. (2006), *Constantinos A. Doxiadis: texts, design drawings, settlements*, Athens, Ikaros, pp.386–403.

[22] The most notable project was the Ford Foundation-funded City of the Future of 1960, ibid. pp.449–463. Kim, J. (2009), 'C. A. Doxiadis and the Ford Foundation', *Hunch* (13): 78–91.

founded in 1953. In its heyday, it boasted hundreds of employees, field offices in two dozen countries and an impressive modernist headquarters, designed by Doxiadis himself and situated in a prominent location in Athens with panoramic views over the Acropolis. Central to DA's business approach was their ability to deliver comprehensive development packages. In a project like Islamabad, for instance, DA would not only prepare a master plan that involved architects, planners, traffic experts, water and power engineers and landscape gardeners, among others, it would also produce blueprints for houses and public buildings, down to the design of door handles and what shade of paint was to be used.[23] DA suggested and negotiated supplier contracts, helped to secure funding, supervised the building itself and provided in-house training.

Doxiadis's activities moved effortlessly between the disciplines of architecture and urban planning on one side, and the discourse of development on the other. His much more famous contemporary Charles-Edouard Jeanneret 'Le Corbusier' may have been the first architect to build on several continents simultaneously,[24] but he did not see himself as a 'development consultant', which was the official self-designation of DA. This advantage made Doxiadis a fortune in the 1950s and early 1960s, but also explains why he has not received the same kind of posthumous attention accorded to many of his rivals. As the world grew more sceptical about the wisdom of large-scale planned interventions in the name of development, Doxiadis was left without new projects and without a striking legacy. His mass housing units around the world, reproduced very cheaply by the hundreds of thousands, pale in impact when faced with his rivals' opera houses, museums and headquarters of international corporations.[25] His decline began as the United States scaled back development assistance in the late 1960s, relying more than ever on strategic partnerships with dictatorial regimes that were meant to control rather than solve the contradictions of social change.[26] By the time of Doxiadis's early death in 1975, the rich West had just experienced a massive recession that marked the end of the post-war welfare state, and

---

[23] Sarkis, H. (2005), 'Dances with Margaret Mead: planning Beirut since 1958', *Projecting Beirut: episodes in the construction and reconstruction of a modern city*, H. Sarkis and P. G. Rowe (eds.), Munich; New York, Prestel: 187–202, p.191.

[24] Frampton, K. (2001), *Le Corbusier*, New York, Thames & Hudson, Chapter 6.

[25] Bromley, R. (2006), 'From global urban futures to America's urban crisis: Doxiadis in the United States', *Space and progress: Ekistics and the global context of post World War II urbanization and architecture*, Athens, unpublished conference paper.

[26] This change was accelerated by Nixon's election to the US presidency and heralded intellectually within development policy discourse by Huntington, S. P. (1968), *Political order in changing societies*, New Haven, Yale University Press.

ushered in a new age of neo-liberalism in which interventionist visions of reconstruction and settlement no longer had a place.

Ekistics and development

A crucial element in Doxiadis's modus operandi was his attempt to shore up business success through the excessive branding and mystification of his personality and work. His theoretical discourse abounded in neologisms and unique technical terms – 'Ekistics', 'ecumenopolis', 'machine', 'shell', 'dynapolis', etc. – which were meant to lend an air of distinctiveness to proposals that often shared more with prevailing architectural fashions than he was ready to admit. This was far from an unusual strategy for a man in his position. Like contemporaries such as Le Corbusier and Buckminster Fuller (and present-day star architects like Rem Koolhaas), Doxiadis wished to be known for his writing and visionary thoughts at least as much as for his projects on the ground.

Doxiadis's theoretical universe rested on conservative foundations. As he pointed out in his most comprehensive publication *Ekistics: an introduction to the science of human settlements* of 1968,[27] living conditions for humankind had been much better in the past, despite all the improvements brought about by the coming of modernity. Life was better organized and more homogenous, individuals did not yet settle in a way that made them lose all contact with each other.[28] However, developments from the eighteenth century onwards upset the harmony that had once existed between Man and Nature, between society and its artefacts. One of the negative side effects of this process, which Doxiadis returned to repeatedly in his writings, was a 'disastrous spectrum of choice'[29] bound to confuse human beings and to make them feel uprooted in their environment. The epitome of this sorry state of crisis was the 'Inhuman City' with its disconnected and 'discontinuous spaces' where ideals of 'happiness, safety and freedom' had been rendered impossible.[30] As he put it with rhetorical self-condemnation in his iconic manifesto 'Confessions of a criminal', planners and architects had singularly failed to bring this disorder under control. They had increased the dimensions of urban settlements beyond what human beings could bear, for instance in high-rise buildings; they had destroyed any cultural

---

[27] Doxiadis, C. A. (1968c), *Ekistics: an introduction to the science of human settlements*, London, Hutchinson.
[28] Ibid. pp.44–56.
[29] Doxiadis, C. A. (1971), 'Confessions of a criminal', *Ekistics* **32**(191): 249–254, p.251.
[30] Doxiadis, C. A. (1968b), 'A city for human development', *Ekistics* **25**(151): 374–394, pp.376–377.

continuities between past and present, and sacrificed 'Man himself' on the altar of speed, monumentalism and progress.[31]

This failure of urban planning as it existed, was not simply down to bad intentions, it was an epistemological problem. Despite their ever-increasing ambition, planners and architects had become singularly unable 'to comprehend the totality of a human settlement'.[32] While they had long learnt to think in three dimensions, for instance, they had forgotten to incorporate the fourth dimension, time, into their planning.[33] Their efforts could only provide momentary relief from urban problems such as traffic gridlock or congestion, but not really make cities or whole regions future-proof by properly anticipating how people would chose to settle in decades to come. The kind of over-specialization that Doxiadis saw around him was by definition the wrong way to deal with the planning of human settlements. A more holistic approach was needed. In order to demonstrate just how complex things really were, he identified five elements in the 'molecular' structure of a city: 'Man', 'Nature', 'Society', 'Shell' (his term for building) and 'Network'; which in their varying combinations could be perceived according to five functions: the economic, sociological, political, techno-logical and cultural, thus opening up 33 million possible combinations to consider. If one added fifteen possible 'units of space' which a planner had to account for – stretching from a single room, via a house, neigh-bourhood, to the metropolis, region and the planet as a whole – one would in fact have to think about 'billions and trillions of combin-ations'.[34] With their energy flows and interconnection the world of human settlements approximated complex biological organisms rather than the kind of orderly grid structures so beloved by modern planners.[35]

Doxiadis's emphasis on complexity did not lead him into an accept-ance of the planner's impotence, however. In a remarkable discursive switch, he actually promised that his trademark approach could handle what was almost by definition too difficult to handle. If one only broa-dened the scope of the planner beyond specialist knowledge and turned him into the kind of generalist social scientist that his new science of 'Ekistics' (or originally 'Oekistics'[36] after the Greek οἶκος or 'household,

[31] Doxiadis, C. A. (1971), 'Confessions of a criminal', *Ekistics* **32**(191): 249–254.
[32] Doxiadis, C. A. (1968c), *Ekistics: an introduction to the science of human settlements*, London, Hutchinson, p.47.
[33] Doxiadis, C. A. (1959), 'The rising tide of the planners', *Ekistics* **7**(39): 5–10.
[34] Doxiadis, C. A. (1968b), 'A city for human development', *Ekistics* **25**(151): 374–394.
[35] Doxiadis, C. A. (1970), 'Man's movement and his settlements', *Ekistics* **29**(174): 296–321, p.311.
[36] CADA: Pakistan Volume 1, p.12.

family') aspired to be, modernity itself could be made safe. The multiple possibilities of future planning could be made conceptually manageable on what he called the 'Ekistics grid'. [See Figure 1]

The 'Inhuman City' of the future could be tamed and turned into a utopia – or rather *entopia*, as Doxiadis preferred to call it – a real place for humans to live in harmony with themselves and nature.[37] Extended families could be revived and the fabric of neighbourhood contacts be protected and nurtured. The dangerous 'machines' (Doxiadis's preferred term for the motorcar) could be removed from the most intimate spaces of human interaction; happier children could be raised in an environment where choice was mitigated by order.[38] Above all, cities could be created to correspond to the 'human scale' where 'aesthetic dimensions corresponded to the aesthetic abilities of the average human being'.[39]

At the very centre of Doxiadis's vision of 'development' stood a project of knowledge. The work of the consultant began with the collection of information that in its ambition of omniscience far surpassed the often invoked planner's mantra of 'survey before plan'. The quintessential part of Doxiadis's *oeuvre* did not consist in stone, asphalt and concrete, but in the form of an extended archive of diaries, research dissertations, photographic albums, maps and reports, which *in toto* embodied the mastery of the Ekistics grid. It is significant and revealing that much of the material contained in this archive was written in English rather than in his native Greek. It was not meant to be just a private repository of information that Doxiadis or his Greek collaborators could draw on to solve whatever problems they faced. The archive itself was an architectural creation[40] and therefore, at least in theory, had to be open to a much wider audience. His trademark diaries, for instance (which will be discussed in some detail in the next chapter), were not the daily reflections of a private man, but highly stylized and carefully crafted pieces of public work that could be shown to donor organizations and potential clients.

The archive as a whole had a strong aesthetic quality. Its most important parts adorned the shelves in Doxiadis's own office, establishing an immediate visual interaction with his light-grey modernist desk (which he

---

[37] Doxiadis, C. A. (1968a), *Between dystopia and utopia*, London, Faber, pp.49–50.
[38] Doxiadis, C. A. (1971), 'Confessions of a criminal', *Ekistics* 32(191): 249–254, pp.253–254.
[39] Doxiadis, C. A. (1968b), 'A city for human development', *Ekistics* 25(151): 374–394, pp.391–393.
[40] Boyer, C. (2006), 'The archive of Ekistics', *Space and progress: Ekistics and the global context of post World War II urbanization and architecture*, Athens, unpublished conference paper.

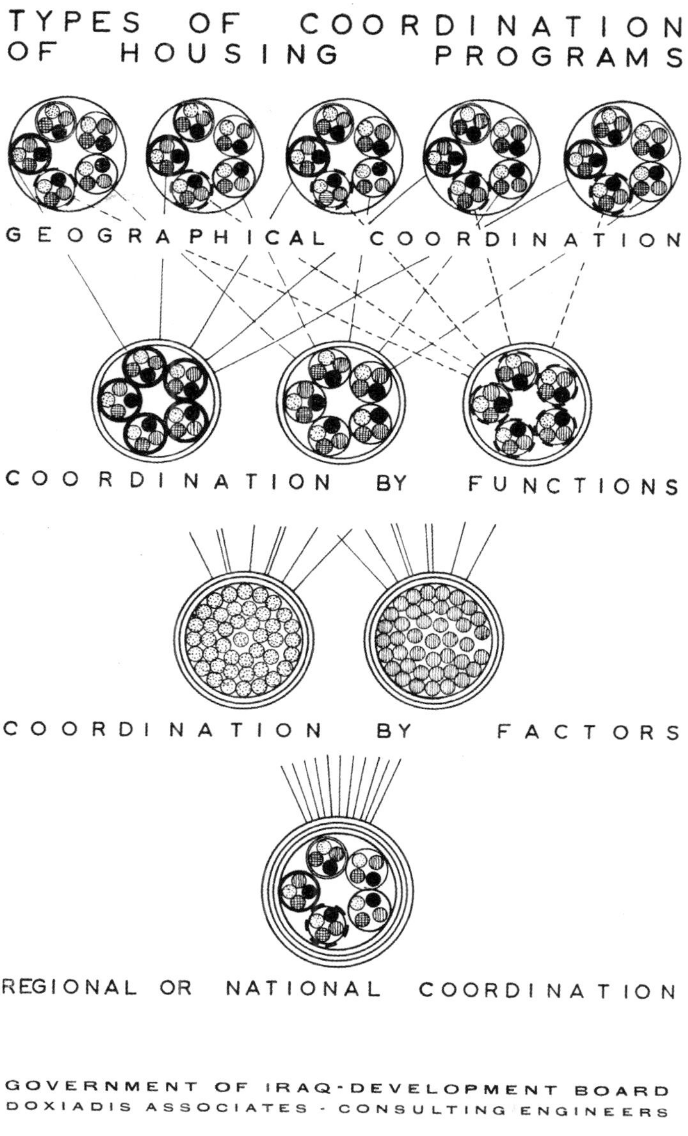

Figure 1 Handling complexity through planning – a graphic representation of Doxiadis's Ekistics principles for official use by the Iraqi government.
Source: CADA: 'Iraq housing program' – DOX-QA 26, 31.7.1956, p.5, Iraq vol.12 (Archive Files 23883).

Figure 2 Doxiadis at his desk in his office at DA headquarters on
Lycabettus Hill, Kolonaki, Athens, overlooking the Acropolis. Some of
his archive volumes are visible on the shelf behind him.
Source: CADA: Photograph No. 32591.

had designed himself), a large globe and exotic *objets d'art* on the shelves
surrounding the room, and the panorama of the Acropolis visible through
a large window outside. [See Figure 2]

Most of the archive volumes were pleasingly colour coordinated with
the desk, and labelled according to a referencing system that was at once
arcane and suggestive of a giant organization – a volume number
followed by codes for individual document series; it also impressed
Doxiadis's reach upon the casual observer – displaying the name of the
country of Doxiadis's activities in a prominent manner on the spine.
The sheer significance of Doxiadis's work in Pakistan, for instance, was
made immediately apparent by the fact that there were no less than
287 identical bound volumes – some containing up to 700 pages of
documents each – lined up next to similar series on other countries.
To the prospective customer who came to see him, Doxiadis's macro-
architectural *oeuvre* – the building itself – was thus intrinsically linked to a

microarchitecture of global expertise – the archive – and a spectacular historic reference point to hold it all together.

It is at once evident that Doxiadis's mission amounted to much more than the provision of good buildings or a pleasant urban environment. In a spatial analogy of Marx's vision of the human being as producer, Doxiadis conceived a meta-history of the human being as a settler. Ekistics would have to cover all aspects of human activity because all human activity was in the last instance an act of settlement or dwelling. Solving the conundrum of how to plan the modern city was nothing less than achieving salvation for humankind. Although Doxiadis was always deeply critical of revolutionary thought in general, and of utopias in particular, he clearly believed in a human capability to master the future. The more he painted the present in dark and apocalyptic colours, the more this future assumed connotations of transcendence. The role Doxiadis claimed for himself extended beyond that of the planner and architect to that of a prophet.[41]

This vision of a new urbanism as salvation was, of course, by no means original to Doxiadis. It had become an iconic ingredient in architectural practice over the course of the twentieth century, epitomized by the most famous architect of all: Le Corbusier himself. The idea that a human future rested on finding a cure for the diseased modern metropolis had been around since at least Victorian times. The relationship between moral panic, Christian ideas of transforming the lives of the poor and hopes for a future closer to nature had been a dominant theme in the history of urban planning from the first mass housing initiatives of the 1880s, through the development of zoning legislation and the construction of Ebenezer Howard's Garden Cities.[42] Le Corbusier formulated trenchantly radical solutions to the same problem in his major publications, *Urbanisme* (1925) and *La Ville Radieuse* (1935), assuming the role of the merciless surgeon who would treat the urban cancer not with limited interventions here and there, but with a wholesale destruction of the urban fabric as people knew it. The new urban environment he envisioned with its trademark high-rise 'machines to live in' lined up along high-speed motorways, allowed for little spontaneous human contact and even less political participation by its recipients. It was top-down

---

[41] It is no coincidence, here, that he would invoke the French Jesuit and New Age philosopher, Pierre Teilhard de Chardin in his writings, a very odd presence in a discourse about development and city planning with its often highly technical language. Doxiadis, C. A. (1968b) 'A city for human development', *Ekistics* 25(151): 374–394, p.374.

[42] Hall, P. (1988), *Cities of tomorrow: an intellectual history of urban planning and design in the twentieth century*, Oxford; New York, Blackwell, Chapters 2, 3 and 4.

in the extreme.[43] Le Corbusier was in many respects Doxiadis's great 'other'. While (most of the time) the former stressed radical intervention and a radically different way of life, the latter stressed consultation, individual human agency and the protection of tradition. But the two visions shared a common ground: a belief in the semi-divine role of the urbanist. Only the manifestations of omnipotence differed, not omnipotence itself; it could consist in the ability to create radically different worlds as in Le Corbusier, or the ability to magically account for a trillion possible human futures through a new form of science, as in Doxiadis.

The secret behind Doxiadis's appeal lay in the fact that he never let his conservatism degenerate into reactionary nostalgia or wholesale cultural pessimism. While deploring their ill effects in a *badly planned* environment, he did not reject the 'machine', the aeroplane or the modern conurbation as such. Despite all his condemnation of the perils of the modern age, Doxiadis remained a lifelong modernist. He was keenly interested in technological advances of all kinds. Most significantly, he preferred a functional style in architecture, which in his rejection of ornamentation or monumentalism differed little from international modernism. Above all he believed in the limitless possibilities of planning – if only carried out according to the correct approach. His building to a 'human scale' could be delivered in thousands of identical and prefabricated units while his visionary plans would encompass entire countries. There was nothing backward looking at all in his famous vision of 'ecumenopolis', an interconnected belt of metropolitan conurbations stretching from Northern England through Central Europe, the Middle East and India all the way to Japan, and then around North America, which he believed would represent the future of humankind.[44] What Doxiadis promised, and what accounts for his great appeal in his heyday, was that he made people believe in his ability to bridge or reconcile fundamental contradictions: between the individual and community, between local cultural tradition and global modernity, between rootedness and dynamism. In so doing he addressed the central political problem of his most enthusiastic backers: anti-communist policy makers in the rich West and conservative nationalists in the developing world

---

[43] Le Corbusier's sense of control was proverbial and is much lampooned in the planning critical literature, e.g. Sarin, M. (1977), 'Chandigarh as a place to live in', *The open hand: essays on Le Corbusier*, R. Walden (ed.), Cambridge, MA, MIT Press: 374–410; Scott, J. C. (1998), *Seeing like a state: how certain schemes to improve the human condition have failed*, New Haven, CT; London, Yale University Press, pp.103–146.

[44] Doxiadis, C. A. and J. G. Papaioannou (1974), *Ecumenopolis: the inevitable city of the future*, New York, Norton.

who saw that rapid social change was both necessary and inevitable, but also highly dangerous to the established order.

Doxiadis's promise to master the process of modernization through 'development' depended on his assumption of an omniscient vision. Wherever he went, he would draw up a comprehensive and all-encompassing agenda for intervention that was directly informed by his ambition for Ekistics: to fully take into account the geographic, social, historical, cultural, political, technological and religious features of the people concerned. This was the primary rationale behind the archive that occupied such an important place in his overall *oeuvre*. For each country of activity there would be an extensive collection of material, including anything from household surveys into consumer behaviour and prayer attendance to tabulations of wages for different social classes and enquiries into energy consumption, industrial output and levels of education. And if such data could not be collected because of time pressures or lack of personnel, Doxiadis would seek to fill the gap single-handedly by compiling elaborate travel diaries and photographic albums on the go. This project of knowledge was central to the emergence of 'development' as a discursive formation from a heterogeneous and often transparently 'ideological' array of ideas about history, politics and culture. Through surveying and categorizing, Doxiadis helped to produce and solidify the categories of 'underdevelopment' that Arturo Escobar and James Ferguson have located at the very heart of the political efficacy of development. The very idea behind 'Ekistics' was to create an 'order of things', which possessed scientific truth value; where any recommendation or prescription made would no longer appear as the potentially politically motivated utterance of a self-interested individual but as something that was independently true, because it derived – apparently – from an understanding of how the world 'really' was.

Underdevelopment comes to Pakistan

When Doxiadis began to develop his trademark approach, Pakistan was still far from a ready-made discursive 'subject' of development. As has already been suggested at the very beginning of this chapter, 'development' did not yet possess sufficient discursive foundations to operate coherently and beyond political suspicion. This was hardly surprising, as the term was still closely associated with the propaganda efforts of the colonial regime forced out of South Asia only a few years earlier. Over the course of World War II, the British had begun to promise louder than ever before that, once the hostilities were over, their government would at last take seriously its obligation to create a better future for all its citizens regardless of colour. But little was achieved in actual practice, and a problematic intellectual ballast remained.[45] 'Development' in colonial parlance was by no means easily distinguishable from nineteenth-century ideas of 'progress' and 'improvement'[46] that justified continuing European control rather than a new world united in prosperity and freedom from foreign domination. The growing pressure of anti-imperialist nationalism may have forced a loosening of the ideological foundations of such earlier agendas for change under foreign tutelage. They could no longer be presented as being so long term as to be practically never ending, putting paid to Victorian notions of a 'permanent Raj'.[47] But this shift was never complete enough to make the new possibility of 'development' believable as 'true' above ideological obfuscations.

Development scepticism remained widespread throughout Doxiadis's career. We have already heard of the leading Pakistani bureaucrat who did not believe that industrialization was really a worthwhile goal for his country, and other examples will follow in due course. The impression of a seamless turnaround from colonialism to 'development' that we get from neighbouring India, where Nehru sought to make scientific planning the ideological bedrock of his regime, never applied in Pakistan. If there was a discursive formation in place that was still widely believed to describe things 'as they truly were', it was not 'development' but colonial social science and the doctrines of governance derived from it. Not coincidentally, this formation had produced its own formidable archive over the previous century or so that served as a striking antecedent of Doxiadis's own ambitions. It included the famous Census of India, one of the earliest and most precise anywhere in the world, a vast collection of official Gazetteers covering everything from history to architecture, geology, land economy, demographics, folklore and politics about each and every administrative district of the subcontinent, not to mention the specialist archaeological, meteorological, botanical, linguistic and geological 'Surveys of India', and the ever-expanding descriptions of the assumed characteristics of 'castes' and tribes across the country.[48]

---

[45] See Zachariah, B. and S. Bhattacharya (1999), '"A great destiny": the British colonial state and the advertisement of post-war reconstruction in India, 1942–45', *South Asia Research* **19**(1): 71–100.

[46] Zachariah, B. (2005), *Developing India: an intellectual and social history, c. 1930–50*, New Delhi, Oxford University Press, pp.80–157; Ludden, D. (1992), 'India's development regime', *Colonialism and culture*, N. Dirks (ed.), Ann Arbor, Michigan University Press: 247–287.

[47] Wurgaft, L. D. (1983), *The imperial imagination: magic and myth in Kipling's India*, Middletown, CT, Wesleyan University Press, pp.2–4.

[48] There is an extensive literature on colonial knowledge in India. Classic examples include Inden, R. B. (1990), *Imagining India*, Oxford; Cambridge, MA, Basil Blackwell; Cohn,

Colonial science rivalled the omniscient ambitions of Ekistics and of 'development', but the two discursive formations could not simply coexist for any extended period in time.[49] Their basic categories and historical sensibilities remained incompatible. The assumption of an essential and unchangeable difference between castes, tribes, religions and races ruled out the kind of expectations of rapid 'catch-up' that new social indicators drawn up on the basis of dynamic statistical averages made possible. In order to be truly victorious, development would have to eventually replace its predecessor as a source of truth. Pre-existing notions about the relationship between the perceived basic building blocks of the social world and people's ability (or inability) to affect the course of history had to be fundamentally changed. This was never altogether easy. Even the most self-avowed proponents of development sometimes fell back into colonial modes of thinking, and their fundamental belief that anybody regardless of cultural background had it in their grasp to become like the most advanced parts of the West, was often revealed to be shaky when the going got tough. For Doxiadis's Pakistani patrons and partners to leave colonial knowledge behind and to endorse something new was a harder task still, and one that in many ways never came to fruition.

The development of development into a discourse began with the politically motivated reconstruction of colonial slogans of development into a new worldview. In its origins, development, even in its new postcolonial form, remained deeply 'ideological', an easily readable response to immediate political problems. But soon ideology began to be solidified with the help of a new heuristic toolkit, a new way of making sense of the world, even if it took a good deal longer – if it ever happened at all – for this discourse to acquire the widespread acceptance and power/knowledge that Foucauldian analysts customarily ascribe to it. The story of how 'underdevelopment' came to Pakistan, is not an account of its economic or political malaise, which remained as deep as ever for much of the 1950s, but of how foreign experts and policy makers, and in a

---

B. S. (1996), *Colonialism and its forms of knowledge: the British in India*, Princeton University Press; Dirks, N. B. (2001), *Castes of mind: colonialism and the making of modern India*, Princeton University Press.

[49] Despite clear continuities especially in Britain, see Kothari, U. (2005), *A radical history of development studies: individuals, institutions and ideologies* London; New York, Zed Books. For a subtle take on similarities and differences between colonial and post-colonial usages of development see Cooper, F. (1997), 'Modernizing bureaucrats, backward Africans, and the development concept', *International Development and the Social Sciences*, F. Cooper and R. M. Packard (eds.), Berkeley, University of California Press: 64–92.

much more haphazard way also locals, began to change their basic reference frame for making sense of the world around them.

What set this process into motion over the late 1940s and early 1950s was not the result of a profound victory of anti-colonialism, and even less the clarion call to a new way of running the world, but rather the relatively limited attempt of squaring some foreign policy difficulties of the period. The trigger for this attempt at re-organizing the world was an intensification of the Cold War around the world, epitomized by Mao's march towards victory in the Chinese civil war, followed soon after by increasing tensions over Korea and Vietnam.[50] This raised the spectre of large swathes of Asia 'going communist', which was not only of concern to the new hegemon the United States, but also for Britain which still had extensive colonial possessions in the region. While the actual resources dedicated to such a strategy remained limited for the time being, at least at the level of propaganda and official ideology an attempt had to be made to stop the communist bloc from exploiting the question of decolonization further for their own advantage. A way had to be found to keep the still non-communist nations and colonial territories of Asia at least nominally united behind Western leadership.[51] This was no easy task as there were not only considerable political tensions between some members of this group – not least between India and Pakistan – but also a great deal of natural sympathy for China's achievements and a natural inclination to see France and Britain relinquish control over their remaining possessions in the region.

It was a reflection of this wider geopolitical context that the first concerted policy reference to 'development' was made by an American president speaking to reconfirm his country's commitment to NATO and the United Nations. His overriding objective was to alleviate fears of another world war, which had become acute and widespread in times of high tension between East and West. Almost as an afterthought, Harry Truman added a 'Point Four' to his famous presidential address in January 1949, announcing that forthwith the United States would be 'making the benefits of our advances and industrial progress available for the improvement and growth of underdeveloped areas' around the world. This was the first time the term 'underdevelopment' was used outside expert discourse by a major political leader. Although not yet fully

---

[50] Packenham, R. A. (1973), *Liberal America and the Third World: political development ideas in foreign aid and social science*, Princeton University Press, pp.35–45.

[51] On the collusion between the United States and a continuation of British colonialism after World War II see Louis, W. R. and R. Robinson (2006), 'The imperialism of decolonization', *Ends of British imperialism: the scramble for empire, Suez and decolonization*, London, I.B. Tauris: 451–502.

worked out and under-resourced as a policy, Truman's declaration turned out to be a step change both in conceptual terminology and ambition.[52]

Initially, the United States concentrated on aid for East Asia, which was seen as most at risk by communist advances. Leaving aside the growing involvement of what was to be Doxiadis's first employer – the International Bank of Reconstruction and Development – in the affairs of 'developing countries',[53] it fell to a British-led initiative to translate Truman's promise into more than a declaration in other areas of Asia. In January 1950, the prime ministers of several Commonwealth countries met to inaugurate the Colombo Plan. Over the following years, this inter-regional development initiative brought together the newly independent nation states of the Indian subcontinent – India, Pakistan and Ceylon (which taken together accounted for four-fifths of the total Plan provisions) – the United Kingdom and Canada, Australia and New Zealand, and areas further East, some of which were still under colonial rule like Malaya and Vietnam, and yet others that had also recently become independent like Indonesia and the Philippines. In concrete policy terms the Plan demanded the drafting of a six-year development plan by all member countries, which would then be scrutinized by joint expert committees, with a view to facilitate an exchange of expertise across the group. The members of the Plan had very little in common apart from the fact that they posed a geostrategic problem for the capitalist West. This raised the question of how one could refer to this highly heterogeneous group of nations and territories in a politically expedient way. It certainly could not be based on language, culture or even a shared colonial history, as there was no common ground on any of these considerations. Given that the preservation of the last remnants of colonialism in the region was at least in part the objective of the Plan, there also could not be any strong reference to anti-imperialism; and a hard anti-communism along Cold War lines was equally out of the question, as some member countries – notably India and Indonesia – had powerful and domestically legitimate communist constituencies of their own.

One way to define a common attribute for the Colombo Plan recipients were new geographic terminologies that turned out to be confusing

---

[52] Rist, G. (1997), *The history of development: from Western origins to global faith*, London; New York, Zed Books, pp.70–75.

[53] The first World Bank Mission to aid a developing country was sent to Colombia in 1949, Escobar, A. (1995), *Encountering development: the making and unmaking of the Third World*, Princeton University Press, p.24.

and explained very little. Guy Wint, veteran India correspondent of the *Manchester Guardian*, for instance, used the term 'South Asia' to refer to the region from 'Karachi to the Philippines' in a 1952 publication introducing the Colombo Plan to a wider public.[54] The arbitrary nature of such designations was highlighted by the fact that writing at the same time for the left-leaning Bureau of Current Affairs, one John Lyons went the opposite way and referred to India, Pakistan, Vietnam, Malaya and Indonesia collectively as 'South *East* Asia'. In yet other accounts, the simple term 'Asia' was seen as most appropriate as a shorthand.[55] This confusion was to engender all sorts of strange, and at times comical, suggestions in the early development literature, including, as we shall see, in the very reading material that someone like Doxiadis had at his disposal before setting out for Pakistan.

The lack of a clear geographic definition of the Colombo Plan countries highlighted the need for an alternative which was not rooted in simple description but also encapsulated the kind of project that the plan represented. In this context Truman's term 'underdevelopment' attained a central role. After sketching the vast geographic and cultural differences that exist in the area between Pakistan and the Philippines, one D. G. Bridson working for the UK treasury information division observed that all these differences could be made to disappear in one stroke if one looked at them not as a geographic area of unclear description, but as a single 'problem'. All countries in question were 'industrially, scarcely developed at all', while 'methods of cultivation are little in advance of what they must have been two thousand years ago', he argued. This state of affairs, he continued, if left unchecked, entailed a 'certainty of eventual starvation' and thus a threat to world peace.[56] According to another writer, the Plan was 'a comprehensive attack upon the problem of poverty and under-development'.[57]

Such a project was, of course, not exclusive to the areas brought together under the Colombo Plan. What was so special about these *South*

[54] Wint, G. (1952), *What is the Colombo Plan?* London, Batchworth Press, p.7.
[55] Lyons, J. (1951), *The Colombo Plan*, London, Bureau of Current Affairs, p.3. His pamphlet appears as an extended paraphrase, often with identical expressions, of one produced without author by the Treasury Department, suggesting identical authorship. While no strong opinion is expressed in the 'official' pamphlet, Lyons is very critical of the Colombo Plan in the one published under his name. The publisher 'Bureau of Current Affairs' published a range of left-leaning and sometimes pro-Soviet material at the time.
[56] Bridson, D. G. (Great Britain, Treasury, Information Division) (1953), *Progress in Asia: the Colombo Plan in action.* (Prepared for the Information Division of the Treasury by the Central Office of Information. Text by D. G. Bridson.) [With plates.] London, pp.5–8.
[57] Blackton, C. S. (1951), 'The Colombo Plan', *Far Eastern Survey* **20**(3): 27–31, p.28.

East Asian countries? asked the aforementioned John Lyons, after pointing out that 'underdevelopment' was also the hallmark of Latin America, the Middle East, China and even parts of Europe that were not included in the Plan. His answer was that they were *especially* 'under-developed', which could be proven on the basis of a range of universally applicable indicators. One of the key characteristics of the 'development' discourse was clicking into place here: that the distinction between countries that really mattered in the post-war world was no longer of an essential kind – religion, culture, language, race, etc. – but of a differential kind – a relative position on a single sliding scale of 'underdevelopment'.[58]

Pakistan was literally constructed as an 'underdeveloped' country when international commentators and experts began to measure the depth of its problems and the extent of its progress under the Colombo Plan with the help of universal development indicators of this kind. An early example was an article by the American economist Jerome Cohen, written in early 1951, just after the first contours of Pakistan's make-shift 'Six-Year Plan'[59] required under the overall Colombo Plan scheme had been published. 'Throughout South Asia the standard of living is lamentably low and the economies gravely underdeveloped. Poverty and hardship are the rule rather than the exception',[60] Cohen asserted before providing a series of statistics, which no longer required any justification or explanation, but simply created 'underdevelopment' through their invocation alone: per capita income – 51 US dollars per year in Pakistan and 57 in India, as compared to 1453 in the United States; daily calorie consumption per head –1750 in South Asia versus 3250 in the United States; literacy rate – 10 per cent in Pakistan, 15 per cent in India. Other 'development indicators' followed: 73 million agricultural workers in India are engaged in cultivating an area that requires less than 8 million workers in the United States with superior green technology; the consumption of steel per 1000 population was 1.3 tons in Pakistan, 3.8 in India and 364 in the United States, indicating a near complete lack of manufacturing industry and, more importantly, modern construction activities; electricity consumption per 1000 population was 13 kwh in

---

[58] Lyons, J. (1951), *The Colombo Plan*, London, Bureau of Current Affairs, pp.4–6.
[59] This Six-Year Plan was a requirement of membership in the Colombo Plan and actually predates Pakistan's first Five Year Plan drafted under the aegis of the Harvard Advisory Group. The Six-Year Plan was in many ways not a plan at all, but simply a list of desirable projects. See Curtin, P. W. E. (1954), 'The effect of the Colombo Plan', *Pakistan Horizon* 7(2): 76–79.
[60] Cohen, J. B. (1951), 'The Colombo Plan for Cooperative Economic Development,' *Middle East Journal* 5(1): 94–100, p.94.

India versus 1033 kwh in Britain and 1.9 kwh in Pakistan. The latter, as Cohen noted, was one of the lowest uptakes of electricity anywhere in the world, making Pakistan one of the most 'underdeveloped' or least 'developed' countries on the planet.[61]

This construction of 'underdevelopment' was linked to another ideological manoeuvre that betrayed that at the bottom of the new universalist and culturally neutral way of describing the poor South stood a renewed assumption of essential difference. '... the problem before these countries [in the Colombo Plan] is very different from that which Western Europe faced at the end of the war', an official British government information booklet argued in characteristic fashion; while 'most of the European countries were already highly developed before the War, and it was mainly a question of restoring what the war had destroyed' the 'real task of development' in Asia 'had barely begun'.[62] The tacit assumption was that the aspects of 'development' that really mattered were so deeply rooted in European culture as to be virtually indestructible by even the most catastrophic vagaries of history. Or, put differently, these characteristics were – despite all talk of a sliding scale of development – not really 'develop-able' at all.

Pamphlets like these were designed to cut off policy choices that had previously been available to people in the poor South, and were not simple endorsements of 'development' as it now emerged. Instead of conceiving the task ahead as one concerted effort to overcome a specific historic crisis – as had been the case with much of Europe after World War II – Pakistan's problems were now addressed as some universal notion of backwardness that Western commentators had begun to find anywhere from Colombia to the Philippines. Pakistanis were now told that only Europe and Japan could entertain the notion of a time-limited single great push to make things better; for everyone else there was only 'development', depicted as a far less straightforward and protracted task that required a complete overhaul of all of social, cultural and economic life in the poor South. There was a directly disingenuous undertone in such arguments, as they were advanced at the precise time when the big spending spree epitomized by the Marshall Plan that had helped the countries of Europe to get back to their feet had ended. Enforcing a shift from ideologies of 'reconstruction' to 'development' was intimately tied with a scaling back of resources, as if the growth of an

[61] Ibid. p.95.
[62] Commonwealth Consultative Committee on South and South-East Asia (1950), *New horizons in the East: the Colombo Plan for Co-operative Economic Development in South and South-East Asia*, London, HMSO, p.9.

idea and its transformation into a meta-historical discourse could compensate for actual lack of commitment.

This new political language was flexible enough to serve the ideological needs of old colonial powers like Britain because it allowed the old idea of an essential 'otherness' of the colonized to be reformulated. The reason for the great divergence between 'developed' and 'under-developed' went back not only to a time before the war, but obliquely also to a time before the imposition of European colonial rule, thus gently absolving the Western powers from all responsibility for the problems they now so valiantly claimed to address. While the inhabitants of the 'underdeveloped world' were good at 'fashioning lovely things with their hands' and lived a life of 'dignity and faith', the aforementioned pamph-let argued in a charming echo of common colonial sentiments, they had still been 'little touched by the revolution in methods of production which in 150 years has so transformed the face of the Western world.'[63] Alongside references to agricultural practices that allegedly had been unchanged for thousands of years, such statements produced the impres-sion of some inherent causes of 'underdevelopment' that existed above and beyond global power politics or geostrategic interests.

Liaquat in Washington

The new language of development was flexible enough to allow nationalist governments in the newly decolonized world to make the opposite claim: that it was first and foremost the colonial presence that had produced underdevelopment, and that the rich world had a special obligation to help remove its own toxic legacy. Such references were, in fact, widespread in official Pakistani government documents, par-ticularly in contexts where the Pakistan government itself was accused of 'underdeveloping' certain regions under its control. When speaking about the 'backwardness' of East Pakistan, for instance, it was com-monplace to invoke the old accusation that the British had deliberately destroyed a burgeoning local textile industry to impose their own factory-made cloth on a forcibly created mass market of new con-sumers.[64] But such arguments could only ever play a supportive or secondary role in Pakistani state ideology. Even if this may have been a highly desirable new project for the nation *after* independence, Pakistan had not been *created* to overcome 'underdevelopment'. Its

---

[63] Ibid. p.6.
[64] Ahmad, N. (1958), *An economic geography of East Pakistan*, London, Oxford University Press, pp.71–88.

raison d'être was to provide a location of sovereignty for the Muslim nation in the Indian subcontinent. Pakistan depended on a discourse of cultural 'difference' for its very existence, and the discourse of 'underdevelopment' with its global language of social transformation was unable to express this adequately. If anything, it wrote such differences out of the picture. The Pakistan that the aforementioned Jerome Cohen conjured up in his country report, was curiously devoid of any references to Islamic history, Jinnah's Two Nation Theory or the experience of standing up to 'the Hindus' which would have featured highly in a nationalist textbook; it was an 'underdeveloped' county like any other.[65]

It is important to note here that the problem of culture was far greater for Pakistan than for its neighbour India. Indian nationalists had argued for their independence on economic grounds for a considerable time before 'development' was officially adopted as one of the signature policies of the Congress movement and later Congress governments. British colonialism was never only seen as bad because it was foreign, but because it had negative effects on India's society and welfare. Arguments like the deindustrialization thesis that later also featured in some Pakistani material were especially important for India because they bypassed the far more difficult and ultimately impossible task of defining the Indian nation clearly and unambiguously on grounds of culture, religion or language. 'Development', in the estimation of Partha Chatterjee, was not an added extra to Indian nationalism, something that could be attempted after the question of national identity had already been settled, it was absolutely central to settling this question itself.[66] In the case of Pakistan, in contrast, economic considerations were often collapsed into ethno-religious arguments. Middle-class Muslims in the Punjab, frustrated landowners in Uttar Pradesh, business tycoons in Bombay, and penniless farmers in East Bengal could all blame their grievances on exploitation 'by the Hindus', which could be overcome only through the establishment of a separate state.

---

[65] Such inconsistencies become apparent in 'official' Pakistani publications that seek to deal with development. Haroun er Rashid, a West Pakistani CSP official, spends large parts of his introduction to the economic geography of East Pakistan on condemnations of Hindu 'bigotry' (p.97) and even on the essential racial features distinguishing 'Hindus' from 'Muslims' in the region (pp.104–105). It is only in the final chapter on 'Development planning' that he slips into a discourse of calories per head of population and other 'development' indicators, but even here somewhat incoherently (pp.367–368). Rashid, H. E. (1965), *East Pakistan: a systematic regional geography & its development planning aspects*, Lahore, Sh. Ghulam Ali & Sons.

[66] Chatterjee, P. (1997), 'Development planning and the Indian state, *State and politics in India*, P. Chatterjee (ed.), Delhi; New York, Oxford University Press: x, 576, pp.271–276.

The problem of how a 'nationalist' and a 'developmentalist' language could be combined produced notable tensions in Pakistani state discourse of the early post-colonial era. A good example is the way in which Pakistan's first Prime Minister, the Nawabzada Liaquat Ali Khan, talked about the subject of 'development' on his visit to the United States in May 1950, the first by any Pakistani leader. It is important to understand the geopolitical impetus behind Pakistan's drift into this political language. American attitudes towards Pakistan had been lukewarm when the country first appeared on the world map. Although there was growing interest in establishing an anti-communist block of Muslim nations along what came to be known as the 'northern tier' against the Soviet Union – Turkey, Egypt (initially), the Gulf States, Iraq and Iran – most US policy makers were looking to multireligious India rather than Muslim Pakistan as their most suitable ally in South Asia.[67]

Pakistani diplomats and negotiators had attempted to enlist American political and financial support very early on. The then Finance Minister and later Governor General, Ghulam Mohammad, had requested a loan of over 2 billion US dollars via his envoy Mir Laiq Ali in October 1947,[68] while the Karachi mayor Genubai Allana appealed for Marshall Plan funding to be extended to Pakistan when speaking as a delegate to the International Labour Organization in San Francisco in summer 1948.[69] In both cases, the unresolved conflict with India in the aftermath of Partition was the main motivation for seeking assistance: help with building up a viable Pakistani military on the eve of its first war over Kashmir in the first instance, aid for the rehabilitation of refugees in the second. Neither case persuaded the Americans at the time.[70] Even though they were not actively ill-disposed towards Pakistan, they had no time for the country's desire to pose a challenge to Indian hegemony in the region. Instead they consistently argued for friendly relations between the two dominions, brushing aside any challenges this may have

---

[67] See Rotter, A. J. (2000), *Comrades at odds: the United States and India, 1947–1964*, Ithaca, NY, Cornell University Press; McGarr, P. M. (2013), *The Cold War in South Asia: Britain, the United States and the Indian subcontinent, 1945–1965*, Cambridge University Press, Chapter 1.

[68] Jalal, A. (1990), *The state of martial rule: the origins of Pakistan's political economy of defence*, Cambridge; New York, Cambridge University Press, p.55. Feroz Khan Noon, landowner and diplomat (and later Prime Minister of Pakistan) also approached the Americans for aid in 1947, already using the argument that India was untrustworthy as 'it would go communist soon'. NARA: State Department Central Files, Pakistan, M1448, File 845F.00/12-2747 Despatch 276, Karachi 27 December 1947.

[69] Khan, M. A. (1996), Pakistan, the first twelve years: the *Pakistan Times* editorials of Mazhar Ali Khan, Karachi; New York, Oxford University Press, p.441.

[70] Kux, D. (2001), *The United States and Pakistan, 1947–2000: disenchanted allies*, Washington, D.C., Woodrow Wilson Center Press, pp.20–21.

posed to Pakistan's own sense of sovereignty and viability. It was only commensurate with these strategic priorities that it was Jawaharlal Nehru of India, and not any Pakistani statesman, who was first invited to Washington for a state visit.

Liaquat's trip to America would not have been possible without twisting the arm of a reluctant superpower. In an acute awareness of the new geopolitical realities of the post-war period, the Pakistani foreign policy establishment responded to being cold-shouldered by the United States by making overtures to the Soviet Union. Although the most powerful bureaucrats in the central government remained strongly pro-Western, and despite the Soviet Union and Pakistan not even having diplomatic relations at the time, Liaquat secured an invitation to visit Moscow in autumn 1949.[71] It was this action, and not any particular alignment of interests with Pakistan, that prompted a counter-invitation from the United States. Stalin's earlier offer, as it happened, was never followed up. The whole episode was meant to be a boost for the Prime Minister himself, desperate to increase his own profile through appearances on the international stage. The world did not make it immediately easy for him, as it were. According to *The Times*, Liaquat was 'not a spectacular figure', at best a man of 'quiet slow charm';[72] much like his country at large, he would forever remain outclassed by his Indian rivals in terms of international public relations.

Liaquat's Washington trip was well suited to providing prestigious photo opportunities. It had all the trappings of a state visit in a now bygone era when the United States would pull out all the stops to present an image of equal recognition and hospitality to its guests from the poor South. The Prime Minister, accompanied as ever by his elegant and politically active wife Raana, was picked up from London by Truman's presidential plane, the *Independence*.[73] Liaquat's tour programme was extensive in its geographic reach and included a large number of public speeches, but little in terms of actual negotiations with high-ranking American officials.[74] It took him to several major American cities – besides Washington to New York, Chicago, Kansas City, Los Angeles, Houston, New Orleans and Boston – with a good amount of sightseeing, a reception in Hollywood and at the very end of the visit, several days of surgery and medical check-ups in some of America's best

---

[71] Kazimi, M. R. (2003), *Liaquat Ali Khan: his life and work*, Karachi, Oxford University Press, pp.291–297.
[72] *The Times* (London), 1 May 1950.   [73] *The New York Times*, 4 May 1950.
[74] Kux, D. (2001), *The United States and Pakistan, 1947–2000: disenchanted allies*, Washington, D.C., Woodrow Wilson Center Press, pp.34–35.

hospitals.[75] *The New York Times* covered the visit in some detail, paying particular attention to the activities of the Begum Liaquat, who made several speeches about women's rights and was repeatedly pictured visiting American children's homes and other philanthropic institutions.[76] Not everyone was equally enthusiastic about the visit from Pakistan, however. Liaquat did not receive anything like the attention accorded to his Indian counterpart Nehru who had come the previous year.[77] According to one commentator, when Liaquat was to address the US Senate there was so little interest in hearing him speak that senators had to be rounded up in the corridors to make the body quorate.[78]

The primary purpose of Liaquat's speeches in the United States was to introduce Pakistan's national interests to an American public in ways that the latter would find sympathetic, while also keeping an eye on how on his representations were perceived back in Karachi. This meant taking a sufficiently robust nationalist line stressing religious difference, without offending the broadly pro-Indian sympathies of his Western audience. When describing the Pakistan project to the members of the US Senate, Liaquat highlighted themes that resonated with US history: the struggle for freedom from colonialism followed by a constitutional settlement, the prominence of religion that did *not* mean theocracy, a constant emphasis on individual responsibility and rights. Economic difficulties were only mentioned towards the end of the Senate speech, in the context of 'handicaps, both natural and man-made' that the new country had to face. But revealingly, the term 'underdevelopment' or any of its derivatives was not used in the speech at all, nor was there any emphasis on the need for outside development assistance; instead, Liaquat highlighted an ethic of 'hard work', 'fortified' by 'faith' that would see Pakistan overcome its birthing pangs.[79]

Liaquat did make use of the new discourse of 'underdevelopment' in other contexts, however. In one of his longest speeches, at the Town Hall in New York City, he portrayed Pakistan as a 'primitive' and an 'Asiatic' country that was in need of new technologies and scientific knowledge from the West in order to achieve 'industrial' advancement from its

[75] *The New York Times*, 8 May 1950, p.18; 9 May 1950, p.1; 10 May 1950, p.22; 28 May 1950, p.30.

[76] *The New York Times*, 5 May 1950, p.11; 7 May 1950, p.41.

[77] Kux, D. (2001), *The United States and Pakistan, 1947–2000: disenchanted allies*, Washington, D.C., Woodrow Wilson Center Press, p.36.

[78] Cauhdrī, Z. H. and H. A. J. Zaidī (1989), *Pākistān kī siyāsī tārīkh*, Lāhaur, Idārah-yi Muṭāla'ah-yi Tārīkh, Volume X, p.290.

[79] Khan, L. A. (1950), *Pakistan, the heart of Asia: speeches in the United States and Canada, May and June 1950*, Cambridge, MA, Harvard University Press, pp.7–8.

agricultural base. This would ultimately enable even the poorest of its residents not to be 'unhappy to compare himself with the more advanced peoples of the world.'[80] Another, even clearer reference to the new discourse of development came when addressing a luncheon meeting at the National Press Club on the topic of Pakistan's 'foreign relations'. Here, Liaquat listed as one of Pakistan's major interests 'our dire need for economic development', including the need for 'goodwill and cooperation, which the rest of the world may choose to offer us, to make up, not for lost years but for lost centuries in trade, in advanced agriculture and advanced industry.'[81] Crucially though, this was only the third and least important of Pakistan's 'world interests' and the one described with the smallest number of words and the least rhetorical flourish; the first was an aggressively formulated defence of the 'territorial integrity of Pakistan' against any potential enemies on the international scene, and the second the realization of the 'thirteen hundred years old' religious ideals of Islam in a modern state. Equally significantly, the reference to 'underdevelopment' was not made in the context of describing the aspirations of Pakistan as a country, but when delineating its relations to others. 'Development', in other words, was not a domestic issue that had arisen from Pakistan's own historical experience in the same organic way as let us say the question of religion in politics. It was a way of how these problems could be related to the wider world.

In a number of pronouncements, Liaquat sought to weave the topic of 'underdevelopment' more closely into the fabric of Pakistani national mythology. For instance, he argued that while Hindus had been the 'developed' people of colonial India – 'traders, technicians, engineers or doctors' – Muslims had been the most 'backward' and 'undeveloped' [sic] who were now faced with the task of 'setting up shops' and learning 'about imports and exports', a challenge they took to with the values of determination, personal responsibility and 'working without holidays'.[82] What is expressed here, and echoed in several other speeches made during the state visit, is a communal rendering – a deuniversalization – of development theory which made Muslim Pakistanis look more deserving of help than 'Hindu' Indians.

Although this may not have been as obvious to an American audience, Pakistani listeners would have immediately picked up on a strange and almost inverted relationship between 'backwardness' and moral rectitude here. As anyone familiar with Muslim League propaganda over the last decade would have known, many sections of Indian Muslim society,

---

[80] Ibid. p.29.   [81] Ibid. p.12.   [82] Ibid. pp.44–46.

especially the better educated ones, saw Hindu commercial and professional success as the result of an inherent 'moneylending' mentality, imagined to be full of subterfuge, greed and 'cunning', resembling anti-Semitic stereotypes in Europe. Precisely because 'development' required a gigantic effort and did not come 'naturally' to them, Muslims had a chance to cultivate values of self-sufficiency, equality of opportunity and reward according to initiative as part of the development experience, which tallied perfectly with American popular appreciations of why providing development aid was worthwhile. A universalist discourse about European pathways to modernity could be utilized in such ways that it actually expressed a mythology of self-expression and religious chauvinism, at least to ears who knew what to listen for.

Liaquat's references to 'underdevelopment' in his speeches in the United States demonstrate the weakness of this ideology at the time: they could never be deployed consistently, and were often literally 'underdeveloped' in terms of conceptual clarity and rhetorical sophistication. But the future potential of this new political language was also already apparent. 'Development' was to prove itself very valuable indeed to paper over the partial deafness and limited commitment that continued to exist on either side of an emerging Pakistan–US alliance. It allowed both parties to talk about aid to Pakistan in ways that skirted around the thorny issue of whether this aid was actually going to be used to strengthen Pakistan's military position vis-à-vis its neighbour India, which continued to remain in the good books if not of all subsequent US administrations then at least among US public opinion at large. When conceptualized as an 'underdeveloped country', Pakistan was not only stripped of its specific (and inherently anti-Indian) experience and aspirations, but also placed in a context of universal history that would effortlessly include both India and Pakistan as fellow aspirants for human betterment rather than as rivals on the brink of war, a vision that suited the American inability (or unwillingness) to make a clear choice between them particularly well.

A game of 'few dollars and fewer people'

In the early 1950s, 'development' provided a useful language to create common ground for a whole range of international players with different and at times opposing interests: post-colonial leaders like Nehru or Liaquat Ali Khan, still unsure about how to relate to the new global order, American Cold War warriors eager to build coalitions against communism but unwilling to get dragged into regional conflicts like that existing between India and Pakistan, and late colonial administrators reluctant to cede control over their remaining dominions. Within this limited framework, the initial character of development as an ideology was still easily discernible, and would remain so for years to come. Liaquat was by no means the only one who deployed the new idiom in a self-serving and haphazard fashion, use in the United States was equally piecemeal and 'ideological', and would remain the subject of savage internal criticism until the end of the decade (see Chapter 4). What made this surface flimsiness of development all the more striking was the fact that very few resources were actually allocated to give the new global project real traction.

Harry Truman, the most prominent proponent of 'development' as a key to US foreign policy was particularly sluggish in putting his money where his mouth was. The total amount of US development aid to Pakistan between 1949 and 1952 was a paltry 11 million US dollars.[83] Crucially, the United States did not get significantly involved in the financing of the Colombo Plan,[84] which, as mentioned before, was Pakistan's first real occasion to engage with matters of development and economic planning. As some critics pointed out at the time, despite all the talk of warding off starvation and political collapse through state-managed socio-economic progress, the resources actually dedicated to 'development' by any Western party were always going to be wholly inadequate, and only a fraction of those spent in the immediate aftermath of post-World War II.[85] 'Development' was, in the words of an internal American document of the time, a game of 'few dollars and fewer people', which nobody outside the newly created Technical Cooperation Administration (TCA) took very seriously.[86] This state of affairs stood in stark contrast to other parts of the world where the United States did mean business when it came to using aid for extending its political influence. In the wake of the Truman Doctrine of 1947 – a separate initiative widely regarded as a precursor to Point Four, and formulated to prevent the countries of the Eastern Mediterranean falling under Soviet influence – Doxiadis's Greece alone had received 300 million US dollars (with a population of 3 million as compared to Pakistan's 80 million), and the Marshall Plan countries as a whole 13 billion US dollars.[87]

[83] USAID *Greenbook*, data, https://eads.usaid.gov/gbk/data/country_report.cfm [accessed 10/10/2011].
[84] Blackton, C. S. (1951) 'The Colombo Plan', *Far Eastern Survey* 20(3): 27–31, p.30.
[85] Lyons, J. (1951), *The Colombo Plan*, London, Bureau of Current Affairs, pp.17–18.
[86] NARA: RG469, Subject Files 1, 1951–54, E-556, Box 2, File OP-1 TCA/W-US Govt. Agencies Letter TCA to Weston Drake, Project Officer, 8 September 1952.
[87] Packenham, R. A. (1973), *Liberal America and the Third World: political development ideas in foreign aid and social science*, Princeton University Press, p.26. By the mid 1960s, Greece had received 4 billion US dollars, p.32.

When he introduced himself as a development expert coming from what was itself a developing country, Doxiadis had failed to mention some gross differences in resource availability.

Any notion of planning big and of justifying massive spending on large infrastructure projects with a hope of recouping this initial investment through future growth remained out of touch with reality over much of the period. Before Truman's successor Eisenhower at least attempted to loosen America's purse strings, aid to the countries of Asia and Africa in the form of massive development grants or soft loans was still practically unknown. The only real game in town was the World Bank, offering hard credit with all its requirements of transparency and oversight. Its demands for proper up-front documentation for every project for which funding was sought was directly responsible for a country like Pakistan sticking to colonial era development schemes, which were ready in the files and could be sent with only a limited amount of reworking.[88] In theory, there was also direct foreign investment from private companies as an additional source of development finance. Whenever Pakistan's first Prime Minister, Liaquat Ali Khan, went on state visits like the one to Washington, he attempted to seduce potential investors by portraying Pakistan as firmly committed to free market ideals, almost to the point where his praise of balanced budgets, thrift and self-reliance all but eclipsed any tentative reference to development he may have made. Unsurprisingly he found few takers as order books were already filled to capacity because of ongoing post-war reconstruction in Europe itself. Even threats to secure funding from the Eastern Bloc if companies were not more forthcoming could not change the basic fact that investments in Pakistan were at the time in few people's interest.[89]

Many of Doxiadis's predecessors and colleagues working in Pakistan on the United States' behalf experienced the empty and rhetorical nature of much of their work all too personally. Although their missions could be adventurous and full of camaraderie, they were also paid late, had

---

[88] Most hydro-electric power developments celebrated as successes of Pakistan development in the 1950s and early 1960s were in fact simply continuations of colonial project initiatives, e.g. the Karnaphuli scheme in East Pakistan and the Warsak Dam in West Pakistan. NAB: File No. 14E-62/48, Organization of Central Engineering Authority in Pakistan to deal with the development of electrical power on the basis of Pakistan Plan. Proceedings of the Hydro-Electric Power Conference, held at Karachi on 28 and 29 April 1948. For similar examples for irrigation projects in Sind, see Haines, T. D. (2013), *Building the empire, building the nation: development, legitimacy, and hydro-politics in Sind, 1919–1969*, Karachi, Oxford University Press, Pakistan.

[89] E.g. *The Times* (London), 7 May 1949, p.3; 13 May 1949, p.8. In the end, direct foreign investment in Pakistan remained confined to a General Motors assembly plant in Karachi and a Burmah Shell refinery in Chittagong.

unclear contractual obligations and often felt entirely out of their depths. Examples abound in the archival legacy of the early US aid presence in Pakistan. Staff were forced to travel by ship for lack of air-tickets, and often found it impossible to find accommodation in Karachi, Lahore or other cities where they were based. When one TCA expert, James Dockins, arrived at the Consulate in Dacca, East Bengal, in 1952, the regular embassy was not even aware of his existence and had made no preparations for his accommodation or upkeep.[90] An internal memo from the same year was highly critical of the 'unfortunate attitude of the [regular] Embassy staff in Karachi' towards the US development agency, and went on to argue that 'placing TCA's Director under Ambassador would put [the] whole program at the mercy of uninterested Embassy Staff. Also the effectiveness of independent technicians ... is seriously weakened by such direct association with the US Embassy – Paks regard Embassy as a foreign listening post.'[91] Not even the custodians of foreign policy – where technical assistance and development were after all meant to function as important ideological tools – were apparently very interested in entering a new age of international cooperation.

Doxiadis's own career in Pakistan unfolded precisely over the roughly ten years that linked Truman's game of 'few dollars' of the early 1950s with Kennedy's 'development decade' in the 1960s, when spending did in fact expand rapidly (in Pakistan's case to roughly 400 times that of the Truman era) and half-amateurish organizations like the TCA transformed into highly professional giants like USAID. It marked, in ways that were by no means straightforward or without friction, the kind of transition from development as an ideology to development as a Foucauldian discourse; from something that was easily criticized by any keen observer because of the self-serving, 'buzz-wordy' and half-baked ways in which it was invoked – not to mention the utter lack of commitment with which it was implemented – to a formation that had sunk such deep foundations into people's thinking that one could at best launch an internal critique, pitting 'good' development ambitions against 'bad' development practices, but no longer any possible alternatives to development itself. We have started this chapter by hinting at Doxiadis's intelligence gathering as a typical activity where this creation of development as a discourse took place. The argument was that the careful cataloguing of developmental problems in a gigantic database of failures actually created a self-explanatory representation of Pakistan as a subject

---

[90] NARA: RG469, Subject Files 1, 1951–54, E-556, Box 2, Operations Memorandum 2 July 1952.
[91] Ibid., May 1952.

of developmental intervention. The same process was already observable in early appreciations of Pakistan's performance under the Colombo Plan, even though they were published at a time when policy makers and a general public around the world still had a relatively clear sense of the ideological nature of this endeavour. The next chapter will show with a wealth of empirical detail from Doxiadis's own work how such suspicions were tackled and overcome.

Let us consider a final piece of evidence from the early records of the American aid effort in Pakistan. In September 1952, TCA headquarters sent a letter of admonition to Weston Drake, a Pakistan-based project officer. He was urged to limit 'official-informal' types of correspondence which were (and we have quoted part of this passage already) 'good enough in the days when there were few dollars and fewer people involved in the Pakistan program, but that's water over the dam ... such documents have been difficult to index, file and find when we later need them.'[92] As far as Washington was concerned, development could no longer be continued as an 'official-informal' activity, where everyone knew everyone else and shared a common experience of work abroad, and when largely undocumented personal contacts formed the backbone of what was going on. The point here is not that such practices ever went away over the following decade – there is ample evidence to the contrary both from US agencies and Doxiadis – but that they were no longer officially acceptable. To be successful in the future, development required an archive – a carefully indexed repository of all available infor-mation – rather than a loose collection of letters. Don Stoops, head of the Pakistan desk at the TCA in Washington, exhorted John Tallman, the TCA representative in Karachi, around the same time to send even inconclusive interim reports back to Washington to be filed: 'I under-stand how much time it can take to get a definitive statement or final action from the GoP [Government of Pakistan]. It will facilitate our dealings with other agencies and with individuals to whom we have made commitments if we can keep them abreast of those activities in Pakistan which concern them. In those cases where we cannot give them a clear cut answer, it will be better to tell them why we cannot, rather than to leave them in the dark. This would also avoid the impression of inactivity on the part of the TCA.'[93]

What sounds like practical advice was actually the first turn of the wheel in the process of turning development from an ideology into a

[92] NARA: RG469, Subject Files 1, 1951–54, E-556, Box 2, TCA to Weston Drake, 8 September 1952.
[93] Ibid., TCA to Karachi, 5 November 1952.

discourse. From now on, the newly constituted development archive had to be well ordered and complete as to produce a full representation of both development agency and development need. What is more, it was no longer enough to remain silent where one had no information; the gap itself had to be clearly identified as a gap, to be filled at a later date, setting up a self-policing and self-propelling system of further and further information gathering and documentation. Far from an ideological smokescreen for political difficulties, 'development' was now a colonizing force where further documentation would automatically lead to calls for further action and vice versa. While creating an archive and new systems of classification, development as discourse also created a new kind of person/subject at the very heart of the development effort: no longer 'official informal' but one from which any suspicion of 'inactivity' had been dispelled through self-control and documentary discipline. The time was set for the arrival of the consultant, both literally, with Doxiadis starting to observe and plan in Pakistan, and metaphorically, as in the wider collective effort of development discourse to place at its centre a new subjectivity.

2   The consultant's gaze

The 'development consultant' first emerged in the context of the League of Nations during the interwar period, but acquired a more distinct historical presence in the late 1940s – both as a concept and as a community of people working on the ground.[1] There had to be somebody who actually carried out the transfer of technical expertise to less fortunate parts of the world, which Harry Truman had so valiantly evoked in his Point Four address. It had to be a discreet presence. Consultants were expected to serve a collective and worldwide venture, which derived a good deal of its sense of historical inevitability from its somewhat abstract and impersonal character. In order to function as a discourse, as a self-validating project that stood above specific interests, any insinuation that development may have furthered the designs of any particular political force had to be dispelled. The definitive question of ideological criticism – *cui bono*, who benefits? – had to be made nonsensical. This is why so often these consultants were freewheeling independents of one form or another, like Doxiadis often from third countries not directly associated with major global donors. Even those who were in fact institutionally associated with the new superpowers – like the early United States TCA operatives mentioned in the previous chapter – tried their best not to be representatives of the foreign policy of their country. While complaining that they were neglected by their regular diplomatic institutions, America's development emissaries also expressed their wish not to be too closely associated with them for fear of dragging the lofty cause of development itself into the quagmire of geopolitical suspicions. As one of them noted: 'Paks regard Embassy as a foreign listening post.'[2]

---

[1] Rist, G. (1997), *The history of development: from Western origins to global faith*, London; New York, Zed Books, pp.58–60. Some authors trace the idea of expert missions even further back into the nineteenth century, Johnston, D. S. (1991), 'Constructing the periphery in modern global politics', *The new international political economy*, C. N. Murphy and R. Tooze (eds.), Boulder, CO, Lynne Rienner: 149–170, pp.156–158.

[2] NARA: RG469, Subject Files 1, 1951–54, E-556, Box 2, Operations Memorandum, 21 May 1952, Problems of the Pakistan Program.

Development had to become a centreless formation of truth like 'medicine' or 'sociology', and for that it required a new location of agency equivalent to the doctor or the social scientist. As this chapter will demonstrate, it took a good deal of discursive productivity to work out even the contours of who and what exactly these new agents of development should be, and how their codes of conduct should reflect the larger project they were engaged in. As it happened, they never became quite like 'doctors' or 'sociologists'. Their sense of authority remained weighed down by internal contradictions, and required to be propped up by potentially damaging references to modes of validation beyond the reach of development discourse itself. In order to convey a thematically tight and yet suitably illustrative sense of what was involved, the discussion begins with a close reading of materials produced by the United Nations, one of the key institutions associated with the new world order. Leaving aside a first example selected for providing necessary context, this material is not picked at random; it is what Doxiadis himself actually read for instruction when he first set out to become a development consultant; and what any of his contemporaries, even those working in entirely different fields of development consultancy, would have read as well. This material helps to locate Doxiadis's own writing, which is subjected to a close textual (and visual) analysis in the second half of this chapter. Doxiadis was – for reasons to be explained more fully in due course – a somewhat special case of development consultant, but he had to grapple with problems that were shared by most if not all consultants of his time.

In aid of 'Mr. Underdeveloped Region'

Two years before Doxiadis embarked on his first fact-finding mission to Pakistan, UNESCO published a pamphlet – somewhat sentimentally entitled *They can't afford to wait* – that sought to convey the problematic of development consultancy to a wider public. It consisted of four stories describing the experiences of Western experts working in Ceylon, India, Thailand and Pakistan at the beginning of the 1950s. Among other accounts, we are introduced to a Dr Karl Wiener from Germany, a Dr Gunnar Norjaard from Denmark and several other meteorologists from Australia and the United Kingdom as they conduct seismic experiments on the Bolan Pass in Baluchistan and predict future rainfall with the help of methods developed by the late Victorian scientist Edward Fournier d'Albe of Birmingham University.[3] Their work is hard – the

---

[3] Behrman, D. (UNESCO) (1952), *They can't afford to wait. (A story of UNESCO technical assistance in South-East Asia. By Daniel Behrman.) [With plates.]*, Paris, pp.25–28.

environmental conditions are severe – but it is also vital to help the newly established Meteorological Survey of Pakistan to its feet, and to facilitate the introduction of scientific agricultural techniques and provide some sense of security against natural catastrophes.

At first glance, this was a textbook case for the universalizing and depoliticizing power of development discourse. After laying out the usual blanket definition of 'underdevelopment' on the basis of objective and universal development indicators, the pamphlet went as far as introducing a 'Mr. Underdeveloped Region': a personification of the global South that in its deliberate denial of any cultural or historical distinctiveness could hardly be surpassed.[4] But, as it turns out, such confidence was only apparent. If anything, the material presented in the pamphlet demonstrated just how fragile and open to resistance the central ideological dictum of development actually was. The confident deculturation of 'Mr. Underdeveloped Region' is soon fatally undermined. A Pakistani meteorologist working with Wiener and Norjaard's team is quoted as saying: 'The purpose of our development programme is to enable us to preserve *our own* system and *our own* outlook, not to discard it for something not adapted to *our needs*.' A Sinhalese expert similarly points out to his UNESCO colleagues from Europe that he may dress like them in the office, but that he still prefers to be different at home, where he dons a sarong, eats curry and rice with his hands and chews betel nut.[5] In short, the transfer of technical expertise is not quite as 'neutral' as it first seemed. There are, in fact, boundary anxieties at play here that are not obviously and easily resolved by the conjuring trick of that 'Mr. Underdeveloped Region' as a stand-in for Pakistanis, Thais, Sinhalese or whatever other case at hand. The distinction between what is purely 'technical' and can easily be shared and what belongs to the 'cultural' that needs to be respected and bracketed off is never entirely clear (if it were, the whole issue would not have been raised by the aforementioned local men), and imposes on the development expert a special burden to tread carefully when confronted with such a reassertion of local identities.

The underlying logic here is worth unpicking. Although underdeveloped countries may all have different cultures, it is also assumed they represent a unified region of the world where culture uniquely mattered; where, unlike in their home environment, the technical experts had to be especially on their guard. It was only a small step from this assumption to one we have already encountered in the last chapter when discussing

---

[4] Ibid. p.7.   [5] Ibid. p.8.

colonial leftovers in development thought, an assumption that had the potential to undermine the very parameters of development ideology itself: if it was only in the 'underdeveloped' world that one had to be especially concerned with 'culture' when offering technical solutions, could this very 'culture' then not also be one of the main causes of underdevelopment itself? And if indeed it was, did this not mean that there would always be something in the essential being of 'underdeveloped' peoples that made them by definition resistant against development? That would mean that 'technical assistance' could at the very best only be a labour of Sisyphus heroically attempting the impossible, or at the worst a cynical ideological diversion that was never even meant to be successful. It was precisely in order to resolve such contradictions between culture and 'development', and to ward off the danger they posed for the very notion of development agency, that a carefully calibrated code of conduct had to be formulated for the new kind of hero at the heart of the UNESCO pamphlet: the 'development expert'.

To understand more clearly what was involved, it may be useful to contrast this figure, as it emerged in discussions over the 1950s, to its predecessor of sorts: the colonial administrator. After all, the latter also received his self-justification from a mission that at least at the level of ideology pertained to be a transfer of knowledge from the advanced North to the backward South, the often invoked 'civilizing mission'. But his code of ethics and qualifications could not have been more different. As suggested in the UNESCO pamphlet, the new figure of the consultant relied very heavily on the valorization of *'technical'* know-how, an esoteric but limited body of scientific truth that the expert mastered completely and to which he was expected to stick exclusively when on a mission. Dr Wiener and his team knew their Fournier d'Albe but as far as Pakistan was concerned they were absolute novices. The latter was not a flaw but precisely what was expected of them. The very definition of the 'purely' technical depended on a clear differentiation from 'culture' or 'politics'. While a lack of technical know-how defined the 'underdeveloped world', too much local knowledge could only lead the consultant into the murky terrain of 'culture' that he was advised to avoid. Colonialism, in contrast, demanded a well-read generalist who could work in any part of the colonial state apparatus regardless of training, while also translating some ancient inscriptions in his spare time, collecting exotic plants and perhaps shooting a tiger or two besides. The very topics that development thought sought to suppress – politics, history and culture – were the colonialist's bread and butter. Moreover, unlike the expert who mattered only for the contents of his or her brain (there were indeed women involved, and precisely because of this somewhat disembodied notion of expertise they could be), the executive of Empire – always a he – also had to shine by virtue of his hardened physique and willpower, surpassing the effeminate native in his power of endurance, and as a charismatic leader, commanding compliance by power of personality alone.[6]

The juxtaposition between development expert and colonialist pinpoints the unstable heart of development discourse. As we shall see over the course of this chapter, the expert was not simply the colonialist's 'other' and successor in terms of historical progression; the colonialist was also the expert's 'ghost', posing a constant danger of regression and backsliding, which the consultant somehow had to manage in his or her mission. Just as culture entered development discourse through the backdoor and posed an ever-present problem, so was the development consultant under constant danger of becoming like a colonialist – which is of course immediately borne out by the all too common accusations that development recipients made against those sent out to help them.

Constantinos Doxiadis found this ideological minefield particularly hard to negotiate. His chosen field of activity – architecture and physical planning – could never be easily reduced to 'pure' and decultured 'know-how', unlike, let us say, power engineering, development economics or the meteorology mentioned in the UNESCO pamphlet. 'Housing and settlements' was something that anybody from local homemaker to post-colonial bureaucrat could have a superficial opinion about. This made it more difficult to sustain the mystique of the specialist, so easily generated by the invocation of a new language about new seed varieties, malarial vectors or savings coefficients in other more 'scientific' disciplines. The time period under review was of course famous for architects and housing experts who more than any of their colleagues before or after strove to achieve a status as scientists and engineers. But such aspirations could never work entirely – even Le Corbusier's universal modernism had to be tempered by 'culture' when he set out to build Chandigarh as a state capital in India[7] – and in Doxiadis's case the usual difficulties were compounded. After all, it was his selling point and trump card against the likes of Le Corbusier that his planning took full account of local cultural and historical peculiarities. Doxiadis was always proud of

---

[6] On masculinity and imperialism see Sinha, M. (1995), *Colonial masculinity: the 'manly Englishman' and the 'effeminate Bengali' in the late nineteenth century*, Manchester University Press; Collingham, E. M. (2001), *Imperial bodies: the physical experience of the Raj, c. 1800–1947*, Cambridge, Polity Press; Stoler, A. L. (2002), *Carnal knowledge and imperial power: race and the intimate in colonial rule*, Berkeley, University of California Press.

[7] Prakash, V. (2002), *Chandigarh's Le Corbusier: the struggle for modernity in postcolonial India*, Seattle, University of Washington Press.

his technical expertise and sought to portray his solutions as technical solutions, but he also consistently promised to deliver more: happy communities, worthy expressions of national identity in architecture, physical means by which the cultural aspects of modernity could be kept in check. To achieve such aims, he had always emphasized that a good planner and architect was precisely somebody who was *not* just a mono-dimensional expert but rather an *Ekistician*, somebody who had all the flexibility and curiosity also demanded of a colonial official.

Doxiadis had to take his battle into the field of culture that other consultants were advised to avoid, while simultaneously policing the very borders of technical expertise that his basic self-justification as a consultant depended on. But when doing so, he could never hide behind an established institutional culture, neither the old inherited from colonial times nor the new that was emerging around notions of development science. Doxiadis had to speak for himself, as a self-sufficient and highly distinctive individual. The remainder of this chapter is about how he went out to create a standpoint from which he could master this challenge. It begins with a survey of some of the actual readings that were to guide him when he went to Pakistan, and then moves on to a close analysis of his diaries depicting in word and image what he saw in Pakistan and how he saw it, for it was through this novel genre of developmentalist writing that the foundations for Doxiadis's own authority were constructed.

Briefings for development

Let us imagine for a moment the future creator of Islamabad as he is relaxing in his first-class seat en route to New Delhi. It is early 1954, at the very beginning of his career and still some months away from securing work in Syria and Pakistan. Relatively unknown outside his native Greece, he is flying to the United Nations conference that is to lay the foundations for his later success. This is his first real encounter with South Asia, although he may have stopped over on his way to Australia where he had failed as a tomato farmer the previous year. On his lap is a leather-bound information pack issued by the UN, which was later to find a place in his personal library. It contains a curious mixture of documents providing historical, social and cultural background information for all newly appointed United Nations operatives deployed in India, which includes him as a conference delegate. Doxiadis is, as far as work in any region of Asia is concerned, still a novice. He is not expected to stay long term and not required to learn any local language. His wider educational background has preciously little to say about what awaits him beyond some platitudes that could have applied anywhere from Morocco to the Moluccas, with perhaps a little more awareness (and bias) reserved for the Islamic world and Greece's old enemy Turkey. Unlike a trainee colonial administrator, Doxiadis is not about to be inducted into a century-old institutional culture with its extensive literature, its District Gazetteers, anthropological compendia, expositions of local religious customs and well-tested, if self-serving vocabulary of 'tribes', 'castes', 'martial races' or 'communal fury'. All he has at his disposal to begin his fraught and delicate encounter with South Asia as a consultant is the information contained in the United Nations pack – supplemented by some other background readings he had acquired from elsewhere, for instance T. H. Lawrence's wartime memoir *Seven Pillars of Wisdom* (see below).

Doxiadis takes out the first bundle of pages, the transcript of a speech, entitled 'Principal concepts of South Asia' by one Pieter K. Roest, a Dutch-born sociologist and anthropologist who served in an influential position on the advisory team to the US occupation authorities in Japan.[8] After familiar clichés about 'the poverty and the disease, the ignorance and the attachment to tradition'[9] afflicting the region of 'India and Pakistan', the paper goes straight to an inherently 'oriental' entanglement with religious cosmologies as something that a consultant in Doxiadis's position will have to watch out for:

A good many people brought up in our civilization fiercely resent the idea of exploitation because they have learned that men are born free, and equal, and are entitled to pursue happiness. That is by no means an oriental idea. The oriental idea is rather that you are born in a certain caste or layer of society, that is your place, the place that has been given to you by the powers that rule the universe, and your only chance for happiness is to fullfill [*sic*] your function in that place according to the rules laid down from times immemorial.[10]

Development assistance in such an environment had to be provided with care because of the extreme differences in the basic outlook on life. While Halloween was only a joke for Westerners, the briefing paper argues, 'to the vast majority of the people of the Orient spirits, disembodied entities are very real, and they have to take them into account just as we take into account the visible people around us.'[11]

[8] Williams, J. (1979), *Japan's political revolution under MacArthur: a participant's account*, Athens, GA, University of Georgia Press, p.52–63.
[9] Roest, p.2, included in United Nations: *Technical Assistance Administration: manual of instructions*: India 1953 File 34705.
[10] Ibid. p.3.   [11] Ibid. p.4.

What follows is a schematic explanation of South Asian society in terms of its broad religious traditions, which are dealt with one by one, and often with meaningless scripturalistic observations: there is plenty of 'karma' in a description of Hinduism, for instance, while the Indian Prime Minister Jawaharlal Nehru is linked to the 'Vanaprastha stage'[12] of Indian society, as if the fourfold division of *varnas* ('Brahmins', 'Warriors', 'Traders' and 'Cultivators') represented a real social formation on the ground. (As most colonial officers would have known, 'caste' – let alone Indian politics – is a far more complex affair). Islam is 'a very powerful and intense creed', and nationalism and communism are judged to be 'very attractive to the strongly anti-capitalistic Orientals'.[13] Roest frequently reaches back into the most shallow and most widely publicized aspects of the Orientalist repertoire; there is India as the land of 'seven hundred thousand villages' untouched by any cultural exchange whatsoever.[14] Katherine Mayo's infamous *Mother India* of 1927, a tract defending colonialism on the grounds of the ill-treatment of women by native culture, makes an appearance even if not fully endorsed by the author of the briefing paper; as does R. V. C. Bodley's World War I adventure memoir *Wind in the Sahara*, cited to explain the inner workings of the Islamic world as if it were an undifferentiated unit from North Africa to South Asia.[15]

What is most striking about Roest's interpretation of South Asian society, and about the fact that he was invited to give a speech of this kind in the first place (to the US Foreign Service Institute, no less), and that this speech was later distributed to all United Nations personnel serving in South Asia is his eccentric and eclectic background. As far as it is possible to judge from the few traceable publications of his, Roest had worked as an anthropologist on oriental magic in the 1920s and later conducted some fieldwork in Afghanistan while also commenting on affairs in Egypt and Ceylon.[16] The only common thread in his musings was a nebulous notion of 'oriental' culture interwoven – not always seamlessly – with the idea that development sociology was a general discipline that could somehow be applied to 'backward' areas anywhere in the world.

Roest's discourse represents the dark side of that careful separation between 'culture' and 'technical know-how' that lay at the very heart of

---

[12] Ibid. p.7.   [13] Ibid. p.20.   [14] Ibid. p.2.   [15] Mentioned ibid. pp.14, 8.
[16] He contributed to Wilber, D. N. (1956), *Afghanistan*, New Haven, CT, Human Relations Area Files. See also Roest, P. K. (1927), *Glimpses of anthropology: abstracts of lectures delivered at the Brahmavidya Ashrama, Adyar, 1926–27*, Adyar, Brahmavidya Ashrama.

the code of conduct of the development consultant. As we know from the UNESCO pamphlet outlined earlier, the consultants most likely to be accepted without much opposition by their host society were ones who stuck strictly to the field of expertise they were trained in. Being ignorant about local customs may well have posed some practical problems in the daily life of such figures, but it also ensured that no backsliding into the bad old ways of the colonialist know-it-all would occur. But far from exorcising the ghosts of previous times, they were actually simply suppressed into the underbelly of development ideology where they could dwell and develop a potency unthinkable under colonialism itself. Consultants who, like Doxiadis on his first journey to Delhi, knew little about the area they were to be deployed to required information that was truly basic, pieced together by half-digested stereotypes and assembled in short résumés of the kind just described. After all, *pure* experts could not be expected to have *any* idea of what awaited them when they started on their missions. Anything too nuanced, too much grounded in historical or anthropological analysis was bound to challenge the model of consultancy itself.

But why did even basic briefing documents like Roest's have to endorse such an unrelenting picture of the development recipients as utterly 'other', which after all was hardly in line with more politically correct notions of a 'Mr. Underdevelopment Region'? The lecture points to a deep-seated suspicion at the heart of the development encounter. The mission of leading the poor South to a better future had to be insured against failure, against the possibility that the seemingly unproblematic transfer of technical expertise did not work out as expected. This was a potentially dangerous situation capable of undermining all that the development consultant stood for. If technology could not work its magic, the authority of the consultants evaporated in one stroke, and all that was left was an unfathomable chasm between East and West. Colonial thought had used a similar device when faced with a loss of control, for instance, during the paradigmatic 1857 'Mutiny' in India which revealed the true nature of the local population as fanatical barbarians beyond the appeal of reason.[17] But at least in the colonial context, such instances of loss of control did not happen very often; for most of the time, the colonial administrator was secure in a position of superior

---

[17] Wagner, K. (2013), 'Treading upon fires: the mutiny motif and colonial anxieties in British India', *Past and Present* **218**(1): 159–197. For a similar dialectics in colonial French West Africa see Conklin, A. L. (1998), 'Colonialism and human rights, a contradiction in terms? The case of France and West Africa, 1895–1914', *The American Historical Review* **103**(2): 419–442.

power that allowed him to make sense of his subjects in more nuanced and less panic-stricken ways. The development consultants, in contrast, rarely had the luxury of being protected by a state that could deflect challenges in a similar way; they were only ever a small step away from encountering a world of the native they could not and were not meant to handle. Mutual respect for difference and political self-determination did not eradicate Orientalist stereotypes; it simply pushed them into the murky domain of the unspeakable and unfathomable where they could survive relatively unchallenged.

The still unsettled nature of post-colonial 'developmental' knowledge is further confirmed by the material that follows Roest's speech in Doxiadis's United Nations information pack: a paper by Claire Holt entitled, 'Principal mores of South-East Asia'. At first glance, Holt's qualification to advise an official traveller to New Delhi is even more tenuous than Roest's; she had lived in *Indonesia* – not India – before World War II, and in the decades up to her death in 1970 was to become one of America's leading experts at the centre for *South East* Asian research at Cornell University. The conflation of South Asia and South East Asia was also common in the literature about the Colombo Plan, as we have seen, but usually with a clear understanding that it denoted not an area of cultural unity but was used simply as a shorthand for a region of great diversity. But this was meant to be an information pack for personnel serving in India, and they were given first-hand experiences of what it meant to live in Indonesia, clearly a confusion of substance. This blurring of regional differences is compounded further by random references in Holt's article to Hopi snake dancing, Mexican archaeology and the free progression of development expertise from 'the pueblo' to Iran.[18]

It quickly becomes apparent that what matters here is not so much Holt's knowledge of local culture, but the ways in which she negotiated the culture clash between West and non-West. Her paradigmatic example is her own son, who had lived in Indonesia with her, learnt to speak Indonesian within nineteen days, and upon their return to the United States is a 'totally Indonesian boy of 14' who has to 'meet headlong our American technological civilization and cope with it.'[19] Culture, here, clearly appeared to be not quite as much of an essentialist hurdle as in Roest's account of 'the oriental'. Long immersion made it possible to appropriate other cultures and revert back to one's own, although Holt

---

[18] United Nations: *Technical Assistance Administration: manual of instructions*: India 1953 File 34705, Holt, pp.11, 12, 19, respectively.
[19] Ibid. p.1.

also conceded that such knowledge could never be total.[20] Much of the piece then turns into a conversation about the new relationship between the Western expert and the host society he (or she) is meant to serve. New nuances that were less apparent in either the UNESCO pamphlet or Roest's lecture are introduced and interrogated. Should the development expert really be a 'consultant', defined here, as it was in the UNESCO pamphlet, as somebody who acts as a repository of knowledge altogether external to the host society and without any strong interest in the host society as such? Or should he be an 'advisor', somebody who not only has expertise but also gets actively involved in how it is applied and thus needs to possess a certain amount of local cultural knowledge? And if one was to be an 'advisor', how could one overcome the basic problem that with regard to one's technical expertise one was automatically more knowledgeable than the locals, while in terms of local knowledge one would always remain in a learning position, something that inherently undermined one's status as expert?[21] As we shall see, these were questions right at the centre of Doxiadis's own attempts at self-stylization.

Much of the practical information that makes up the rest of the United Nations information pack for South Asia is obviously modelled on the idea of the 'consultant', the technocrat who would not openly interfere in local debates but wishes to sustain a luxury lifestyle away from home for the limited time period he (or she) is in the field. Apart from some general rules for how the new United Nations officials have to behave – emphasizing a 'willingness to be without prejudice or bias with persons of all nationalities, religions and cultures' – there is an 'Area Report' containing basic information about New Delhi tailored to the needs of this new category of expat consultant. New Delhi was 'one of the handsomest cities to be found anywhere' Doxiadis (and others in a similar position) are informed. 'There is enough social life here to satisfy anyone's appetite, although it is possible not to be overwhelmed by it'.[22]

A description of living standards is clearly measured against US norms: 'There is not always hot running water, but with servants this inconvenience is not troublesome.' Vacuum cleaners and washing machines were not needed because of the cheapness of domestic labour, but 'servants are hard on Pyrex, plastic and other breakable equipment'.[23] The following essential goods may be hard to obtain:

---

[20] Ibid. p.14.   [21] Ibid. pp.16–19.
[22] United Nations: *Technical Assistance Administration: manual of instructions*: India 1953 File 3470, 3 Nov 1952. United Nations Field Operations Service – Area Report, p.6.
[23] Ibid. pp.10–11.

apple butter, apple juice, apricots, asparagus, Airwick, baby foods ... bacon (because local bacon never tastes the same), baked beans, baking chocolate, baking powder, baking soda, corned beef, blackberries, blueberries, cake mixes (unnecessary if you have a good cook), cereals, cheese spreads, maraschino cherries, cocoa, corn, bleaches – preferably powdered, DDT, detergents, dextri-saltose, dry cleaning fluids, ham, horseradish, insecticides, jams, jellies and juices ... soft toilet paper.[24]

This concern for how the everyday needs of average North American suburban life could become luxuries in the developing world encapsulated what the developmental encounter in these early post-war decades was often like: experts who had been selected by virtue of their technical 'know-how' were transplanted into an entirely new environment where they would occupy an always precarious position between vulnerability and prestige.

The return of the adventurer

It is quite clear from these documents (there were others of lesser relevance in the pack that we can skip over here) that Doxiadis – even if he dutifully read them en route to his first visit to India – was not really particularly better informed about his place of deployment. But he would have been alerted to a basic contradiction in the role of 'development consultant', which was to preoccupy him for the rest of his life. In the first instance, there was this notion of the new 'consultant' with no meaningful connection to local cultures. He or she was legitimate in the post-war development business precisely because he or she knew so little, because this would make him or her stick to narrowly defined technical expertise and avoid any infringement of the cultural autonomy of development recipients. This absence of knowledge is what briefing papers of this kind actually helped to construct, as they clearly pre-assumed (and thereby created) a particular kind of reader. One would not have given such material to an anthropologist embarking on his first stint 'in the field', and equally, they would have never been deemed sufficient or well grounded enough to sustain a colonial 'Old India' hand.

But there is a twist to this kind of ideological production. People like Holt also invoked a romantic ideal of cultural exposure and a mystique of the 'real' expert; after all *she* had spent almost a decade in Indonesia, spoke the language and knew the place inside out. So while essential for delineating the necessarily ignorant 'consultant' as an 'other', the greater 'experience' of the truly embedded area specialist was also going to cast a

---

[24] Ibid. p.13.

dark shadow over the former's work and legitimacy. Consultants could all too easily be – as post-developmental critics have come to argue with such vehemence – culturally insensitive, misinformed, beholden to a 'one-size-fits-all mentality', removed from local wishes and preferences and so on.[25] This line of attack was by no means the invention of a post-modernist sensibility at the very end of the twentieth century; it was as old as the age of the development consultant itself. Doxiadis, for one, having barely made a start to his own career, already singled out the 'exported' technocrat as a figure of condemnation: 'The usual type is the magician – he brings formulae, he has all the solutions up his sleeve and he pulls them out like rabbits. He certainly cannot serve as there are no solutions of universal value.'[26] Doxiadis felt that his visions for a better urban future were superior to let us say those of Le Corbusier, because unlike the latter, he was no such 'exported' technocrat without any regard for local requirements.

The mystique of going native, of coping with a difficult cultural and physical environment, reintroduced considerations to the code of the consultant that were reminiscent of the hard masculinity of the colonial official. Increasingly, as the basic ideological parameters of development became solidified and changed into a discursive formation, there was recognition of that magic quality of 'experience' that sat very uneasily with the idea of an expert in need of soft toilet paper or maraschino cherries invoked in the United Nations information pack. When development experts looked back at their careers many decades later, it was often this element of adventure and hardship that they found most important for their self-definition. An interesting illustration with a loose connection to the case at hand appeared recently in the German magazine *Der Spiegel*. It told of the reminiscences of a German carpenter by the name of Friedrich Thimm from the provincial town Lambsheim in the Palatinate, who volunteered for development service, and over the early 1960s spent several years in a small village outside Multan in southern Punjab in order to teach the locals basic artisanal techniques.[27] Like Doxiadis, Thimm had arrived in Pakistan with no prior knowledge of the country he was meant to serve. But, after several years of coping

---

[25] E.g. Latouche, S. (1996), *The westernization of the world: the significance, scope and limits of the drive towards global uniformity*, Cambridge, Polity. Or with less development scepticism: Altaf, S. W. (2011), *So much aid, so little development: stories from Pakistan*, Baltimore, Johns Hopkins University Press.

[26] Doxiadis, C. A. (1959), 'The rising tide of the planners', *Ekistics* 7(39): 5–10, p.6.

[27] Mikhail, B. (2008), 'Ich hatte Angst dass Schlangen meine Söhne anknabbern', *Spiegel* online, Eines Tages, http://einestages.spiegel.de/static/topicalbumbackground/13741/1/_ich_hatte_angst_dass_schlangen_meine_soehne_anknabbern.html [accessed 31/10/11].

with a new and hostile environment – including an episode of fending off poisonous snakes attacking his infant sons, and his wife's perennial battle to procure unspoilt meat from fly-infested butchers' shacks – he had emerged as a new kind of person, someone who was happy to 'sit with the locals on the floor and eat millet porridge', as he proudly recounted his life's mission himself. This attitude turned him from mere expert into a seeker of an alternative way of life. His 'experience' ensured that he never again became a normal German carpenter, but remained engaged in 'development' work in other countries after his assignment in Pakistan had ended.

It was precisely this adventurous and romantic aspect of development consultancy that the newly instituted administrators of the United States TCA sought to control with the imposition of a regime of complete archival accounting, as seen in the last chapter. But a sense of adventure was also both irrepressible and somehow essential to the validity of the consultant's project; even the UNESCO pamphlet derived much of its persuasive power from juxtaposing meteorological science to the romantic location of the Bolan Pass.

The problem for somebody like Doxiadis was that he would have to generate at least three competing character traits before he even arrived on any assignment in the poor South. His position as a technical expert was only relatively secure. He spent of course much of his time inventing a new science, Ekistics, which he naturally would be a master of; but despite his efforts, this science was never universally accepted as such, and by the middle of the 1960s would often be criticized as mere commercial soundbitery. Then, by virtue of his trademark claim to cultural sensitivity, he had to be something of an expert in local cultures, which was perhaps easy enough when operating in the corridors of power in Washington D.C. but fraught with resistance in encounters with his clients, who after all owned this cultural knowledge directly. Finally, Doxiadis had to be an 'experienced' consultant to be hired in preference to his many rivals. He could enlist his work in Greece as a foundation for this 'experience' but as far as work in Asia and Africa was concerned he had to find a way to pre-emptively auto-generate 'experience' before he had any chance to acquire it the hard way, as carpenter Thimm had done while living in Multan. Doxiadis's solution to these problems lay in his particular style of writing and seeing, which he first developed in his encounter with Pakistan, and which he turned into a veritable genre of discursive productivity.

Doxiadis's mission to create authority for himself stood at the very heart of his written output. A signature document in the Doxiadis Archive is a 329-page diary of his first voyage to Pakistan, complete with numerous sketches and more than a hundred photographs.[28] In a striking self-referential turn, this diary takes us back not only to the beginning of Doxiadis's encounter with Pakistan, but also to the very decision of making travel diaries central to the Ekistics project in any part of the world. Before investigating this foundational moment further, it needs repeating that there is nothing spontaneous or personal about this diary. It is written in English, not Greek, neatly typed out and bound, and carefully edited to something approximating publication standard. The overall text feels homogeneous and seamless, although it is in fact an amalgamation of various different materials, 'notes' from the journey, as well as retrospective 'recollection', and finally, Doxiadis's trademark verbal sketches spoken to the portable tape recorder he took with him wherever he went.

'Flying from Athens to Cyprus and Beirut in the first evening of my Pakistan trip, I am thinking of the Syrian experience just finished [serving on a World Bank mission, his first assignment outside Greece]' – the diary starts with a recreation of what went through Doxiadis's head as he watched the sunset on the first day of his journey long before he even reached Karachi; despite the obvious editorial reworking of all that follows, the account is narrated in the present tense and from a first-person perspective. Having just filed his report, the narrator asks:

how could I submit a complete report in which I would pass over to other people the maximum amount of the *experience* gained and preserve this *experience* [emphasis added] for me not only in its general lines, which are very seldom lost, but also in its details? . . . should I walk some centuries back and try again the form of diaries kept by travellers, the importance of which has been always recognized by the coming generations but never by the present ones? Is the diary a dead form of presentation of our impressions? Can we revive it and can it be useful not only for the people to come but also for the people now concerned about these problems? I cannot give an answer to these questions now[29]

The next morning, back on his flight to Karachi, the narrator feels closer to a solution:

Looking out of the plane's window I face the red soil of Arabia, the hills and the wabies [wadis?]: the Arabian landscape, a landscape that I have never visited but I know very well! And then I remember Lawrence's 'The Seven Pillars of Wisdom', which is really the book, a book in the form of a diary, even if not called so, which has brought me into contact with the Arabian world, which has taught me the nature of the land and the people and their culture from Mecca to Damascus. It is the book which has allowed me to understand the Syrian

[28] CADA: Pakistan Volume 2, Dox 20, Diary 12 October–23 November 1954.
[29] Ibid. p.2., emphasis added.

countryside before ever visiting it. This book is a diary, a diary which does not answer problems of future policies, does not propose programs but opens the eyes for the understanding of problems and the ways to meet them. Here is the case of a successful diary which allows me to take the decision and try and write a Pakistan diary.[30]

These passages are carefully crafted narratives of self-empowerment as much as an attempt to fill the Ekistics archive before there was time to conduct more systematic and extensive surveys of underdeveloped lands and populations. Although we do encounter various Pakistani officials and take nicely documented tours of cities and the countryside in the several hundred pages that follow, the primary subject matter of these diaries is not Pakistan, its culture and developmental needs, but Doxiadis himself. This is about 'his experience' of a country (this term is in itself highly significant, as 'experience' is what the really successful development 'advisor' has and what the 'exported' consultant lacks), 'his' wealth of observations and 'his' legacy among 'coming generations'. He wishes to step into the footsteps of the adventurer-travellers of the past – 'Lawrence of Arabia' and unnamed others – who have played such a central role in the construction of the kind of Orientalist knowledge that Doxiadis was to draw on frequently. Although he does not mention this here or elsewhere, there is another source of inspiration lurking in the background: Le Corbusier, as ever the model of the heroic master architect of the modern age, started his own career with a 'Grand Voyage' to '*l'Orient*' (in 1911, taking him to the Balkans, Greece and Turkey) on which he reflected in carefully constructed diaries, photographs and travel sketches.[31]

By carefully constructing the first-person narrator in an epic encounter with an alien and unfamiliar country, Doxiadis wanted to appropriate some of the heroism, endurance and, of course, access to local knowledge that the heroic traveller represents. Needless to say, there was a glaring incongruity at play here: Doxiadis usually travelled with five-star comforts along a carefully pre-planned route where every one of his whims was taken care of; moreover, he never spent more than a month 'in the field', as it were. If there was any relationship between his diaries and adventurous experience, it was an inverse one. The diaries became such a cherished and carefully produced part of Doxiadis's work precisely because he, more than anyone else, actually lacked the kind of additional pathos and heroism that separated the ordinary 'consultant' from the truly successful development advisor. In order to get round

[30] Ibid.
[31] Le Corbusier, C. E. (2007), *Journey to the East*, Cambridge, MA, MIT Press.

such glaring inconsistencies, the narrator-self in Doxiadis's diaries makes much of a novel site of self-fashioning that was both befitting for its wider historical environment, and also very different from the Orientalist antecedents so often invoked in the diary: the aeroplane.

The romance of aerial surveillance

It is no coincidence whatsoever that the crucial moment of deciding to keep a diary takes place at thousands of metres above ground. Doxiadis not only returned to the motif of air travel compulsively, he also accorded a central role to the aerial view in his larger epistemology. Before exploring this further, it is worth mentioning a seemingly marginal but actually very telling episode included in another diary covering one of Doxiadis's Pakistan trips in 1955. One of the very few occasions on which the stance of Doxiadis's carefully crafted protagonist/narrator slips to reveal Doxiadis, the real man and traveller, is related to aviation. While he never talked about problems such as food, ill health or inadequate accommodation in his diaries, there is a curiously emotional account of being unjustly thrown off a flight – despite turning up in good time for check-in – while local politicians are observed to have bribed their way on to the passenger list at the last moment. This is then followed by an equally unnecessary account of the humiliating experience of having to pay for excess baggage the next morning.[32] Not only is Doxiadis's status as a powerless outsider clearly revealed in both episodes, it is revealed in the context of his most cherished source of sophistication and power.

'Aerial life' – as Peter Adey called it in a recent path-breaking intervention[33] – was an important and complex site where new mobilities and possibilities of space emerged side by side with new ideas of the human body and personal identity and new modes of governance, which all have some relevance for the case at hand. 'Development' as a global project was embedded in the kind of spatial perception and experience produced by the easy availability of air travel. While generalized ideas of 'backwardness' had existed in colonial times, and sometimes drifted from place to place – let us say India to Africa within the British Empire – local differences and peculiarities would always be emphasized because of the relatively long periods of exposure to a single geographic setting. The idea that all parts of the Third World were somehow united by the

---

[32] CADA: Pakistan Volume 4, Dox 40, Athens March 1955, Diary 20 January–24 February 1955, p.49.
[33] Adey, P. (2010), *Aerial life: spaces, mobilities, affects*, Chichester; Malden, MA, Wiley-Blackwell.

simple fact of 'underdevelopment' – couched at least at the surface in non-cultural terms – corresponded directly to a more 'aerial' experience in post-colonial times. Doxiadis is the best example. He controlled an empire of 'development' projects from a single base in Athens, and spent most of his time flying from site to site to reconnoitre, exercise oversight, negotiate contracts and so on. It was only because of air travel that Doxiadis could be in Syria one week, in Pakistan the next, and in Iraq and Ghana thereafter. Moreover, it was only thanks to the daily airmail pouch that DA could ever manage projects like Islamabad, whereby maps could be posted to Athens for consideration by a team of engineers, and finished drafts posted back within a matter of days.

Also of relevance was the fact that the places Doxiadis visited – Baghdad, Karachi and Dacca – were usually stopovers on long-distance air routes that led to the new hubs of the world economy – London, New York and Tokyo. In the early 1950s, it was simultaneously an expression of special favour and a mark of subordination that American presidents would have to send their own private aeroplanes to pick up heads of state like Liaquat and Nehru to enable them to visit the United States. Being connected up – preferably by a national flag carrier of their own – was one of the main preoccupations of post-colonial government the world over. Pakistan's PIA, for instance, was founded in 1951; and in June 1954, only several months before Doxiadis arrived at Karachi airport, first used a Lockheed 'Super-Constellation' to connect Karachi in the Western Wing of the country with Dacca in the East without having to make any stopovers in the hostile Indian territory between. The first international service – to London, the erstwhile colonial metropolis, via Cairo, epitome of Muslim grandeur – started some months later in early 1955.[34] As a country divided into two distant wings, with grave repercussions for national unity, Pakistan was perhaps always more interested in aeroplanes than others.

Aviation also demanded a new kind of personal identity. The 'airman' was of central importance for constructions of heroism in a highly 'modernized' setting, driving America's 'winged gospel' as much as French literary sensibilities, and Italian Fascist and German National Socialist ideals of a 'New Man'.[35] While such ideas were most powerful in the 'golden' age of aviation when the likes of Charles Lindbergh, Antoine de Saint-Exupéry and other pilot aces still roamed the skies, they still

[34] Ali, A. (2011) 'History of PIA', www.historyofpia.com/history.htm [accessed 21/03/11].
[35] Corn, J. J. (1983), *The winged gospel: America's romance with aviation, 1900–1950*, New York, Oxford University Press; Wohl, R. (2005), *The spectacle of flight: aviation and the Western imagination, 1920–1950*, New Haven, CT, Yale University Press.

exercised some attraction in later decades. Even as a relatively comfortable passenger in an airliner, Doxiadis saw the unbound space above the clouds as the site where he most easily connected with the likes of Lawrence of Arabia, and where he acquired the same status as the senior diplomats and captains of industry that shared his first-class cabin with him. This romanticism and fascination was by no means confined to the rich West. In South Asia, aeroplanes had become the obsession of maharajas and industrialists. Nationalists like Jawaharlal Nehru and M. A. Jinnah, likewise, had sought to appropriate the mystique of the aeroplane when it was first used in election campaigns of the late 1930s and 1940s.[36]

'Aereality' also presented new methodologies of power and control, the most obvious being new modes of warfare such as aerial reconnaissance and bombardment. There were also radically transformed possibilities for the architect, city planner and archaeologist. In colonial Palestine, Iraq and Malaya, aerial visions provided for the first time a framework to systematically perceive and exploit the economic potential of forests and other resources.[37] Le Corbusier published an iconic monograph entitled *Aircraft* in 1935, in which he ruminated about the new possibilities for regional planning afforded by an all-penetrating aerial view – as well as on the new dangers and possibilities that destruction from the air posed for urban centres.[38] According to him it was only from the air that the true perniciousness and irrationality of the premodern city became apparent, and from where the benefits of a modern city layout could be properly appreciated. This aerial view covered an important aspect of what James C. Scott has called 'seeing like a state', an attempt to perceive the world in such a way that it becomes subject to a great 'plan', a vision in which unwelcome complexities on the ground are filtered out so as to produce an image that can be entirely comprehended and thereby facilitates concerted intervention from above.[39] An important aspect of this manner of seeing was, as Adey has pointed out in the context of colonial era aerial surveying of forests, the right choice of 'resolution'; despite the claim to omniscience underlying the very methodology of the aerial gaze,

---

[36] For instance Nehru as 'Hindustan ke badshah' posing next to the aeroplane that took him on a whirlwind election tour round India in 1937, *The Tribune* (Lahore) 19 January 1937, p.1.

[37] Adey, P. (2010), *Aerial life: spaces, mobilities, affects*, Chichester; Malden, MA, Wiley-Blackwell, pp.86–94.

[38] Boyer, C. (2003), 'Aviation and the aerial view: Le Corbusier's spatial transformations in the 1930s and 1940s', *Diacritics* **33**(3/4): 93–116.

[39] Scott, J. C. (1998), *Seeing like a state: how certain schemes to improve the human condition have failed*, New Haven, CT; London, Yale University Press.

it could not be too fine, as it would then literally prevent the observer from seeing 'the wood for the trees'. But with a resolution just right, aerial pictures could reveal new patterns which could be decoded and used for development purposes, for instance by establishing the overall types of vegetation in a particular area.[40]

While this methodology was crucial for Doxiadis, as we shall see, his case also throws up important limitations in Scott's and Adey's understanding of the aerial gaze with important implications for our reading of the governmentalities of development more generally. One of the great insights of Adey's work is to link aerial surveying to the surveying of aerial bodies – passengers undergoing automated biometric security checks at airports – in which similar problems of 'resolution', pattern recognition and total visibility are involved, and which according to him constitute something like a singular 'aerial' mode of control. Central here is what he himself called with reference to an expression by feminist theorist Donna Haraway 'seeing everything from nowhere',[41] a form of seeing in which the observer has vanished, and which – as in the case of certain forms of aerial surveillance and of biometric testing – can actually be carried out by computer software. A similarly depersonalized reading is also central to Scott's interpretation of the instrumental rationality of development more generally. It also underpins the notion that 'development' was a 'discursive formation' in Foucault's sense, a centreless constellation of power. As the following account of Doxiadis's use of the aerial gaze will demonstrate, such readings are not entirely on target – for ultimately it is not an automated version of visibility/control but a highly personalized and ultimately 'non-discursive' form of authority that underpinned much of the development encounter. Closer reflection will lead us away from Escobar or Ferguson's idea of development as centreless discourse and into an alternative and more complex reading around the creation of new centres of sovereignty within 'development', a major theme of the book that will have to be addressed again and again.

Doxiadis's aerial vision appeared repeatedly and prominently in his travel diaries. Air travel is never only a way of getting from place A to place B: it is the very space where the expertise of the consultant comes into its own. At the very end of his first Pakistan diary Doxiadis records – while waiting for the connecting service from Cairo to Athens on his last leg home – the key difference between his own perspective and the

---

[40] Adey, P. (2010), *Aerial life: spaces, mobilities, affects*, Chichester; Malden, MA, Wiley-Blackwell, pp.94–98.
[41] Ibid. p.85.

conventional view, which he calls 'bureaucratic administrative'. His final conclusion is worth quoting at length:

[W]e should try and get disconnected from the actual problem, increase the distance between it and ourselves. This has been attempted in several ways in several cases, from the ancient Greek author who shaved half of his head in order to be unable to go out in the agora ... to people who have retreated in monasteries ... These look to me rather antiquated ways. At present the plane which takes me to a big geographical distance helps me to see more and more clearly my problem.[42]

There are many examples of how an aerial perspective was one of Doxiadis's key methodological ploys. Flying high over India on one of his trips, for instance, the consultant's aerial gaze sharply dismisses what must be British colonialism's crowning achievement in the field of city planning: Edwin Lutyens and Herbert Baker's New Delhi (planned between 1912 and 1930):

The view of New Delhi is distressing from the air. We fly over the big axis of it and the Victoria monument [sic], over the round squares and the stern-like [sic – should be 'star-like', D. slips into German here!] streets and I see again how complicated the town-planning is for anyone who would really like to move into this city, in spite of the fact that it looks planned with geometrical exactitude. How better planned are the villages of the small towns which have escaped from the school of town-planners and decorators.[43]

Apart from the fact that Doxiadis does not let a little geographic inaccuracy dampen his confidence – the famous Victoria monument is actually located in Calcutta, not Delhi; what he was looking at was most likely the great triumphal arch on King's Way (later Raj Path) – this vision seeks to draw a clear dividing line between Doxiadis and whatever came before him in terms of city planning. While the 'decorators' Lutyens and Baker were after creating an image of imperial control regardless of what it would be like to live in such a city, Doxiadis wanted to provide a new urban space where the problems of modernity could be resolved for ordinary people; it was exactly that which made him a 'development consultant' rather than an architect. The aerial view is no longer the key to aesthetic enjoyment, as it had been for the creators of New Delhi with their elegant star-like road patterns, but now provides a key analytical tool where consultancy expertise can be generated. In this sense, he was in complete agreement with Le Corbusier's *Aircraft*, even if the condemnation of 'modern' town planning and the celebration of the

---

[42] CADA: Pakistan Volume 2, Dox 20, Diary 12 October–23 November 1954, p.330.
[43] CADA: Pakistan Volume 4, Dox 40, Athens March 1955, Diary 20 January–24 February 1955, p.185.

'naturally' grown village in Doxiadis's quote was an exact – and in all likelihood entirely deliberate – inversion of Le Corbusier's aesthetics.

Staying with the diary narrative of Doxiadis's second trip to Pakistan, we are frequently treated to more views out of the plane window – often meticulously recorded by the consultant's Leica and combined with hand-drawn diagrams designed to decode the 'meaning' of the landscape patterns observed. [See Figures 3 and 4] Setting out from Karachi to Dacca, the capital of East Pakistan, Doxiadis first records and ruminates about the landscape and architecture of North India; and later on – now on a shorter trip in an amphibious biplane – on the nature of Bengal and Bengali society. The aviator's gaze first meets large natural features – a *beel* (a saucer-like depression where surface water accumulates and forms a wetland or marsh) now in dry season, its vegetation and surrounding 'islands' – and then moves effortlessly to deep cultural interpretation:

Some of these islands are very densely [*sic*] built in a way that you can scarcely recognize any openings between the small huts. It is here that the patriarchal structure of the Bengali family becomes very apparent. The grouping of several huts around a rectangular courtyard proves the existence of several single families (each owning a hut) inside the greater unit of the patriarchal family who is living in the same enclosure around the same central courtyard, in the most prominent place on which is usually built the hut of the family's leader. This element of patriarchal life grouping more families into one has been completely overlooked in modern planning of villages and towns and this is one of the most important elements which should be looked at if we want to avoid big upsets of the pattern of life overnight. We should be definitely thinking of community planning and town-planning solutions which will express in a physical way the idea of living in groups of families which we recognize here[44]

After continuing on his flight for another hour (during which the narrator remains silent), Doxiadis goes on to identify 'Zamindars or different land-owners' as the main obstacles of progress and concludes with ideas about 'appropriate leadership', 'voluntary participation' and necessary 'catalysts':

It is when flying over such areas that we think more and more of the need of such people who will put in motion the forces lying idle in all these small human islands of which there are a hundred thousand in East Bengal[45]

By the time Doxiadis finally meets the inhabitants of the area face-to-face – there is a very revealing photograph concluding his aerial impressions which shows curious children and other villagers lining the river-bank where the plane has landed [See Figure 5] – he has already not only

---

[44] Ibid. pp.167–168.   [45] Ibid.

```
                    - 180 -

                FEBRUARY 6, 1955
                ================
```

FROM DACCA TO LAHORE

Dacca-Dalhi

At 9 o'clock in the morning I leave by Orient
Airways for Lahore via Delhi.

During the first 15 minutes we fly continuously
over extended hills where settlements are build on the top
of small or big areas. On their slopes there are gardens
covered with high types of vegetation, bushes, etc. There
are also some trees.

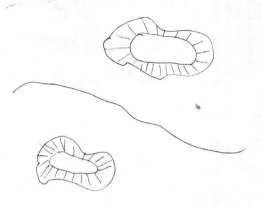

In between these islands there are light green
fields with very clearly cut divisions between them. Here
and there there are beds crossing these fields to different
directions and in between these small hills, in the deepest
line of the landscape, there are rivers and small canals
with water still in them.

Fifteen minutes later we fly over the landscape in
which there are no more settlements on islands, probably no
hills at all and all settlements are linear and full of
trees. In between these settlements there are fields
without any trees at all or with some few trees.

At exactly 30 minutes we fly over the Ganges full
of sand-covered banks and relatively low-level of water.

Past the Ganges, the landscape remains the same as
before. There are only linear settlements again, many
rivers completely dry at this time of the year and no trees
at all outside of the settlements and the immediate
surrounding of the ponds. These ponds are of irregular
shapes and very seldom rectangular.

Figure 3 Aerial topography sketched and interpreted by Doxiadis in his
diary en route from Dacca to Lahore.
Source: CADA: Pakistan vol.4, Diary DOX-PP 40, Jan.–Feb. 1955,
p.180 (Archive Files 23556).

Figure 4 Doxiadis's trademark impromptu aerial surveying –
photograph taken on a commercial flight over East Pakistan (today's
Bangladesh).*Source:* CADA: Pakistan vol.4, Diary DOX-PP 40, Jan.–
Feb. 1955, p.74 (Archive Files 23556).

decoded their main problems with the combined help of aerial analysis
and, presumably, some undisclosed background reading, he has also
created the space (the 'catalyst') that he as the outside expert could
occupy.

Deciphering the consultant's gaze

Doxiadis's use of the new possibilities of the aerial gaze, which allowed a
remote observer to see more accurately than whoever was both literally
and metaphorically too close to the ground, was highly representative of
his preferred epistemology more generally. It consisted of two elements:
a sharp separation between an active observer and an entirely passive
subject; and an emphasis on the visual decoding of surface realities.
We have already seen this methodology at work in the context of
Doxiadis's thoughts about 'feudalism' in East Bengal, which tied the
perception and interpretation of certain shapes in the landscape (the *beel*
and surrounding huts) directly to social and cultural analysis. In order to

Figure 5 The consultant has landed; Doxiadis captures the crowds awaiting his arrival by amphibious biplane in Rajshahi, East Pakistan. *Source:* CADA: Pakistan vol.4, Diary DOX-PP 40, Jan.–Feb. 1955, p.92 (Archive Files 23556).

know what was going on, Doxiadis did not need to mingle with a local population, let alone enter into a potentially two-sided and challenging discussion with native informants. His access to knowledge was immediate and depended primarily on his superior ability to 'see', rather than on any process involving measurement, interaction or listening.

The following episode that took place on Doxiadis's first fact-finding mission to Iraq illustrates this nicely. As he had done in Pakistan shortly before, Doxiadis went to tour the country and met local officials and foreign development experts, including an Iraqi bureaucrat and planner with the name of Hasan Muhammad Aly Moustapha, or 'Hasan Bey' according to Ottoman conventions of address. On one of their car journeys north of Baghdad the following exchange occurred (as reported by Doxiadis's first-person narrator in not entirely perfect English):

During our drive on the *band* Hassan Bey can show to me [*sic*] some houses and he tells me that [whether?] they are inhabited by people coming from the north or the south. I ask him how he can make this distinction and he tells me that he says so because of the colors of the clothing which is hung outside of the different buildings. Now I notice that the houses which he believed have been built by people coming from the north are not single story ones. Many of them, although they are built with mud, look to have two or three storys. This may be a wrong impression as they may be on a slight hill-side. Anyhow, such houses of the people of the north show much greater craftsmanship than the houses of the southern people. I assume that the northern people are better masons. Hassan Bey agrees with me.[46]

Doxiadis once again notices something fundamental about the culture of the people whose resettlement he was about to plan simply by taking a quick but sharp look at a feature of the urban landscape. What is more, he is at once able to offer a more comprehensive reading of local culture than his companion, whose recognition of different styles of clothes on the washing line represents a somewhat inferior version of the consultant's gaze. Hasan Bey can also do the kind of visual decoding that Doxiadis has made his trademark tool, but he gets stuck at the level of easy familiarity and does not penetrate to deeper levels of meaning. In the end, the local knowledge he represents is not there to inform but only to reaffirm Doxiadis's own analysis.

Doxiadis employed his trademark consultant's gaze in order to challenge the cultural knowledge of local experts, and also to judge and dismiss the work of his rivals. When visiting Le Corbusier's landmark achievement – Chandigarh, the newly built capital shared between the two Indian Union states Punjab and Haryana – his entire critique of the project consisted in an exercise of sign-reading (albeit now carried out at ground level) which played out the ill-informed intentions of the great planner against visual evidence of local 'resistance'. Driving around the site with his camera, Doxiadis documented and commented upon the failure of many of Le Corbusier's most celebrated contributions. The 'bat-chit' or 'gossip squares' – Le Corbusier's nod towards community life in India – were not only far too big and devoid of residents; Doxiadis also detects the traces of unplanned paths in the trampled-down grass, cutting diagonally across these squares – signs for Doxiadis that the planner had been out of touch with the daily routines of the local inhabitants who saw in these squares transitional spaces (or places to dry their laundry in) rather than spaces to rest and gossip.[47] The back lanes of lower- and middle-class housing blocks are found to be full of boxes and furniture, leading Doxiadis to comment sarcastically: 'they need more space for storing, but the engineers disagree'.[48] Typically, he acts as the advocate for taking local realities seriously, and places the agency of local

---

[46] CADA: Iraq Volume 1, Dox-Q2, July 1955, p.43.
[47] CADA: India Volume 3, Notes II, October–November 1955, p.54.   [48] Ibid. p.104.

people centre stage; but neither is he *of* the local people – in fact his whole *raison d'être* is that local people themselves are incapable of doing their own urban planning – nor has he had, in any way, any close social interaction with them.

Nothing brings this relationship between planner and development recipient out more clearly than an analysis of the numerous photographs in Doxiadis's diaries, usually prints from 35 mm black-and-white film and mostly 11 cm by 7.3 cm. They are in a documentary mode, taken at eye-level with a standard 35 mm or 50 mm lens; this looks 'natural' and downplays the authorial input of the photographer; some concern for good composition is nevertheless evident – as it would be in the work of a trained architect – for instance, in the use of the golden ratio wherever possible. But there is nothing fancy or artistic about these images. The editing is deliberately scant, keeping a number of photographs on display that the accomplished tourist photographer would probably discard – for instance, those with areas out of focus, backs of heads in the way and sub-ideal exposure.

The primary function of these images is to visualize the 'Ekistics problem' of Pakistan, i.e. to catalogue as widely as possible the different landscape patterns, forms of habitation and urban environments in the country. The coverage is biased towards urban spaces but otherwise fairly comprehensive: unusually for much material on Pakistan of the period, we get a very good sense of both wings, East and West, and most importantly, of all the different historical layers in the built environment. There is little romanticization of an 'oriental' setting, with modern multistorey blocks of flats, industrial estates, grain silos, mud huts and colonial office buildings and railway embankments featuring alongside well-known monuments and street scenes. [See Figure 6] While everything in this material points towards the importance of the subject photographed and downplays the input of the photographer, the man behind the camera is, of course, also always present. Apart from Doxiadis telling us 'this is Pakistan!' he is also telling us 'I was there!'; more to the point, he is there as an expert with no time for artistic frivolities, all-absorbed, as it were, in finding and documenting the kind of visual clues that were the key to his knowledge production.

Unlike the kind of anthropological photographs of 'native populations' which predominated in the colonial use of photography,[49] Doxiadis's pictures do not include many images of people; they are mainly of buildings and landscapes in which people may feature as coincidental additions. This

---

[49] See Pinney, C. (1997), *Camera Indica: the social life of Indian photographs*, University of Chicago Press, pp.24–71.

Figure 6 Street view of the Walled City of Lahore, West Pakistan,
autumn 1954. Note that this picture is taken from a car-accessible
location, reflecting Doxiadis's preferred mode of transport.
Source: CADA: Pakistan vol. 2, Diary DOX-PP 20, Oct.–Nov. 1954,
p.230 (Archive Files 23554).

appears sometimes as unwanted by both photographer and photographed,
for instance in shots of the interior of huts, with local inhabitants either
turned away from the camera's gaze or the place too dark to discern
anything properly. [See Figure 7] On other occasions, the photographer
clearly focuses on something else, while local bystanders – often children –
are seen to have squeezed into the picture at the margins and stare or smile
at the camera. If we exclude the small number of group photographs of
officials that sometimes include Doxiadis himself, there are only very few
shots that depict Pakistanis deliberately and 'head-on'. Where they do
occur, their subjects show a clear awareness of the camera by their way of
posing, sometimes with an embarrassed smile, but more often in a compos-
ure of stark earnestness. Doxiadis commented on this with humorous asides
in the captions, as if to say that these images were only included for comic
relief, while, of course, also highlighting the gulf that separated ordinary
Pakistanis and their outdated – often static and officious – relationship with
photography to the quick-footed snapping away of the consultant.

For Doxiadis's photographic evidence to work as he intended, there
had to be as little interaction as possible between the subject photographed

Figure 7 Photograph taken during one of Doxiadis's surveys of vernacular building styles in Rajshahi, East Pakistan.
Source: CADA: Pakistan vol.4, Diary DOX-PP 40, Jan.–Feb. 1955, p.93 (Archive Files 23556).

and the photographer himself. The majestic distance of the aerial gaze and its superior ability to 'see' could only be transposed from the skies to the ground if a similar distance could be maintained. This is the reason why Doxiadis preferred pictures of inanimate objects over pictures of people who could never be entirely relied upon to remain passive. Even when the actual subject matter is people's agency itself, it was depicted and interpreted almost exclusively on the basis of its representation in the material environment, as in the pictures of buildings, of washing on the line, of water spilt around a communal tap, of traces on the lawn, etc.

Nothing – and in particular, no trace of the photographed subject 'talking back' at the photographer – was to be allowed to intrude in the act of cataloguing and sign-reading that underpinned the authority of the consultant. If we remember Ariella Azoulay's advice to recognize time as an added dimension in the interpretation of photographs – 'watching' them as if they were still images from a film with a before and after, rather than merely 'looking at them'[50] – we can easily imagine how the photographs masked out a very different reality. Doxiadis, far from being a lone

[50] Azoulay, A. (2008), *The civil contract of photography*, New York, Zone Books, p.14.

Figure 8 Rapid surveying – snapshot of mud houses in south-western Punjab. Note the motion blur and the railway fencing, suggesting this was taken from a speeding train.
Source: CADA: Pakistan vol.4, Diary DOX-PP 40, Jan.–Feb. 1955, p.233 (Archive Files 23556).

master observer, is actually surrounded by a whole coterie of companions and government minders standing outside the angle of view when he points his camera at the subject of his expert gaze; his limousine is parked by the roadside behind him, surrounded by fascinated locals; and Doxiadis has to wait for the right moment when taking his picture to ensure that there aren't too many passers-by or onlookers accidentally included. Because of his light editing, this 'photographic situation' is sometimes directly visible in the photographs themselves; for instance, when there is the aforementioned back of the head obstructing the view or, even more strikingly, when we can clearly observe motion blur or reflections from train or car windows in some images. [See Figure 8]

Doxiadis the Olympian expert, contemplating with such penetration the inner secrets of a foreign country, is clearly revealed here as the travelling salesman that he really was, whisked from place to place at great speed and shielded from the outside by the vehicle he is riding in.

Doxiadis's diaries and photographs were designed to turn Pakistan from a difficult terrain with complex political realities into a grand canvas of developmental intervention, a country where 'colossal' problems awaited to be solved by a heroic expert and the dedicated backing he received from metropolitan funding organizations or charities. Even when local peculiarities and respect for local people's wishes were placed centre stage – as they often were in Doxiadis's *oeuvre* – a carefully cultivated 'gaze' and epistemological stance managed to concentrate all agency in the person of the consultant himself, while reducing the very people in whose name development was carried out to a passive silence. In some ways, his diary was the direct equivalent of the District Gazetteer of the colonial period; a great archive that presented a territory as a problem while also providing the necessary tools for its resolution. But there were important differences in both emotional flavour and sense of subjectivity here. While the colonial archive underwrote the will to power of a regime of several hundred years' standing with little reference to the personalities of the officers involved, Doxiadis's archive underwrote a similarly broad project – 'development' – in a way that made it the terrain of a single and highly distinctive personality, Doxiadis himself.

Contrary to first appearances, Doxiadis's technique of reading visual signs and clues was never really an example of an 'aerial' governmentality as endowed with such great impersonal power by the likes of Adey and (more implicitly) Scott; this was not a case of a god-like 'seeing everything from nowhere', it was a case of *Doxiadis* seeing everything from wherever he happened to be, while pretending that he saw things somehow from a superior vantage point. The observer was not only present implicitly, the entire mode of seeing was designed to make his presence as strongly felt as possible. The whole point about the sketches, photographs and verbal interpretations of visual evidence in the archive was that they were not simply the result of expertise in the decultured, depersonalized sense recommended by UNESCO or similar development agencies at the time. Doxiadis's visual diagnosis was a self-conscious work of his own *genius*. He derived his authority from the ability to perceive what others could not. Although anybody would be able to see what Doxiadis saw after he had pointed it out – as was the case of Hasan Bey on the outskirts of Baghdad – the initial revelation belonged to him alone. His ultimate authority did not lie in his technical expertise at all, but elsewhere, in a more imponderable mix of heroism and aesthetic sense.

A striking echo from a related but different context can help illuminate what was going on here. In *Tristes Tropiques*, his iconic autobiography-cum-field-journal-cum-philosophical-treatise published to great public acclaim just around the time Doxiadis was exploring Pakistan and Iraq, Claude Lévi-Strauss noted how the momentary glimpse of some seemingly unimportant piece of circumstantial evidence – 'chance fragments of landscape, momentary snatches of life, reflections caught on the wing' – make it possible to suddenly understand something that otherwise offers little information.[51] More specifically, he made the following observation while recounting the various impressions of the shoreline that he gleaned from the deck of the ship that took him from France to Brazil in the 1930s:

I was, as yet, so little of an anthropologist that I never thought to take advantage of these opportunities. I've learnt since that these brief glimpses of a town, a region or a way of life, offer us a school of attention. Sometimes – so great is the concentration required of us in the few moments at our disposal – they may even reveal to us characteristics which in other circumstances may have long remain hidden.[52]

These moments of 'seeing', like those central to Doxiadis's own methodology, cannot be acquired from reading books or attending lectures; they are illuminations produced by 'experience': of travel, of hardship, of living through challenging encounters with the unfamiliar. This is precisely what Doxiadis himself placed at the beginning of his diary project: not his training as an architect or engineer, but his spiritual kinship with Lawrence of Arabia. But even when considering that Lévi-Strauss's own period 'in the field' was short by any standards, he still stood on much stronger ground than Doxiadis. At least initially, the latter had nothing more than some ill-informed United Nations pamphlets and a few weeks' interaction with bureaucrats and politicians to show for himself. His claim to authority was in the first instance an invocation pure and simple, by reading signs like an initiate he could make people believe that he was in fact an initiate, a consultant of 'experience', not a magician pulling inappropriate technical solutions from up his sleeve.

The consultant's authority

Doxiadis pointed out repeatedly, starting with his earliest policy papers on Pakistan, that the development consultant was never merely a scientist following a certain methodology. To be truly effective he had to be willing to act in a self-consciously transgressive and irrational manner when the situation required. Every situation in a developing country was by definition new and irreducible to existing templates; it immediately

[51] Lévi-Strauss, C. (1961), [Tristes tropiques.] A world on the wane. Translated ... by John Russell. [With plates.], London, Hutchinson, p.50.
[52] Ibid. p.66.

threw up problems 'that have not existed before'. 'It is here that *imagination* must come and complement the study of the past and present', Doxiadis wrote in a programmatic passage; 'it is at this moment that ... [w]e must *free our minds* and try to conceive new solutions without fearing to be considered *crazy*. There are always *crazy ideas* necessary when one has to break new ground and find new solutions.'[53]

But how could such a bold self-assertion of authority that deliberately refused to seek refuge behind the truth dispensations of development discourse be insured against opposition and failure? Part of an answer emerges in another highly significant passage in Doxiadis's first diary, bracketed off from the main travel narrative by its strange title: 'Musical Intermezzo'. As so often, the discussion is framed as a moment of reflection while normal sensory perceptions are restricted. Doxiadis is resting in the hot humid air of a small bungalow in Rahimyar Khan in southern Punjab. He seeks relief and opens the verandah door, only to be assaulted by the constant beat of a drum that is continuing for hours on end – and nicely incorporated into the writing by the repetition of the phrase 'the drum-beating continues', in order to pace and punctuate the unfolding argument. First, Doxiadis turns to his hosts and learns that this is a wedding in progress, but they do not comply with his wishes to take him there, arguing that he would not understand and that this was not for him. Doxiadis can only imagine what is going on – 'a sexual dance', he suspects – and has to go back to his room; but plagued by fundamental questions he cannot sleep, with ideas coming 'continuously in my mind as if raised through drum-beating from sub-consciousness.'[54] 'I start thinking how alien I must look to these people who do not believe I can understand their music, their dancing, their weddings and be taken there. But my contact with all these people here has proved to me that I am not alien; although expressions of our lives may be different we are completely the same.'[55] It follows a long meditation on the problem of the consultant. How different can the post-colonial consultant be from his host society? How can he offer solutions if there is an unbridgeable gap between them? How does difference affect the power relationship between consultant and host? Or, as Doxiadis himself puts it, 'Is there any justification for this attempt for development and for our presence in this unknown land amongst unknown people?'[56]

---

[53] CADA: Pakistan Volume 3, Dox 21, January 1955, Pakistan Ekistics – Problems, Policies and Programs, p.35.
[54] CADA: Pakistan Volume 2, Dox 20, Diary 12 October–23 November 1954, p. 202.
[55] Ibid.   [56] Ibid. p.203.

Doxiadis's answer – and a successful self-justification for his role as consultant in Pakistan – hinges on the invocation of a notion of popular authenticity that allowed him to eradicate any notion of essential difference between him and his host society, and also to ward off any threat to his authority as expert. It is the 'common' people, the poorest, least educated and least developed, that on closer inspection turn out to be exponents of a single and universal sense of humanity. Doxiadis counters his frustrations about being excluded from the wedding by his local handlers by invoking an immediate and direct connection with ordinary folk around the world:

> Every time I meet the plain people of the countryside or the poor people of the towns I have the feeling that I meet people of my own country or of other countries I have visited. It is true that the more educated the people are, the greatest the distance between them is [sic] … I think that almost all the people I have met – from the single peasant discussing the techniques of his farm to the farm laborer, to the people building the roads, or the dams, or the houses and ports which I have visited, to the people using the new projects and living in new housing schemes – were interested in what was happening and they expressed in every possible way their participation in the big revolution which is taking place.[57]

What made this immediate connection possible was of course the simple fact that the 'ordinary' Pakistani was less likely to challenge Doxiadis's authority in the very limited circumstances where direct exchange took place. He or she was always more of a construction in Doxiadis's own mind than a real human being on the ground, as it were, and even then the carefully constructed expert's gaze made too much direct interaction superfluous. The well-educated and articulate member of the elite who would encounter Doxiadis on a daily basis and in potentially challenging conversations was more of a direct threat, either because this kind of interlocutor was a planner and an expert himself, or because he viewed Doxiadis's developmental do-goodery with a great deal of cynicism and suspicion, as was the case with many of the bureaucrats and politicians who so elegantly subverted the chief consultant's authority. Both these stock characters are carefully demolished in Doxiadis's account, the first with the argument that as a Western-trained expert, the home-grown planner was really in no way closer to the people of Pakistan than the Western-trained expert born elsewhere; and the second, by equating development scepticism with fundamental character flaws. (There is a wonderfully evocative description in the diary which we shall save for a later chapter.)

[57] Ibid.

Doxiadis's manoeuvre of separating a troublesome and pesky elite from the more congenial 'real' people was far from original, of course. It has been deployed to create a sense of legitimacy for autocrats and right-wing populists around the world (the branding of the educated liberal left as 'out of touch' with 'real people', so dear to conservative tabloid editors in the United Kingdom is as good an example as any), and was a cornerstone of colonial self-justification. Just like the types that Doxiadis depicts in his diary, educated Indians with a propensity to answer back were in the colonial view either self-interested demagogues or misguided westernized agitators who spoke for no one but themselves; the most loyal of all subjects of the Raj meanwhile were frequently seen to be the common peasantry untouched by new ideas and developmental progress. Once again, the colonialist lurks behind the development expert, even if the latter was Greek and had no historical connections with British rule whatsoever.

Through identifying the ordinary Pakistanis as 'his' people and natural allies while dismissing the Pakistani elite as illegitimate, Doxiadis had prepared the ground for his most treasured intellectual weapon: his endorsement and celebration of folk culture as where the genius of the people and the genius of the consultant could ultimately be fused. He would return to it again and again in his great building projects of later years, after discovering it as an extension of the earlier discovery of a universal brotherhood of common people: 'The simplest forms of local architecture are practically always and everywhere the same that is *if climate and physical conditions are the same*. But the more developed an architecture is the more if differs from country to country, from civilization to civilization.'[58] This is a typical rendition – in terms of architecture – of the basic ideological function of 'development': just as development problems were the same around the world regardless of history, politics or cultural specificity, so were the nature of people and their architectural language. If there were differences, they were not inherent and insurmountable but caused by external variables – the 'climate and physical conditions' in Doxiadis's quote. Instead of acting as a limitation to development, these variables actually provided an access point for the expert to deploy his technological superiority. Behind the deceptive specificity of folk architecture – what after all could be a better incarnation of a people's particular collective spirit? – lurked the imposition of uniformity so typical for development thought.

[58] CADA: Pakistan Volume 2, Dox 20, Diary 12 October–23 November 1954, p.202, emphasis added.

The realm of folk architecture as conceived here by Doxiadis offered a safe framework where the encounter between outside expert and development recipient could be formulated with more or less secure role expectations for each. Throughout his survey work, Doxiadis went out of his way to catalogue the local building practices of farmers and craftsmen, petty shopkeepers and food sellers, shanty town dwellers and boat people. More often than not he is full of admiration of what he sees, and uses the people's architecture to criticize what the state or the rich and powerful have built at the same time. While 'French-style' villas on a model farm were a dreadful waste of resources as well as next to uninhabitable in Bengal's climate, a row of bamboo huts for farm labourers were a model to be developed. 'It is a pity that such traditional types which are serving the people so well have to be abandoned for new construction without any previous effort for their betterment.'[59] Folk architecture not only was a more genuine expression of the identity of the people but also demonstrated a great deal of technical expertise. The protective properties of Bengal mat-huts were superior to the latest glazing technology used in the West, 'as they do not have any big openings for light, rain or insects to come in'.[60] About a house on the beachfront in Karachi, Doxiadis wrote:

For any western trained architect, I would also say for any western man, a window is an opening in the wall, starting two or three feet above the floor; it is just where sitting men would like to have the opening on their walls. But here I find myself in front of a house the windows of which start just from the floor and go only four feet high. Is this not the ideal solution for a house, the inhabitants of which sit on the floor? We may laugh at it but this is a rational house allowing the breeze not to blow over the heads but on the people living in this house. Such expressions of real need are easily overlooked and hidden behind the heaps of westernized buildings.[61]

Praise for local practices like this did not mean that the work of the expert had in any way become obsolete, of course. Nobody was more interested than Doxiadis in actually providing mass housing to the poor, and no other planner in Pakistan at the time had as much an impact on actual everyday living spaces as him. The reason why the development consultant was needed, even in a country with well-developed intermediate technologies, was coordination. It was only the foreign planner who had the ability to observe and identify best practice across the land and to combine it with superior technology that had not previously been used but could help to save precious resources, for instance the use of cement guns on bamboo or jute structures,[62] or the objective measurement of the heat transfer properties of a particular type of mud wall. In short,

[59] Ibid. p.58.   [60] Ibid. p.77.   [61] Ibid. p.5.   [62] Ibid. p.53.

Doxiadis's emphasis on folk architecture made it possible to jump between difference and sameness in his argumentation as the situation required. Whenever there were questions about whether he as a Greek with little prior knowledge of Pakistan had any right to speak on Pakistani development matters at all, he could enlist some notion of universality as demonstrated by the material just quoted; when, on the other hand, he wanted to dismiss his rivals – either outsiders like himself, or 'western-ized' Pakistani planners – he could harp on about avoiding universal and outside solutions and demand that local specificities were taken seriously.

Development could not transform itself from a self-interested political ideology into a world-making discourse without a robust but at the same time self-effacing notion of personal authority at its centre. The argument has been made repeatedly already: we can unmask what is merely an 'ideology' – a politically motivated misrepresentation – by asking who has created it; and by investigating the social origins or political interests of this figure, we can then identify the purpose of an ideology and therefore destroy its validity.[63] We can easily explain why the British Foreign Office in 1949 would jump at the concept of 'underdevelopment' to find a new language to relate to its erstwhile colonies, for instance, or why Liaquat Ali Khan would made a reference to 'underdevelopment' when explaining Pakistan to American businessmen, and this realization makes us suspicious of any inherent truth-claim 'development' may have. Nobody could perform such an easy critical operation with 'discourse', however. We do not ask (or at least not usually) what kind of self-serving purpose a doctor has at the back of his mind when he diagnoses a heart attack and asks the patient to be placed on a defibrillator. The reason is not simply that medical science somehow works independently of the authority of any of its representatives; after all, medicine does not admin-ister itself, it is still a particular doctor who has to carry out a credible diagnosis and chose a credible course of action in accordance with this diagnosis. The reason the authority of the doctor is not challenged is that it is vouchsafed by a code of conduct, through procedures of training and initiation and models of behaviour.

Doxiadis came to the problem of how to fashion the role of a develop-ment consultant from a somewhat unusual angle. Unlike most other development consultants active at the time, he was a trained architect and a self-employed businessman and entrepreneur, which gave his handling of dilemmas such as cultural immersion versus technical expertise, or disembodied consultancy versus new romantic adventurer,

---

[63] As pointed out with exceptional clarity in Mannheim, K. (1929), *Ideologie und Utopie*, Bonn, F. Cohen, pp.35–47.

a harder edge than usual. But the dilemmas themselves were not unique. The case of Doxiadis, and of the literature he read about the question of development consultancy, demonstrated that what vouchsafed the authority of the expert was not necessarily only related to his or her expertise. In fact – and in blatant contradiction of what much of the development literature appeared to argue at first sight – the authority of the consultant was sometimes even directly opposed to relying solely on expertise. The 'purely technical' expert, transplanted from his normal American suburban habitat to a place like India or Pakistan and requiring a steady supply of soft toilet paper, to quote Doxiadis's United Nations information pack once again, was not a suitable centre of authority for development, whereas the carpenter Thimm, who made use of what he was given in a Pakistani village, was. Ultimately, what vouchsafed development discourse was an old-fashioned sense of hardness in the face of adversity, a willingness to face the oriental 'other' – as it was portrayed in such stark colours by advisors like Roest and Holt – while heroically pretending that it was merely 'Mr. Underdeveloped Region', and an ability to take on development even if in the background their lurked a pre-emptive realization that it was all really a great charade. Development had more than a hint of Shakespearean drama about it and was far from exhausted in discursive productions around new categories of knowledge such as GDP per capita or the Ekistics grid.

The conception of development as 'discourse', as it stood at the heart of the analysis of critics like Escobar or, by extension, James Scott, fails to fully account for its subject. Although every attempt was certainly made to push it into this direction, development' never really became a formation like medicine and its key practitioners never became like doctors. The power of development was never only, or even primarily, the power of power/knowledge in Foucauldian diction, but an extension of the non-scriptural and highly personalized power of its practitioners. In anticipation of where the discussion will be heading over the next chapters, we can call this power 'sovereign' (in the sense Foucault used it to describe the way early modern kings and noblemen exercised power, rather than in the more common notion of sovereignty as a category of international law). It is not hard to see why this should be the case: a consultant like Doxiadis claimed to see everything from a perspective high up in the skies – which Foucault in his later work came to regard as the 'greatest dream of the greatest sovereign'[64] – and he developed a methodology of

---

[64] Foucault, M., M. Senellart, F. o. Ewald and A. Fontana (2007), *Security, territory, population: lectures at the Collège de France, 1977–78*, Basingstoke; New York, Palgrave Macmillan: République Française, p.66.

relating directly to 'his' people. Moreover, when working as a consultant in Pakistan his primary preoccupation became to behave like a 'big man' or a 'little king', constantly seeking to challenge and squash rival locations of authority. This conclusion demands a change in methodology and focus. 'Development' needs to be recast as an eminently *political* project, in the sense of being driven by the cut and thrust of irreducible conflict, rather than by a will to truth or discursive productivity. It is Doxiadis the aspiring power broker, rather than Doxiadis the writer and theoretician of development that will stand centre stage in the next chapter.

3   From 'great plan' to great project

Doxiadis's self-stylization as a 'Lawrence of Arabia' of development was inseparable from his actual experience of working in Pakistan. His travel diaries – where the image of the heroic, even self-avowedly 'crazy' consultant was constructed with such care – had an immediate practical purpose. They were to document and justify Doxiadis's activities for the benefit of his financial backers who had underwritten his mission to the country. They formed the first building blocks of a much larger collection of material. As Doxiadis got his teeth into his new role as chief consultant to the Pakistan Planning Commission, his records also came to include official files of state, extensive correspondence with a network of contacts from Washington to Karachi, as well as technical plans and reports. Taken together, this material allows us to tell a story of what 'development' actually meant at ground level and in practice. It is a story full of twists and turns, of expectations and disappointments, of alliances made and broken. The historical record is still largely silent on such matters, not least because not very much 'happened' as far as the larger development history of Pakistan was concerned. The years between 1954 and 1958 did not produce any tangible successes, either for Doxiadis as a person or for the country in general. The First Five Year Plan, on which Doxiadis was working at the time, is universally recognized as a 'failure', retaining some historical significance solely for the fact that it was compiled at all. Development 'take-off', as it were, began only from 1958 onwards. And yet, behind the failures of this early period, important future directions already began to emerge. Although it felt more of a road to nowhere at the time, Doxiadis's journey towards Islamabad – his greatest achievement – actually began in those years, among the policy contortions that surrounded urban reconstruction in the old capital Karachi at the time. The failure of the 'great plan', for which he had come to Pakistan in the first instance, propelled Doxiadis towards a new commercial strategy: a focus on 'great projects' that would eventually enable such major achievements as Islamabad and Korangi.

106

To get us set on our journey through the ups and downs of Doxiadis's political engagement in Pakistan of the 1950s, a few more words on historical context are useful. His arrival in 1954 followed hot on the heels of Pakistan's first *annus horribilis* and the subsequent evolution of an ever-closer strategic relationship with the United States. The year 1953 was arguably the end of the hot phase in Pakistan's decolonization process. It had begun a few years before the declaration of independence with the formation of a mass movement for separate nationhood that was competing with the nationalism of the All India Congress. This momentum was now fading into a bleaker but more clearly post-colonial future.[1] Following the end of the Korean boom in commodity prices, the new nation had run into severe economic difficulties, with endemic food shortages leading to widespread riots and discontent around the country. First attempts to engage with development planning under the aegis of the Colombo Plan had to be aborted, long before the six-year timeframe that the Plan envisioned was up. In political terms, the loose and uneasy coalition that had achieved the creation of Pakistan was about to break up. Whatever remained of the mass mobilization that had given the Muslim League movement its original strength was now turned into an enemy of the new state. Unsatisfied hopes and dreams that had been central to the Pakistan demand were first vilified as ideological deviance and then crushed by force: first, in the Bengal language riots that ended the possibility of easily combining being Bengali and being Pakistani; then in March 1953, in the suppression of the anti-Qadiani agitation in West Pakistan that condemned popular notions of Islamic communitarianism as contrary to Pakistan's ideology.[2]

As their electoral support base was beaten off the streets, provincial politicians found themselves at loggerheads with unelected central bureaucrats, who for the first time felt powerful enough to dissolve parliamentary bodies and dismiss a prime minister with a working majority. Their assumption of power in tandem with the military leadership,

[1] For more historical background on this period see Sayeed, K. B. (1968), *Pakistan, the formative phase, 1857–1948*, London, New York, etc., Oxford University Press, Part II; Jalal, A. (1990), *The state of martial rule: the origins of Pakistan's political economy of defence*, Cambridge; New York, Cambridge University Press; Talbot, I. (2012), *Pakistan: a modern history*, London, C. Hurst & Co. Publishers Ltd, Chapters 1 and 2.

[2] This is not the view most often represented in the literature, where the question of finding the right kind of national identity for Pakistan (How much Islam? How much regional identity?) is usually foregrounded, while the element of demobilization and control of popular agency is usually missed. Both the agitation for Bengali language rights and the anti-Qadiani riots are seen as 'deviations' from what Pakistan 'really' meant, as anti-state intrusions launched by pro-Indian secularists and anti-Pakistan 'Mullahs'. See Munir, M. (1980), *From Jinnah to Zia*, Lahore, Vanguard Books.

already represented by Pakistan's future dictator General Ayub Khan, went hand in hand with a stepping up of American aid efforts in the wake of Eisenhower's assumption of office that same year. The summer of 1953 saw the quick passing of a massive wheat loan package in aid of Pakistan, a first sign of turning away from the stinginess of the Truman era, and over the remaining months of the year the first contours of a closer aid relationship – both military and civilian – were hammered out. It took another four years, however, to make the newly emerging state structures permanent and viable, a tortuous process in which development ideology increasingly played an important role. The eventual publication of the First Five Year Plan which had brought Doxiadis to Pakistan was both a testament to the new US–Pakistan relationship and its weakness. The Prime Minister who signed the preface, Feroz Khan Noon, not only was Pakistan's seventh in only ten years but also would be the last civilian to be nominally in charge of the country until the early 1970s. Pakistan was back in crisis mode when Doxiadis's first period of engagement came to an end, and at least at the surface, the changes to affect the country later in 1958 would prove even more momentous than those of 1953.

Chief advisor for housing and settlements

Doxiadis's entry to the Pakistan development scene was connected to the formation of the Harvard Advisory Group for Pakistan, a body of experts financed by the Ford Foundation. This philanthropic organization had over the previous decade transformed itself from a tax-saving measure of only local importance into a global operation with a total endowment of 417 million US dollars, a sum that dwarfed the financial capabilities of international organizations like the United Nations and many US government departments.[3] Such financial muscle drew a great deal of suspicion from conservative sections of the US political class, who at the time were enflamed by a moral panic over suspected 'liberal' and 'communist' subversion. A particularly delicate point in the fortunes of the Foundation was reached in 1952, when it was investigated for 'un-American activities' by a House Select Committee chaired by Edward Cox and later Carroll Reece. Although no malpractices were found, this generated considerable pressure to put Ford's philanthropic power in the service of America's Cold War. Despite being increasingly central to US global strategy, 'development' expenditure was still far from being

3 (1952), 'The Ford Foundation', *Social Service Review* 26(1): 90–92; Sutton, F. X. (1987), 'The Ford Foundation: the early years', *Daedalus* 116(1): 41–91.

easily justified in a domestic political context, which made its 'farming out' to wealthy non-state bodies particularly attractive. Eager to prove its patriotism, Ford became heavily involved in the funding of educational institutions and the training of educational experts in the emerging Third World, including Pakistan.

The Harvard Mission was by far the most ambitious of all Ford programmes in Pakistan. Although officially limited to a role as 'advisors', Doxiadis and his colleagues effectively became the core of the newly constituted Pakistan Planning Commission. In this capacity they practically drafted the country's First Five Year Plan. Designed to cover the years 1955–1960, this was the first serious attempt of its kind in Pakistan and, although deeply flawed in many ways, went substantially beyond the mere compilation of short wish lists that had passed for 'plans' before. While most of the experts were North Americans and worked on different aspects of development economics, Doxiadis was the man responsible for housing and urban planning during the initial stages of the mission. This role would provide him with a bird's eye view of virtually all urban planning and government construction activity in the country, as well as offering direct access to the wider Pakistani political establishment. His appointment appears to have been largely a coincidence. The Ford Foundation's preferred housing expert had become ill, and the job was offered to Doxiadis instead.[4] It must have helped that he had had contacts with the Foundation before, most notably with its former colourful chairman Paul G. Hoffman, who previously had been in charge of the Marshall Plan and knew Doxiadis from his work in Greece.[5]

If Doxiadis was the right man for the Ford Foundation in 1954 because he possessed the right kind of political background and added a welcome international and non-governmental flavour to what was in effect an extension of US foreign policy, the Ford Foundation in turn was also essential for Doxiadis's success as a development entrepreneur. Unlike most of the economists or engineers on the Harvard Mission, he saw his appointment not as an end in itself, but as a way of expanding his consultancy business through follow-on contracts both in Pakistan itself and elsewhere in the world. Without the financial backing by a powerful donor from the world of international development finance, he would have been unable to pursue a commercial strategy of this kind. Previous

---

[4] Kim, J. (2006), 'C. A. Doxiadis and the funding of the ecumenopolis', *Space and progress: Ekistics and the global context of post–World War II urbanization and architecture*, Athens, unpublished conference paper.

[5] Kyrtsis, A.-A. (2006), *Constantinos A. Doxiadis: texts, design drawings, settlements*, Athens, Ikaros, p.357.

indirect contacts between Doxiadis and Pakistan – unconnected to the Harvard Mission – had already established that the Pakistan government was both unwilling and unable to procure the services of foreign experts unless the latter brought their own funding with them.

Immediately after the Delhi housing conference that had marked Doxiadis's international breakthrough, his friend Jacob Crane had tried to get him in touch with the Pakistani Ministry of Works and Health through its Permanent Secretary G. Mueenuddin,[6] whom Crane had met on a visit to Karachi in early 1954. In his capacity as administrator of the United States Housing and Home Finance Agency, Crane could act as an international middleman, brokering contacts between prospective experts like Doxiadis, possible sources of funding and prospective clients like the Government of Pakistan. In a letter to Mueenuddin, Crane introduced Doxiadis as somebody 'who played a major role in the reconstruction of Greece after World War II ... particularly in the housing phase' and who had 'wide international experience in Europe and Australia', before pointing out that he had learnt about an 'increasing interest of the International Bank for Reconstruction and Development [the 'World Bank'] in the feasibility of helping to finance the development of building and housing, perhaps particularly the production of housing materials and equipment.' Since Doxiadis had then just gone on a World Bank mission to Syria, he would be the man the Pakistanis should contact if they wanted to benefit from the Bank's largess as well. In Crane's words, '... the work of Mr. Doxiadis for IBRD in Syria constitutes the most important current interest of IBRD in housing and related matters.'[7]

Around the same time Crane had also got in touch with Doxiadis, reporting back to him the impressions he had gleaned on his Pakistan trip. He had tried to get the Pakistani delegation at the New Delhi housing conference to contact Doxiadis directly, which seems to have had some effect as Doxiadis referred to some of the members of the delegation as 'old friends' when he came to Pakistan later that year.[8] Among them was Zaheer ud-Din Khwaja, a man who was to become one of the most prominent planners/architects of Pakistan over the following decades.[9] At the time Crane was less sure about the prospects

---

[6] As so often with Pakistani surnames, there is not a single agreed romanized spelling even when talking about the same person. I have used 'Mueenuddin' even where other spellings are used in the primary documents to avoid confusion.
[7] CADA: File 19255 Correspondence between C. A. Doxiadis and J. L. Crane (1954–57), Letter Crane to Muin-ud-Din [February 1954].
[8] CADA: Pakistan Volume 2, Diary 12 October–23 November 1954, p.234.
[9] Ibid. p.267.

of success: 'It is very hard to say what may come of this, but I hope I have made the most appropriate moves.' In his advice to Doxiadis, he immediately focused on the most important factor that would determine Doxiadis's business career in a country like Pakistan: the availability of funding. 'The Pakistanis said that it is almost impossible for them to pay for foreign experts directly, because of the very tight exchange problem', Crane poignantly added to one of his letters, while suggesting the World Bank route as best commercial strategy.[10]

Doxiadis's success or failure depended not so much on his quality as a consultant but on his skill as a middleman. Over his decade-long involvement in Pakistan, he would typically first approach a donor body like the Ford Foundation to pre-approve a particular project, before offering it – with cash in hand so to speak – to the Pakistani side, who were then less likely to look the proverbial gift horse in the mouth. He was, of course, not the only consultant in his field to operate in this manner. Doxiadis had to contend with the presence of other foreign housing experts in Pakistan, among them the British firm Minoprio–Spenceley–MacFarlane assigned under the Colombo Plan, Otto Koenigsberger, German-born veteran of urban planning in the former princely states of colonial India and now in Pakistan for the UN, the Americans John E. Zemanek and John Bell on the payroll of the US Foreign Operations Administration (FOA), and the aforementioned Frenchman Michel Ecochard, also attached to the UN.

The relationship between these consultants was often highly competitive, and in some cases outright hostile. But there was also a good deal of cooperation geared towards a shared common purpose: the advancement of urban reconstruction as a worthwhile commercial project in itself. This was best achieved through a network of consultants that faced the often sceptical host governments as a united front, rather than as individuals that could be divided and ruled. While Doxiadis, for instance, had little good to say about Minoprio–Spenceley–MacFarlane,[11] who also directly competed with him for commissions in Iraq and the Middle East, he sought to build bridges with Ecochard, whose work he admired but who he believed lacked the necessary communication skills to sell himself in a non-expert policy environment.[12] On his fact-finding tours for the Harvard Mission, Doxiadis frequently asked his Pakistani

---

[10] CADA: File 19255 Correspondence between C. A. Doxiadis and J. L. Crane (1954–57), Letter Crane to Dox, 18 February 1954.
[11] 'I have never seen a worse planner in my life.' CADA: Pakistan Volume 31, Correspondence, Letter to Rudduck, 4 July 1957.
[12] CADA: Pakistan Volume 2, Diary, pp.8, 329.

interlocutors if he should put them in touch with experts in specialist
fields who were unrelated to his own company; thereby furthering his
own career as well as those of others.[13] A further illustration of this
climate of quiet collusion among rivals was Doxiadis's access to classified
documentation prepared by the FOA, a US government body, for the
exclusive use of the Government of Pakistan. Although he was only
shown the report in question 'for a few minutes', Doxiadis felt confident
enough that his company 'should get it', suggesting much wider possibilities of informal information sharing in contradiction of legal
restrictions.[14]

Throughout his fact-finding tours in Pakistan, Doxiadis continuously
attempted to use his position on the Planning Board in order to identify
potential future projects for his own company. On his visit to the US-
funded Ganges–Kobadak scheme in East Pakistan, for instance, he could
not help making the self-serving comment '... here is the chance for a
regional plan which should not be missed';[15] and when discussing the
possibility of FOA funding for housing in Pakistan with David Bell of the
Harvard Mission, he noted not without glee that 'several millions of
dollars could be spent very profitably for all kinds of housing schemes
and services. This is a good start of a day.'[16] George Gant, the Ford
Foundation's leading man in Pakistan at the time, admitted with remarkable candour that a not unimportant consideration in Doxiadis's engagement in the First Five Year Plan was to have the succession phase 'all
lined up' so as to create 'a *huge* job for the next five years.'

Lobbying for the 'great plan'

The lynchpin of Doxiadis's lobbying strategy, both in terms of planning
ideology as well as in terms of its practical usefulness as a generator of
follow-on contracts, was his trademark vision of Ekistics – predicated, as
we have seen, on an all-encompassing 'great plan'. In characteristic
fashion, Doxiadis had at first declined the Harvard job because it
appeared too limited to him. Only when his brief was extended from
urban reconstruction in the narrow sense to cover all issues concerned
with 'housing and settlements' did he accept.[17] As Doxiadis pointed out
in virtually any document he wrote on the subject, planning was an
activity that did not stop at the local level or with the provision of

[13] Ibid. p.222.   [14] Ibid. p.54.   [15] Ibid. p.56.   [16] Ibid. p.17.
[17] CADA: Archive File 28548: Scrapbook, 'Our New Programme in Pakistan' [translated
from the Greek by Klairi Mavragani], 15 January 1959, point 2.

a certain number of housing units. A comprehensive intervention conceived on the trademark Ekistics approach would include a national master plan, several large urban reconstruction schemes running in parallel, education and training initiatives, as well as architectural blueprints for a whole range of buildings, from single-room housing units to university campuses. Attention to local detail had to be linked to a perspective that took regional and even international considerations into account, or the planning effort as a whole would fail altogether.[18]

In January 1955, Doxiadis put his highly ambitious case to the Pakistan Planning Board, on which he now served in his capacity as chief advisor for housing and settlements. His intervention came in the form of a 356-page document with the enigmatic title 'Pakistan Ekistics – problems, policies and programs'. Although still designated as a preliminary draft, and based only on impressionistic evidence, the very scope and internal structure of this document was designed to lead Pakistani housing policy onto a development path that would commit it to Doxiadis's consultancy services for years, if not decades, to come.

'I have made an attempt to create a pattern for presentation of *all* [emphasis added] problems, policies and programs which could be followed and serve *any* type of area from the whole country to the single settlements', he pointed out in the preface, before arguing further:

This is the reason why I have presented chapters and sectors which are not at present of the greatest importance or although of big importance cannot be presented in any concrete way due to the lack of necessary data. A *systematic* approach though required *reference to everything* which would be necessary for the *complete understanding and solution* of ekistic problems.[19]

In other words, where planners of a different bend of mind would have started with the most pressing problems Pakistan faced in terms of housing policy – for instance, the resettlement of refugees – Doxiadis proposed a comprehensive vision that at every point sought to formulate policy at the most abstract level and from first principles. The document was divided into four parts: the overall 'Ekistics problem', the 'basic elements', the 'geographic units', the 'factors of these problems', which followed Doxiadis's own Ekistics grid rather than established policy procedures. In order to inject a sense of implementation and urgency into this representation of Pakistan's housing problems, Doxiadis systematically added little summary sections divided into 'problem', 'policies' and 'program'.

[18] Doxiadis, C. A. (1959), 'The rising tide of the planners', *Ekistics* 7(39): 5–10.
[19] CADA: Pakistan Volume 3, Dox 21, p.5, emphasis added.

Such an ambitious vision of planning was going to require the sustained intervention of a team of planners and a huge data-gathering exercise, which Doxiadis knew would be hard to justify in a country short of trained personnel and foreign exchange. In order to advance his point he occasionally felt compelled to replace technical jargon with apocalyptic metaphors of natural disaster:

The tide is rising. If we dig canals in time we will regulate and control it, the effort will be small and the expense reasonable and the results important. If we do not act in time then the rising tide will cause destruction and we will have to fight for repairs.[20]

The argument here was that huge investments in housing and settlements were inevitably made even if no planning at all took place. Ordinary Pakistanis would simply build new shanty towns or elite colonies, create new markets on the roadsides, or set up small industries wherever they deemed fit, using their own initiative and access to capital. Although the state would have to invest nothing into any of these activities, this would not really save anything in the long run. Unplanned housing development would not only create urban problems that would turn into real obstacles for further 'development', but also entail a potential waste of resources across the board. Ordinary Pakistanis did not possess the necessary overview to coordinate their individual activities in the most rational manner. While the houses of the rich would end up being 'overly heavy' while still not providing the best possible comfort to their inhabitants, the shanty towns of the poor could not benefit from the latest intermediate technologies that made best use of cheap materials.[21] In consequence precious capital ended up being wasted on housing which could have been reinvested, for instance, in the industrialization effort. What is more, only comprehensive planning could actually ensure that scarce resources were allocated in such a way as to ensure the greatest happiness of the greatest number; only an overall plan could tell whether the money sufficient to build 100 houses should actually be spent on building 100 houses, rather than on improvements in building codes or on research into building techniques which could in the long run benefit many more people.[22] In short, the expense spent on an ambitious foreign consultant at the beginning of the development process would actually end up as the more 'economic' option in the long run.[23]

As a development entrepreneur constantly in search of future assignments, Doxiadis had a natural interest to push expenses on consultancy services as high as could be justified within the very constrained economies

---

[20] Ibid. p.10.   [21] Ibid. pp.11–12.   [22] Ibid. p.33.   [23] Ibid. pp.11–12.

of a 'developing nation'. When he made his proposal for a grand plan, Pakistan government investment in what was then imprecisely referred to as 'town improvement' had been miniscule. Although cumulative figures since the foundation of the country in 1947 had risen from a mere 2 million rupees in 1952/53 to about 60 million by 1954, this sum was dwarfed by the 980 million rupees spent on defence or 820 million on irrigation over the same period.[24] Doxiadis proposed to raise the total expenditure on housing drastically over the next five years, starting with a first additional annual investment of 10 million US dollars (or 32 million rupees).[25] Out of these, at least 3 million rupees (or 1 million US dollars) were to be spent on additional consultative services required by the Ekistics approach,[26] an expense directly earmarked for the order books of DA.

One of his biggest tasks was to find allies on the Pakistan Planning Board to which the Harvard Mission was attached. Most of the people in question held briefs that had a much better claim to receive government resources than housing and settlements. When Mahmud Alam – the man in charge of transport and communications, and one of the few members who were favourably inclined towards Ekistics – broke his leg, Doxiadis was quick to organize a permanent assistant for him, who would also lobby Doxiadis's case in wider policy circles.[27] On tour to East Pakistan, he had come across Mohammad Noman, underpaid municipal engineer in Dacca and a man who appeared to be especially perturbed by the lack of an overall plan in his region of activity.[28] Under pressure from Doxiadis he was dutifully installed in his post as town planning assist-ant on the Planning Board – a 'nucleus' from which further Ekistics activity could spread in the future, as his patron commented full of expectations.[29]

Doxiadis's expansionist reading of his brief set him on a collision course with the dominant section of development economists on the Harvard Mission, however. The Housing and Settlements Plan that he proposed to the Planning Board was in many ways a spatial rendition of a separate Five Year Plan in its own right. This made perfect sense in the Doxiadian universe where it could be assumed that no less than '100 per cent' of all investment in developing countries was in one form or other an investment in 'settlements'; after all, industrialization started

---

[24] Ibid. p.19. The total figure spent on housing of every description and across different government departments – including as its lion share housing for government officers and employees – could be estimated at a not quite so unimpressive 300 million rupees, although this figure relied on shaky statistical foundations.
[25] Ibid. p.45.   [26] Ibid. p.46.   [27] CADA: Pakistan Volume 2, Diary, p.147.
[28] CADA: Pakistan Volume 1, File Dox 9, 3 November 1954.
[29] CADA: Pakistan Volume 5, File Dox 43, 17 November 1955.

with factory buildings and agricultural revolution with the provision of stables.[30] It is not surprising, however, that the economists in the Harvard Group saw Doxiadis's plan as an encroachment upon their very own work. Their discipline shared with Ekistics a tendency to subsume almost all human activity within its methodological reach and scope of influence; but unlike Ekistics that depended on very detailed intervention on the ground, economics could generate control by pulling a limited number of levers at the highest levels of government. In order to get Pakistan to developmental 'take-off', it was crucial to concentrate resources on activities that would break Pakistan's low-level equilibrium trap. This meant, in the words of the leading Harvard Advisory Group economist Gustav Papanek, that the 'peasantry' had to be 'squeezed' through artificially low prices for agricultural commodities that could be turned into savings for industrialization.[31] Within the economist's universe, investment in a great housing and settlements plan was not a corollary of investment in 'development' as Doxiadis saw it, but an investment in welfare, which was at best only a defensive measure against potential social unrest and at worst an unnecessary distraction.

Although he later voiced admiration for Doxiadis's ability to understand the needs of local people,[32] Papanek was consistently critical of the amount of government expenditure that a comprehensive national settlement plan would demand; he saw housing as the 'least remunerative' form of development activity and would not support the reassignments of trained engineers to such a purpose.[33] He further observed that the Pakistanis themselves were not particularly interested in the promise of flowering cities and happily housed people that Doxiadis was trying to sell them. Despite some recognized need for welfare provisions in other fields such as 'education, health, irrigation', Papanek commented, 'there has not so far been any demand from any quarter for making a beginning with the national housing programme.' 'The idea of a national housing programme has still to find a root and grow', and under the prevailing circumstances should only receive the lowest possible priority.[34] Moreover, in Papanek's assessment 'ill-considered and haphazard development would bring discredit to the programme of the Planning Board which will impair the prospects of the evolution of an orderly

[30] Doxiadis, C. A. (1959), 'The rising tide of the planners', Ekistics 7(39): 5–10, p.5.
[31] Papanek, G. F. (1967), Pakistan's development: social goals and private incentives [S.l.], Cambridge, MA, Harvard University Press.
[32] In an e-mail exchange with the author in spring 2007.
[33] CADA: Pakistan Volume 5, Dox 57, Comments 6 October 1955, p.329.
[34] Ibid. p.326.

and ambitious programme in the future.' In other words, in the interest of successful planning itself, the Planning Board and the Harvard Mission could not support any policy that was 'less than perfect', and in the field of housing 'perfect can't be had'.[35] Under pressure from the Planning Board, the projected volume of the Housing and Settlements Plan was drastically revised downwards;[36] and Doxiadis soon found himself cold-shouldered by both the Harvard Group and the Pakistani administration.

By late 1955 Mohammad Noman, the city planner on the Pakistan Planning Board whom Doxiadis had practically hand-picked for the job, stopped sending him government documents and explained that 'he had no instructions to communicate'.[37] Other key officials are described in Doxiadis's correspondence as not having any time or interest 'for housing' or as wilfully ignoring all the new ideas and planning principles which Doxiadis had enthusiastically introduced on his earlier visits to the country.[38] Meanwhile, his Pakistani 'fixer' Syed Babar Ali – later one of Pakistan's leading industrialists and philanthropists – did little to react to Doxiadis's increasingly desperate promptings to tip him off about Pakistani initiatives in the housing sector before they would be put out to public tender.[39] Ali later recollected that he never felt compelled to make more than 'a couple of phone calls' on Doxiadis's behalf, and that the latter was deeply distrusted by many Pakistanis as a potential spy. Be this as it may, it is significant that such scepticism came from a man who was well connected to both the Ford Company – he was their monopoly importer – and an insider in Pakistan's political elite. His brother Syed Amjad Ali was a somewhat controversial finance minister at the time, known for both his staunchly pro-American position but also his somewhat development-sceptical stance.[40]

Doxiadis's problems were in no small part down to the fact that his lobbying power was effectively constrained by the time he was able to spend in the country. Unlike other foreign experts like Papanek or Bell, he was never based in his theatre of operations long term, but only ever came to visit on trips lasting no more than a month. It was only later, when his strategy had become less advisory and more directly

[35] Ibid. p.328.   [36] Ibid. pp.326, 330.
[37] CADA: Pakistan Volume 85, Diary of Third Trip to Pakistan, p.130.
[38] CADA: Pakistan Volume 5, Note Mushtaq Ilahi, Government of Pakistan, Housing and Settlements Section, p.544; Letter Noman to Doxiadis, 7 September 1955.
[39] CADA: Pakistan Volume 31, Correspondence, Letters to S. Babar Ali, 9 February 1957, 9 January 1958, 31 March 1958.
[40] He was against the construction of a Pakistan steel mill favoured by other sections of the bureaucracy at the time, Interview S. Babar Ali (Lahore, 10 November 2007).

project-based, that several dozen of DA experts would work on a semi-permanent basis in offices in Karachi, Rawalpindi, Lahore and Dacca simultaneously. While Doxiadis's clout remained relatively strong in the corridors of power in the United States – thanks to connections with men like Jacob Crane and continuing sponsorship by the Ford Foundation – his initial encounter with Pakistan, at least, was marked by frustration and failure. Apart from some personal contacts and an appreciation of the byzantine nature of local politics, there was nothing in this experience that would suggest, let alone directly facilitate, later successes like the Islamabad project.

'Colossal problems'

The eventual failure of Doxiadis's 'great plan' was not only the result of unsuccessful lobbying among bureaucrats, businessmen and other experts, but also the inevitable outcome of deep structural incompatibilities between his Ekistics vision and ground realities in a country like Pakistan. The problem was not only insufficient funds to support an ambitious housing and settlements plan, which could have been tackled relatively easily with more international aid. Far more intractable were institutional weaknesses at all levels that would have made it virtually impossible to implement even the most well-funded housing policy without first making deep-reaching and politically highly contentious changes to the way government operated.

At the most basic, trained urban planners who could work alongside foreign experts on the Ekistics project could literally be counted on the fingers of two hands.[41] Out of all Pakistani cities, only Karachi, Lahore, Chittagong and Dacca had a full-time planner, while Rawalpindi and Khulna could draw only on part-time officials on secondment from the provincial governments. Sukkur, which had experienced particularly drastic change as a result of the influx of Partition refugees, did not even have a municipal engineer;[42] Multan, despite its population in the hundreds of thousands, no technical staff at all.[43] In Rahimyar Khan, an emerging industrial city in southern Punjab, the chief engineer of the district irrigation department doubled up as the chairman of the local town improvement trust, mistakenly assuming easy transferability of skills from one area to the other.[44] In Doxiadis's own assessment, out of all Pakistan's major cities only one, Lahore, could be described as reasonably functional in terms of its town planning arrangements, and

---

[41] CADA: Pakistan Volume 1, Dox 8, 2 November 1954, p.19.
[42] CADA: Pakistan Volume 2, Diary, p.176.   [43] Ibid. p.234.   [44] Ibid. p.190.

even there the local authorities were unable (or perhaps unwilling) to produce basic documentation of their activities when visited by him on one of his tours.[45]

Levels of technical education were still generally poor. Some promising young Pakistani planners and architects were already operating in some areas when Doxiadis first appeared on the scene. Chittagong in East Pakistan had a town planner with a degree from the University of Edinburgh, for instance;[46] Bombay-educated Zaheer ud-Din Khwaja – later chief engineer on the Islamabad project – was attached to the Thal Development Authority in north-western Punjab; and US-educated Muzharul Islam – doyen of vernacular modernism in future Bangladesh – was rising through the ranks of the East Pakistan administration. But it was to take until the end of the 1950s and the early 1960s before a significant number of home-grown experts could take on more ambitious planning tasks.

Part of the problem was the near absence of effective municipal government and a highly complex and often confused replication of local responsibilities across several government institutions. Virtually everywhere there was a basic split between a municipal corporation, nominally in charge of town planning legislation, and an improvement trust, engaged in actual physical planning and construction. Not only was the relationship between these two bodies entirely unresolved, but also the institutions had different (and sometimes overlapping) geographic areas of responsibility. This was a hangover from colonial policies to control the cities of British India. Municipal corporations had been set up in order to provide limited self-government to ambitious Indians that the British wanted to keep away from any access to real power. Their councils were elected but restricted in their field of activity to what the British called 'native' or 'black' towns, usually the most overcrowded parts of indigenous cities. Improvement trusts, on the other hand, were unelected and commercial bodies and, at least originally, overseen by the British themselves.[47] Their field of responsibility was the creation and defence of new urban spaces adjacent to the native cities. In the greater Delhi metropolitan area, for instance, this split still corresponds neatly to the division between 'Old Delhi' – part of a municipal corporation – and 'New Delhi' – set up and administered by a 'development agency'. In the cities that became part of Pakistan after 1947, municipal corporations

[45] Ibid. p.234.   [46] Ibid. p.87.
[47] This dual structure is typical for the British colonial world, see King, A. D. (1976), *Colonial urban development: culture, social power, and environment*, London; Boston, Routledge & Paul.

were often so bogged down in local political rivalries as to make them entirely dysfunctional. In Dacca elections remained suspended for long periods, while in Lahore, Karachi and Sylhet local self-government actually had to be disbanded altogether for some time, and rule by a central executive officer was imposed.[48]

Municipal corporations and improvement trusts (or later 'development agencies') were not the only bodies exercising some element of control over some part of a city's physical area. Port trusts and central authorities like the railways and the military had their own respective spheres of control, again dating back to colonial divisions. Cantonments, or military enclaves, were originally designed to keep soldiers away from civilian populations but had in later years grown to include prime real estate for housing and buzzing commercial areas. When visiting Bahawalpur, for instance, Doxiadis observed that the cantonment – one of Pakistan's most grandiose – had expanded to such an extent as to push up against the boundaries of Bahawalpur town itself.[49] This expansion had occurred without any input from any civil town planning authority, serving as a striking metaphor of what was to happen to Pakistani civil–military relations at large as the age of development unfolded. Another complication arose from the presence of special agencies, usually under central government control, that were expected to take charge of some specific aspect of urban reconstruction, for instance the rehabilitation of Partition refugees or victims of cyclones and floods. Little or no coordination existed between these bodies and local authorities.[50]

The problem was worst in the capital Karachi. The Karachi Municipal Corporation (KMC) and the Karachi Improvement Trust (KIT) operated in exactly the perverted ways their colonial progenitors had originally intended: as punitive agencies with no interest in welfare provision. Assistant Secretary Akber from the Ministry of Health and Works told visitors from the Planning Board that while both institutions were preoccupied with the enforcement of building legislation, demolishing several hundred badly needed housing units every year, neither had any capacity to provide much new housing, particularly to the poorest inhabitants of the city.[51] The Chief Engineer of the KMC pointed out in defence of his institution that it was catastrophically underfunded. Municipal income had not grown substantially since 1947, *before* an influx of refugees more than doubled its original population. This amounted to a cut in real terms by four-fifths, leaving it with

---

[48] CADA: Pakistan Volume 2, Diary, p.124; Pakistan Volume 4, p.145.
[49] CADA: Pakistan Volume 2, Diary, p.219.   [50] Ibid. p.43.
[51] CADA: Pakistan Volume 1, Dox 11, p.53; Volume 2, Diary, p.14.

only 18 rupees to spend per inhabitant in 1954.[52] When he went to visit the KIT, the body that was at least in theory responsible for carrying out urban development activity in Pakistan's capital city, Doxiadis discovered that there were only two town planners at work and that they obviously could not be spared to dedicate any time at all to anything more ambitious than local crisis management. Moreover, the presence of a central government official – which Doxiadis now in effect was – appeared to be most unwelcome:

> They could not give us any data or any answers, they would not even show us round the capital unless they were ordered by the Ministry of Works and Health. They do not believe that they could also have any more meetings with us. All these [foreign] experts wanted data and more data about Karachi . . . were certainly not available.[53]

There were no maps for Karachi, or indeed any other of Pakistan's major cities, presenting sufficient detail to begin with proper planning activity. Whatever existed was either of colonial era vintage or based on aerial topography not supportive of a small enough scale. As Pakistan's surveyor general told Doxiadis, his office's budget would have to be increased by over 50 per cent in order to have any chance of producing the maps required to prevent 'a complete failure of any development program during its first years'.[54] In the meantime, his office would work on city plans only when 'they had nothing else to do'.[55] Things were little better as far as regional planning for urban expansion in East Pakistan was concerned. When asked about the best source of information for a regional housing plan, technical staff pointed to a colonial report drawn up in the early 1940s, of which some copies 'may still be available in Calcutta'.[56] Population statistics as compiled by Pakistan's decennial census were as meticulous as they were useless; although there was exact – or at least aspiring to be exact – data about total population (75,842,000) and total number of buildings (1,734,864 no less) as it existed in 1951, this was of little use to the urban planner. There was no reliable information about any increase since the census date as both birth rate and refugee movements remained largely unmonitored; and there was no information about family size in different regions and among different social groups, which would have to serve as the baseline for any meaningful estimation of the housing needs of Pakistan.[57]

If the Ekistics vision had no foundation at the bottom of the bureaucratic ladder, it was also unsupported as far as the top was concerned.

---

[52] Ibid. pp.147–148.   [53] Ibid. pp.6–7.   [54] Ibid. pp.151–152.   [55] Ibid.
[56] Ibid. p.44.   [57] CADA: Pakistan Volume 1, Dox 11, pp.46, 48.

The recurrent problem of Doxiadis's involvement in Pakistan was the lack of a suitable government agency that could plausibly commission or evaluate the kind of ambitious master plans that he hoped would attract international funding and spawn long-term follow-up contracts. According to one of his first impressions, '. . . the country does not have up to now any central authority in charge of any of the problems . . . it has not even any authority which could look at the problems as problems . . .'.[58] Several ministries were affected by the scope of settlement planning as conceived along Ekistics principles: health, education, communication, refugee rehabilitation, power and public works. They all viewed each other with distrust and either – as was the case with the Public Works Department – wanted to have nothing to do with planning at all,[59] or sought to appropriate it exclusively for their own institutional expansion. Secretary Akber from the Ministry of Health and Works presented himself as a strong supporter of Doxiadis's idea of a National Housing and Settlements Authority, as long as it was under his Ministry's control, while also urging Planning Board member Mahmud Alam to pressurize the Finance Ministry into releasing the necessary funds.[60] The Ministry of Refugee Rehabilitation, meanwhile, claimed that there was no worthwhile urban development activity other than the settlement of refugees, and therefore demanded to be put in charge of whatever central authority was set up.[61]

An important dimension in this kind of lobbying politics was the relationship between the central government and the provinces. When Doxiadis's plan began to be discussed in terms of official Planning Board policy, there were calls from all parts of the country to raise allocations to their respective areas. After the creation of the One Unit Scheme comprising all former provinces of West Pakistan in 1956, bureaucrats from the erstwhile North West Frontier Province felt short changed due a misrepresentation of their needs by Punjabi bureaucrats in the new Unit capital Lahore. Voices from East Pakistan, meanwhile, were particularly consistent in expressing their misgivings with current policy, continuously asking for a larger allocation of resources and inflating their own projections of development needs to prove their point.[62]

The East argued that more should be spent on housing per capita in the East than in the West, because building conditions were much more

[58] Ibid. p.98.
[59] CADA: Pakistan Volume 5, File Dox 65, 15 November 1955; Pakistan Volume 8, GoP Housing and Settlements Report 58, 4 July 1956, p.262.
[60] CADA: Pakistan Volume 2, Diary, pp.13–14.   [61] Ibid. p.194.
[62] CADA: Pakistan Volume 5, File Dox 70, p.424.

difficult there.[63] This opened an old debate within development economics about whether allocations should be based on need or on the ability to use resources to the best possible effect. Though having received much less than the West in terms of development resources in the past, East Pakistan had also been singularly unable to spend its allocation, at times to the ratio of 50 per cent. Eastern bureaucrats countered claims of incompetence by deflecting accusations back to the centre, explaining to the Pakistan Planning Board that 'meagre spending in the past was due to various reasons, one of which was the Central Government officials appeared to be very keen on turning down estimates of the Provincial Departments'.[64] The central authorities remained insistent, however, that in order to deserve additional spending in the field of housing and other areas, the East would first have to clean up its administrative mess.[65] But, as the Planning Board added somewhat disingenuously, it would not support the establishment of any additional administrative structures that actually increased control by the provincial government, citing the argument that 'in a democratic country local bodies have to play a great part ...'.[66] To Eastern ears this must have sounded sanctimonious, to say the least, as the bypassing of dysfunctional municipal corporations and improvement trusts by special government agencies of a higher order had been standard practice in the West for years.

Involvement in the Pakistan Planning Board as one of its chief advisors sometimes turned Doxiadis from a client – in the sense that he did what he was told by local authorities and could profit from the remuneration – into a patron – a key political player in his own right, who was responsible for the allocation of resources himself, and as a result petitioned by local power. He was often saddled with the task of evaluating major project proposals as there was 'no authority of the Central Government in charge of them or ready to face them'.[67] With news spreading of the first national Five Year Plan being compiled, the Planning Board/Harvard Mission turned into an arena in which to stake claims that bypassed the normal administrative hierarchy. The chairman of the board had to point out in a meeting with Eastern bureaucrats that 'there was some misapprehension among the officials of the provincial government about the

---

[63] CADA: Pakistan Volume 4, File Dox 40, p.66.
[64] CADA: Pakistan Volume 8, Government of Pakistan, Minutes of the meeting of the Planning Board, Dacca 7 January 1956, p.35.
[65] Ibid.
[66] CADA: Pakistan Volume 8, Minutes of the meeting of the Planning Board, 10 January 1956, p.62.
[67] CADA: Pakistan Volume 4, Diary, p.42.

status and the function of the Planning Board' which as a technical body 'had no power to issue sanctions of any kind and ... could not speak with the authority of the Central Government'.[68]

Such admonitions notwithstanding, power holders at various levels of the administrative hierarchy sought to manipulate access to the Board to their advantage. When on tour in Chittagong, East Pakistan, Doxiadis was met by the district engineer of faraway Comilla who had come all the way to see him and to point out that he 'needed planning very badly' and 'needed assistance'. This journey to plead for resources was likely to have taken him several days by train and steam boat.[69] Adopting something of the opposite strategy, the District Commissioner of Sukkur, an all-powerful figure within his local environment, kept Doxiadis and his entourage engaged in conversation for hours in his house, while deliberately not telling them that a group of industrial experts from the Sind provincial government had been waiting to see them as well. The issue they wanted to discuss – the planning of a local Sind Industrial Corporation scheme to provide employment to Partition refugees – actually interested Doxiadis a great deal, but in consequence of the Commissioner's ruse, never received the hearing its initiators had hoped for.[70] Older structures of power were well entrenched enough to throw a spanner into the works. In a way so revealing of how the Pakistani post-colonial state operated, they would not have to confront 'development' in any direct way at all. It was perfectly sufficient to engage in the right amount of inactivity at the right time.

From 'great plan' to great project

The period from 1955, when his relationship with the Planning Commission had effectively disintegrated, to his breakthrough moment in October 1958 in the wake of Ayub Khan's military takeover saw a much less intense involvement with Pakistan for Doxiadis, with much of his attention shifting to Iraq and elsewhere. But he was still engaged in lobbying activities to somehow achieve a revival of his fortunes. As always, he would discuss his strategy with his friend and long-term partner Jacob Crane in Washington, who kept him regularly informed about important personnel changes in bodies such as the Ford Foundation as well as in US government institutions. Crane had been closely involved with US government initiatives in housing policy and watched out for any

---

[68] CADA: Pakistan Volume 8, Government of Pakistan: Minutes of the meeting of the Planning Board with East Pakistan Government, 7 January 1956, p.32.
[69] CADA: Pakistan Volume 2, Diary, p.77.   [70] Ibid. p.174.

possible US government funding that could support Doxiadis's work in Pakistan. His attempts to gain a foothold with the FOA – the development arm of the US government – were thwarted when the organization was recast as the International Cooperation Administration (ICA) and placed under the directorship of John Hollister, a Republican who, in Crane's assessment, 'may not be sympathetic toward international cooperation in social affairs, housing etc.'.[71] Further bad news emerged when Crane's interlocutors confirmed that the ICA mission in Pakistan was not considering entering into a contract with DA as it could not directly collaborate with a non-American company. This meant that, at least for the time being, Doxiadis was unable to benefit from the increase in directly government-funded development activities that went hand in hand with ever-closer political and military ties between Washington and Karachi.

Although Crane was able to assure Doxiadis that he maintained excellent contacts with ICA staff – when one of Crane's acquaintances was leaving the organization he was happy to report 'I consider all [potential successors] to be good friends' – he also made it clear that for Doxiadis to have any future in Pakistan at all, he would have to lobby the Karachi government directly and then cobble together some joint funding initiative involving the Ford Foundation. The latter had been his long-term supporter, after all, and was less constrained by issues of nationality than the ICA. This was precisely the course of action Doxiadis actually embarked upon when he shifted his emphasis in Pakistan from a comprehensive housing and settlements plan to the building of a new capital city. His change in strategy proved to be prescient as the ICA, under severe political pressure from politicians hostile to development aid to Pakistan, radically slashed their designated support for housing in the country in early 1956.[72] Meanwhile, Doxiadis's hopes that he would be able to use his position on the Planning Commission to secure other major contracts produced nothing. Both the master plans for Lahore and Dacca, for which he was on the verge of signing a contract, were at the last minute and entirely unpredictably awarded to other companies. Dacca went to his bitter rivals Minoprio–Spenceley–MacFarlane, apparently for the sole reason that as a British company they could be brought to Pakistan on Colombo Plan funding.[73]

Doxiadis's strong reliance on Ford Foundation funding imposed its own peculiar logic on his project proposals. The Foundation saw its activity in

[71] CADA: File 19255 Correspondence between C. A. Doxiadis and J. L. Crane (1954–57), Crane to Doxiadis 6 August 1955.
[72] CADA: File 19255 Correspondence between C. A. Doxiadis and J. L. Crane (1954–57), Cable DA (Athens) to C. A. Doxiadis, Karachi, 21 February 1956.
[73] CADA: Pakistan Volume 31, Correspondence, Letter to Crane, 15 January 1957, Letters to Syed Babar Ali, 20 February 1957 and 9 April 1957.

the field of educational assistance and emphatically not in development aid,[74] where the kind of projects Doxiadis had in mind would normally be located. In consequence, Doxiadis had to couch his ideas in 'educational terms'. Just as the First Five Year Plan itself proved less promising as a generator of future assignments, Doxiadis's Pakistan files began to fill up with blueprints for Ekistics training institutes, mass-produced primary schools, universities and technical colleges – a flurry of proposals that made Ford Foundation officials wonder about overstretch and overambition.[75] But importantly, urban reconstruction projects could still be smuggled in through the backdoor, as it were, if they could be presented as 'pilot projects' for the purposes of Ford Foundation regulations. Rather than as direct contributions to 'development' in their own right, they were sold as exemplars of good planning practice that served as pedagogic models for follow-up activities elsewhere. Much of the Korangi project, for instance, was later financed by the Ford Foundation on such terms: as a demonstration project and work placement of choice for students enrolled at Ekistics training institutes run by DA both in Pakistan and at their company headquarter in Athens.

Taken together, political pressures in both the local and international context propelled Doxiadis towards a new strategy of securing the 'huge job' he needed for commercial success. Instead of relying on the 'great plan' as the main generator of follow-up projects, he began to focus on grand prestige assignments which offered a number of advantages: they could be easily relabelled as 'pilots' or 'models', required little institutional backup from the host country beyond the approval of a few very highly placed government officials, and perhaps most importantly, they could tap effectively into the ideological needs of post-colonial regimes that were otherwise unconvinced by the need for urban planning as a development strategy. Nothing fitted this bill better than the reconstruction of Pakistan's capital city, which at the time did not necessarily mean the construction of an entirely new settlement in the north of the country – which is what 'Islamabad' eventually turned out to be. Rather it involved a whole range of proposals from a new administrative centre-cum national monument within the existing city boundaries of Karachi itself (here called capitol following precedent in some of the architectural literature),[76] or a satellite township somewhere close outside it.

---

[74] Gant G .F. (1959), 'The Ford Foundation Programme in Pakistan', in *Annals of the American Academy of Political Science*, Volume **323**, pp.150–159.
[75] CADA: Pakistan Volume 5, File Dox 50, 26 August 1955, Note by David Bell.
[76] E.g. Gordon, D. L. A. (2006), *Planning twentieth century capital cities*, London, Routledge, pp.25–30.

In search of a new capital

Debates about the location and nature of Pakistan's capital city had been on and off the boil for many years before Doxiadis's arrival, in fact ever since the months leading up to independence in August 1947. As a new territory, Pakistan did not have the luxury of inheriting a capital city with a developed administrative infrastructure and long-standing symbolic importance. It was both a testimony to the prevailing nostalgia for the Mughal past as well as a sign of desperation that Jinnah originally thought that New Delhi could in some form be shared with India. He proposed that Pakistan's first constituent assembly should meet there rather than in any of the cities on Pakistan's own territory. But the idea was unsurprisingly rebuffed by a Congress leadership keen to forestall any possible association between Pakistan and historical claims to imperial sovereignty that could challenge India's own pre-eminence.[77] Delhi had, after all, been the seat of the subcontinent's most powerful dynasties since the thirteenth century, and Congress regarded itself as their only legitimate successor. This move not only made Pakistan appear as the somehow less 'historically grounded' of the two successor states of the Raj, but also left it bereft of a clear historical legacy and national identity – issues that would have to be addressed whenever plans for the construction of a new capital area were put forward.

There were only a handful of cities that could even be considered to be Pakistan's new capital at the time, and most of them had strong disadvantages: Dacca in East Bengal was no more than a country town before 1947 and struggled to even cope with its new role as a provincial centre; besides, a location in the East did not appeal to Urdu-reading nationalist circles for whom Pakistan's national culture was intimately connected with the old Mughal heartlands in the north-west. Lahore, the provincial capital of the Punjab, was both a large and highly modernized city and an important seat of culture, but its location was strategically unsuitable; at the moment of Partition it was still unclear whether it would be part of Pakistan at all, and even after this was confirmed to be the case, the Indian border was less than 20 miles to the East. In addition, there were political anxieties about an undue influence of the local Punjabi elites and their highly mobilized mass followers over national leaders like Jinnah and Liaquat Ali Khan, who had no local constituency of their own. Rawalpindi in the north was important as a major military base and would become the General Headquarters of the Pakistan Army, but like

[77] Khan, Y. (2007), *The great Partition: the making of India and Pakistan*, New Haven, CT; London, Yale University Press, p.129.

Dacca it was no more than a large country town with few administrative facilities at the time. There have been suggestions that Jinnah himself liked the idea of a capital in the north in principle,[78] and there is documentary evidence that Pakistan's first native Commander in Chief, General Ayub Khan, had entertained such plans from the early 1950s onwards.[79] But in the event, the only really credible choice available in summer 1947 was Karachi, a large and reasonably functional port city and capital of the southern province of Sind. To endow this selection with some symbolic significance, it was stressed that it was the Qaid-e Azam's own city of birth – although he had left when he was a teenager and was culturally much more at home in Bombay.

Karachi's nomination as capital triggered a gigantic movement of people that imposed a heavy strain on the fabric of the city as it then existed. As Sarah Ansari has pointed out in her extensive and detailed study of the period, Karachi had already experienced rapid urban growth over the course of World War II – swelling its population to more than 400,000 people – which had not been properly absorbed by the time Partition took place. Now, it was not only the 7000 designated civil servants of the new Pakistan government with their families that began to arrive, but also tens of thousands – later hundreds of thousands – of refugees who left their homes in the cities and country towns of northern India to seek employment in the lower echelons of Pakistan's newly emerging state apparatuses, or to eke out a precarious living as craftsmen and shopkeepers.[80] By the census year of 1951, Karachi's population had reached 1.5 million, three times its number before Partition. Refugee colonies – often little more than shanty towns – had sprung up everywhere, on every piece of available land in the very heart of the city and close to key government institutions, and further out in dry river beds prone to flooding and in semi-deserts without facilities. Political tensions rose, not only between old-time residents and newcomers, but also between different religious groups and sects, fuelled by the agitational politics of radical nationalists disgruntled with the new post-colonial order.[81]

Attempts to bring Karachi under control began with the announcement of a 'Greater Karachi' scheme in January 1948, which increased Karachi's designated metropolitan area six-fold, and was soon followed by proposals to turn the city into a federally administered area independent

[78] Noon, F. K. (1993), *From memory*, Islamabad, National Book Foundation, p.220.
[79] See Footnote 102.
[80] Ansari, S. (2005), *Life after Partition: migration, community and strife in Sindh 1947–1962*, Karachi, Oxford University Press, pp.49–50.
[81] Ibid. pp.122–141.

of the surrounding province of Sind.[82] The task ahead was formidable: not only would hundreds of thousands of refugees have to be rehoused, but also the entire city infrastructure, including its drinking water and sewerage system, would have to be reshaped, and above all, the main institutions of the Pakistani state would have to be accommodated in a dedicated administrative centre: a capitol of some sort that would also express the national identity and sovereignty of the new nation to foreign visitors and Pakistani citizens alike.

The genesis and eventual demise of the Greater Karachi scheme already set the tone for much of what Doxiadis was to encounter a few years later. Foreign consultants were brought in with a brief so extensive as to beggar belief, which they were entirely unprepared for in terms of experience. As Doxiadis was to say, the Pakistani bureaucrats who brought them in were effectively incapable of even accurately perceiving 'the problem as a problem'. Once the inadequacy of the proposed plans and projects became apparent, the Pakistani state machinery had no ability to turn things around. It could only attempt to claw back some measure of control by adopting a stalling strategy. While any meaningful implementation process was indefinitely delayed in a quicksand of bureaucratic interventions, the project would rumble on on paper – even acquiring a public presence that could be used for ideological purposes. This was development stalemate as an intended policy outcome.

The unlucky consultants involved in the Greater Karachi scheme were an international conglomerate called Merz Rendel Vatten Pakistan (MRVP). In a Cabinet decision that must appear extraordinary by today's standards, this company had been appointed universal 'consulting engineers' to the Government of Pakistan in 1948. This meant that all technical advice on a whole range of different issues was to be provided to both the central and provincial governments by a single supplier.[83] In fact, the range of activities covered by this exclusive contract included almost all aspects of development policy then carried out by the Karachi administration: water power, thermal power, railways, docks and harbours, aircraft bases, government ordnance factories, industrial development and, almost as an afterthought, also town planning.[84] The idea behind such a concentration of consultancy in one hand was to

[82] Ibid. p.60.
[83] NDC: Case 564/78/48, Appointment of Messrs. Merz Rendel Vatten as Consulting Engineers to Government of Pakistan, 27 October 1948, Records of Cabinet Meetings held during the year 1948, film 1405, p.2567.
[84] NAB: Sl 1, Commerce & Industry proceedings, Bundle 6, File 3A-72/48 Appointment of consulting engineer to Govt for the execution of power development schemes in East Bengal – MRVP, GoP, Circular Letter, 20 January 1949.

preserve scarce foreign exchange reserves, and to extend central government control over whatever provincial governments were up to in terms of their own separate development policies. MRVP thus played a direct role in the gradual concentration of most development functions in Karachi with far-reaching consequences for regional disparities and political discontent in the provinces. In a sign of things to come, its original appointment was already strongly criticized by bureaucrats in East Bengal because of cost.

The conglomerate consisted of three separate firms that had made common cause to fill the role demanded by the Pakistan government. First, there was Merz & McLellan, a British company with a long track record in the power sector in various parts of the British Empire and also the United States, Greece, Japan and Iceland. They were joined by Rendel, Palmer & Tritton, another colonial company with long experience in India, working primarily on harbours, railways and other infrastructure projects. Both companies satisfied the stated criteria of having '... not only experience and worldwide connections, but also ... first hand knowledge of the conditions in the Indo-Pakistan subcontinent and preferably contacts with provincial administrations.'[85] In fact, so close had such connections been in the past that there were concerns around the Cabinet table that the two companies may still be beholden to old partners who were now located across the border in India, and could reveal Pakistani state secrets to the enemy. In the end these concerns were set aside with the argument that this link could also work in the opposite direction: that Pakistan would, via their consultants, learn more about the inside workings of India's development policy.

The third partner in the group was an outsider to the subcontinent. It was Vattenbyggnadsbryan (VBB) of Sweden, one of the world's leaders in the field of hydroelectric engineering. It had been brought on board primarily for this reason as this was the time when hydroelectric power acquired the status of a miracle cure for the development effort, and when the first post-colonial high dam projects were initiated. Ironically, it was also VBB that would on demand provide a capability in the field of city planning.[86] This was by no means their core business, and there appears to have been doubts over their suitability. One VBB executive felt himself compelled to write to the chairman of the Central

---

[85] NDC: Records of the Cabinet Meetings, January–December 1948, Case 564/78/58 Appointment of Messrs. Merz Rendel Vatten as Consulting Engineers to Gov. of Pakistan, 27 October 1948.

[86] NAB: Sl 1, Commerce & Industry proceedings, Bundle 6. File 3A-72/48 Appointment of consulting engineer to Govt for the execution of power development schemes in East Bengal – MRVP, GoP, Memorandum 1 June 1948.

Engineering Authority of Pakistan that his company had in fact some experience in this field after working in Sweden, Latvia, Estonia (presumably before Stalin's annexation) and the Soviet Union.[87] What clinched the deal in the end was that MRVP could offer a comprehensive package that would not only draw up the new Greater Karachi Master Plan, but also provide designs for a new airport and docks. This allocation of responsibilities demonstrated once more the low priority the Government of Pakistan gave to city planning. It also meant that where the knowledge of local conditions would have mattered most, it was the least available.

VBB's inexperience clearly showed in the Greater Karachi scheme, as it was drawn up over the following year. Their provisions for a new city centre in Karachi were strikingly out of kilter with both South Asian traditions and with the political needs of their clients. In their combination of monumental national buildings, multistorey mass housing and giant public spaces, their visions were more reminiscent of the Soviet Union than anything seen in the region at the time. Other aspects of the plan – the delineation of the city area, tentative zoning proposals and the main layout of roads and other infrastructure networks –remained too ill-defined to serve as more than a very rough approximation of what might be done in the future.[88] Considering the lack of information and shortage of trained personnel Doxiadis still encountered in Karachi six years later, this was hardly surprising.

'Cardiac embarrassment' in New Karachi

Like Doxiadis's First Five Year Plan a few years later, the Greater Karachi Master Plan quickly became a ghost document. It was finally published in 1952, three years after its completion and original submission to the authorities, but despite carrying glowing acknowledgements to dignitaries like Abdus Sattar Pirzada, future Chief Minister of Sind, and Prime Minister Liaquat Ali Khan himself,[89] had actually no legal status whatsoever. Up to its first consideration by Cabinet in late 1949 its

---

[87] NDC: File No. 385/CF/48 Land Control – Capital of the Federation, Letter RL Evans, 13 November 1948.

[88] For a more detailed discussion of the plan, see Daechsel, M. (2014), 'Islam and development in urban space: planning "official" Karachi in the 1950s', *The city in South Asia*, C. Bates and M. Mio (eds.), London; New York, Routledge, section 1. See also Hasan, A. (1997), 'The growth of a metropolis', *Karachi: megacity of our times*, H. Khuhro and A. Mooraj (eds.), Karachi, Oxford University Press: 171–196.

[89] Merz Rendel Vatten (1952), *Report on Greater Karachi Plan 1952*, Stockholm, A.B. kartografiska institutet.

arrival had been eagerly awaited by bureaucrats who wanted to know on what basis they could allocate land to cooperative societies for refugee rehabilitation, and what areas should be reserved for the building of a future administrative centre. When the draft plan finally arrived, however, it drew a barrage of criticism and then got lost in the quicksand of administrative intrigue all the same, without ever being either directly repealed or replaced.

First, the provisions for water supply were rejected as inadequate on the recommendation of a 'development' advisor speaking on behalf of the Foreign Ministry, and operating separately from MRVP.[90] Then, later in 1950, the ever-vigilant Ministry of Finance under the fiscally conservative and future Governor General Ghulam Muhammad requested that 'financial implications be clarified' and that no comment would be forthcoming to speed up approval for another six months.[91] When the Ministry finally reported back later that year it expressed grave concerns about the potential cost of the Greater Karachi scheme and, without a clear sense of what a master plan actually was, suggested that 'even New Delhi took 20 years to build'.[92] They treated the plan as a blueprint for the construction of an entirely new city, rather than a framework document coordinating future expansion of an existing one. They reiterated this view several times over the next months, stating that they could not accept the plan without further financial data.[93]

An increasingly exasperated Ministry of Health and Works attempted to point out that a master plan was a 'very rough and ready sort of estimate' and not a 'development project' which had to precisely costed in terms of budgetary allocation. Fearing that it may take 'several years' before the Finance Ministry would finally correct their misapprehension, the same official noted with alarm that 'this Ministry [Health and Works] ... finds it very difficult to enforce orders [in Karachi] ... simply because it is contended by the parties that the Cabinet have not accepted so far the principle according to which decisions are taken'. In other words, land speculators and construction businesses could not be legally prevented from grabbing land that was earmarked for other purposes. In the words of the official, 'in the absence of an approved master plan we are unable to stop creation of slums, haphazard location of factories, the construction of wrong buildings at wrong locations'. Even the area set

---

[90] NDC: File 103/CF/50 Greater Karachi Master Plan, Minutes of the Cabinet Meeting, 31 May 1950.
[91] NDC: ibid., Minutes of the Cabinet Meeting, 14 June 1950.
[92] NDC: ibid., Note, Ministry of Finance, 7 November 1950.
[93] NDC: ibid., Note, Ministry of Finance, 5 May 1951.

aside to accommodate the new administrative centre for the nation, let alone those areas earmarked for refugee rehabilitation schemes, was increasingly lost to land grabbing due to administrative paralysis.[94]

Such warnings fell on deaf ears. According to one bureaucrat, the Finance Ministry would 'stall completely' unless at least costs for road building, road lighting and water supply – as suggested by the tentative outlines included in the Greater Karachi Master Plan – could be worked out precisely, as if the fate of a future city layout depended on whether the government had enough money to put up a sufficient number of lanterns to illuminate streets that only existed as lines on a map.[95] In the event the plan was referred back to discussions at Secretary level and was still not approved in winter 1953, a full three years later. By this time, the nature of the main obstacle to taking the matter forward had changed, however. The problem now was that proposals for a new administrative centre in Karachi had become unstuck as well, leading to an impossible chicken-and-egg situation; the capitol area could not be properly conceived without a master plan, and a master plan could not be formally approved until the exact nature and location of the capitol was finalized.

The Finance Ministry, as always, sought to influence the debate with parsimonious suggestions. After Ghulam Muhammad's promotion to Governor General, it was headed by the future Prime Minister Chaudhry Muhammad Ali, a man of similar development-sceptical views as his friend and predecessor. In autumn 1954 they proposed, and got approved, the idea of searching for an 'entirely new site for the capital', 'as far away from the sea as possible' to protect the civil servants' fragile health.[96] 'Far' was a relative term here, however, as the same Ministry only slightly later also opined that that anything more than 20 miles inland would be too costly. What they had in mind was a replica of what the British had achieved in New Delhi: the creation of a new administrative city that could grow in tandem with an already existing metropolis.[97] This view was regarded as nonsensical by both the Chief Engineer of the Public Works Department and by Michel Ecochard, who was then in Karachi as United Nations advisor on housing and had just touched base with the recently arrived Doxiadis. The Frenchman argued that if health was the main reason why a capital should be shifted further inland, it would only make sense if a site at a considerable

---

[94] NDC: ibid., Briefing Note, Ministry Health and Works, n.d.
[95] NDC: ibid., Letter Osman Ali to A.R. Khan, 18 June 1951.
[96] NDC: File 232/CF/47 II – Site for the Federal Capital, Minutes of Cabinet Meeting, 14 September 1954.
[97] NDC: File 232/CF/47 II, Minutes of Cabinet Meeting, 18 December 1954.

distance from Karachi was chosen, but when pressed on the matter selected a location in Malir-Pipri (today part of Greater Karachi) as least bad of the options on offer.[98]

The strange concern for health in the capital location debate was a particularly striking throwback to colonial era thinking. It was only a step removed from the miasmas and climatic effects on 'humours' expressed in the more popular fringes of late nineteenth-century medicine, with the major difference that arguments usually reserved for 'whites' were now adopted for Pakistani bureaucrats. A Ministry of Health memorandum authored by its Permanent Secretary G. Mueenuddin (the same person Crane had tried to put in touch with Doxiadis when the latter was at the very beginning of his career) argued that Karachi's location by the sea, 'badly affected the health' of civil servants: 'they get up with a feeling of tiredness and lassitude and they admit that consequently they are unable to work at a high level of efficiency'. The result was a condition of 'cardiac embarrassment', effecting a fall in blood pressure and a 'collapse of the nervous system'. In a striking fast forward to the age of development, Mueenuddin wanted this condition to be investigated by the World Health Organization.[99] M. Jafar from the Directorate of Health offered a similar argument about Karachi's high humidity and temperature, but added an explanation involving the excess consumption of tea and coffee endemic among civil servants.[100] For the Civil Surgeon of Karachi, a Lt. Col. M. H. Shah, meanwhile, the matter was even worse: the city not only bred eczema, but also produced malnutrition and anaemia 'amongst the families of the junior employees', even tuberculosis, because eggs and milk were especially expensive at this location. And this was not all, 'filing work' between 10 a.m. and 5.30 p.m. in a place like Karachi was 'extremely tiring', impeding the development of a 'proper ego ideal' and culminating in psychological 'functional disturbance'.[101]

Over the next years, the debate about the most appropriate location of the new centre somehow got sidetracked by the somehow more tangible and exciting question of which international architect should be hired to design the main government buildings making up the proposed capitol. The debate centred on questions of how to represent Pakistan's Islamic spirit in architecture, while also expressing a modernist ethos. With the location debate rumbling on in the background, some unconventional

---

[98] NDC: ibid., Note Chief Engineer, PWD, 8 April 1954.
[99] NDC: File No. 385/CF/48 – Land Control – Capital of the Federation Memorandum, 25 March 1952.
[100] NDC: ibid., Note 10 April 1952.   [101] NDC: Note M. H. Shah, n.d.

ideas came from the Ministry of Defence, headed by none other than the future military dictator and patron-to-be of 'Islamabad', Muhammad Ayub Khan. He suggested that the search should be widened to include any suitable site in West Pakistan, and not only locations close to Karachi itself. This was a transparent attempt to steer the debate closer to Rawalpindi, where he was based as Commander in Chief of the army, and from where he had to fly to Karachi whenever he attended Cabinet meetings in his other role as minister. Unsurprisingly, the Finance Ministry as ever poured cold water on such ideas, judging them as too costly, and reiterating the view that Pakistan's capital should be a 'New Karachi' comparable in design to New Delhi across the border.[102]

This was also the time when Doxiadis was on the hunt for new strategies to secure his personal fortune in Pakistan, and began to get personally involved in the 'new capital' debate at the highest political level.[103] In October 1955 he met the Prime Minister, none other than ex-Finance Minister Chaudhry Muhammad Ali, enforcer of parsimony in previous administrations and reputedly possessed by a particular reverence for Britain's colonial legacy.[104] They discussed both the need for a new capital area and the rehousing of refugees. Naturally, Muhammad Ali was reportedly much more interested in the resettlement issue than in the idea of a new capital city as such. It was a specific and acute problem which could conceivably be solved through concerted action and at limited cost, and did not demand much of the blue-sky thinking or crystal ball gazing involved in a 'take-off' developmentalism that many sections of the Pakistani establishment deeply distrusted. Indeed, if the Prime Minister had much enthusiasm for the idea of a new capital at all, it was directly seen as a means to solve the refugee crisis.[105]

Doxiadis used a variety of arguments to refocus the Prime Minister's mind, with the most revealing (and powerful) tagged on at the end:

> I said ... that the creation of the new capital was of the greatest importance from the economic, social, political, cultural and educational point of view. Such a capital is going to become the symbol of the nation if we want it or not. The challenge is between creating a good or a bad example which will influence the

---

[102] NDC: File 232/CF/47 II Site of the Federal Capital, Minutes of the Cabinet Meeting 14 April 1955, Cabinet Committee Meeting 29 June 1955, Cabinet Meeting 2 July 1955.

[103] See CADA: Pakistan Volume 5, Report Dox 67, On the Creation of the Federal Capital, p.402.

[104] Gauhar, A. (1996), *Ayub Khan, Pakistan's first military ruler*, Oxford; New York, Oxford University Press, p.81.

[105] CADA: Pakistan Volume 7, File Dox 90, p.199.

country's physical development. Then I explained the *educational* role of such a project and *the role the Ford Foundation could play in it.*[106]

The Prime Minister left the conversation with a request to think about the matter, but when he and Doxiadis met again some weeks later, the financial argument appears to have stuck:

> The HPM [Honourable Prime Minister] was interested; it seems that he has agreed on the principles presented and he told me that he will study the matter further ... The HPM authorised me to tell Mr. Gant [the Ford Foundation operative in Pakistan] that he was very interested in a Ford Foundation project and wanted to know whether the Ford Foundation was willing to finance such a project for the creation of a Federal Capital. He told me that this was not committing him to accept any solution as he did not have yet a decision of the cabinet but as a Prime Minister he was definitely interested in this project and wanted to know the Ford Foundation's position.[107]

In the meantime, Doxiadis had himself suggested to Gant at the Ford Foundation that the involvement in a potential Federal Capital Project could work as a vehicle for commissioning more long-term educational projects; this would secure Doxiadis's continuing presence in Pakistan, while also allowing the Ford Foundation to defend their profile as America's foremost supporter of pro-Western political values.[108] Far from simply acting as a service provider to local political power or international funding bodies, Doxiadis used the role of mediator between two sides to instigate a project of which he himself was the main beneficiary. Although it would be an overstatement to argue that Doxiadis – rather than Pakistani politicians, generals and bureaucrats – wholly *invented* what later took the form of 'Islamabad', there can be no doubt that he offered powerful reinforcement for the idea, not least in a context where the potential cost of a project could easily override even the most important of national priorities. As an internationally renowned expert he was able to argue at the highest political level that such a project would command respect in the rich West and, what is more, open up sources of funding that in the event would benefit both him, the consultant, and the country they were meant to develop.

The initial enthusiasm so eloquently expressed in Doxiadis's own reminiscences of his meeting with Chaudhry Muhammad Ali was soon dampened, however. According to Doxiadis's own records, the Pakistan

---

[106] CADA: Pakistan Volume 5, File Dox 61, Meeting with the HPM 21 October 1955, p.350.
[107] CADA: ibid., File Dox 69, p.421.
[108] CADA: Pakistan Volume 7, File Dox 86, Diary of the fourth trip to Pakistan, 16 October 1955–19 October 1955, p.13.

government did formally approach the Ford Foundation to approve an agreement on a new Federal Capital Project in March 1956,[109] as he had suggested, and in subsequent meetings even discussed possible locations, all in the vicinity of Karachi itself.[110] Pakistani government sources make it clear, however, that Doxiadis's name had largely dropped out of these discussions. DA was not included on a preliminary shortlist of possible foreign contractors for the capital scheme. First placed was – a bitter irony from Doxiadis's point of view – none other than his perennial bête noire Le Corbusier, working, as it happened, in tandem with Doxiadis's good acquaintance Michel Ecochard. The latter was chosen – according to an internal Pakistan government recommendation – because he had 'picked up a Muslim flavour' when working in Morocco and hence could look after the 'identity' side of the project, while Le Corbusier would provide 'modernity' and international prestige. Second placed was the British company Raglan Squire who had had prior contact with one of Pakistan's best home-grown architects Mehdi Ali Mirza, and as a British company could to a large extent be brought in on Colombo Plan funding, as the shortlisting document did not fail to mention. Further down the list were Pereira & Luckman from the United States and Niemeyer and Marx, the creators of Brasilia.[111] In the event, none of the above was ever invited to design a new capital city. After Chaudhry Muhammad Ali's resignation and the assumption of office by Shahid Huseyn Suhrawardy, a radical nationalist from Bengal, the project itself was downgraded to a mere ensemble of new government buildings in Karachi itself – a capitol without a new capital, in other words – and even this much reduced scheme disappeared in a morass of political indecision soon afterwards.[112]

While Pakistan's political and administrative system was sliding ever deeper into an authoritarianism without real governmental capability, Doxiadis's talent for conjuring up the prestige assignment that he needed for commercial success yielded fewer and fewer results. In increasingly sharply worded letters to lobbyists and local stringers, Doxiadis urged the use of 'energetic follow-up and aggressive promotional tactics'[113] to get a foot back in the door, while he also attempted to invite highly placed officials in the Public Works and Planning departments to spend some

---

[109] CADA: Pakistan Volume 7, File Dox 88, p.57.
[110] CADA: ibid., File Dox 90, p.200.
[111] NDC: File 213/CF/47 Federal Capital, Progress Report 1 August 1956.
[112] NDC: ibid.; Minutes of Cabinet Meeting, 19 December 1956; Briefing Paper, Ministry of Health and Works for Cabinet Commission Meeting, 19 December 1956.
[113] CADA: Pakistan Volume 31, Correspondence, Letter to Syed Babar Ali, 9 January 1958.

time in Greece as part of fully sponsored 'information trips'.[114] In several letters to Crane written at the time, Doxiadis appears close to have given up on Pakistan altogether. The ICA architect John Bell, who had been touted as a potential partner for collaboration, had 'failed in Pakistan' with no news about any possible replacement, while the Ford Foundation had slipped out of touch and turned 'quite secretive' towards Doxiadis himself. The Pakistani regime, meanwhile, was, in Doxiadis's words, 'not able to face the creation of major agencies and undertake major programmes. All the initial enthusiasm in overall planning is lost because of politics.'[115]

The 'great plan' fails

C. A. Doxiadis's work for the Pakistan Planning Commission came to a formal conclusion with the belated publication of Pakistan's First Five Year Plan in May 1958. (As mentioned earlier, the Plan was meant to cover 1955–1960.) Being a consultant, his name was not mentioned anywhere in the document, but his fingerprints were all over the sections relevant to his advisory brief. The fact that a dedicated chapter was named 'Housing and Settlements' and not simply 'Housing' had been the direct result of his wishes. As we will remember, he had insisted on such a wide interpretation of his remit before he even agreed to be hired by the Ford Foundation to serve in Pakistan. Trademark terms such as 'Ekistics' did not find their way into a publication that had to embody the language and vision of the Pakistan government and not that of an individual consulting company. But it is immediately clear from the wording and general thrust of argument that none other than Doxiadis himself had actually drafted the relevant chapter.[116] 'The expression "housing and settlements" ... means the sum-total of physical facilities essential to the development of a harmonious, healthy and happy community life', we read in the very first line before encountering a characteristically long list of areas involved: houses, public buildings, factories, markets, schools, places of worship, water supply and sewerage,

---

[114] CADA: ibid., Letter to G. Ahmad, Chairman of WAPDA, West Pakistan, 30 June 1958; Letter to A. Khaleeli, Secretary Works, Irrigation, Power, 16 July 1958; Letter to Said Hassan, Deputy Chairman Planning Board, 6 August 1958.

[115] CADA: ibid., Letter to Crane 15 January 1957, p.30.

[116] David Bell, a leading member of the Harvard Group, told George Rosen explicitly that Housing and Settlements was among the Plan's topics where the outside consultant was the effective author of the Plan, with no more than editing being performed by the Pakistani head of the Planning Commission. Rosen, G. (1985), *Western economists and Eastern societies: agents of change in South Asia, 1950–1970*, Baltimore, Johns Hopkins University Press, p.154.

hospitals, electricity supply, streets, road and communication systems. 'In developing settlements ... one cannot think of houses alone' the document continues, 'a government development programme for housing people ... has to be planned in terms of the whole settlements [read 'Ekistic'] problem ... They are perhaps the first type of investment carried out in any society, and in a developing economy the amount of public and private investment in housing and settlements frequently is larger than in any other field.'[117]

None of this ambition to make Ekistic planning a central component of the wider development effort was ever realized. Although his words may have survived in the Plan almost unchanged from his very first draft submissions, their actual lack of importance was reflected in the fact that they appeared way down the list of priorities in Chapter 26 of 31. To drive the point home, the executive summary of the Housing and Settlements section drafted by the Pakistani head of the Planning Commission, Zahid Husain, not only was short enough to be quoted in full here, but also stipulated in strikingly un-Doxiadian terms:

The country's needs for more and better houses, and for community services such as water and sewerage systems, are enormous. During the present Plan period, priority in both rural and urban areas is given to providing pure water supplies and sewerage systems, because of their importance for health. The Plan provides also for about 250,000 new housing units in urban areas, 120,000 of which will be set aside for refugees. This work will be done in new ways designed to serve the needs of the people better at less cost, by the maximum use of local materials and 'self-help' methods of construction.[118]

Apart from the reference to new methods of construction, which were also dear to Doxiadis's heart, this could have been written at any point before his arrival in Pakistan, even by a British colonial official of World War II vintage. There is the customary interest in public health, a matter that had been seen as intricately linked to urban governance in India ever since the first tentative steps towards town planning were undertaken in the aftermath of the infamous 1857 'Mutiny'. Similarly old-fashioned was the commitment to build a number of dwelling places for the deserving poor – nearly half of which were dedicated to the specific problem of refugee resettlement rather than to tackle the growing crisis of urbanization more generally. Meanwhile there is no mention whatever of an overall planning vision or even the need for any form of

[117] Pakistan, Planning Board (1958), *The First Five Year Plan, 1955–60*, Karachi, Manager of Publications, p.517.
[118] Ibid. p.17.

integrated urban reconstruction also involving schools, markets, mosques and whatever else Doxiadis had mentioned in his chapter.

If Doxiadis's vision had already been marginalized within the planning framework, it was marginalized further still by the fact that the First Five Year Plan as a whole was not really a major concern of the government in the first place. It speaks volumes that what should have been an important milestone in development policy was not published for more than a year after it had been officially approved by the National Economic Council – and about three years after individual sections like Doxiadis's had in effect been completed.[119] As Prime Minister Feroz Khan Noon freely admitted in his official letter of endorsement, the first three years covered by the Plan had not only already expired but also fallen well short of target, thus imposing an impossible game of catch-up for the remaining two. In a further twist, Noon added a reference to attaining 'self-sufficiency in food' as his first priority in government, which actually contradicted the relative emphasis on industrialization expressed in the Plan itself. There was nothing here that could and would ever be implemented, casting a big question mark over what – if anything – the document was actually meant to reflect.[120]

The members of the Harvard Mission had been given considerable freedom of action. Doxiadis was not the only one among them who ended up directly drafting sections of the Plan rather than merely advising on technical issues. In ways utterly incomprehensible to their colleagues dispatched to neighbouring India at the same time, foreign experts were seldom challenged or constrained by the Pakistani authorities. Doxiadis himself was almost treated as a senior member of the Karachi government at times. But this autonomy did not express the consultants' actual authority but rather their utter irrelevance. The Pakistani state apparatus had yet to accept development as a self-evident policy goal for a post-colonial state, or at any rate development as a grand global venture that was not immediately and visibly tied to matters of security, sovereignty or the well-being of the state elite itself. Although questions can be raised about the actual implementation of the Five Year Plans that Nehru's government was drawing up with such urgency and professionalism across the border, there is no doubt that, unlike its Pakistani counterpart, the Indian state saw the act of development planning as an important expression of its autonomy and power

---

[119] Rosen, G. (1985), *Western economists and Eastern societies: agents of change in South Asia, 1950–1970*, Baltimore, Johns Hopkins University Press, pp.65, 153, 158.
[120] Pakistan, Planning Board (1958). *The First Five Year Plan, 1955–60*, Karachi, Manager of Publications, Foreword, unpaginated.

in itself.[121] The Pakistanis seem to have appreciated this association somewhat more after General Ayub's military takeover later in 1958, even if Doxiadis's subsequent experience in Pakistan offers a cautionary note even on this widely accepted impression. But this is getting ahead of the argument. The Greek planner was no longer involved with Harvard and five-year planning at this point, and as far as the remaining members of the Ford-funded mission were concerned, they were increasingly seen as an unwelcome presence. By 1970, they were completely sidelined and left the country in acrimony, partly because establishment voices were beginning to discredit many of the experts on grounds of their Jewish backgrounds.[122]

The art of doing nothing

When investigated with a historian's sensibility for finely grained empirical evidence, the grand claim that 'development' took over the world during the 1950s must appear as highly questionable. Doxiadis failed in almost everything he set out to do in Pakistan, and his driving force appeared to be professional greed as much as anything else. The continuation of the story into Doxiadis's more successful period of the early 1960s will not substantially change this impression, as the next chapter will demonstrate. The fact remains that when seen from ground level, there was always something quixotic or positively disingenuous about the quest to make a country like Pakistan catch up with European metahistory. But it is not the intention of this book to merely offer a critique of 'development' based on the trivial insight that empirical detail is always more complex than any larger theoretical argument. Doxiadis's story does by no means force us to conclude that the transformation of development from ideology to discourse as described earlier in this book was only apparent, some kind of unreal surface phenomenon, while what really mattered underneath, or behind the scenes, was 'hard' politics. Rather, Foucauldian analysis reveals something more interesting and complex: an interplay between different kinds of power, incorporating both the confrontation between different kinds of 'sovereign' individuals *and* the power of discourse. In order to develop this argument further, it is useful to conclude the largely 'political' narrative offered in this chapter with a return to more theoretical considerations, before returning to more 'straight' history again in the next chapter.

---

[121] Khilnani, S. (1998), *The idea of India*, New York, Farrar Straus Giroux, pp.81–89.
[122] Rosen, G. (1985), *Western economists and Eastern societies: agents of change in South Asia, 1950–1970*, Baltimore, Johns Hopkins University Press, p.192.

C. A. Doxiadis's great Housing and Settlements Plan was designed to resolve all of Pakistan's problems as far as they could be approached from the angle of physical planning. In his characteristically ambitious view this covered little less than the entire range of activities normally referred to as 'development'. In one integrated sweep, Pakistan's landscape was to be reconfigured as a well-ordered and rationally organized space, fit to face the challenges of the future, from an East Bengal homestead to the metropolis of Karachi, and from a single housing unit to international highways and air routes. There was no way such a vision could actually be implemented. Pakistan in the 1950s not only lacked the institutional structures required for this task, but also was run according to a particular modality of statecraft that was not immediately compatible with the kind of macromanagerial project proposed here. But despite such failure, Doxiadis's plan was not without consequences. Failure was in a certain sense 'productive'.

One of the most striking facts about Doxiadis's early travails in Pakistan is that they were so extraordinarily well documented in his extensive records. Much of the evidence demonstrating that his great planning venture was indeed doomed to failure – the scarcity of competent and committed bureaucrats, the games of ministerial intrigue, the scarcity of almost all necessary resources – came from material written or collected by the man himself. Considering the high status that Doxiadis accorded to his archive, and remembering further that this material was made accessible to his peers in the global development establishment, this was not a coincidental collection of facts, a case of speaking candidly in private while adopting a more optimistic line in public. Doxiadis was engaged in some sort of elaborate and pre-emptive damage limitation exercise here. He catalogued his problems so as to be able to explain to himself, as well as to colleagues and his sponsors, why his role on the Pakistan Planning Commission could not achieve many tangible results, or rather, never could have produced any tangible results in the first place. After all, the cataloguing of problems was so intricately interwoven with the formulation of the Plan itself as to preclude any clear distinction between a 'before' and 'after'. The Plan (taken here to include the final published document as well as the many drafts and dossiers preceding it) could simultaneously be read as an account of what had to be done, and as an indictment of just how catastrophically bad things already were. This constant juxtaposition produced a highly significant ideological effect that is crucial to our understanding of how a 'developmental' governmentality came to operate in Pakistan of the 1950s and 1960s.

Part of the broader argument proposed here is already familiar from the previous two chapters: what emerges very clearly from the documents in the Doxiadis Archive is that the account of his experiences in a way created 'underdevelopment' in Pakistan or, more precisely, helped to solidify an ongoing production of 'underdevelopment' that had only started shortly before Doxiadis's arrival. Prevailing inadequacies in the built environment and all sorts of other indicators of misery like poverty, ill health, low per capita income and underemployment were stitched together into a singular pathological vision, which immediately called forth a concerted international effort to remedy it. Pakistan was thus recast as a specific object of intervention, which went hand in hand with a specific mode of knowing and understanding it. This is the same argument that has been proposed in the classic development-critical studies of Egypt, Lesotho and Columbia mentioned in the Introduction, and with somewhat less theoretical sophistication by a recent case study of Pakistan's Village Agricultural and Industrial Development (V-AID) scheme that was rolled out under American tutelage at the very same time as Doxiadis was active.[123] A failed development project was never going to question the wisdom of development, but rather lead to an intensified and ever-expanding effort to bring development to areas of life that had been left untouched before; as the search for the causes of development failure progressed, it went from economics to politics, from nutrition and education to gender roles, from state agencies to the individual agency of every single inhabitant of the developing world. Failure keeps discourses like development busy and while busy they are less easily challenged.

While we can once more observe how Doxiadis's activities contributed – or at least sought to contribute – to a consolidation of development as discourse, the counter-attack by representatives of the local state is also amply documented in his files. The latter could clearly feel that a new power was tightening its grip around them. In their day-to-day lives, they were now accosted with requests for additional work: the provision of statistics that they had no power to collect or the drawing up of maps, for which they had neither the time nor the necessary skills. Moreover, a succession of foreign dignitaries and their allies in the central government began to intrude into their running of affairs and to undermine their authority. From district commissioner in Sukkur to irrigation officer in Bahawalpur and municipal councillor in Chittagong, they all had to face the travelling court of development that Doxiadis and the Pakistan Planning Board on their fact-finding mission represented, and be accountable to new standards. To make matters worse, these encounters

---

[123] Bhuiyan, A. H. A., A. H. Faraizi and J. McAllister (2005), 'Developmentalism as a disciplinary strategy in Bangladesh', *Modern Asian Studies* **39**(2): 349–368.

even provided opportunities for their rivals and subject populations to have their demands voiced and recorded.

The more development ideology became a discourse the more it became immune to direct political attack by its opponents. But a new tactic of resistance emerged. One would affirm development in principle, at the level of official announcements and even policy procedures, but at the same time attempt to derail its implementation through inactivity. In a beautiful twist of irony, this inactivity could itself be perfectly justified with reference to development discourse. The fact that Pakistan was so patently 'underdeveloped' also meant that the Pakistani state could not really be expected to carry 'development' through. In the words of an American policy maker operating in Pakistan at the time when Doxiadis's first assignment came to a close:

When taxed with embarrassing questions about the internal policies, practices and conditions, the average GoP [Government of Pakistan] official will, at best, assert that the actions necessary to cope with these matters are precluded under the existing conditions of political and economic instability. Therefore, inasmuch as corrective action is impossible, US aid must come to the rescue and bail the Government and the nation out of its dilemma. We find this type of reasoning increasingly unpalatable ... *the only sure way to play safe for the would-be administrator is to do nothing ... While Pakistan has no monopoly of this condition, it has developed to a degree of refinement beyond any former experience encountered by this officer.*[124]

Unlike the 'common folk of Pakistan' who Doxiadis had so skilfully constructed as the subjects of development and who, for this very reason, could not be expected to be anything but in full agreement with a venture carried out for their benefit, Pakistan's political establishment was a recognized source of trouble. There was something about their modus operandi, about their very sense of being, that made them resistant to development. Their fightback was of course conditioned by the power of development as discourse, but they sought to outflank it, shake it off balance and drag it into a terrain where it lost its magic immunity. In theoretical terms, and we will come back to this with a more substantial discussion in Chapter 6, resistance was about making the dispersed subject of discursive power reappear in a location where it was visible and could be attacked. Doxiadis felt this tactic many times in his time in Pakistan and offered several memorable descriptions of it.

Who could possibly be against development? Doxiadis asked in one of his diaries and answered with an anthropological description that captured the nature of opposition perfectly. His account is worth quoting at length:

---

[124] NARA: RG469 Pakistan Desk Subject Files, Box 4, ICA Memorandum 15 October 1958, Economic Aid Program in Pakistan.

He is an official of the Government with whom I had dinner. Tall, dark and pompous, he came wearing [a] dinner jacket of the latest London fashion. He smoked over 10 big cigars the whole evening, lighting one using a small part of it and then leaving it in the ashtray only to light another in a very few minutes. He is a big man in this area. He explained to me that I have come to Pakistan fifty years early ... Conditions he believes are excellent and people do not need anything. He then goes out to come back after a few minutes, smelling strongly of whisky. He probably drinks it on doctor's prescription but it seems that the prescription orders a good dose to be taken every 10 to 15 minutes, as my host leaves me in such intervals to come back smelling more and more of whisky, speaking more and more strongly against any ideas which would come from abroad and upset the people's life. A couple of hours later, with the assistance of whisky I learn that apart from being a high civil servant he is also a big land-owner who does not believe in agricultural reform. People are happy with present conditions, he says, ... why don't you come back in fifty years' time?[125]

Against development, it turns out, were the 'big men' of Pakistani politics, local potentates whose power relied on an intricate web of relationships of domination – caste, economic power, family, even religion – as well as on an official position in the state hierarchy. Such men were hard to handle for the discourse of development; they could not be reduced to spokesmen of a past that would inevitably be swept away by the modernization process – they were too 'westernized' for that – and their sources of power were too complex and political to be reduced to a mere assemblage of development indicators or other social descriptives. When faced with such men, it is now Doxiadis's turn to feel a power that he cannot easily rebuff. His angry tone and disgust make this clear. The challenge does not come from better arguments – 'come back in fifty years' time, the locals are happy' is laughable as an intellectual challenge to development – but from a mode of behaviour that produces power at a different level altogether.

The power of the 'big man' was something that discourse could not reach or break down. At the same time it irritated the non-discursive elements in the consultant's persona – the masculine hardness, the heroism, the willingness to indulge 'crazy ideas' – with deadly precision. It relied on what Doxiadis described as 'pomposity', even rudeness, when dealing with high-status foreigners. It flowed from imposing phys-ical features (why else did Doxiadis have to mention that this man was 'tall and dark'?) and from conspicuous consumption (consider the fash-ionable dinner jacket and the cigars deliberately wasted, half smoked). Above all this mode of power relies on transgression. Hence, the whisky, banned by religious injunctions and available only on medical prescrip-tions, and the insulting manner of getting up every quarter of an hour to

---

[125] CADA: Pakistan Volume 2, Diary, pp.203–204.

drink while the guest's glass remains empty. No set of rules – and what else is 'discourse' – can diminish the stature of someone who defines himself through openly and theatrically breaking the rules.

In the final analysis, the power of those who were against development was 'sovereign' power: the power of kings and 'feudal lords'. Sovereign power is in many ways what discursive power is not: while the former is concentrated in a clear location, the latter is dispersed across a complex network making its workings invisible. Demonstrating who is boss is precisely what sovereignty is all about, as is still clearly indicated in the peculiarly British use of the term as a designation of the legal personality of the monarch. 'Discourse' works through creating deliberately non-politicized, 'normalized' epistemological categories – by making a world and making it appear 'natural'. In contrast, sovereign power is primarily performative, even theatrical; it is exercised in often spectacular actions that far from seeking to appear 'natural' (or 'normal' or 'beyond politics') are meant to strike their recipients as extraordinary acts of force, as demonstrations of power that are openly acknowledged as such. While discursive power is operating in a meticulous and constant manner – the medical power of the doctor does not stop in the doctor's absence; a country does not stop being underdeveloped when no expert is looking – sovereign power is time limited; it is only effective at the moment when it is applied, and perhaps while the memory of its effects are fresh and tangible. Not least because of this temporal constraint, sovereign power is never total. As Foucault demonstrated with such richness of detail in his most famous book, sovereign power could come up with the utmost cruelty to execute a man accused of regicide, but it could only hit the condemned man's body; his mind remained free and untouched.[126]

It is a similar sense of 'sovereignty' that anthropologists and political scientists of South Asia have put centre stage in their analysis of how politics works in the region, be it the politics of neighbourhood bosses in Bombay or Karachi, or the politics of crowds from colonial Lahore to contemporary Calcutta.[127] This is, of course, not the commonsense

[126] Foucault, M. (1977), *Discipline and punish: the birth of the prison*, New York, Pantheon Books.
[127] Hansen, T. B. (2002), *Wages of violence: naming and identity in postcolonial Bombay*, Princeton, NJ; Chichester, Princeton University Press; Chatterjee, P. (2004), *The politics of the governed: reflections on popular politics in most of the world*, New York, Columbia University Press; Verkaaik, O. (2004), *Migrants and militants: fun and urban violence in Pakistan*, Princeton, NJ; Oxford, Princeton University Press; Daechsel, M. (2006), *The politics of self-expression: the Urdu middle-class milieu in mid-twentieth century India and Pakistan*, London; New York, Routledge; Chakrabarty, D. (2008), '"In the name of politics": sovereignty, democracy and the multitude in India', *Varieties of world making*, N. Karagiannis and P. Wagner (eds.), Liverpool University Press: 115–124.

meaning of the term 'sovereignty' as derived from international relations and international law that locates such an attribute exclusively in the ontology of the Westphalian ('modern') state, but such a multiplicity of meanings is not necessarily a problem. It actually facilitates the creative use of the concept of sovereignty at different levels of the analysis. We can use it to describe – following some ideas of Carl Schmitt[128] – the political logic of *coup d'état* and military dictatorship, or we can reduce its scope to describe the behaviour of political institutions like the CDA or the Ministry of Finance or of individuals: Ayub Khan, a landowner bureaucrat in lower Punjab, the community leaders in the slums of Karachi, even Doxiadis himself. They are all 'sovereign bodies' albeit of different orders, to use the title of an influential collection of essays representing this approach.[129] Doxiadis's encounter with the whisky-drinking and cigar-smoking bureaucrat was a single iconic instance of what this book seeks to capture at large: the inevitable collision of 'developmentality' with 'post-coloniality' in a grand clash of different sovereigns.

---

[128] Schmitt, C. (2005), *Political theology: four chapters on the concept of sovereignty*, University of Chicago Press, pp.38–50.
[129] Hansen, T. B. and F. Stepputat (2005), *Sovereign bodies: citizens, migrants, and states in the postcolonial world*, Princeton University Press.

4   On the road to Islamabad

Doxiadis's ultimate triumph, the creation of the new capital city of Islamabad, was put on its way to realization less than a year after the publication of his ill-fated Housing and Settlements chapter in the First Five Year Plan, and about five years after he had first argued for extending his Ekistics vision to Pakistan. There was no direct connection between these earlier efforts and his newly found success. His sudden luck was entirely due to the dramatic events of October 1958: Ayub Khan's *coup d'état*. When success finally came, it came not only with breathtaking speed but also at an unprecedented scale. Islamabad was not Doxiadis's only notable achievement to materialize within months after the generals taking over: there was also Korangi, the new university campus for Punjab University and several other assignments. How is the historian to explain this sudden reversal of fortunes? It is tempting to see his experience as part of a larger story commonly found in the literature, and often confirmed by popular memories of the period. We have already encountered it at the very beginning of this book: it is the story of General Ayub Khan as Pakistan's hero of development. According to this story, Pakistan's past problems had been primarily down to shortcomings in domestic political morality. The civilian governments of the previous decade had lacked both the will and the ability to knock the state apparatus into shape. There was too much 'politics', too many special interests, too much jockeying for personal gain, too many ideological divisions. Only a regime of 'non-political' and unflinchingly nationalist officers was able to cut through the Gordian knot of administrative incompetence and finally get down to business. Ayub, in short, acted as a game-changer and introduced Pakistan into a new age where development and post-colonial statehood fitted hand in glove.

This is not the explanation offered in this book. As this chapter will demonstrate, the immediate driving forces of Doxiadis's success were short-term political trends not long-term changes in structures of governance, and even these short-term trends were not primarily concerned with what happened in Pakistan, but rather originated several thousands of miles away in events in the United States. The structural contradiction between 'developmentality' on one side and 'post-coloniality' on the other, meanwhile, did not diminish over Ayub's time in office, but actually became strengthened.

Washington calling

Doxiadis's bonanza of prestige assignments in Pakistan between 1958 and 1961 owed a great deal to the changing circumstances of US aid policy, both in general terms and with particular reference to Pakistan. This is hardly surprising as the ambitious Greek had always been some kind of outrider for US international interests, even if most of his funding had to be routed through the private Ford Foundation rather than through a government institution in Washington D.C. Few in Pakistan doubted that he had been chosen as a consultant for his pro-Western and anti-communist stance rather than for his technical competence, while some even suspected that he may have had direct links to the CIA.[1] It was not only in Pakistan that development was under suspicion, however; many – if not a majority – of policy makers and the general public in the United States itself remained deeply sceptical about the newly formulated dream to transform the world. Their misgivings shaped official American policy and by the late 1950s had led it into a deep ideological and administrative morass. Unresolved battles between different interpretations of Washington's strategic role posed at least as many challenges to American aid representatives in Pakistan as the hostility and evasive manoeuvrings of the Pakistani elite. Perhaps counterintuitively, it was not a successful deepening of the US–Pakistan relationship that provided the context for Doxiadis's meteoric rise, but rather the catastrophic failure of American development assistance, a matter that requires to be discussed in some detail.

Dwight D. Eisenhower's assumption of office in January 1953 had at least the potential to bring fundamental change to a still decidedly underwhelming American aid presence in Pakistan under his predecessor Harry Truman. He was to be America's most pro-Pakistani president until Ronald Reagan joined hands with General Zia ul-Haq in the wake of the Soviet invasion of Afghanistan in 1979. By the time Eisenhower handed over to John F. Kennedy in 1961, Pakistan had become the 'most allied ally' of the Americans in South Asia, and joined not only one but two pro-Western defence pacts against the Soviet Union

---

[1] Interview S. Babar Ali (Lahore, 10 November 2007).

(Baghdad Pact/CENTO and SEATO). This growing military relationship was accompanied by an expansion of US development activities, starting off with a wheat loan agreement in summer 1953, followed by the transfer of economic and military assistance in the magnitude of 1.4 billion US dollars over Eisenhower's two presidential terms, and an expansion of American aid projects funded and managed either directly by a US government agency or by one of their proxies like the Ford Foundation. But throughout the period, aid for Pakistan remained a political hot potato as far as American domestic politics was concerned, and few if any of the projects concerned ever achieved the kind of success on the ground that would have justified their continuing existence.

Development aid to Pakistan was caught between two ideological positions that were both, for their own separate reasons, not particularly conducive to its wider success. On one side was a growing camp of policy makers – mostly but not exclusively 'liberals' in the North American sense – who saw economic assistance as a key weapon to contain the spread of communism in Asia. Prominent among them were the founding fathers of 'modernization' theory: Walt Whitman Rostow and Max Millikan at the MIT Center for International Studies, who were to become the leading voices behind a proactive development policy in the late 1950s and throughout the 1960s. On the other side of the political divide stood an uneasy combine of (mainly) 'Southern' Democrats and right-wing Republicans who were equally strongly committed to the Cold War, but understood it in different terms. In their assessment, the threat of Chinese and Soviet communism in Asia was primarily military in nature, as exemplified by the Korean War just concluded. This necessitated the creation of military alliances with willing partners in the region, beefed up, where necessary, with direct military aid and 'defence support': economic aid given for the express purpose of freeing up resources that the country in question could then use for strengthening its armed forces.[2]

In their eyes, any aid not tied to a clear pro-American stance and to military utility smacked of an international extension of Roosevelt's

---

[2] For a participant account of their rise see Rostow, W. W. (1985), *Eisenhower, Kennedy, and foreign aid*, Austin, University of Texas Press. Also Gilman, N. (2003), *Mandarins of the future: modernization theory in Cold War America*, Baltimore, Johns Hopkins University Press; Adamson, M. R. (2006), '"The most important single aspect of our foreign policy": the Eisenhower administration, foreign aid and the Third World', *The Eisenhower administration, the Third World and the globalization of the Cold War*, K. C. Statler and A. L. Johns (eds.), Lanham, MD, Rowman & Littlefield; Kaufman, B. I. (1982), *Trade and aid: Eisenhower's foreign economic policy, 1953–1961*, Baltimore, Johns Hopkins University Press.

reviled New Deal: a policy that rewarded lack of initiative and was potentially harmful to the economic interests of the United States itself. For people like Clarence Randall, chairman of an early government commission on the value of development aid, George Humphrey, Eisenhower's first Treasury Secretary, or Otto Passman, chairman of the Congress subcommittee on foreign aid, 'trade' was emphatically preferable to 'aid'.[3] As vividly recounted in Rostow's own reminiscences of the period, these sceptics managed to scupper any meaningful extension of US development policy until well into Eisenhower's second term. Presidential requests for aid allocation were either vetoed or downgraded by Congress every single year of the period, and early proposals for a United Nations-led fund of development finance – the somewhat inappropriately named SUNFED – or the ambitious proposal by the FOA director Harold Stassen for an 'Arc of Free Asia' had to be shelved altogether.[4]

Fatefully for Pakistan, the paradigmatic battleground between the pro- and anti-development positions was the question of whether the United States should give aid to India. This issue so dominated discussions that landmark shifts in policy were expressly formulated with this country in mind. Nehru's India was large enough to be a rival for Mao's China, which, disconcertingly for the West, had at the time just celebrated (apparent) developmental successes. India was also at least constitutionally democratic and, were it not for the difficult matter of also desiring good relations with the Soviet Union, would have made an ideal partner for any Washington administration. Although modernization theory would soon acquire the theoretical flexibility to justify development aid to military dictatorships as well as democracies, India was in all respects their ideologically most persuasive case. Popular accounts of Indian heroic backwardness like Mehboob Khan's 1957 blockbuster *Mother India* and Satyajit Ray's *Pather Panjali* were inspiring educated Americans. Nehru himself was well known and well liked, especially by the liberal establishment. The importance and popular appeal of the matter was such that John F. Kennedy, working very closely with Rostow and Millikan, actually made aid to India a central component of his presidential election campaign. Ironically for someone who only a few

---

[3] Adamson, M. R. (2006), '"The most important single aspect of our foreign policy": the Eisenhower administration, foreign aid and the Third World', *The Eisenhower administration, the Third World and the globalization of the Cold War*, K. C. Statler and A. L. Johns (eds.), Lanham, MD, Rowman & Littlefield, pp.49–50; Rostow, W. W. (1985), *Eisenhower, Kennedy, and foreign aid*, Austin, University of Texas Press, pp.92, 114–119.

[4] Rostow, W. W. (1985), *Eisenhower, Kennedy, and foreign aid*, Austin, University of Texas Press, pp.93, 116.

years later was to have one of the *worst* relationships of any US president with Jawaharlal Nehru, his professed pro-Indian enthusiasm offered an easy way of outflanking pro-Pakistan Democrat rivals like Stuart Symington in the primaries, and (somewhat unfairly) to castigate Eisenhower's Republican party for their obsessive military focus and ineffectual foreign policy.[5]

To sum up the situation for much of the 1950s, those in the United States who were broadly in favour of large-scale development aid were also favourably inclined towards India and, by extension, suspicious of Pakistan's progress. Working on the assumption that India should be the natural recipient of US aid, they viewed any aid given to Pakistan as the misjudged corollary of a useless military alliance, in fact worse than useless as it actually made the primary objective of forging a closer relationship with India more difficult. If American aid for Pakistan was to find any approval by this group of opinion makers at all, it had to be seen as especially effective and successful, which for most of the time it was emphatically not. For those broadly sympathetic to Pakistan, on the other hand, there was usually little appreciation of the value of development aid beyond military or geostrategic parameters. They liked Pakistan because they trusted and valued the pro-Western credentials of its leadership: men like General Ayub Khan or President Iskander Mirza, whose son even got married to the daughter of the fervently pro-Pakistani US Ambassador Horace Hildreth.[6] While these sceptics were happy to let defence support and military aid rumble on in the background, as it were, they also brought a quite narrow understanding to debates about what other forms American development aid in Pakistan should take.

Too many masters to please

Ongoing battles between these two camps made the lives of America's men and women on the ground in Pakistan very difficult. Battling to preserve their own sense of mission, while also appealing to the needs of development sceptics back home as well as to a range of Pakistani public opinions, often made it impossible to get anything done. Even after Eisenhower brought a new impetus to foreign assistance policy, US aid operatives in Pakistan found little positive to note in their files.

---

[5] Pearce, K. C. (2001), *Rostow, Kennedy, and the rhetoric of foreign aid*, East Lansing, Michigan State University Press, p.21; Barrett, R. C. (2010), *The greater Middle East and the Cold War: US foreign policy under Eisenhower and Kennedy*, London, I.B. Tauris, pp.2–4, 284.

[6] Kux, D. (2001), *The United States and Pakistan, 1947–2000: disenchanted allies*, Washington, D.C., Woodrow Wilson Center Press, p.75.

A predictable litany of laments over double-dealings, ungratefulness, corruption and more generally 'the slow tempo at which the Pakistan government moves'[7] went hand in hand with an increasingly critical assessment of how aid was conceived and delivered by the Americans themselves. The overall amount of aid was not the issue – if anything there was now too much of it rather than too little. As an audit report of 1955 pointed out: 'The delays in program implementation are attributed by the agency [FOA/ICA] at least in part to the substantial increase in the level of aid which it claims was dictated principally by international political considerations. The agency was not prepared at that time to put into timely action and effectively administer a program of the size called for by the sharply increased level of aid.' The sums involved were now 'beyond the financial and physical capacity of the agency and the foreign country', while whatever efforts had actually got under way remained 'too dispersed ... to administer them effectively'.[8]

The failure was wider than the problem of aid absorption due to institutional weaknesses, so well known from standard development economics. An additional and much less well publicized source of complications was the constant need for US aid agencies to chart a course around hostile interventions from development sceptics back home. According to internal complaints, the high number of visiting delegations of elected representatives from Congress and other US state institutions disrupted the activities of the local ICA staff, and undermined their status in the eyes of the Pakistani administration.[9] One of the most prominent visitors, the aforementioned Southern Democrat Otto Passman, chairman of the powerful Congress Foreign Aid committee, had come to Karachi to inspect the activities of local US aid agencies in autumn 1955. Although he was reportedly quite impressed with 'Pakistan, Pakistani and US personnel' encountered on his tour, he also expressed some trenchant criticisms. His hosts may have taken some succour from his opinion that any aid to India should be stopped immediately and completely, if he had not expressed similar ideas about all economic aid to Pakistan as well. For Passman, American development activity should be restricted to the kind of technical assistance originally envisaged in Truman's Point Four, the provision of experts and educational facilities. Everything else should be financed through

---

[7] NARA: RG469 Records of the US Foreign Assistance Agencies 1948–61; O/NEASA& AFRICA Ops, Pak Br. SubFiles 1, 1951–54, Box 2: File OP-5 Intra TCA, p.5.
[8] NARA: RG469 Pakistan Subject Files, Box 15, Audit Report to the Congress of the United States: United States Assistance Program for Pakistan, ICA, 27 December 1955, p.1.
[9] NARA: RG469 Pakistan Subject Files, Box 12, Despatch Karachi 479, 26 January 1957.

increased domestic income tax by the Pakistani state itself. When his ICA interlocutors pointed out that no real technical assistance was possible without more economic assistance given the present state of institutional weakness in Pakistan, Passman made only minimal concessions, allowing a gradual scaling back of aid commitments over the next two years.[10] When an increase in aid to Pakistan was discussed in 1956, Ambassador Horace Hildreth expected it to run into tough opposition in Congress.[11]

In order to counter impressions that development assistance was a 'hand-out', aid was often restricted to covering the foreign exchange component of a particular project venture, assuming that it was not a lack of resources in general but primarily the inability to import essential investment goods from hard currency markets (or pay foreign experts in hard currency) that impeded the realization of Third World development ambitions. Aid dollars were provided on the condition that so-called 'counterpart funds' would be made available by the recipient country to cover local costs. Any increase in American assistance thus meant a corresponding increase in financial obligations for the Pakistan government as well, which was bound to lead to acrimonious disputes over whether the kind of projects the Americans were keen to fund were also the ones the Pakistanis themselves would have prioritized.[12] In consequence, US-financed investment goods often arrived before the necessary counterpart funds had been allocated. Expensive machinery would rust away in government godowns and Western experts remained idle because the local workforce meant to carry out the heavy lifting could in effect not be paid. The reverse problem – that local work was stalled because experts or machinery did not arrive in time – was equally common, and squarely put down to the incompetence of US aid operatives charged with the difficult task of coordinating the various participating partners in jointly financed projects. Pakistani bureaucrats often felt that a particular project in question was actually much dearer to the American aid operatives charged with its execution than to their own hearts. In consequence, as one TCA representative observed, there was 'a tendency on the part of Pakistan to put off responsibility for its part of the undertaking, to look to

---

[10] NARA: RG469 Pakistan Subject Files, Box 12, File Pakistan – programs 1955–56, Confidential Comments on Foreign Aid Program, Rep. Passman (D-La.) 26 October 1955.

[11] NARA: RG469 Pakistan Subject Files, Box 11, File Pakistan – Politics, Despatch 683, 29 March 1956.

[12] NARA: RG469 Records of the US Foreign Assistance Agencies, 1848–61, Deputy Director of Operations, Near East Central Files, Pakistan Subject Files 1952–58, Box 9: Pakistan Health 1957–58, Report Milliam F. Mayes, Chief Health Adviser USOM, 18 May 1955.

TCA and Ford to do most or everything for them, with consequent unfavourable complications and unwarranted delays'.[13]

Pakistani bureaucrats and politicians understood only too well that the men and women of the ICA had acquired such a vested interest in the success of their own endeavours that they would not allow a project to fail even if rupee counterpart funds were not forthcoming. In some cases, for instance V-AID – an integrated rural development scheme much favoured by American development experts in the region but deemed somewhat less essential by Pakistani bureaucrats – the Ford Foundation would step in to avoid political complications.[14] Elsewhere, other ways had to be devised to rescue ailing projects without upsetting development-sceptic sensibilities. One was, unsurprisingly, the redesignation of economic assistance for Pakistan as 'military assistance', which satisfied Congress but made the funds involved more difficult to administer and utilize for civilian project operatives.

Another way of expanding development assistance to include rupee counterpart funds in ways palatable to a home audience was Eisenhower's Public Law 480 (later renamed 'Food for Peace' by Kennedy). It worked as follows: the United States would provide agricultural commodities such as wheat and cotton at highly concessionary rates to a government like Pakistan's which the latter could then sell to its own people at a profit, which in turn had to be reinvested as rupee components of agreed development projects. While the ostensible trade component in this arrangement satisfied ideological opponents of aid, American farmers in the South and Midwest also found a welcome way of disposing of their own agricultural surpluses. Moreover, because aid was provided in the form of agricultural commodities (even if it was in the end not used as such), it fitted perfectly into a discursive framework that only the most stone-hearted of sceptics could ignore: that of emergency assistance in times of 'hunger', a carefully constructed category central to the ideological effectiveness of the 'development project' as a whole.[15]

Arrangements like PL 480 led to considerable problems for America's representatives in Pakistan, however, as they got drawn into battles not

[13] NARA: RG469 Records of the US Foreign Assistance Agencies 1948–61, O/NEASA& AFRICA Ops, Pak Br. SubFiles 1, 1951–54, Box 4, File R-2–3 Monthly Report to Field, Memo 8 July 1953.
[14] NARA: RG469 Deputy Director for Operations, Office of Near East, South Asia and Africa, Pakistan & Afghanistan Division, Political Desk, Subject Files, Box 12, File Pakistan – programs 1955–56, memo of conversation Ford Foundation and TCA, 23 July 1953.
[15] Escobar, A. (1988), 'Power and visibility: development and the invention and management of the Third World', *Cultural Anthropology* 3(4): 428–443, pp.434–436.

only between themselves and the development sceptics back home, but also between different interest factions vying for control of the Pakistani state. The dumping of America's agricultural surpluses, particularly when involving crops like wheat and cotton, could potentially depress prices for these commodities on domestic markets and hence lower profits for Pakistani farmers, particularly in West Pakistan where they formed one of the most powerful political constituencies. Besides, commodity aid of this sort was a distraction from the need to grow and modernize Pakistan's own agricultural sector, where for many American experts the emphasis of the Pakistani development effort should lie. Their recommendations reflected a dominant stream in developing economics (as ever contemporary policies in India were at the forefront of debate) and also made direct sense in the face of heightened food insecurity in Pakistan. But an 'agriculture first' strategy remained contrary to official US policy. With a view to satisfying the likes of Passman and Midwestern farming interests, there was actually a direct ban on any kind of development assistance capable of undermining America's ability to export its own agricultural products around the world.[16]

The matter of industrial versus agricultural development also divided opinions in Pakistan, but ironically did not prevent the proponents of either camp to launch savage criticisms against American aid policy itself. Whatever US experts proposed, they would find themselves discredited. While some members of the Pakistani elite, particularly those well connected to agricultural lobbies in the provinces, wholeheartedly agreed with an 'agriculture first' view, they were still deeply distrustful of American intentions because many of the actual policies remained, in accordance with Washington directives, industry focused. This was the case, for instance, with the First Five Year Plan drawn up by the Harvard Advisory Mission and, of course, also with subsequent instalments of wheat loans and direct food aid that were among the most publicized of all aid measures at the time. Speaking for this opinion from a radical left perspective (but nevertheless not skipping the opportunity to share his views with US consulate staff in Lahore), the Sindi peasant organizer Hyder Bux Jatoi blamed the United States squarely for the pro-industrial and anti-agricultural bias of the Iskander Mirza

---

[16] NARA: RG469 Records of the US Foreign Assistance Agencies, 1848–61, Deputy Director of Operations, Near East Central Files, Pakistan Subject Files 1952–58, Box 13 File – Pakistan Programs Evaluation D. Lahore 165 Ernest F. Fisk's farewell assessment 3 May 1957. Box 5, Despatch 28, Karachi 9 July 1957. Pakistan Subject Files, Box 15, Audit Report to the Congress of the United States: United States Assistance Program for Pakistan, ICA, 27 December 1955, p.4.

administration.[17] Similar accusations were also voiced by more
mainstream voices in the Pakistani press.[18]

At the same time, many Pakistani bureaucrats directly involved in
development policy at the central government level reacted with equal
suspicion against any proposals made in favour of 'agriculture first'.
For men like the 'go-getting' chairman of the Pakistan Industrial Development Corporation and later of the newly established Water and Power
Development Authority (WAPDA), Ghulam Faruque, an emphasis on
agricultural productivity voiced by some American experts contained a
hidden agenda to deprive Pakistan of the kind of industrial base necessary to defend its sovereignty, a view which unsurprisingly also found
ready acceptance in the military. One iconic battle that raged for most of
the 1950s and into the 1960s was over the question of whether Pakistan
should build its own steel mill. The main question was whether Pakistan
should invest a considerable amount of its resources into a venture that
could never be economically viable: given its paucity of raw materials,
steel produced in Pakistan would always be more expensive than
steel imported from abroad. For the notoriously pro-American Finance
Minister Syed Amjad Ali – the brother of Doxiadis's local agent Syed
Babar Ali and proprietor of one of the main import houses for cars and
similar commodities in Pakistan – the economic case sunk the project,
particularly at times of food insecurity.[19] His views were publicly backed
by American economists working for the ICA. One 'junior official',
Robert L. Clifford, was roundly castigated in the pro-central government
newspaper *Dawn* for speaking out publicly against the steel mill, to which
he as a foreigner had no right, especially as no funding had been sought
from American sources at the time.[20]

Ghulam Faruque, in contrast, did not believe that any economic
arguments against the project really mattered as, for him, the survival
of the nation was as much threatened by dependency on outsiders in a

[17] NARA: RG469 Records of the US Foreign Assistance Agencies, 1848–61, Deputy
Director of Operations, Near East Central Files, Pakistan Subject Files 1952–58, Box
12, File Pakistan Programs 1957–58, Lahore D. 145, 22 March 1957, Memorandum of
conversation with Hyder Bux Jatoi.
[18] *The Times* (Karachi), 8 July 1957, attached to NARA: RG469 Records of the US Foreign
Assistance Agencies, 1848–61, Deputy Director of Operations, Near East Central Files,
Pakistan Subject Files 1952–58, Box 5, File Pakistan – Disasters 1955–58, Despatch
28 Karachi 8 July 1947.
[19] Interview S. Babar Ali.
[20] *Dawn* (Karachi), 16 July 1957. ICA advisor Robert Clifford, for instance, wanted more
agricultural development but no steel mill, NARA: RG469 Records of the US Foreign
Assistance Agencies, 1848–61, Deputy Director of Operations, Near East Central Files,
Pakistan Subject Files 1952–58, Box 9 'Telegram State to Karachi' 30 July 1957.

strategically important area of industrial capability as by a hungry population.[21] For him, views like Clifford's proved that the American's were attempting to keep Pakistan 'underdeveloped'. His views were not confined to the nationalist right. The communist proprietor of the influential *Pakistan Times*, Mazhar Ali Khan, similarly accused what he saw as a pro-US coterie of 'feudal' interests around Amjad Ali as wishing to delay Pakistan's 'take-off' into the industrial age.[22] The waters were muddied further by the fact that German, Japanese and US corporations were at the same time attempting to muscle their way into the debate with the help of local lobbyists in order to gain commissions.[23]

Aid under scrutiny

By 1957, US development policy for Pakistan had got so bogged down in irreconcilable ideological contradictions that it was vehemently attacked by all sides, while also becoming increasingly impossible to administer due to its piecemeal, project-by-project orientation and over-complex funding arrangements. Further embarrassment emerged when 10 million US dollars had gone missing in the Pakistan aid effort, with the ICA ending up funding machinery for fertilizer and pesticide factories that did not in fact exist. In response, James Langley, the new US ambassador to Karachi, went as far as to suggest to 'cut off economic aid to Pakistan' pure and simple.[24] His view was not only a direct reaction to specific problems in Pakistan; it also reflected the general mood in America.

[21] Farooq, S., Ed. (2004), *Ghulam Faruque Khan: revolutionary builder of Pakistan*, Peshawar, Unique Books, pp.147–152, *passim*. He was also reluctant to allow the participation of the Pakistani private sector in the project because he believed this to undermine his strategic 'nationalist' vision. Historisches Archiv Krupp: File WA 51/5917, Aktenvermerk Besprechung mit Herrn Rangoonwala, Essen, 23 March 1956. The informant, Mohamed Aly Rangoonwala, was President of the Federation of Pakistani Chambers of Commerce at the time.
[22] 'Economic policies', *Pakistan Times* 20 February 1957, reprinted in Khan, M. A. (1996), Pakistan, the first twelve years: the *Pakistan Times* editorials of Mazhar Ali Khan, Karachi; New York, Oxford University Press, p.617.
[23] The Krupp steel corporation of Essen, Germany, was involved in lobbying for the Pakistan steel mill project from 1953 to 1967. See Historisches Archiv Krupp: Files WA51/5881, 5915, 5916, 5917, 5935, 5936. Also from a US perspective NARA: RG469 Records of the US Foreign Assistance Agencies, 1948–61, Deputy Director for Operations, Office of N.East, S.Asia&Afr, Pakistan & Afghanistan Division/Pakistan Desk, Subject Files Box 1, Meeting Notes on German and US Steel Industry in Pakistan 14 September 1953, Magis, Ed Dahl, SOA, Jo Drake, Larry Nahai.
[24] NARA: RG469 Records of the US Foreign Assistance Agencies, 1848–61, Deputy Director of Operations, Near East Central Files, Pakistan Subject Files 1952–58, Box 12, File Pakistan programs 1957–58, Telegram Dulles to US Embassy Karachi, 2 November 1957.

At the very same time as when the scandal broke, George Meader, Republican Congressman for Michigan, had published a highly critical article entitled 'Our foreign aid program – a bureaucratic nightmare' in *Reader's Digest* magazine[25] (the pro-development lobby took careful note; a copy of it was included in the files of the ICA mission in Pakistan). Meader's article suggested that any development policy that went beyond Truman's narrow promise of technical cooperation with the underdeveloped world should be scrapped. Later in the year, a congressional mission was dispatched to Karachi to investigate all United States aid operations, a deeply uncomfortable moment for the ICA and its experts in Pakistan, which was bound to intensify doubts about the values of US-led development policy even among otherwise pro-Western Pakistani politicians.[26]

By 1958 a point was reached when the future of the entire development aid programme in Pakistan appeared questionable. In August – some months after the final publication of the ill-fated First Five Year Plan, and at a time when Doxiadis had in many ways reached the depths of frustration as far as his relationship with Pakistan was concerned – the Pakistan government began to openly cast doubt on its continuing relationship with the United States. To the great consternation and alarm of the local American mission, the pro-government Karachi daily *Dawn* published a leak from what was purported to be a 'top secret' Pakistani report in which the aid effort was savagely criticized. Development aid was described as the self-serving game of US contractors and experts who were only interested in filling their own coffers while not even possessing the capacity to effect any positive change on the ground.[27] Even though leading bureaucrats and later even the Prime Minister and Finance Minister were called in to apologize for the sensationalist and unbalanced tone of the press article, members of the American mission themselves had to concede that the actual report on which the leak was based had been fair in its criticism.[28] According to a memo drafted a few weeks later, and only days after Ayub and Mirza staged their *coup d'état*, the US aid programme had failed comprehensively and lost all popular appeal:

---

[25] 'Our foreign aid program – a bureaucratic nightmare', *Reader's Digest*, April 1957.

[26] NARA: RG233, Hearings before a Subcommittee of the Committee on Government Operations, House of Representatives, Eighty-Fifth Congress, Second Session, Part II, pp.1059–1071.

[27] *Dawn* (Karachi), 19 August 1958.

[28] NARA: RG469 Records of the US Foreign Assistance Agencies, 1848–61, Deputy Director of Operations, Near East Central Files, Pakistan Subject Files 1952–58, Box 10 – Industry and Information, Telegram Embassy Karachi to Secretary of State No. 387, 19 August 1958.

The glamour has worn off after six years; there is little visible evidence of its operation; only the already rich seem to have gained from it; there is an ever stronger feeling that it is designed to tie Pakistan to the US by fostering her economic dependence on the US; it is accused of undermining Pakistan's political independence; and the psychological resentment against the benefactor is becoming more and more a factor in the public mind. The extent of Pakistan's economic dependence on US aid serves to embitter relations between self-respecting Pakistanis and the Government which are alleged to have permitted this dependence to develop.[29]

As had been clear to the ICA operatives in Pakistan for some time, the only way forward was to reduce the scope of direct US involvement in development policy, while simultaneously also simplifying and depoliti-cizing aid to Pakistan. 'Development' had to be transformed from a missionary effort led by outside consultants to a policy of encouraging Pakistan to develop itself. Any criticism that sought to insinuate a direct link between America's commitment to help Pakistan attain a better future and the geostrategic desire to keep it allied to the Western camp had to be disabled. This had, of course, always been the objective of development enthusiasts like Rostow and Millikan who now managed to rise to pre-eminent positions in US politics, first with the covert blessings of Eisenhower, and later with a very public endorsement by Kennedy. Their idea that 'development' aid had to be non-political and free from any geostrategic ties to work in the US national interest was based on nothing else than the magic of development as 'discourse': as the kind of depoliticizing, scientific intervention that proposed 'objective' and value-free solutions; an intervention that could be gladly accepted by the most keen defenders of their national independence, even by non-aligned statesmen like Jawaharlal Nehru.

The practical implications were soon spelt out by ICA officers operat-ing in Pakistan. Non-performing projects – and according to ongoing audit reports this included virtually everything the Americans were actu-ally involved in, from dam projects to malaria prevention, road building to drinking water and sewerage schemes[30] – had to be pruned and the list

---

[29] NARA: RG469 Records of the US Foreign Assistance Agencies, 1848–61, Deputy Director of Operations, Near East Central Files, Pakistan Subject Files 1952–58, Box 4 Pakistan – Defense Expenditure, Memorandum ICA, 15 October 1958, Economic Aid for Pakistan.

[30] See lists in NARA: RG469 Records of the US Foreign Assistance Agencies, 1848–61, Deputy Director of Operations, Near East Central Files, Pakistan Subject Files 1952–58, Box 15, Audit Report to the Congress of the United States: United States Assistance Program for Pakistan, ICA, 27 December 1955. Audit Report to the Congress of the United States, United States Assistance Program for Pakistan, ICA, Fiscal Years 1952 through 1957.

of top priorities streamlined. The widespread impression that there was an 'excessive number of US technicians in Pakistan' had to be countered, even if only to call the bluff of Pakistani bureaucrats complaining about undue influence. Most important of all, the great deal of autonomy previously enjoyed by American experts on the ground had to be restricted and a greater amount of oversight granted to the central government. While the Pakistani Ministry of Economic Affairs had always nominally been in control of foreign-run projects, it operated as no more than a 'post office' in practice, which left individual consultants free to deal with individual ministries and even departments as they deemed fit, encouraging the same kind of factionalism and intrigue that Doxiadis had also experienced when he sought to locate a suitable partner for his comprehensive Housing and Settlements Plan.[31]

Doxiadis saves the day

Doxiadis's extraordinary turn of luck began, barely weeks after Ayub's coup, with the assignment of the Korangi 'Pilot' project – as mentioned earlier, a massive urban resettlement scheme located 12 miles outside Karachi, and at the time one of the largest of its kind in Asia. Its main purpose was to resolve one of the most pressing as well as politically sensitive problems plaguing previous administrations, the integration of poor refugee migrants from India that accounted for most of Karachi's urban poor. Immediately after the takeover, Ayub Khan appointed Lt. Gen. Muhamad Azam Khan as new Minister for Refugee Rehabilitation. The latter had acquired something of a special interest in architectural and planning matters, and enjoyed a 'go-getter' attitude within the military. He had commanded the troops that had taken control of the streets of Lahore back in 1953 in order to quell the infamous 'anti-Qadiani riots' under Pakistan's first (and short-lived) Martial Law. How Azam Khan in turn came to pick Doxiadis as the main brain behind the Korangi project is not fully documented. What is beyond doubt, however, is that in stark contrast to the fruitless lobbying of previous years, everything happened very quickly and within weeks of the coup itself. American diplomatic sources mention his appointment as chief consultant to solve the refugee crisis already by December 1958. According to them, witnesses observed how Azam Khan had met Doxiadis at an event organized by the Ford Foundation, liked the look

---

[31] NARA: RG469 Records of the US Foreign Assistance Agencies, 1848–61, Deputy Director of Operations, Near East Central Files, Pakistan Subject Files 1952–58, Cablegram Killen to Bell and Stevens, TOICA 290, 28 August 1958.

of him and hired him on the spot. Doxiadis was told that 15,000–20,000 houses would have to be constructed in six months in the Greater Karachi region, and was not even given time to register the doubts he had at the time about the viability of the project.[32]

Doxiadis's own account provides important additional detail. His actual contract only came through a few months after his fateful meeting with Azam Khan. Meanwhile, the mass housing project had already been started by engineers of the Karachi Development Authority (KDA) and the Public Works Department without his direct involvement. Under acute pressure from the military government they began constructing houses with no overall plan, much as they had done over the previous decade. It was only in January of 1959 that Doxiadis, backed by ICA experts, fully took charge of the project and massively enlarged its scope from merely providing housing units to planning an entire new satellite town. A good 1000 newly erected concrete shells already on the ground actually had to be destroyed, because they stood in the way of the future road network of Korangi. From then on over the next three years, Doxiadis was fully in charge.[33]

A good deal of political folklore has grown ever since about the military's ability to exceed even its own ambitious targets.[34] The project was declared completed in June 1959, and the first buildings proudly presented to the world when Generals Eisenhower and Ayub Khan flew over the site by helicopter in December of the same year.[35] 'Here is a real demonstration of the new regime and what they can do', Doxiadis wrote enthusiastically in his travel diary and added with satisfaction that the main ideological flavour behind this new 'pet scheme of the Government' was a reorientation of city planning away from 'the designers' and towards 'the economic level' and 'social level' – in other words, the kind of practically minded and comprehensive planning he had always advocated under his trademark doctrine of Ekistics.[36] Similarly delighted were representatives of the American aid establishment. In April 1959, when the first houses were already visible on the ground, the ICA mission in Pakistan had a meeting with General Ayub which was widely reported

[32] NARA: RG469 Records of the US Foreign Assistance Agencies, 1848–61, Deputy Director of Operations, Near East Central Files, Pakistan Subject Files 1952–58, Box 9, File Pakistan-Housing, Box 9, File Pakistan-Housing, TOICA 901, 24 December 1958.

[33] CADA: Pakistan Volume 14, Dox-PA 17, Development of the Korangi Area, pp.2–6.

[34] See Ansari, S. (2005), *Life after Partition: migration, community and strife in Sindh 1947–1962*, Karachi, Oxford University Press, p.190.

[35] *Dawn* (Karachi), 7 December 1959.

[36] CADA: Pakistan Volume 12, File Dox 95, Pakistan Diary from 15 to 19 December 1958.

in the press. The Chief Martial Law Administrator himself spoke, praising American Secretary of State John Foster Dulles and highlighting Pakistan's importance as a strategic partner for the United States. Ambassador Langley confidently declared that the highly critical (and self-critical) ICA report into aid in Pakistan was now 'ancient history', and the early successes of the new regime had turned a new leaf in the relationship.[37]

The refugee rehabilitation scheme was the first instance after the coup when the generals could prove their mettle, when the overwhelmingly bad impression that development policy had previously cast on both the Pakistani state authorities and their ICA partners could be dispelled. For both sides there was much to lose. Between their assumption of power in October 1958 and the successful implementation of Pakistan's Second Five Year Plan from 1961 to 1965, the junta found itself particularly vulnerable. Although greeted by many in Pakistan with great expectations and enthusiasm, the generals had in fact few means to publicly deliver what they promised. The economic situation was bad and unlikely to improve fast enough to shore up regime support in the short run. In consequence Ayub's regime was, for a few years at least, particularly reliant on American backing, and therefore especially receptive to their patron's developmental expectations. The stakes were also high on the American side. It was not only the ICA mission to Pakistan itself that was in danger of being dismantled, the continuing provision of development aid to Pakistan was increasingly threatened. Its traditional backers among military-focused geostrategists were highly unimpressed by what had been achieved, and their pro-development rivals remained as ever too enthralled by neighbouring India to give Ayub much time.

The very sensitivity of the moment was to be Doxiadis's golden opportunity. He became the man of the moment because his involvement allowed both the Pakistani generals and their American backers to hedge their bets. Doxiadis was reliably pro-American, but, crucially, not American himself, and nor was he directly sponsored by any US state institution. Revealingly, it was once again the Ford Foundation that had brought him back to Pakistan, and under circumstances that were far from straightforward. Not only did Doxiadis's dispatch happen with extraordinary speed, it was also not really justified by his less than successful previous track record. Although the ICA were finally willing to make a not unsubstantial financial commitment of half a million rupees to help with local labour costs, they were keen not to enter into any

---

[37] *Dawn* (Karachi), 21 April 1959.

contractual agreement with Doxiadis or his company directly. All of his expenses – 300,000 US dollars per year – were to be met by Ford.[38] Once again, the private foundation appears to have stepped up to the plate to look after US foreign policy interests when official institutions found the situation too hot to get involved. If Korangi had not worked as spectacularly as it did, at least over the first two years of its execution, both Ayub and his generals and the men of the ICA could have safely disowned the project.

An equally important factor was the nature of Doxiadis's expertise itself. While housing and settlements had been seen as a mere luxury earlier in the decade not only by Pakistani bureaucrats but even by development economists like Gustav Papanek, it now emerged for the first time as a field of activity that could satisfy the most diverse of opinions and constituencies. It transcended the battles of 'industry first' versus 'agriculture first' and, leaving aside building contractors and the cement industry, was not associated with any of the more powerful vested interest groups operating in Pakistan. Development sceptics could see a project like Korangi as a simple humanitarian intervention, as a way of putting a roof over the heads of the most destitute. Development enthusiasts, at the same time, could follow Doxiadis's own arguments and see it as the first stepping stone of the modernization process, and the Pakistani public, meanwhile, could see it as an important part of their sovereign project of providing a home for the Partition refugees, who had made the largest sacrifice for the creation of the nation, a reterritorialization measure par excellence. Korangi, in short, was a perfect compromise for this moment in history; not so much because it represented a larger global trend or structural force, but rather because it helped to resolve a bundle of previously intractable conflicts between highly 'political' and sectional interests in Washington and Karachi.

The last stretch on Doxiadis's road to Islamabad, so to speak, also appears to have begun less than a month after the coup, possibly as future reward for his willingness to shoulder the risk of the politically sensitive Korangi project. With the new capital there was, however, a great deal less international politics involved. In fact, according to DA representative Orestes Yakas, the Americans remained long sceptical about the very possibility of abandoning Karachi for a new location in the north.[39]

---

[38] NARA: RG469 Records of the US Foreign Assistance Agencies, 1848–61, Deputy Director of Operations, Near East Central Files, Pakistan Subject Files 1952–58, Box 9, File Pakistan-Housing, Box 9, File Pakistan-Housing, TOICA 901, 24 December 1958.

[39] Yakas, O. (2001), *Islamabad, the birth of a capital*, Karachi, Oxford University Press, Note 1, p.151.

Be this as it may, Doxiadis already referred to the dispatch of two plans for a new federal capital to Pakistan in October 1958 – one internal and the other for public consumption. The proposed location of the new capital at this point was officially still kept open. Doxiadis had stated the conventional wisdom the previous year when he wrote in a private letter that 'Pakistan ... badly needs a new federal capital outside but in connection with present Karachi'.[40] As his handwritten comments on the secret 'Report on the Location of the Federal Capital of Pakistan' indicate, Doxiadis did not see a particular need to shift the capital to the north, as was proposed by the military leadership, and privately disagreed with the reasoning among his patrons. With regard to the aim of prohibiting any social contact between civil servants and the commercial and business elites – which was the most important secret (or not so secret) argument in favour of locating a new capital city away from the commercial hub of Karachi – Doxiadis pencilled in a simple but clear 'οχι!' (No!). None of these disagreements were visible in Doxiadis's other records from the time, however. All we find is a series of impressive brochures in which he provided a pseudo-scientific gloss to support the official decision to relocate; as well as a series of photographs and unusually sterile travel diaries that take us straight to the site already chosen by Gen. Yahya Khan, Ayub's chair of the newly established Federal Capital Commission (FCC) (and the man who was to succeed him as Pakistan's second Martial Law Administrator). Doxiadis's master plan for 'Islamabad' was formally approved in October 1960.[41]

Among other commissions of the immediate post-1958 period was the new campus for Punjab University in Lahore, contracted in May 1959.[42] After Korangi and Islamabad, this was Doxiadis's most enduring contribution to Pakistani cityscapes, and in architectural terms arguably the most important. Although he produced the foundational master plans and provided project oversight for Islamabad and Korangi, he never actually designed anything more spectacular than mass housing units and basic community facilities in terms of actual buildings there. Other projects followed soon after. In 1961, DA was assigned to oversee a massive school building programme in East Pakistan funded once again by the Ford Foundation, which envisioned the construction of nearly 10,000 schools and training colleges. In the words of the *DA Monthly Bulletin* this was to be 'one of the most extensive national educational

---

[40] CADA: Pakistan Volume 31, Correspondence, Letter to Syed Babr Ali, 9 April 1957.
[41] Yakas, O. (2001), *Islamabad, the birth of a capital*, Karachi, Oxford University Press, p.85.
[42] CADA: Pakistan Volume 17, Document MR-PA8, 9 June 1959.

Figure 9 In business together – Minister for Refugee Rehabilitation (and later Governor of East Pakistan), General Azam Khan, meets Doxiadis at DA headquarters in Athens in June 1959. Azam Khan was Doxiadis's most powerful backer in Pakistan, and this was the high-water mark of Doxiadis's success.
Source: CADA: Archive Files 28557.

programmes ever drawn up'.[43] The contract must have been greatly facilitated by the fact that Doxiadis's old patron Azam Khan – who had in the meantime become friendly enough to visit Doxiadis at his headquarters on Lycabettus Hill in Athens [See Figure 9] – had been appointed as new governor of the province the previous year, a position he filled with characteristic enthusiasm until he fell out of Ayub's favour in 1962.[44] Just before the 1965 war there followed further and comparatively minor assignments: a West Pakistan agricultural university in Lyallpur (now Faisalabad), the Rawalpindi Polytechnic and a memorial to mark the place where Pakistan's first Prime Minister, Liaquat Ali Khan, was

[43] CADA: *DA Monthly Bulletin*, No. 52, February 1963.
[44] *Daily Star* (Dacca), 7 October 2010, republished at http://pakistaniat.com/2010/10/12/azam-khan/#more-15220 [accessed 9/01/2012].

slain back in 1951.[45] The nature of these projects (with the exception of the last) already indicated that Doxiadis's status in Pakistan had declined and shifted after Azam's demotion: they were all educational institutions directly funded by the Ford Foundation, and represented more an enduring loyalty towards Doxiadis on their account rather than any serious interest or commitment on behalf of Ayub's government.

While it lasted, Doxiadis's success had in fact rescued US development policy in Pakistan. Korangi was arguably the first and certainly the most visible of all Pakistani development schemes that actually 'worked'. The involvement of direct US funding, which had been so carefully leveraged as not to take on too much responsibility, was now openly propagated as the project became an emblem of US–Pakistan collaboration, with the Greek consultant's contribution more and more only mentioned in passing. But Korangi was in many ways the last project of its kind. The overall thrust of development policy moved away from too close an association with individual projects under direct control of foreign consultants. At precisely the same time as Eisenhower came to admire Korangi and endorse Ayub's military regime for an American public, radical changes to aid provision in the future were already under way. In reaction to the passing of Kennedy's path-breaking 'Aid to India' initiative in the US Senate, the President of the World Bank, Eugene Black, sent a mission of three prominent bankers to India and Pakistan in order to survey the possibility of large-scale development aid that would be paid directly to recipient governments, and although tied to Five Year Plan commitments would largely remain under local control.[46] The golden age of the development consultant was about to come to an end. When he went to tackle his biggest project of all – Islamabad – the relationship of power between consultant and state, between development as an ideology and development as discourse, had fundamentally changed.

Spectacles of development

The importance of short-term propaganda value over considerations of long-term development success was amply illustrated in DA's copious publicity material. Much of it was focused on Doxiadis as a person, as heroic hero of development whose arrival in Pakistan helped to create a

---

[45] These contracts were all signed in spring 1965, completion took into the early 1970s, see *DA Review*, February 1965, p.15, March 1965, p.6, April 1965, p.13.

[46] Packenham, R. A. (1973), *Liberal America and the Third World: political development ideas in foreign aid and social science*, Princeton University Press, p.62.

Figure 10 Doxiadis presents aspects of his master plan for Islamabad to the Capital Development Authority, Rawalpindi, in May 1961.
Source: CADA: Photographs No. 30917.

new world. Photographs taken at the time show scenes of development theatre: the great consultant flies in from Athens and arrives at Karachi (or Rawalpindi) airport, walking down the aircraft steps with a briefcase bulging with papers. His smile betrays that he knows that his coming is eagerly anticipated. He brings with him blueprints and designs that everybody has been waiting for with bated breath for weeks. After being taken by limousine to the president's office or similar place, he then presents this material to a gathering of Pakistani state dignitaries. There is the obligatory briefing in which Doxiadis appears in one of his most favourite poses: with pointing stick in hand lecturing to an audience that is facing him attentively and with admiration. Then there is the clinking of glasses among men of power, and a besuited chat over whisky and cigar. [See Figures 10 and 11] Before the consultant can be challenged and before the bonhomie on display can dissipate, Doxiadis is gone

Major General A. M. Yahya Khan and Dr. C.A. Doxiadis
Pindi/11.2.60

Figure 11 Doxiadis having a friendly beer with the chairman of the Federal Capital Commission (and Pakistan's future president), General Yahya Khan. Rawalpindi, February 1960.
Source: CADA: Photographs No. 30916.

again, his appearances carefully timed not to let his presence turn into routine, not to lose his creative vision in the humdrum disorder of everyday project management.

Complementing this chamber piece was another spectacle laid on in the open air and involving a much larger but largely impersonal cast of actors: the transformation of the project sites themselves. DA's *Islamabad Newsletter*, which was sent to an extensive list of bureaucrats, academics, politicians and planning professionals, was full of descriptions conjuring up how the city was gradually coming to life. 'Hundreds of labourers are working on the Highway giving a real biblical picture to the quiet landscape of Islamabad. The two highways earth works are now well progressed with the help of new machinery procured by the CDA', we read in one issue. One could even observe traffic jams in Pakistan's new capital, with private cars and horse-drawn tongas already piling up at the site.[47] 'Soon houses would begin to be occupied', the newsletter says a few months later,[48] and then, 'Community life has started', followed by a colourful account of how a branch of Habib Bank has been set up in one of Islamabad's first residential sectors, alongside the first post office, police post and a cooperative store.[49] Some weeks later still, the reader learns that a bus service has begun to ply on what is still Islamabad's only road to cater for more than 3000 workers, craftsmen and builders.[50] We can see, in a time series of panoramic observations, how the city itself emerges as a heroic subject of development – 'the birth of a capital', as DA's publicity material put it with succinct grandeur.[51] The miracle of development was conjured up with the coming together of the two theatrical productions just described: of Doxiadis dramatically arriving with new plans, and of a landscape being transformed in the wake of his presence. A similar sense of development drama based on the juxtaposition of a state 'before' and a state 'after' was propagated to the world in the context of the Korangi project. [See Figures 12 and 13]

The theatrical nature of Doxiadis's projects as they unfolded over time depended on the constant presence of witnesses, on an audience who could see the spectacle as a spectacle. Not coincidentally, a large part of the correspondence of DA site offices was taken up with the matter of organizing visits by domestic and foreign dignitaries. In Korangi, great

---

[47] *Islamabad Newsletter* attached to CADA: Pakistan Volume 157, File C-PI 3008, 1 February 1962.
[48] CADA: Pakistan Volume 157, File C-PI 3112.
[49] CADA: Pakistan Volume 159, File C-PI 3799, 6 July 1962.
[50] CADA: Pakistan Volume 158, File C-PI 3639.
[51] CADA: Pakistan Volume 114, File C-PI 2769.

AN ASPECT OF THE PROBLEM: THE LYARI AREA

DOXIADIS   ASSOCIATES — CONSULTING   ENGINEERS

Figure 12

DOX – PA 1
Page   14

51

A VIEW OF THE ACHIEVEMENTS: THE KORANGI PROJECT

DOXIADIS   ASSOCIATES — CONSULTING   ENGINEERS

Figure 13

Figures 12 and 13 The drama of development exemplified – DA
publicity material depicting chaotic housing conditions in the Karachi
slums cleared by the Ayub Khan regime in late 1958 and 1959 and the
new township of Korangi designed by Doxiadis to resettle their
inhabitants. Note the contrast of the orderliness of the new settlement
with the desolate and deserted feel of its environs.
Source: CADA Pakistan vol.14, DOX-PA 1, 8.4.1959, p.4 and p.14
(Archive Files 23565).

care had been taken to finish a 'demonstration sector' as quickly as possible that could be shown to touring dignitaries. Doxiadis's men planned the aesthetic experience they wanted to convey down to the last detail. They identified a set route through the township that directed the visitors' gaze away from any apparent problems, while also offering an exciting range of impressions: there had to be close-up views of neighbourhoods, community facilities and actual residents – they would even plant greenery to hide trouble spots or convey a more homely picture.[52] Demonstration houses could even come fully furnished (in characteristic fashion, the Pakistani state later refused to reimburse DA for the outlay).[53] Of equal importance were great sweeping vistas of the sheer size of the development as a whole. All visitors were taken on to the roof of a particular building in the demonstration sector from where the 15,000 new housing units seemed to stretch in endless row after row to the horizon. If the visitor in question was important enough, the master plan itself could be altered. While residents had to stick to Doxiadis's housing designs in all details, it was not too much trouble for the men of the Korangi site office to add an extra door to a local community building so that the Duke of Edinburgh when he came to visit could 'always walk under cover'.[54]

What DA and their partners had constructed in Korangi within record time was quite literally a gigantic stage set rather than a functioning urban community.[55] At least initially, there was only a rudimentary water supply, no electricity, no transport connections with Karachi, no proper drainage. While all of these provisions were duly planned, alongside an extensive industrial zone where the Korangi residents would eventually find employment, the timing was out of kilter. Residents were moved into the township first, in a series of clearance measures that were themselves carefully staged and highly theatrical in nature, and then expected to fend for themselves until development finally caught up with their lives. By the time this was expected to happen, Korangi had already fulfilled its duty as a development spectacle, and was no longer wanted by Ayub's regime. In fact, the project had in a sense found its completion at the very moment US President Eisenhower took an inspection flight by helicopter over the site in December 1959, thus renewing his commitment to Pakistan and paying homage to the generals as heroes of

---

[52] CADA: Pakistan Volume 107, File C-PKH 2292, 7 January 1961.
[53] CADA: Pakistan Volume 154, File C-PKH 4456, 27 April 1962.
[54] CADA: Pakistan Volume 107, File C-PKH 2378, 21 January 1961.
[55] For a fuller elaboration of this argument see the companion article to this book, Daechsel, M. (2011b), 'Sovereignty, governmentality and development in Ayub's Pakistan: the case of Korangi Township', *Modern Asian Studies* 45(1): 131–157.

'development'.[56] When foreign funding ran out for Korangi, and when it became clear that it would be impossible to finance the project through contributions from the residents themselves, the state simply withdrew support.[57] It was time to move on to Islamabad as the next big showcase of the government's developmental credentials.

A document written in January 1962 listed the following official visitors to the capital site over a single fortnight alone: Naseer Ahmad Faruqui (Ayub Khan's Principal Secretary and later Chairman of the CDA), a group of journalists from Saudi Arabia, the Defence Minister of Saudi Arabia, police officials from Iran, a German television crew and finally the Foreign Minister of Burma.[58] There were many more throughout the year. Virtually any official foreign visitor to Pakistan from the King of Nepal to Crown Princess Beatrix of the Netherlands to the President of the Philippines and the Prime Minister of Japan were taken to see Islamabad come to life.[59]

Just as in Korangi, one of DA's overriding objectives in Islamabad was to complete a visually impressive 'demonstration area' (subsector G 6/1–4) as quickly as possible so that Islamabad could be declared open, and actual residents in actual houses be shown to visitors. As always, everything had to look exactly like Doxiadis had intended it to be. Just at the time when Crown Princess Beatrix of the Netherlands was about to come, a Doxiadis inspection team noted with great alarm that some boundary walls had not been constructed to the appropriate height, and 'thus the architectural and aesthetic aspect from the road on two sides of the block is not satisfactory'.[60] While this was presumably easily rectified, there were other cases when important parts of work would not be carried out as they could not be executed while preserving the demonstration character of parts of the site. The laying of 'facility lines' for water and power in one of the first demonstration sectors was judged to be inadvisable, for instance, after sewerage and drainage had already been completed and pavements laid to a neat and presentable finish.[61]

---

[56] Ibid. p.152.
[57] Daechsel, M. (2011a), 'Seeing like an expert, failing like a state? Interpreting the fate of a satellite town in early post-colonial Pakistan', *Colonial and post-colonial governance of Islam: continuities and ruptures*, M. Maussen, V. Bader and A. Moor (eds.), Amsterdam University Press: 155–174, pp.159–161.
[58] CADA: Pakistan Volume 157, File C-PI 2907.
[59] CADA: Pakistan Volume 113, File C-PI 2448, DA Newsletter, 16 September 1962; Pakistan Volume 160, File C-PI 4337, 12 November 1962.
[60] CADA: ibid., File C-PI 4333, 12 November 1962.
[61] CADA: Pakistan Volume 160, File C-PI 4211, Letter to Khalid Shamim, Department of Works, 4 October 1962. Such instances were avoided as much as possible, Interview Frantzeskakis (Maroussi 30 June 2010); Pakistan Volume 157, File C-PI 3112.

At times, there was the impression that the timetable of the project was actually dictated by visits, which DA had the duty to arrange in as smooth and impressive a manner as possible. On one occasion, the DA Islamabad office were urged by high ranking Pakistani officials in the strongest possible terms ('we cannot make headway in this manner!') to prioritize plans for an external drainage scheme that was funded by the Government of Canada, not for any reason to do with the project but simply because the visit by a Canadian delegation was imminent.[62] Tours by Ayub Khan himself or Yahya Khan were important deadlines for the project, as well as occasions of public pageantry. The official account of General Ayub's first official tour in May 1962, on the day after the first residents were scheduled to move into G6, provides a good sense of the great symbolic gestures involved. The first point of call was 'zero point' where the highway from Rawalpindi enters the Islamabad area. Here Ayub, 'looking intently at the landscape around, ... described it as a beautiful site', before going on to inspect some of the first residential quarters and, in a highly significant gesture, to demarcate the locations for two future buildings that taken together were to sum up Ayub's official ideology: one was the future main mosque of Islamabad and the other the central electrical grid station[63] – 'Islam' and 'development' expressed in a single public gesture of city planning.

The political theatre of development actively demanded some conflict and drama. Official tours of Islamabad offered many important Pakistani functionaries an opportunity – almost an obligation – to act out their power and importance at the expense of that of the consultants. Both Yahya Khan and Ayub's right hand man N. A. Faruqui came to inspect newly built government housing and immediately criticized the lack of ventilation, which they attributed to the absence of back lanes that Doxiadis had studiously sought to avoid in his plans. He feared that they would simply get clogged up by rubbish and wasted precious space and building materials; in fact, he had savagely criticized Le Corbusier in Chandigarh for having them.[64] The matter was raised repeatedly and prompted a flurry of reports, all seeking to prove with scientific rigour that tolerable internal temperatures could also be achieved with houses being built back to back. But the leading CDA officials would not give in easily to such demonstrations of the consultants' prowess as experts. A charpoy (traditional wooden bedframe) had to be carried in and out

---

[62] CADA: Pakistan Volume 114, File S-PI 259, 19 October 1961.
[63] CADA: Pakistan Volume 158, File C-PI 3501, 18 May 1962.
[64] CADA: India Volume 3, Notes, p.66; Pakistan Volume 6, File Dox-PP 78 Report on Chandi Garh, February 1956.

of the dwellings repeatedly to demonstrate to N. A. Faruqui personally that there was indeed sufficient space available.[65] Faruqui's stance in this exchange was immediately evocative of an easily recognizable role model: that of the paternalistic leader or sovereign who earns the undying loyalty of common folk by deliberately upsetting pre-staged occasions like these Islamabad site visits, and by showing a down-to-earth concern for details of their daily life that would otherwise seem too unimportant for a man of high position. Seemingly mundane exchanges like those over ventilation and the size of doors actually underpinned complex ideas of power, sovereignty and leadership which we will have to re-examine.

The 'great plan' returns

Doxiadis's shift in strategy from 'great plan' to 'great project' paid him great dividends. While his vision for a comprehensive reshaping of Pakistan's built environment according to the principles of Ekistics had got him nowhere, a more flexible and politically astute recognition of the general's priorities delivered him Korangi and Islamabad. But Doxiadis was too much a believer in his own ideas to remain satisfied with individual projects for long, no matter how grand and prestigious they may have been. Throughout his final five years in Pakistan he sought to return to his original ambition of the 'great plan' and conducted a relentless and aggressive lobbying campaign to this effect.

His ultimate aim was already apparent in one of his first planning documents drafted for the Korangi project. In a report of April 1959 – the time when the building of the first batch of housing units was nearing completion, and when the Americans had very demonstratively come back on track – Doxiadis sought to place the new refugee township within the wider context of a 'National Housing and Settlements Program'.[66] Throughout his time as chief advisor to the Planning Commission he had emphasized the necessity of a National Housing and Settlements Authority as a single agency that could cut through the chaos of overlapping departmental responsibilities, bureaucratic rivalries and disputes between central, provincial and local governments.[67] Knowing the political priorities of his customers, the 1959 report did not address the issue of centralized planning directly. It started off with the safe and familiar

[65] CADA: Pakistan Volume 114, File C-PI 2819, 18 December 1961.
[66] CADA: Pakistan Volume 14, File Dox-PA 1.
[67] CADA: Pakistan Volume 7, Diary 21 February 1956–7 March 1956; Pakistan Volume 8, Housing and Settlement Reports [Pakistan Planning Board], File HS 39, 21 January 1956, p.6.

issue of refugee resettlement and with Korangi as a flagship project, but then sought to generate a drift towards more comprehensive solutions. Refugees needed very badly to be rehoused in Karachi, Doxiadis argued, but then so did all sorts of impoverished city dwellers in other parts of Pakistan as well. Korangi had to be properly planned to make it a functioning urban centre; it had to be integrated into its hinterland and made to provide community facilities and economic prospects to its inhabitants, and the same was the case for cities elsewhere in Pakistan too. Referring to the defunct First Five Year Plan, which at least on paper still had a year to run, Doxiadis identified a substantial underspend in government provisions. Now that the bad years of civilian rule were over, it was time to make a fresh attempt to tackle Pakistan's housing and physical planning problems at a massive scale, he urged.[68]

What emerges from the report is once again the familiar sense that urbanization was an aspect of 'development' that could only be effectively controlled through a long-term planning effort at the highest level. The main problem in Pakistan was not so much the lack of buildings or, for that matter, of construction engineers and cement mixers, but the lack of a proper 'scientific' coordination of all housing-related activities across the land.[69] This was why Korangi was classified as a 'Pilot Project', a place where Ekistics methodology could be tried out before it was rolled out further, and where students from Pakistan and from around the world could be trained hands-on in the new science. Such proposals reflected not only Doxiadian development thinking, they were also, as always, cleverly designed to make the best of the changing financial environment at the time. As already mentioned, the Ford Foundation specialized in educational projects in the emerging Third World, and Doxiadis's emphasis on developing and sharing new methodologies was central to their ability to fund him. This was not all. The revamped emphasis on the 'great plan' was also much better aligned with the policy environment of 1960 than it had been back in 1954. After all, the formation of the great aid consortia under World Bank auspices shifted attention from individual projects to national plans. In the future, the best place for a foreign consultant working in the housing and settlements field would no longer be a brick and mortar project like Korangi – individual ventures of this sort would increasingly be transferred to local control – but precisely as advisors at the top echelons of the planning machinery.

Doxiadis's attempts to bring the 'great plan' back turned into a swan song for his career in Pakistan. Some concessions were made by the Ayub

---

[68] CADA: Pakistan Volume 14, File Dox-PA 1, p.11.   [69] Ibid. p.59.

regime, in part under pressure from the ICA 'to widen Doxiadis's involvement [to] planning for all housing needs of the country',[70] but they never pertained to what really mattered. Housing itself never regained a prime importance in subsequent Five Year Plans, and whatever Doxiadis had achieved over his breakthrough years was gradually wound down. The reasons that had made a project like Korangi so attractive only a few years earlier were now absent. Pakistan was no longer seen as the potential death trap of US development assistance, but as one of its most successful examples. 'Development' in general was no longer an embattled notion in the Washington context, but with Kennedy's assumption of the presidency – and Rostow's elevation to chief advisor to the president – had assumed a hegemonic status of sorts. Aid was flowing freely and in unprecedented amounts to both India and Pakistan, not least because the antagonism between the two countries had at least been temporarily reduced with the World Bank-sponsored compromise over the use of Indus waters. Most importantly, the new flavour of the day was a celebration of 'catching up' rather than spreading moral panic over the direst forms of 'underdevelopment'. Demonstrating success became more important than pulling at development sceptics' heartstrings through the invocation of misery. As a result, for much of the 1960s, Pakistan's 'new middle class' in both the city and countryside displaced the morally deserving slum-dweller in the iconography of development. Urban modernization still mattered to underpin this shift – this was the time when new commercial centres were built in Dacca and Karachi and, of course, when Islamabad itself emerged on the map. But it was an urbanism of modern architecture – of glitzy office buildings, company headquarters and monuments of state – and no longer the kind of welfare urbanism that Doxiadis had made his trademark contribution. Even in his cherished Islamabad, as we shall see, he would soon appear as a man out of place.

Doxiadis's path towards marginalization did not at first appear quite as relentless as it turned out with hindsight. At the beginning of his campaign for a National Housing and Settlements Program in 1959, prospects for a long-term defence of Doxiadis's commercial interests in Pakistan seemed bright enough. The National Housing and Settlements Agency (NHSA) he so cherished was indeed set up by Ayub's government later that year. But it was little more than a personal concession to Doxiadis that could easily be made because the Ford Foundation, as ever, would foot the bill. No actual power was ever given to the new institution.

[70] CADA: Pakistan Volume 34, Letter to Azam Khan, 16 April 1959.

Although an extension was promised for the future, the only project the new NHSA was actually responsible for was the Greater Karachi Resettlement Scheme. This meant, in essence, Korangi, a project already part of Doxiadis's remit. To further illustrate its irrelevance, the NHSA had only a part-time director, Col. N. D. Humayune from the Ministry of Refugee Rehabilitation, who also doubled up as Director General of the KDA. Staffing was otherwise more or less confined to DA's own men already working on the new township.[71] Doxiadis was forced to pursue his ambitions for a future 'great plan' bottom-up rather than top-down, as it were. An opportunity presented itself when it became clear that Korangi was insufficient to resettle all of Karachi's remaining refugee slum-dwellers. Soon, a second major township located in North Karachi, slightly smaller than the first, was added to the NHSA's list of responsibilities,[72] and a few years later in 1963, there was even talk of a Third Township, to be located in the vicinity of the old Malir extension and Karachi airport. Doxiadis quickly seized the opportunity to suggest that the three townships could only be planned appropriately if a comprehensive new Greater Karachi Master Plan was drawn up first, and that even the latter would make little sense if not embedded in a comprehensive national plan – calls that remained unheeded by the regime.[73]

While North Karachi was actually implemented, although with less spectacular speed and less international attention than Korangi, the Third Township never went beyond the planning stage. Even in the existing townships, meanwhile, enthusiasm began to fade soon after Ayub's much-publicized great push of 1958 and 1959. A signal that things would not turn out well came in 1960 when the economic committee of Cabinet reminded the NHSA and DA's field offices that 'only the barest works might start in North Karachi and both the schemes for Korangi and North Karachi Townships should be adjusted so that expenditure remains within the resources allocated for housing in Karachi by the Second Five-Year Plan'.[74] As soon as ICA funding ran out for the two townships, the Pakistan government was unwilling to commit additional resources of its own, and the failure and success of the

---

[71] For this reason, Doxiadis felt unable to take on further responsibilities in East Pakistan when the opportunity presented itself under Azam Khan's governorship. CADA: Pakistan Volume 107, Correspondence, File C-PKH 2324, 12 January 1961, Report on my meeting with the Governor and the Government of East Pakistan.

[72] CADA: Pakistan Volume 69, File C-PKH 1386, 13 June 1960, NHSA.

[73] CADA: Pakistan Volume 108, File C-PKH 2807, 12 April 1961. Pakistan Volume 153, File C-PKH 4052, 4 January 1952, with attachment: Government of Pakistan, Planning Commission, Meeting of development working party; immediate/confidential 11 December 1961.

[74] CADA: Pakistan Volume 69, File C-PKH 1358.

ventures began to rely more and more on the residents' own financial contributions. In 1963 a decision was taken to completely stop further government building in the Karachi rehabilitation projects altogether.[75] In the estimation of one of Doxiadis's employees on the project, 'barely 10 per cent' of the overall targets had been achieved at that time, and nobody apart from DA staff and a dedicated local executive officer, Lt. Col. S. S. Hasan, seemed to care.[76]

Swan song for Ekistics

The year 1963 was not yet the end of the line for Doxiadis's dream of gaining control of the 'great plan' in Pakistan. The Ford Foundation contract for the NHSA still had more than a year to run when Korangi operations were wound down. This gave Doxiadis an opportunity to lobby for an extension of the NHSA's remit. As there was little left to do in Karachi, the unit was transferred to Lahore and renamed *West Pakistan* National Housing and Settlements Agency (WPNHSA). At first glance, this move actually got Doxiadis closer to his cherished goal, as the scope of responsibilities now included planning for the housing needs and urban future of an entire wing of the country. As is evident from the still copious amount of correspondence between DA's new Lahore office and Athens headquarters, Pakistan Ekistics reached a final flurry of activity. There was still a substantial underspend in housing when measured even against the reduced allocation of the Second Five Year Plan.[77] It was time to offer master plans for cities where Doxiadis had not been involved before, for instance, the West Pakistan capital Lahore. Moreover, material was collected on Pakistan's electricity and telephone networks, on house prices broken down to neighbourhood level, on new suburban neighbourhoods and middle-class colonies from Bahawalpur to Peshawar and much more besides, leading to a last and significant expansion of the Ekistics archive.[78]

In actual fact, the newly reorganized agency did not stop Doxiadis's removal from real influence over Pakistan's development policy. This is clearly borne out in confidential letters written to him by his field officers

[75] Daechsel, M. (2011b). 'Sovereignty, governmentality and development in Ayub's Pakistan: the case of Korangi Township', *Modern Asian Studies* 45(1): 131–157, p.154.
[76] CADA: Archive File 19200, File H-PL8, Kakissopolous to Doxiadis, 27 July 1963.
[77] CADA: Pakistan Volume 199, File Dox-PAK A247 Housing in West Pakistan.
[78] E.g. CADA: Pakistan Volume 188, Letter Doxiadis to NHSA, File C-PKH 6167, 27 September 1963; Memo Kakissopolous, New Lahore Township, Town Planning Directorate on 16 September 1963; Pakistan Volume 204, Pakistan Reports R-PAK LH 73–103, 1964.

in Lahore. Composed in the self-consciously elitist and often impenetrable *katharevousa* version of Greek favoured by the nationalist right (and with a handwriting that would prove a challenge even to a trained palaeographer), they must have been beyond the grasp of Pakistani postal censors.[79] Candid assessments of the NHSA's activities were combined with little vignettes about personal relationships with named senior bureaucrats and Pakistani employees that offer a unique glimpse at the consultant's final attempts to defend a foothold in the country. Writing in summer 1963, half a year after the relocation of the NHSA to Lahore, one DA engineer described the circumstances of the shift and its impact on ongoing operations. The main problem was to find and maintain staff that could work side by side with the Greek engineers to fulfil one of Ford's conditions of funding. The environment was not favourable. The new WPNHSA was created through a merger with the Urban Rehabilitation Department of the West Pakistan government, which was seen as a largely useless unit made up entirely of bureaucrats with no technical training whatsoever. To hire additional staff was very difficult as there was no financial incentive. Unlike some executive engineering positions, employment in the new agency did not offer any opportunity for kickbacks – which elsewhere could easily amount to four times the actual salary of a high-ranking civil servant, or up to 10,000 rupees per year. In order to stand any chance in the future, the powerful Finance Ministry would have to be persuaded to increase the pay of Pakistani agency officials to make their position worthwhile.[80] Meanwhile, staff that had proven reliable in the past had a propensity to quit or be transferred out at short notice, making the building of alliances with Pakistani government departments nigh on impossible.

Personal rivalries between well-connected Pakistani bureaucrats associated with the agency further stalled any meaningful progress. First, one of the officers most favourably inclined towards Doxiadis, Lt. Col. Hasan of the Korangi project, was removed.[81] Then, there was a long-running rivalry between the first Director General of the agency, Said Khan, and Mazhar Munir, the Joint Secretary of the Communications and Works Department in the West Pakistan government. The former – described as 'very rich' despite receiving only a modest salary – was a Pathan from Peshawar and saw his Lahore posting as a

---

[79] I would like to thank Giota Pavlidou from the C. A. Doxiadis Archive and Konstantinos Palaiologos from the Institute of Hellenic Studies, Royal Holloway, University of London, for translating and explaining this material for me.
[80] CADA: Archive File 19200, H-PL 10.
[81] CADA: ibid., File H-PL 4, To Doxiadis, 15 May 1963.

form of punishment. He felt that his authority was undercut by other government officials because of his ethnic origin and, after only a short stint on the job, he resigned. Munir, for some time touted to become the agency's new Director General, was the son of Pakistan's famous Chief Justice Muhammad Munir with direct connections to Ayub's top leadership. Doxiadis's men saw him as the 'best friend of our office in Pakistan' and as 'honest but arrogant'. Munir did not want to take up the job, however, because he was in fact more powerful as a Joint Secretary of a government department than as the Director General of a toothless agency. His position was so strong that even his immediate boss and main contact with the Ford Foundation, Secretary Mian Abdul Aziz, reportedly 'felt afraid of him'.[82] Another bureaucrat advised DA to get rid of Mazhar Munir as quickly as possible, as he would not support a new contract with the company.[83] The DA engineers in the agency were repeatedly urged not to get involved in such rivalries but in the end felt like referees between two hostile football teams.[84]

Despite having some channels of influence with men like Munir, work was not going well for DA. K. Kakissopolous of the Lahore office lamented that after years of fighting so hard for having an agency of this kind created, their efforts had now come to nothing.[85] He also picked up a distinct anti-housing attitude among members of the Planning Commission, particularly the economist and future Nobel Laureate Mahbub ul-Haq. While careful to stress that the situation was not actually as 'bad as it seemed', another DA employee in Lahore felt that he had to alert Doxiadis to a significant worsening in US–Pakistan relations over 1963 and feared that this may have knock-on effects on continuing Ford Foundation funding in the future. The latter had shown a certain nervousness about the whole assignment from its inception. Fearing that, true to style, Doxiadis would use the WPNHSA as a Trojan Horse to control urban planning operations by proxy, H. Hanson, the local Ford representative, urged that any activities had to be strictly confined to training only, and that the Greeks must not get involved in any planning work directly.[86] By the beginning of the Third Five Year Plan period in 1965, as the original funding finally ran out, the overall allocation for housing policy was further reduced. Kakissopolous's hope that despite all 'a new era will start, inshallah' was not to be fulfilled. The contract

---

[82] CADA: ibid., File H-PL 10, To Doxiadis, 18 September 1963.
[83] CADA: ibid., File H-Pak 1–16.
[84] CADA: ibid., File C-DA 3657, Letter Doxiadis to Kakissopolous, 8 May 1963.
[85] CADA: ibid., File H-PL3, Kakissopolous to Doxiadis, 7 May 1963.
[86] CADA: ibid., File H-PL 1, Letter H. Hanson to DA Lahore, 10 April 1963.

covering the new agency's activities was not renewed, and any possibility to ever realize Doxiadis's greatest ambition slipped out of reach.[87] All that was left of DA's presence in Pakistan from now on was the Lyallpur Polytechnic project, and a short stint to advise on some limited matters in Islamabad in 1967.

An account of Doxiadis's rise and fall in Pakistan would not be complete without mentioning a further significant field of activity: his efforts in the field of education, which were designed as a direct reinforcement of his quest for the 'great plan'. As ever closely aligned with the requirements of his long-term sponsor, the Ford Foundation, he set up an institution, named with characteristic confidence the Athens School of Ekistics. The school was based at DA headquarters and awarded postgraduate degrees in the scientific discipline Doxiadis himself had invented. The graduates were, in fact, long-term interns, who worked both on project sites in their country of origin and, for a limited period of time, in Greece itself, all paid for through international philanthropy and development aid. Doxiadis consistently argued that none of his major projects could be carried out by staff unfamiliar with his trademark methodology and had a 'training component' included in most of them. Colourful photographs of classes of graduates assembled at the Parthenon would go round the world in DA publicity material, just as Doxiadis's house journal *Ekistics* became required reading for architects and planners in established universities. The long-term aim of this policy was, of course, to make DA the monopoly provider of development solutions for the long-term future. As the Ekistics graduates moved up into influential positions in state engineering departments and on planning boards back home, it was hoped they would ensure a steady stream of projects for the company that originally trained them.

Several dozens of Pakistanis were part of the programme. They were assigned to all of Doxiadis's main projects, from Islamabad to Korangi, and upon graduating were often hand-picked for salaried positions within DA's sphere of influence. An attachment to Doxiadis often carried a sense of prestige. Ekistics graduates are repeatedly reported to have set themselves up as major intermediaries between contractors and local residents, and Pakistani state institutions. In Korangi several of them doubled up as 'social workers', tasked with helping to create community cohesion among the often disoriented first inhabitants. In Islamabad, an Ekistics graduate by the name of Sakil [?] even went to the Rawalpindi chief of police without prior authorization to discuss the allocation of

---

[87] CADA: Archive File 192000, File H-PAK L24, 14 January 1965.

land for the future police headquarters in emerging Islamabad.[88] The most significant legacy of the Ekistics graduates was their research work, however. The Doxiadis Archive includes a substantial list of 'dissertations' in which crucial problems of planning for Korangi, Islamabad and elsewhere were discussed, often based on original survey work. They included everything from detailed accounts of social conditions in the slums of Karachi to a survey of entertainment facilities in the greater Rawalpindi region, complete with a nicely illustrated account of local prostitutes and their living conditions.[89] Like the 'great plan', Pakistani participation in the Athens programme did not survive the non-renewal of Ford Foundation funding.

In the end, Doxiadis felt that he had not being able to earn his rightful reward of more than ten years of assiduous lobbying activity in Pakistan. In a letter to an associate, he made it clear that he did not regard Islamabad and Korangi, important as they were in their own right, as all that could have been achieved.[90] His assessment was certainly correct as far as his long-term influence was concerned. It is striking how quickly after the heady days of 1958 and 1959 his stock had declined again, and how little a lasting legacy he was able to leave behind. Even some of his closest backers among the Pakistani elite did not seek a connection beyond the time when it was politically opportune.

A good indication was Doxiadis's inability to attract many Pakistani delegates to his annual Delos Symposium – a venture he started with great fanfare in 1962. It was part-cruise and part-elitist club, designed to rival Le Corbusier's foundation of the CIAM group several decades earlier.[91] Invited personalities of note included the anthropologist Margaret Mead, the historian Arnold Toynbee and the fellow urbanist Buckminster Fuller, among others, alongside other guests, often bureaucrats and politicians from countries where DA had a presence. They were taken around the Eastern Mediterranean on a private ship,

[88] CADA: Pakistan Volume 112/113, File C-PI 2211, 3 August 1961 and Letter Shakir Hassan to DG Police, Rawalpindi.
[89] CADA: Archive File 20191, S.A.A.B Rizvi: Findings on the socio economic and housing survey of the central flat areas of Karachi, 1960; Ghulam Farid Khan, Identification of attitudes of juggi-dwellers living in Jacob Lines towards Korangi Township (Athens Technological Institute 1970); Ihsan Ullah, A study of a neighbourhood market in Korangi, August 1961; Anwar Jafri, A study of the factors contributing to the problem of overdue instalments in the Drigh Village Township, Karachi, August 1964; Abdul Malik Siddiqi, Locational Pattern and other recreational establishments/institutions in Rawalpindi, June 1961.
[90] CADA: Archive File 19200, C-DA 3637, 25 April 1963, Doxiadis to Kakissopolous.
[91] Kyrtsis, A.-A. (2006), *Constantinos A. Doxiadis: texts, design drawings, settlements*, Athens, Ikaros, pp.456–459.

combining seminars with sightseeing. The symposium culminated in a dramatically staged vow to secure a better urban future for humankind that was taken at the Apollo sanctuary on the island of Delos itself. Only two personalities that had played a role in Doxiadis's Pakistan story ever attended, even though many more were invited, including Gen. Azam Khan and Mazhar Munir. One was Gustav Papanek, the economist on the original Harvard Mission, who had actually been quite critical of Doxiadis. The other was the Sindi politician and lawyer A. K. Brohi. How Brohi got associated with Doxiadis is unclear. He does not feature anywhere else in the archive, but his involvement with the landmark Indus Water Treaty of 1960 in his capacity as Pakistan's ambassador to India may have been a point of contact. What Brohi was famous for in Pakistan was not development, let alone urbanism, but his continuing services to the bureaucratic-military oligarchy. He served as minister for legal affairs several times over his long life, including under General Zia ul-Haq's dictatorship, and provided retrospective legal justification for all military takeovers in Pakistan. Intellectually, Brohi was most interested in Islamic mysticism, which he approached in a decidedly heterodox fashion, and to which he made copious reference when accepting Doxiadis's invitation to Delos.[92]

It served as a fitting conclusion to Doxiadis's career in Pakistan that the only Pakistani willing to engage with him *intellectually* – and intellectual engagement was so clearly the most important part of his lifework – was a juris-consultant of military rule. The irony involved could not be greater. Doxiadis the chief theoretician of development, the grand master of the power of discourse, was embraced by Pakistan's very own Carl Schmitt, an apologist and theoretician of a naked politics of sovereignty.

Pakistan and the birth of biopolitics

Having traced the rise and fall of Doxiadis's career between 1954 and the late 1960s allows another moment of reflection and stocktaking. His experience suggest a larger structural argument that can now be spelt out in a single sweep to serve as the foundation for further exploration and conceptual fine-tuning in the last two remaining chapters of this book.

There can be no doubt that the planning of 'housing and settlements' appeared as little more than fanciful in the eyes of many Pakistani power holders of the 1950s and early 1960s. Pakistan was at the time a state with

[92] CADA: File 6077, Delos Participants, A. K. Brohi, Letter Brohi to Doxiadis, 12 September 1963.

minimal tax-raising powers and as such could ostensibly ill afford perceived 'luxuries' like a national housing policy, unless there was access to
international aid. But there were also deeper and more structural incompatibilities involved, pertaining to the very nature of the state itself.
Doxiadis had drawn his inspiration from the context of post-war reconstruction in Europe, which accorded the question of settlements primary
importance. There was a mass provision of cheap housing by the state
across the continent. Cities destroyed by the war were rebuilt in ambitious urban regeneration projects, which often included the construction
of whole new towns. Such endeavours were politically justified in the
context of the newly created welfare state and as a defensive weapon in
the Cold War. They also made economic sense within the prevailing
Keynesian orthodoxy. Big government spending on building projects put
millions into work and helped generate the demand behind the post-war
economic boom.

Post-war reconstruction marked a step change in statecraft which was
to shape the rest of the twentieth century in most parts of the rich world.
For Michel Foucault, lecturing to the Collège de France in the late 1970s,
the coming of the welfare state constituted what he called the 'birth of
bio-politics', a new order where the state used largely consensual and
non-interventionist strategies to control its citizens.[93] These went beyond
the famous progression from the physical 'punishment' of the mediaeval
principality to reformist 'discipline' in the panopticon prison of the nineteenth century. There was a third modality of state power involved, which
had emerged with increasing clarity in Foucault's later work – something
he initially called 'security'.[94] It designated a way of governing people –
now conceived as 'population', as a statistical assemblage of probabilities
about what people were most likely to do or want – through the gentle
steering of natural desires rather than the heavy-handed interventions
that both the sovereign power to punish and the disciplinary power to
prescribe 'normal' behaviour entailed. His analysis of this 'bio-politics'
was based on a historical case study of post-war Germany, where he felt
the coming of this new 'governmentality' could be observed with special
clarity. As we shall see, his account provides a perfect counterfoil to what
was happening at the same time in Pakistan, and thus enables us to

---

[93] Foucault, M., M. Senellart and Collège de France (2008), *The birth of biopolitics: lectures
at the Collège de France, 1978–79*, Basingstoke; New York, Palgrave Macmillan.

[94] Originally introduced in the previous lecture cycle: Foucault, M., M. Senellart, F. o.
Ewald and A. Fontana (2007), *Security, territory, population: lectures at the Collège de
France, 1977–78*, Basingstoke; New York, Palgrave Macmillan: République Française,
Lectures 2, 18 January 1978.

understand Doxiadis's problems with the Pakistani state establishment in terms of a wider structural problem.

Dissecting the debates around the formation of post-war West Germany after 1945, Foucault observed that the experience of World War II necessitated a whole new way by which the very existence of a state could be justified. Catastrophic defeat and the historic disgrace of Nazi atrocities meant that the West German establishment could not argue for the reconstruction of their country in the old language of sovereign power. The Germans had lost the right to self-determination, the right to have a state with military capability to defend their national interest or, for that matter, the right to enforce their sovereignty internally through disciplinary regimes. The only basis on which they could argue for the creation of a new state at all was economic. After the Western allies realized that they needed economic growth to revitalize the European economy as a whole, they had to allow the creation of some degree of statehood in Germany, if only for the purpose of ensuring that the seemingly limited and non-interventionist task of creating a level playing field for economic actors within a capitalist market could be maintained. This would eventually entail a whole range of new power relations between state and citizen, in which control was exercised largely without reference to state sovereignty or the disciplinary powers of the past. They included multiple ways in which the circulation of goods, people and capital were gently 'managed' through targeted and seemingly non-political interventions, from a national health insurance and unemployment benefits scheme to industry standards, from educational provisions to a well-regulated banking system and, also in prominent place, through the provision of a functioning physical infrastructure and of affordable housing to create a stable and productive labour force.[95]

In deliberately provocative usage, Foucault called this new mode of governance 'neo-liberal' (others would have stuck to the historically more accurate but relatively unfamiliar term 'ordo-liberal'),[96] which at first glance contradicts the commonsense assumption that 'neo-liberalism' was actually opposed to, rather than part and parcel of, the post-war welfare dispensation. In part, this was taking a stance in a debate within the European left at the time which had sought to classify the post-war West German state as 'neo-fascist', not least because of its

---

[95] Foucault, M., M. Senellart and Collège de France, (2008), *The birth of biopolitics: lectures at the Collège de France, 1978–79*, Basingstoke; New York, Palgrave Macmillan, Lectures 4–7. pp.80–84.

[96] Foucault referred to the Freiburg school of Walter Eucken, Lecture 5, 7 February 1979, ibid. pp.103–106.

repressive reaction to the 1968 student rebellion and the radicalism that followed.[97] Foucault disagreed with this assessment on the grounds that the 'fascism' label assumed far too much emphasis on sovereign and disciplinary power in the formulations of post-war statecraft. What was so striking about late 1970s and early 1980s 'neo-liberalism' – in Germany, as elsewhere – was precisely the opposite: that the foundation of a state on economic necessity alone was flexible enough to be either expanded into a web of welfare provisions – as it had been immediately after the war – or to be retracted into a more commonsensical minimalist 'neo-liberal' direction. The line of argument and the essentially managerial modality of power employed in both cases was essentially the same, establishing a clear historical connection.

Returning to the case of Pakistan in the 1950s and 1960s, Foucault's observations throw up an almost perfect juxtaposition. If West German 'neo-liberalism' sought to conjure up a state out of a web of economic relationships with as little recourse to sovereignty as possible, the way Pakistani statesmen saw their task was almost exactly the opposite. They had been given a state on the basis of sovereignty: this is precisely what the 'transfer of power' from colonial overlord to post-colonial nation state actually meant. But this state had no substance beyond a new flag being hoisted or an oath being taken by a governor general. At least initially, there were not even any meaningful ways in which the newly acquired sovereignty itself could be exercised beyond mere symbolism. The Germans were by the specific circumstances of their history barred from linking statecraft to practices of sovereignty; for them, state power had become so circumspect that it had to disappear behind a soft cushion of 'mere' governance and regulation. The Pakistanis, in contrast, were by their very different but equally specific history obsessed with highlighting the presence of state sovereignty in all aspects of life; a 'soft' governmentality was either a hindrance in this context or, as we shall see repeatedly throughout this book, had to be reformulated in such a way as to turn it into a sovereignty game in its own right.

Pakistan's sovereignty obsession was directly rooted in the specific historical experience of decolonization. There was an overriding perception of being under constant threat of annihilation, a compulsive need to 'stand up to' India, and a privileging of power contests with the designated 'other' over a reconstruction of the 'self' in terms of nationalist ideology. While these features were greatly enhanced by the entrenchment of a 'state of martial rule', there can be little doubt that the

---

[97] Ibid. pp.185–189.

prevailing sovereignty obsessions were not a product of the post-colonial order alone but had powerful roots in the political culture of the late colonial period. 'Pakistan' had come into being in the first instance as a largely deterritorialized 'will to power' felt by a not always clearly demarcated nation of Muslims; the translation of this desire into a language of statehood, and even more problematically into a fixed territoriality, became one of the enduring dramas of twentieth-century history, involving some of the worst episodes of ethnic cleansing and population displacement ever witnessed.

Development did have a role to play in Pakistan's national 'project' but only as a subsidiary consideration that flowed directly from the primacy of sovereignty itself. The task was to create a sound enough economic and administrative structure to ensure the country's survival in the face of Indian supremacy in the region. This included the ability to project sovereign state power both to the outside world and against anyone within Pakistan's body politic that could be suspected of 'undermining' or 'subverting' national self-assertion. The politics of development in general, and of development in housing and settlements in particular, was a legitimate concern of the state only insofar as it furthered these capabilities. This is not to say that Pakistani administrators and political leaders were all at heart development sceptics. There were, in fact, numerous and often heated debates about the merits of high dams and steel mills, or the wisdom of deficit finance to increase production capacity. Jinnah himself saw the opening of a textile mill as an integral part of national self-determination, for instance, and Liaquat Ali Khan was convinced that Pakistan could not survive without rapid industrialization,[98] while others in Pakistan's first Cabinet were more doubtful about the merits of industrialization, as they believed that it would undermine stability and control. What is most important for our argument is that such debates were settled in the end over the question of how much these innovations contributed to the defence of Pakistan's sovereignty, just as the vital matter of an alliance with America had settled the question of whether Pakistan should have a proactive housing policy or not in Doxiadis's heyday.

In ways that require to be analysed further in this book, there was no real appreciation of the value of urban planning and mass housing as an integral part of an alternative modality of power. What mattered was the

---

[98] In neither case did such an endorsement mean a wholesale acceptance of 'developmentalism' as it then emerged. Swaminathan, V. S. (1950), 'Pakistan problems and prospects', *Middle East Journal* 4(4): 447–466; Kazimi, M. R. (2003), *Liaquat Ali Khan: his life and work*, Karachi, Oxford University Press, pp.328–330.

fact that the state had to physically establish itself on the ground in the form of government buildings, civil servant accommodation and national monuments. This meant that there was also a certain need for housing and settlements experts. The two most important cities in the country – Karachi, the federal capital old and new, and Dacca, the capital of East Pakistan – were in particular need of urban reconstruction because they had not been administrative centres of note before. Although existing buildings could be requisitioned to meet initial needs, it was clear that neither centre would be entirely functional without realigning the urban fabric more consistently with state needs. The most visible and politically sensitive point of connection between a politics of sovereignty and urban development was the refugee problem. It was the direct outcome of the underlying need to 'territorialize' Pakistan's sovereignty project. In consequence it had become intimately connected with the national story of making huge sacrifices for the new nation, and reflected Pakistan's ability to protect fellow Muslims against 'Hindu' atrocities, and to nurture all those who had taken a conscious decision to leave their homesteads to join the new state project.

The logic with which the Pakistani state elite approached the merits of 'development' was the exact inverse of what was on the mind of a man like Doxiadis. He would start with the identification of development needs first, and then demand the creation of an effective state apparatus to overcome them. This was precisely what his 'great plan' and the meticulous identification of weaknesses in Pakistan's structure of governance was all about. This procedure closely resembled the 'German' neo-liberal approach mentioned before. When Doxiadis started his career in post-war reconstruction during the Greek Civil War, he sought to salvage statehood not out of sovereignty games, but out of a comprehensive effort to rebuild its infrastructure and settle its people. The modality of power that stood at the very heart of all of his proposals, whether targeted at the developing countries or the rich West itself, was a precise rendition of Foucault's 'security'. If Ekistics had a single ideological core it was the collection of data about the natural inclinations of population, which could then be gently controlled through the management of circulation in the built environment. This is exactly where Doxiadis's ambition to see all and know all came together with his insistence on *not* acting as the all-controlling planner in the Corbusian mould, but rather to allow a great deal of agency to individual citizens.

From a Pakistani point of view this new modality of power was not only irrelevant, but also could be positively dangerous. The gentle web of biopolitics was bound to undermine the sheer majesty of the post-colonial state. This was especially the case if state power was dragged into the mire of micromanaging such mundane issues like the building of houses or the planning of cities, which many Pakistani policy makers regarded with particular suspicion as potentially ungovernable spaces. Doxiadis's exchange with Harvard economist Gustav Papanek described earlier represents a particularly significant example for this basic incompatibility of governmentalities. Papanek had rejected Doxiadis's ambitions in the housing and settlements field because he feared that any major investment in this area was bound to undermine the legitimacy of planning itself. A housing policy, he argued, could all too easily lead to unwanted complexities and problems on the ground and should therefore be avoided. Eager to defend his own field of development economics, Papanek was acting more like a member of the Pakistani state establishment than as representative of post-war planning here: if planning was to have any value in Pakistan at all, it had to be a jewel in the crown of state sovereignty, something that represented the state's writ in a top-down manner, and something that could at least in some way be shown to be effective, even if effective did not necessarily mean any improvement in the living standards of Pakistani citizens.

The generals' assumption of control in 1958 did not change this underlying logic. Ayub's regime did not appear on the scene to depoliticize Pakistani statecraft along the lines of a politics of 'security', no matter how often the junta declared that it stood above 'politics' and had come to save the country from squabbling 'politicians'. The overlap between the autocrats' political language and Foucault's new modality of governance was confined to words alone. Depoliticization by means of a new managerialism of experts, as Foucault observed it in West Germany, cannot be based on overt acts of suppression as they happened in Pakistan. Ayub staged a *coup d'état,* an act of deliberate violation of laws and constitutional norms. Then he went on to ban political parties, arrested their leading members and arranged for show trials to pass harsh sentences. None of this had any legitimacy apart from the fact that the coup succeeded. This was sovereign power par excellence, a decision to use force that justified itself. In this respect, Ayub's state acted precisely in the 'fascist' manner that Foucault did *not* see at play in West Germany of the 1970s.

This was not a preference easily reversed. Unlike the power of discourse, or for that matter its conceptual successor, 'security', sovereign power is a discontinuous and highly vulnerable modality of control. It always has a clear location – its whole *raison d'être* is to show *who* is boss – which constantly invites attack by rivals; and its force has to be constantly renewed through repetitions of the sovereign act itself. Like the proverbial bicycle that will topple when it stops moving, this means more repression, declarations of war, or other policy ventures that above all show the will and ability to get things done. The king ceases to be king when he lays down the sword, and likewise, a regime like Ayub's could never let anybody have any doubt as to where real power lay. This is as far removed from the European use of 'security' as one could possibly get. In the case of the latter, the location of power has been obfuscated to the point where nobody seems to be fully in charge of anything – think of the invention of a concept as nebulous as 'people's sovereignty'. The only real power in this context is the power of experts and managers who at face value do not even seem to exercise power at all, only do what is self-evidently or scientifically proven to be right. Unlike rising up against a military dictator, hitting a doctor or a social worker is a testimony of one's own powerlessness, an insane action that makes no difference. But Ayub Khan was no doctor or social worker. If he hired a man like Doxiadis it had nothing to do with the sudden espousal of a fundamentally new strategy of control.

Doxiadis owed his breakthrough moment in October 1958 to his close association with the discourse of development. When he was hired by the generals, and endorsed by their backers in Washington D.C., it was not so much his ability to produce aesthetically pleasing buildings or exciting cityscapes that counted, but his contribution to the speedy resolution of 'underdevelopment' in his particular field of expertise. His first task was to resettle the urban poor of Karachi, removing them from chaotic and impermanent dwelling places where they were seen to live a life of poverty, political irresponsibility and ill health, and transplanting them to new environments where they could be reconstituted as proper citizens: as owner-residents of their houses, small but 'pucca', organized into regular neighbourhoods and held together by amenities such as clean drinking water, markets, mosques, schools and recreation grounds. Korangi was regarded, first and foremost, as a development project, a success story that could save the reputation of an American aid presence in Pakistan, while also showcasing the commitment to development by the new military regime. Korangi made Pakistan acceptable to the new ideological climate of the late 1950s, when it was no longer just a willingness to fight communism that counted, but participation in a collective journey towards a better future for humankind. This was how Doxiadis's first structures in Pakistan were presented to the world, and this was also how he himself would have defined his own contribution to the field of urbanism. After all, his new science of Ekistics was conceived as a discipline of development studies in the broadest sense, closely related in scope and ambition to Millikan and Rostow's modernization theory or Rosenstein-Rodan's development economics that acquired a hegemonic status at the same time.

Doxiadis's close identification with development was not going to see him through a successful career in Pakistan, however. Even at the moment of its seemingly unstoppable ascendency to hegemonic discourse for a post-colonial age, the notion of development was actually deeply incompatible with the ideological needs of newly independent nations, and nowhere was this contradiction more strongly felt than in Pakistan. As has been pointed out repeatedly throughout this book, development produced a world where all countries of the global South were deprived of their respective individual histories and political identities, and recast as uniform cases of 'underdevelopment' that could be arranged on a sliding scale. Doxiadis's problem was that he had to account for this need for cultural distinctiveness while also operating within the discourse of development.

This chapter is about how Doxiadis attempted to come up with a solution to this problem, and how this solution fitted in with established expectations and political needs in Pakistan. Although in the final analysis he could not resolve the fundamental contradiction between 'development-mentality' and 'post-coloniality', he certainly tried. His attempts can be mapped between two other grand conceptual nouns that have become so ubiquitous in the academic literature as to become almost clichéd: 'Islam' and 'modernity'. Pakistan was not only a country that happened to be Muslim; it was a country that came into being to defend the right of Muslims to live in their own space according to their own rules and aspirations, even to turn this space into something like an Islamic state. Religious self-assertion of some kind was the *raison d'être* of Pakistani post-coloniality. And, although this was by no means always synonymous with 'developmentality', as we shall see, Pakistanis of all walks of life wanted to partake in 'modernity' of one form or another. These two ideological requirements had to be represented in the built environment as much as in any other aspect of Pakistani life, but there were many ways in which this could be achieved. What made a cityscape Muslim and modern? Was this by virtue of functionality or by stylistic preference? Did urban space have to be Muslim and modern simultaneously, or could the two requirements be addressed separately at different levels of space creation, for instance one in architecture and the other in city planning? Doxiadis attempted to use these possibilities creatively but, as we shall see, produced formulations that by and large did not satisfy either the Pakistani generals or the prospective inhabitants. In the end, the sovereign aspirations of the international consultant could not be indulged by the sovereign aspirations of a post-colonial nation for long.

Another note on the political context may be useful here. As outlined in the last chapter, Doxiadis achieved his breakthrough moment over the one or two years when Ayub's regime was arguably most 'development' minded. This orientation never went away entirely, but it was soon supplemented and eventually overshadowed by a second strategy of legitimation: a populist nationalism in which religion naturally played an important part. Although the basic facts are well known, the existing literature does not always convey a clear sense of this shift, not least because when compared to the Islamization policies of the late 1970s and 1980s, Ayub still shines as Pakistan's most prominent 'secular' ruler. After all, his constitution of 1962 omitted the designation 'Islamic' from 'Republic of Pakistan' and his Family Law Ordinance did more than any other piece of legislation to advance women's rights against shari^c^a injunctions.[1] And yet – as this chapter will confirm with reference to urban reconstruction – Ayub and his bureaucrats were no strangers to a bit of 'Islamizing' when they felt it would stabilize their hold over power. Ayub's own professed dislike of the religious establishment[2] did not stop him from giving space to Islamic radicals and religious conservatives to keep ethnic separatists and left-leaning secularists in check. In East Pakistan regime support for the Islamist Jama^c^at-i Islami and other groupings of a similar persuasion remained constant throughout the 1960s. Even in West Pakistan there was plenty of official patronage for religion, especially after Ayub had committed himself to some measure of electoral politics, culminating in the election contest for the presidency with Jinnah's surviving sister, Fatima, in 1965. A fanatic hostility to 'Hindu' India was combined with a fervour for Islamic identity in a heady mix, which although not outright 'fundamentalist', facilitated the public articulation of demands for 'more Islam', whether they concerned politics, public morals or private lives. When war broke out in 1965, it was only natural that it would be fought as a 'Jihad' with constant incantations of the Islamic fervour and rectitude of the soldiers involved.[3]

Islam and urban identity – an unresolved battle

The question of how Islam should relate to 'Islamabad' was present in public discourse more or less from the start. This was hardly surprising as the matter of religious identity had already preoccupied minds when the capital city problem was being discussed with reference to Karachi. How to introduce an Islamic element to the design of important buildings of state had become a focal point of official debate at the very beginning

---

[1] For the wider context see Munir, M. (1980), *From Jinnah to Zia*, Lahore, Vanguard Books, Chapter x. Also Rahman, F. (1980), 'A survey of modernization of Muslim family law', *International Journal of Middle East Studies* 11(4): 451–465.

[2] Allegedly, his very first encounter with a 'Maulvi' during his childhood ended in physical violence. Ayub Khan, M. (1967), *Friends not masters: a political autobiography*, London; New York, etc., Oxford University Press, p.17. Also Gauhar, A. (1996), *Ayub Khan, Pakistan's first military ruler*, Oxford; New York, Oxford University Press, pp.179–181.

[3] Daechsel, M. (1997), 'Military Islamisation in Pakistan and the spectre of colonial perceptions', *Contemporary South Asia* 6(2): 141–160, p.153.

of the 1950s.[4] At least initially this came as a welcome diversion from the more challenging and intractable problem of how to plan Karachi to make it more functional as a city. Choosing architectural styles was both exciting and accessible to the non-expert generalists that still dominated the ranks of the highest civil servants, and unlike a master plan that may never work, official architecture offered tangible results within foreseeable time frames. Just as the MRVP 'plan' disappeared in the morass of artful bureaucratic inactivity, the minds of senior civil servants got excited by the question of what a future Pakistani parliament building or presidential palace should look like.

There was an early agreement that the designs would have to somehow represent the aspirations of the nation: that is that they had to be at once 'modern' and 'Islamic'. What this should mean in practice was much harder to determine, however. Increasingly the 'modern' was thought to be automatically taken care of by hiring a famous architect with a European or American background, who would then be asked to make suitable allowances for the 'Muslim spirit' in his proposals. This formula attracted a handful of interested bidders, but never the big names the Pakistani administration had hoped for. The earliest proposals were by has-beens with a conservative stylistic preference. One was the German-born, Old India hand K. Heinz, who had previously designed the United Provinces Assembly building in Lucknow in oriental art deco; another was the Spaniard Jose Maria Muguruza Otaño, a less well-known member of a Francoist family of architects who had acquired some local fame for bringing together traditional elements with modern functionality. When these proposals were passed to Cabinet for a decision, a heated debate ensued among senior bureaucrats over what precisely constituted an appropriate Islamic style for Pakistan, and how this style could be made to look both modern and suitably impressive. Armed with the generalist's knowledge of Islamic history and supplemented with travel impressions and the perusal of coffee table books, these men would confidently propose their own ideas about the necessity of domes, minarets or arches that the invited foreign architects found hard to satisfy.[5] Too often in this debate it was much easier to voice criticism of what had been proposed than to have a clear idea of what was wanted instead, to the point that Secretary G. Mueenuddin (who already made an appearance earlier in this book) actually suggested dropping the

---

[4] Daechsel, M. (2014), 'Islam and development in urban space: planning "official" Karachi in the 1950s', *The city in South Asia*, C. Bates and M. Mio (eds.), London; New York, Routledge.
[5] Ibid. section 2.

Islamic element altogether and focusing exclusively on the modern aspect of state architecture. In the end the matter proved so hard to resolve that no commissions were ever made, while a haphazard commissioning process rumbled on in the background.[6]

Having got lost somewhat in the political dramas of 1957 and 1958, this debate resurfaced almost immediately with Ayub's announcement of the building of a new capital in the north of the country. The fact that this was to be an entirely planned city provided undreamt of scope for all kinds of new suggestions. Not only would the new settlement have to be named, but also everything from its city layout to the design of important buildings was now, at least in theory, a potential marker of what Islam should mean to the people of Pakistan. The custodians of religious righteousness got their interventions in early, in some cases even before Ayub and Yahya chose the suitably vague but nevertheless programmatic name 'Islamabad' in spring 1960.[7] A letter written in October 1959 by one Bakhteyar Husain, an American-educated planner and resident of Jinnah Avenue, Dacca, to Yahya Khan as chairman of the FCC, deserves to be quoted in full:

Dear Sir,
   In designing the layout of the Capital of Pakistan, I hope you will follow a very distinctly Muslim idea. Where no other dominant factor determines the layout of main roads and streets, keep them oriented in the direction of the Holy Ka'ba [sic] or transversely. This would facilitate doing 'Namaz' in any building and would obviate the misfitting appearance of Mosques in any area. Where a mosque is inserted between buildings oriented in other directions, it has to be distorted in various ways to be fitted between the other buildings. We find examples of this all over the world. I hope that this appearance of religion being a misfit in our worldly activities, can be avoided in a town visualized by Muslims and intended to serve the idealised requirements of a dominantly Muslim population. I would appreciate if I could be informed that you have received this letter.
   Yours faithfully
   sgd. B.Husain[8]

A similar request to make the *qibla* (direction of prayer) the main reference point of Islamabad's orientation was also put forward in another letter, dated slightly later and signed by one Raza Ali, 'Bahadur OBE', a retired army captain from Nowshehra in West Pakistan. Writing in the immediately recognizable idiom of the 'native' colonial officer, he

[6] NDC: Cabinet Papers, File 385/CF/48 Land Control – Capital of the Federation, Minutes of the Cabinet Meeting 23 July 1952.
[7] CADA: Pakistan Volume 73, Correspondence, File C-PR 388, Yakas to DA, 8 March 1960. Nilsson, S. (1973), *New capitals of India, Pakistan and Bangladesh*, Lund, Studentlitteratur, p.147.
[8] CADA: Pakistan Volume 72, Correspondence Nov–Dec 1959, Husain to Major General Yahya Khan, 16 October 1959.

concluded his message with the following exclamation: 'I have been praying and pray now most heartily that Islamabad, by Grace of God Almighty, be the Islamabad for the muslims [sic] in its true sense. May God help us all in the service in Islam – the peace on Earth.' [9] What was expressed in these letters was both an uncompromising endorsement of modernity – in the advocacy of strictly orderly and linear road alignments and the rejection of the chaotic mingling of alleyways so characteristic of historic Muslim cities – and a highly evocative urge to make Islam the all-determining direction of every activity of life. Whether or not it was practical or even sensible in terms of city planning, this was a clear expression of a reformist sense of piety that had become widespread in Pakistani middle-class circles at the time. Appearances of 'secularism', which are often unduly stressed in the historical literature and in personal memories of the Ayub era, were in fact misleading. There was a whole spectrum of opinions – from the political Islamism of Abul A°la Mawdudi to the liberal 'fundamentalism' of a Ghulam Ahmad Pervez – that all shared the diagnosis that the cultures and traditions of the past had become incapable of adequately expressing the essence of Islam, and that a renewed search for a perfect alignment of all aspects of life with the commandments of faith was necessary.[10]

The fact that copies of both letters found their way into the Doxiadis Archive in Athens suggests that the FCC took them seriously enough to pass them on to the chief consultant, perhaps even actively encouraging the petitioners. Doxiadis would have found opinions like these hard to stomach as they stood against everything he believed in as a planner, and against everything he was proposing for the Islamabad project. Although he was keenly aware that Islamabad would be a city of Muslims and had to cater to a distinctly Muslim way of life, Doxiadis vehemently believed that such matters could not be appropriately addressed in a city's layout plan. Urban planning was a technical matter and on no account an exercise in drawing symbolic images onto a map. This was the folly of 'ornamentalism' that he had so savagely criticized in New Delhi as well as in Brasilia, where Costa and Niemeyer created a city centre in the shape of a flying bird (or something resembling it).[11]

---

[9] CADA: Volume 74, Letter by Captain Raza Ali Bahadur, MBE (OBI) to Yahya Khan, 22 May 1960, attached to File O-PR 679.

[10] Gauhar, A. (1996), *Ayub Khan, Pakistan's first military ruler*, Oxford; New York, Oxford University Press, p.190. On Mawdudi's Islamism see Hartung, J.-P. (2014), *A system of life: Mawdūdī and the ideologisation of Islam*, New York, Oxford University Press.

[11] See Chapter 2, Footnote 43; CADA: emphasizing differences to the monumentalism of Chandigarh and Brasilia, see Pakistan Volume 239, Dox-PAK A 265, 5 April 1966, Considerations on some questions related to the development of Islamabad.

The direction of roads should be determined entirely by topography, climatic needs, growth projections, traffic flows and other practical considerations. The appropriate place to represent Islamic ideals in city planning, as Doxiadis saw it, lay to some extent in the choice of architectural styles, where he advocated a return to folk culture, but more importantly in the painstaking recognition of Islamic religious and cultural needs in the actual functionality of houses and neighbourhood centres. Planning a Muslim city meant providing mosques, covered markets, tea houses and communal bathhouses for its residents and facilitating the easy observance of the norms of purdah and of a conservative family life.

Towards an urbanism of development

When the Greek planner added his voice to ongoing debates about an urban modernity for Pakistan, he had to position himself strategically against at least two kinds of others. He had to be more convincing than the list of foreign consultants that had gone before or were working contemporaneously with him, but who had by and large failed to offer winning solutions. Apart from conservatives like Heinz and Muguruza, it included planners with a stronger vision of an urban modernity but little awareness of local cultural, political or religious traditions, like the men from MRVP or Minoprio and Le Corbusier. Then there was Pakistan's political class that had strong opinions on how their new national identity should be represented in buildings and cityscapes. Even if their ideas were often contradictory and ill-attuned to new departures in urban theory, they felt that they as the new elite of a post-colonial country were the ultimate custodians of collective aesthetic values, and what they appreciated most easily were spectacular or monumental pieces of architecture. While some emerging home-grown architects like Zaheer ud-Din Khwaja, Mehdi Ali Mirza or Muzharul Islam articulated an enthusiastic espousal of modernist ideas from their usually subordinate positions within the state apparatus, the debate was dominated by bureaucrats and politicians with limited architectural knowledge, or by commercial architects who were still operating within an aesthetic framework shaped by colonial precedent. The question of how exactly such conflicting expectations could be resolved presented the aspiring architect and planner with an ideological minefield, even a no-win situation, as countless examples from then and subsequent decades have proven time and again.[12]

---

[12] See Mumtaz, K. K. (1999), *Modernity and tradition: contemporary architecture in Pakistan*, Oxford; New York, Oxford University Press, pp.28–39, 55–62.

In line with his track record as a consultant to the Planning Commission, Doxiadis chose to base his pitch for pre-eminence in the field of Pakistani urbanism on his expertise in the field of development, rather than on his ability to handle complex stylistic solutions to Pakistan's identity problems. This was of course precisely *not* the natural preference of the Pakistani elite, but had other advantages. Doxiadis could enlist backing from funding bodies like the Ford Foundation or the American ICA, which he knew his Pakistani hosts would find irresistible, and he could use the growing authority and public acceptance of development discourse to sideline the emotionally charged debates about Islam and modernity that forever plagued his rivals. But this outflanking manoeuvre was not without its own problems. Even when he sought to shift the terms of debate into a different direction, Doxiadis had to have something to say about what his clients found most pressing or relevant. He had to argue the case for development in such a way as to also incorporate the question of Pakistan's national identity in a convincing manner; he had to somehow overcome the inherent tendency of development discourse to 'flatten' the specific identities of its subject countries. Driven by the strategic deployment of ideas in line with his commercial objectives, and by some implicit assumptions of his trademark Ekistics methodology, Doxiadis arrived at two conceptual ploys that he hoped would allow him to square the circle of being at once a developmental and post-colonial urbanist: the identification of folk culture as the premier site of cultural authenticity, and the refocusing of attention on the architecture and cityscape of the everyday rather than on monumental spaces of state. This theoretical redirection deserves to be discussed in some detail as it was to have a profound impact on the actual shape of Doxiadis's proposals for Korangi and Islamabad.

In order to reconstruct how Doxiadis argued his case, it is once again useful to return to the very beginning of his mission to Pakistan and career as a development consultant in general, his field diaries of the mid 1950s. As pointed out at some length in Chapter 2, Doxiadis had developed his own trademark methodology, his characteristic expert 'gaze' in his diaries, which allowed him to arrive at far-reaching conclusions about the social, political or cultural needs of his target populations on the basis of moments of inspired contemplation. Let us begin our exposition with one of these moments, which presented the problem of a national urban modernity for Pakistan in a highly evocative image that chimed with established perceptions of both Pakistani policy makers and potential funding organizations in the West. Doxiadis, as always speaking in the present tense and in the first person, describes a walk at the very end of his tour, taking him through Peshawar, the last of West Pakistan's main cities on his itinerary. He spots an old landmark:

It is the old Victoria monument but the statue of Victoria is not there any more. It has been taken away since Partition ... Is it not symbolic of the situation we have to face? Has not Pakistan reached the moment at which it has over-thrown [sic] the old symbols but has not yet created the new ones? ... Has not Pakistan reached the moment when it has to abandon the old type models of its towns and villages and replace them with something new? Something though which has not yet been created?[13]

The question of how to find an appropriate symbol of national aspiration was precisely where the Pakistani Cabinet and architectural juries or commissions entrusted with the rebuilding of the capital Karachi would have started as well; but Doxiadis turns into a new direction. The monument is literally empty, and instead of thinking about what should replace the now missing statue of Queen Victoria, Doxiadis is happy to leave the monument empty. It is now new 'models of towns and villages', not any monument or building, where a radically new symbolic representation of the national genius should be sought.

He had carefully prepared the ground for this shift throughout the diary. Another significant passage occurs weeks earlier in terms of narrative when he is still in East Pakistan, and has just left the port city of Chittagong and boarded a launch of the irrigation department to continue his fact-finding tour up the Karnaphuli River. As always, when he is not actually surveying his surroundings, Doxiadis begins to ruminate about some of the deeper problems of the development encounter. We read:

Looking at Chittagong from the river, from a certain distance, I can see more clearly the general picture of my problem than half an hour earlier when I was crossing the crowded streets of the city or visiting with the town-planners. I close my eyes and see even more clearly the human element of this city. Are these people urban dwellers? Have the people whom I met yesterday in Narayanganz [Narayanganj, a new industrial town south of Dacca] been urban dwellers? They certainly do not look so; but if they are not urban dwellers why should we build urban centres for them? ... There are certainly no urban dwellers yet in these areas but urban centres are under formation. Pakistan, East Pakistan, or any such big area cannot any more live without urban centres of major order and Chittagong, Narayangaz [sic] and several other settlements will become *from one moment to the other* urban. [But] it will ... take *a generation or two* to create *a different type of persons* who will grow into urban dwellers.[14]

Doxiadis creates the ordinary Pakistani city dweller and the city more generally as developmental subjects here. The problem is not, as most

---

[13] CADA: Pakistan Volume 2, Diary, p.301.   [14] CADA: ibid. p.88.

other planners would have approached it, that Pakistan is in need of modernizing its cities. Cities were for Doxiadis a new *social* form *that did not yet exist* in Pakistan. Chittagong, he noted, 'gives the impression of an old town without any urban tradition at all'.[15] Real cities could only be created, from scratch and through development, in the future. But once brought into being, these cities would be the ultimate representations of modernity, simply because they existed at all.

This shift from monument to city, and from architecture to planning, gave Doxiadis the means to escape the kind of debates that had bogged down his rivals. He argued:

I think it will be unreasonable to try and build right from the beginning houses and buildings corresponding to types of persons who have not yet been created ... It looks difficult to solve this problem but it is not ... Let us build the city in the proper way but let us not commit huge amounts of money for types of buildings for which their inhabitants are not yet ripe ... Let us make a basic distinction between city and buildings, create the *city of the future* and the *buildings of the present*.[16]

In short, the greatest monument to modernity is *the city as a whole*, and not any of its buildings. While it was imperative to get the planning issues right – after all they would determine people's lifeworlds for centuries to come – matters of architecture could be approached with a great deal more pragmatism and less symbolic charge. The heated debates about the right kind of architectural language for a Muslim modernity in Pakistan had got their priorities wrong. In reality it was neither possible nor desirable to find more than temporary solutions to what shape the buildings of the present should take. Cities were growing and new cities had to be created because more people than ever were leaving their rural surroundings in search of a new urban life. This led to the problem of 'the lack of the right type of urban dwellers', and anxieties over whether it would be possible 'to precipitate the formation of a new type of urban dweller by creating new types of urban neighbourhoods'.[17] Until the not-yet city dwellers of today had finally become proper city dwellers in future generations, there was no point in seeking permanent architectural solutions. Doxiadis's methodology was designed to make it possible to go back to the safety of tradition while simultaneously embracing the future – a move that led Doxiadis into a mystical embrace with who he saw as the 'real people' of Pakistan.

---

[15] CADA: Pakistan Volume 2, Diary, p.86.   [16] Ibid. p.88, emphasis added.
[17] CADA: Pakistan Volume 4, Dox 40, Pakistan Diary 20 January–24 February 1955, p.11.

The discovery of folk culture

Even in Doxiadis's 'city of the future' which was defined by planning rather than architecture, stylistic decisions and questions about architectural symbolism still mattered. After all, how should the process of developing 'proper' cities and 'mature' city dwellers actually be conceived? The first aspect – creating proper cities – involved difficult long-term decisions and was best left to the expert planner. But the second – the formation of mature city dwellers – involved a two-way interaction between expert and developmental subject, with the aim of an internal transformation of the latter. The not-yet city dweller was expected to gradually gain experience of what living in a modern city was all about, and to develop a new urban identity in due course. The shaping of his or her own living spaces in terms of architecture and style was a crucial aspect of this learning process, and here the planner was not to be prescriptive but pedagogic. Just like the young tree seedling protected by an old oil drum that Doxiadis saw when driving through a shanty town hours after landing in Karachi for the first time, local initiative had to be guided and protected not smothered by outside impositions.[18] Finding the right way for Islam and modernity to come together in urban space required a coming together of the consultant and 'his' people in some form of interchange. They had to enter into an architectural conversation in which the consultant used his observation of local practices to produce exemplary buildings, which in turn could then be adopted back into local practice and developed further.

More often than not, this interaction did not involve any actual encounter between the two sides, but instead happened entirely inside the mind of the planner. The strategic privileging of folk culture had to be combined with an ability to deduce, almost on the spot, what the essence of this folk culture was, in order to translate observations into concrete plans and design proposals that could be used in major commissions like Korangi and Islamabad. What Doxiadis 'saw' on his tours did not always produce results that were easy to sell to his Pakistani patrons, however. Nowhere was such a disconnect more pronounced than when making sense of Pakistan's Bengali-speaking Eastern Wing, where Doxiadis discovery of folk culture led him to a wholesale rejection of almost all existing architecture – be it of Sultanate, Mughal, British, West Pakistani, modernist East Pakistani or post-war developmentalist provenance. It was all against the genius of the Bengali people, as he

---

[18] CADA: Pakistan Volume 2, Diary, p.2 [3].

imagined it to be in his trademark reflections. A sense of almost biologistic environmental determinism predominated. Doxiadis wrote: 'Darkness falls on the river and we enter into the heavy mist. It is at that time that being unable to look even at a distance of a few feet, I can see the whole of Bengal, this vast alluvial plain consisting of soft soil, the surface of which is continuously changing under the influence of the everything-controlling factor: the water.'[19] Bengal thus emerges as a location where any conventional planner and architect would run into severe difficulties, because the very notion of architecture itself had no place in such a fluid environment. No wonder, as Doxiadis goes on to say, that Rabindranath Tagore could feel no emotion when contemplating the great Parthenon in Athens. For the great Bengali poet and philosopher, any attempt to build for eternity was a cruel waste of human labour.[20] There was no place for monumental architecture of any kind in this part of Pakistan.

Doxiadis's discovery of folk culture – strategically convenient as it was to make sense of his position as a consultant at the time – was also politically explosive. It implicitly attacked the very notion that the power and majesty of the Pakistani state could or even should be architecturally represented in a central location, and argued for local or at least regional solutions instead. There was a supreme irony in the fact the future father of Islamabad included the following recommendation in one of his first extensive documents submitted to the Pakistan Planning Commission:

These problems [creating the right kind of built environment] differ as much as bamboo huts of East Bengal differ from the mud fortresses of the Afghans and as much as the clay huts of the big deserts differ from the modern buildings of Karachi or Lahore. *Ekistics phenomena are related to the land and the people* and therefore they vary from place to place as much as *the plants or the animal life*. Whilst we need an overall ekistics program based on a general conception of the country's ekistic problems we do need solutions related to local factors. The conception must be national but the solutions of the above problems should be locally bound.[21]

Doxiadis's priorities were entirely different from those of the Pakistani leadership for whom he worked. The problem went much deeper than the simple insistence on regional specificity and the rejection of 'national' solutions that is directly articulated here. The epistemological building blocks of Ekistics themselves, its unspoken premises and assumptions, already put Doxiadis on a different track from his Pakistani hosts. The first reference point of his methodology is '*the land and the people*',

---

[19] Ibid. p.100.   [20] Ibid. p.101.
[21] CADA: Pakistan Volume 3, Report Dox 21, Pakistan Ekistics p.11, emphasis added.

conceived as environmentally conditioned dwellers of the soil like 'plants and animals'. These were pre-political, even pre-social categories. Urban planning and architecture, as conceived within this discursive framework, was not about the representation of particular ideals of power or religion, or indeed any other primarily aesthetic purpose. Like development in general, it was targeted at what Foucault called a 'population' (we will return to this matter in Chapter 6). Its recipients were human beings in their most pared-back aspects, bodies in need of shelter, health and sufficient nutrition.

What is missing here is precisely what Doxiadis's Pakistani hosts found most important: the state. Pakistan, it needs emphasizing, was first and foremost created as a state, even if its supporters were initially not entirely clear about what this meant beyond a lasting feeling of empowerment.[22] There simply was no Pakistani 'people' that could in any way be assumed to pre-exist their constitution as a political nation and their will to statehood. Without the state of Pakistan demanding and receiving their loyalty, the people occupying its territory would simply be part of the vast array of ethnic and religious groupings that made up the historic region of India. Nothing bears this out better than the great waves of population transfer that accompanied Partition: Muslim residents of Delhi became Pakistani not by any objective ethnic criteria, not even their religion, but simply because they chose to be Pakistanis and made the trek across the new frontier to their promised land. Meanwhile, a Sikh or Hindu who had for centuries been part of the 'land and the people' of what was now Pakistan, became Indian because the Pakistani nation refused to accept them as being one of their own. In short, the Pakistani state was not the executive organ imposing order on an already constituted people; it was what established this people as a people in the first place.

Doxiadis did not accidentally miss this crucial element of Pakistani political identity in his visions; he was explicit in his rejection of it, even when he attempted to flatter his hosts with perfectly judged historical references. In 'Pakistan Ekistics' – that 350-page-plus programmatic statement addressed directly at the Pakistani bureaucratic establishment – we read:

at present Pakistan is proceeding to the creation of new conditions in Settlements with a courage and at a scale which reminds us of the creators of Fatehpur Sikri ... There is a difference though between these two tasks, because, whilst the target of the great Moghuls was much more limited and very *egocentric* the task and the obligation of the present generation are much greater in scale and much

[22] Daechsel, M. (2006), *The politics of self-expression: the Urdu middle-class milieu in mid-twentieth century India and Pakistan*, London; New York, Routledge, pp.75–81.

more wide. Unlike the great Moghuls who were only *empire builders* the present generation has to *serve crores of people* entering into a new phase of political, social and economic development and requiring social justice. Where a big architect could serve the vision of the great Moghuls, a big number of technically trained people is now necessary to face the new problems of this era. *Where architectural design was enough to serve the great Moghuls, science, technique and architecture; administration and legislation are now necessary* to meet the present colossal tasks.[23]

The grandeur of Mughal architecture, exemplified by the act of founding new cities and settlements like Akbar's capital Fatehpur Sikri, was of course precisely what was upmost in the mind of Pakistani policy makers when they embarked on their quest for a Muslim capital fit for the future. Creating a new capital city like Islamabad, or in the pre-Ayub era, a 'New Karachi' of some form or other, stood in a long tradition of state building, epitomized not only by the Mughal capitals but also by New Delhi, which was nothing less than a British attempt to create their own Fatehpur Sikri for their imperial ambitions. For Doxiadis, in contrast, the age for imperial architecture – for the 'egocentric' pursuit of creating great monumental buildings as an adoration of the state – was over. For him the state was no more than a sum of its functions, and these functions were no longer primarily aesthetic or political, as in the era of the 'big architect', but collective and scientific: matters for all sorts of depoliticized, agentless and self-validating discourses, to use Foucauldian language once again.

Doxiadis's espousal of folk architecture was theoretically grounded and part of a consistent developmental worldview. Although a testimony to great cultural accomplishments, Mughal architecture was in the final analysis as unsuited for Pakistan's needs as the British colonial architecture and later Western imports for which Doxiadis reserved his most savage criticism. While he made this point most strongly about Bengal, the overall logic of his argument suggests that he perceived all major examples of state architecture in the region as ultimately alien to its people. The time had come to no longer produce architecture that monumentalized political power, but for 'creating monumental expressions of the people themselves'.[24]

Doxiadis subscribed to the widespread if scholarly discredited narrative of successive invasions shaping the history of South Asia: in his reading, first the Aryans, followed by the Persians, Greeks, Central Asian Muslims and then the British[25] (given that he received a lot of his

---

[23] CADA: Pakistan Volume 3, Report Dox 21, Pakistan Ekistics, pp.8–9, emphasis added.
[24] CADA: Pakistan Volume 4, File Dox 4, p.21.
[25] CADA: Pakistan Volume 2, Diary, p.144.

knowledge from second-rate orientalists, as described in Chapter 2, this is hardly surprising). This vision of history meant that there was a clear distinction between some ancient substratum of 'real' South Asians that had never found their political voice, and subsequent waves of alien states and cultures imposed by foreigners. Freedom for the people of South Asia could only mean a break with the architectural styles of these outsiders, a turn towards something radically new and home grown. Looking around him, as Doxiadis pointed out in a landmark essay on the architectural style for a future Islamabad, there was nothing in the existing monumental architecture of India or the Middle East that could serve as a precedent. The 'only healthy elements are ... where the people have built their own simple houses, mainly in the rural areas, have not been subjected to any outside influence, and influence based on alien patterns, and influence which could not in any way appeal to them'.[26]

The question emerges of how Doxiadis could ever find any takers for this radical anti-statist stance, and for an aesthetic preference that was so deeply out of step with public opinion in Pakistan. Part of the answer is that he never did, and we will see his persistent problems when we follow the story of how his trademark projects were actually implemented. But two of his discursive strategies to make his suggestions more palatable to the Pakistani generals nevertheless deserve scrutiny as they also directly influenced some of his designs. The first, and arguably less profound, was to pay at least lip service to the prevailing nostalgia for Muslim imperial greatness without conceding too much in substance. Doxiadis understood only too well how close the emotional connection between Fatehpur Sikri and Islamabad was for his hosts and accordingly included copious references to the Mughals in his official plans and brochures. At one point he even quoted an almost page-length extract from Abu-l Fazl's *Ain-e Akbari*, a famous Persian treatise on Mughal statecraft, in order to produce a compelling historical 'narrative' which the Pakistani leadership could feed back to educated public opinion as and when required.[27] On other occasions Doxiadis made references to 'Memar Khan' (or 'Khan Mamur') as the great Mughal architect the new Pakistani regime should be proud to emulate, and on yet other occasions, his descriptions of the genius of Muslim architecture seemed at the surface to go quite far

---

[26] CDA Library, Islamabad: Dox-PA 99 (21 January 1961), Volume 39, 'Islamabad: on architecture in Islamabad', p.32.
[27] CADA: Pakistan Volume 16, Pakistan Reports May–December 1959, p.133, other examples elsewhere.

towards endorsing a Mughal stylistic vocabulary, only to reveal their superficiality at the last moment.[28]

More interesting and directly influential for what Doxiadis actually built was another discursive strategy that in its sheer whimsicality provides a unique insight into what the man was all about: his discovery of a *classical Mediterranean* ethos in the Pakistani folk culture that he made the baseline for his architectural recommendations. What is more, he attached a specific sense of being Muslim to this classical sensibility. In the end, it was not only the universalizing power of development that gave the consultant a direct rapport with his subjects, far-fetched as it may seem, there was also a claim to a fundamental and ancient ethnic connection. Alongside all of his other selling points, Doxiadis managed to enlist a feature that none of his challengers could take away from him: his being Greek. At the end of the day, he was not a Western expert like any other; he remained an outsider, for sure, and within the logic of his methodology that was not necessarily a disqualification as it made him better able to perceive what Pakistan needed than many of its home-grown experts. But he was no longer as much of an outsider as the Americans and Frenchmen he was going to trump. He and the Pakistani generals were all branches of the same ancient tree of a shared civilization. It was hardly coincidental that the Greek-ness that Doxiadis discovered in Pakistan was most clearly visible to him in the foothills of the Himalayas. This was, of course, where Islamabad was about to be built, but it was also the area from where the most powerful patron and creator of the city, General Ayub Khan himself, traced his origins. In Doxiadis's vision, the general and the consultant became no less than two descendants of Alexander the Great joined for a great purpose.

Greeks of the Himalayan foothills

Doxiadis's discovery of 'classical' features in West Pakistani folk culture (the East had already revealed itself to be radically different when Tagore failed to appreciate the Acropolis) is traceable to his first Pakistan diary, but emerged in ever more clearly developed forms as his career advanced towards the Islamabad project. En route from Lahore to Lyallpur on his very first trip back in autumn of 1954, Doxiadis was taken to several central Punjabi villages, which he photographed extensively and where he

---

[28] CADA: Pakistan Volume 14, File Dox-PKK 1, 18 December 1958. For his (spurious) argument that Islamic art was 'geometric' and that a city founded on a gridiron pattern was therefore 'Islamic', see CDA Library, Islamabad: File Dox-PA 88 Volume 32–2 Islamabad, Programme and Plan, p.254.

Figure 14 Doxiadis's survey party inspects a mud construction in central Punjab that shows the 'clean lines' and 'functionality' that Doxiadis approximated to the 'classical'. Note the awkward encounter between villagers and bureaucrats incidentally captured in Doxiadis's own photograph here.
Source: CADA: Pakistan vol.2, Diary DOX-PP 20, Oct.–Nov. 1954, p.243 (Archive Files 23554).

had an opportunity to closely survey local houses both externally and internally. [See Figure 14] As so often with folk architecture, Doxiadis was impressed by the craftsmanship and stylistic sophistication he observed, but also felt that what he saw here was better than anything encountered previously on his tour of the East and the South: 'This is one of the few areas where architectural forms are so *clean*, in many cases they remind of *Mediterranean* architecture although materials are completely different', he noted enthusiastically in his diary, establishing a first and tentative connection between quality, simplicity and Southern European heritage that he would develop into some kind of Pakistani folk nationalism later on.[29]

Five years later in 1959 – Ayub Khan had in the meantime taken over as Chief Martial Law administrator and Doxiadis had been commissioned

[29] CADA: Pakistan Volume 2, Diary, p.241, emphasis added.

as chief consultant to the Islamabad project – references to similarities with ancient Greece reappeared in a much more developed form. When surveying the site chosen for the new capital at the feet of the Margalla Hills north of Rawalpindi, Doxiadis commented extensively on similarities between the local architecture and that of the ancient Greeks. He had now progressed from vague Mediterranean resemblances to a precise historical and geographic identification that left him ruminating about influences left by Alexander the Great's great Eastern campaign 2300 years earlier.[30] Doxiadis placed considerable emphasis on the importance of local historical precedent when situating the project both ideologically and theoretically. Of particular relevance and an endless source of fascination was the fact that the Islamabad site was only a little more than 10 miles away from the ancient city of Taxila, one of the centres of the Gandhara civilization that combined Greek stylistic elements with Buddhism, and also one of the very few places in South Asia where an ancient Greek temple had been excavated.[31]

This connection clearly touched Doxiadis at a personal level. He had after all gained his doctorate with a dissertation on city planning among the ancient Greeks, which included the foundation of new colony cities around the Aegean Sea,[32] and here he was, founding a new *polis* himself, as it were, at the furthest reaches of the Greek civilizational orbit. When commenting on landscape features on the Islamabad site, what came most quickly to Doxiadis's mind were similarities with the landscape of Athens.[33] Islamabad was not the only place where the Gandhara/Greek heritage was invoked, however. While also containing somewhat disconnected photographs of landmark Mughal buildings, a brochure introducing the new campus for Punjab University in Lahore depicted

---

[30] CADA: Pakistan Volume 13, Diary 99, 2 October to 11 October 1959, p.181.

[31] CADA: Pakistan Volume 16, File Dox-PA 33, p.169. For a classic account of the ruins and historical background see Marshall, J. H. S. (1921), *A guide to Taxila*, Calcutta, Superintendent Government Printing.

[32] See Doxiadis, C. A. (1972), *Architectural space in ancient Greece*. Translation of the author's thesis, prepared at the Berlin Charlottenburg Technische Hochschule and published in 1937 under title Raumordnung im griechischen Städtebau.

[33] CADA: Pakistan Volume 41, Diary PA 100, Pakistan Diary from 7 to 16 February 1960, p.88. This connection is also recognized more generally by Ahmed Zaib Khan Mahsud, who said of Islamabad: 'Doxiadis attempted to give the city symbolic character based on a combination/fusion of Greek acropolis, mediaeval landscape and Late Renaissance Palatial Formality, but at the same time adjusting the city pattern to the 20th century mode of mobility [the car] makes a hybrid plan but leaves the question of a specific national style for the symbolic representation of the state to be evolved, and which remains, unresolved.' Mahsud, A. Z. K. (2009), 'Extrovert synthesis in the design of Islamabad: Doxiadis's ambition for an evolutionary style of the new capital', *Ο Κωνσταντίνος Δοξιάδης και το Έργο του*, Athens, Τεχνικό Επιμελητήριο Ελλάδας, p.124.

Doxiadis's own outline plan immediately next to a similar-sized map of the Taxila excavation site, inviting the reader to draw the most relevant historical comparisons and parallels from this juxtaposition.[34] [See Figure 15] The most immediate connection that in all likelihood prompted this choice of illustration must have been the fact that Buddhist Taxila was also known as one of the first 'university' sites in South Asia. For Doxiadis, the oldest architectural layers were the most indicative of the spirit of a place, even if they completely exploded conventional Pakistani frames of reference by invoking a historical legacy unconnected to and occurring long before the emergence of Islam. A few years later, when dealing with the stylistic minutiae of the Islamabad project, Doxiadis suggested the use of a logo on manhole covers and bus shelters that went even further back, to the Indus Valley civilization of 3000 BC, because for him this was when the people of the region had first built a sophisticated water supply and sewerage system.[35]

Strange as this may seem, the invocation of ancient historical roots actually proved quite useful within the ideological context of post-colonial Pakistan. Drawing on his observations of what was now explicitly called the 'classical'[36] in Pakistani folk culture, Doxiadis pinpointed the space where the Greek connection fitted in with his wider ideas about the Muslim city of the future: 'In the countryside, where people have been building for long centuries, without any external cultural influences or by rejecting all alien elements and keeping only those which are akin to them and which they develop, the architecture is of a very high standard.'[37] This was what the city planner could use to take Pakistan forward into a new age of urbanization. From his other writings it was clear that the influences that were successfully absorbed by local folk culture referred to the ancient Greek and Islamic, and those rejected, not only to the British colonial but also to anything Indian and Hindu.[38] Doxiadis's path to defining what it meant to be Pakistani and Muslim involved the detour of first juxtaposing the architectural merits of the ancient Greeks to the perceived stylistic inadequacies of Hindu civilization. After describing the intricate decorations on the houses of the Hindu mercantile class which he encountered during a car excursion in lower Sind, for instance, Doxiadis felt compelled to comment:

[34] CADA: Asian Field Boxes, The University of the Punjab, The New Campus of the University of the Punjab, Inauguration Day brochure, 22 November 1963, back page.
[35] CADA: Pakistan Volume 194, File C-PI 5424.
[36] For instance CADA: Pakistan Volume 41, pp.2, 31, 88.
[37] CADA: Pakistan Volume 16, File Dox-PA 33, p.188.
[38] CDA Library, Islamabad: File Dox-PA 99 (26 January 1961), Volume 39, Islamabad: on architecture in Islamabad, pp.26–39.

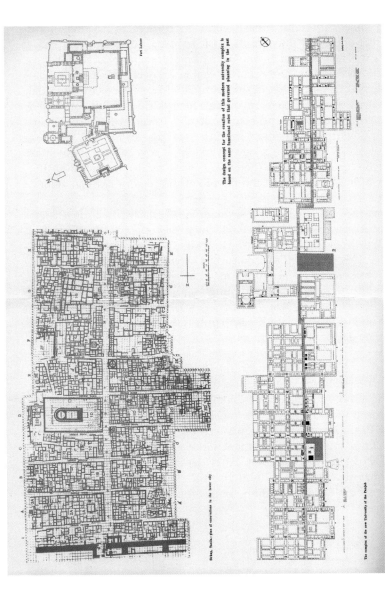

Figure 15 DA publicity material representing the historical inspirations for Doxiadis's new Punjab University campus, Lahore. Note the prominent position given to the ancient Buddhist 'university' of Taxila, located close to present-day Islamabad, while the addition of an 'Islamic' element with a footprint of Lahore Fort in the top right corner is almost incidental.

Source: CADA: *DA Monthly Bulletin* No. 56, July 1963.

The Greeks who were sailors and merchants of the world had neither such a type of decorations nor any similar type of architectural expression, but these here are the inhabitants of the jungle, initially the natural jungle and later the artificial and cultural one. They have created this artificial surrounding by mimicking subconsciously the jungle from which they initially came ... – the natural habitat of the Hindus.[39]

Similar references recurred through much of Doxiadis's oeuvre, whether it was a photograph of an over-decorated 'Hindu' door being disparagingly dismissed as *'l'art pour l'art'*, or balustrades and balconies on houses condemned for their flowery styles, all in line with Doxiadis's generally held antipathy to anything in city planning that was ornamental without being directly functional.

This detour to a Muslim folk essence via ancient Greece was a stroke of genius. Doxiadis managed to directly address the defining trait of Pakistani national identity – the juxtaposition between 'Hindu' and 'Muslim' – and to endow it with a notion of great historical depth and importance, as well as some direct connections to the non-Muslim consultant himself. More importantly, Doxiadis could now argue that the problem of Islam and modernity was not in effect as difficult as it had seemed to so many of his rivals, as at least in architectural terms there was a natural affinity between the clean lines and functionalism of modernism and the defining sensibility of Muslim folk art. In order to be truly modern – even outright modernist – the aspiring architect for Pakistan needed to search no further than in the country's villages and peasant homesteads. And if this was not enough, Doxiadis managed with great astuteness to tap into an ideological stream of Pakistani nationalism that was still somewhat subterranean at the time, but was to emerge with great strength in later decades: a glorification of the 'sons of the soil'.[40]

At first sight there was a problem. The valorization of folk culture that Doxiadis espoused was closest in political terms to a collection of groups and parties that were seen with particular suspicion by the Ayub Khan regime. They were ethnic nationalists from Bengal, Sind and the North West Frontier Province, for whom Pakistani identity was not simply a question of having a state that protected against Hindu perfidy, but one

---

[39] CADA: Pakistan Volume 7, Pakistan Reports and Diaries, Dox-PP 85–93, August 1955–November 1956. File Dox-PP 88, Diary of My Sixth Trip to Pakistan 21 February 1956–7 March 1956, p.98.

[40] For a classic formulation of the geographic nationalism of the people of the Indus, see Ahsan, A. (1996), *The Indus saga and the making of Pakistan*, Karachi, Oxford University Press.

that also possessed a certain positive substance in terms of regional language and cultural inheritance.[41] The problem with these formulations was that they often cut across religious boundaries: both Bengali and Sindi nationalists made it an explicit point to give equal recognition to Hindus and Muslims within their respective ethnic groups. In addition they excluded any easy accommodation of the millions of Muslim refugees from India, who were by definition not 'sons of the soil', but constituted one of the most politicized and at the time still state-loyal constituencies. And to make matters even worse, ethnic nationalism had a reputation for never having fully subscribed to the idea of Pakistan when it was first muted by Jinnah and the Muslim League, and for being clandestinely pro-Indian and pro-communist.

However, the antagonism between these ethnic nationalists and important sections of the Pakistani establishment concealed the fact that a different and pro-state 'son of the soil' position was gradually taking hold within official nationalism as well. It was more or less similar to opposition ethnic nationalism in its desire to give a strong regional cultural substance to what it meant to be Pakistani, but being 'official' it had to do so without any major backsliding into cross-communal harmony or 'secularism'. This was precisely what Doxiadis provided in his architectural visions: a folk culture that was as much locally rooted as it was anti-Hindu. It was only possible to locate such an identity in areas where anything Hindu could be easily dismissed as alien and different; this excluded Sind or Bengal, where the Hindu presence was clearly visible even in rural areas. But Doxiadis's vision worked relatively well in Punjab, from where almost all Hindus and Sikhs had been expelled at Partition, and particularly well in the northern regions where Hindus had rightly or wrongly been most closely associated with moneylending and petty trading – professions that were by definition more disconnected from the soil than farming. The only 'Hindu' spaces in this area were the cities. Rawalpindi, the urban area closest to Islamabad, for instance, had once been a Hindu-majority city, with countless temples that were still visible at Doxiadis's time. But this is precisely why Doxiadis's identification of the rural as the only legitimate resource of Pakistan's past and his condemnation of cities as urban 'jungle' was so helpful. In the final analysis, the rural folk of northern Punjab and the North West Frontier Province – not coincidentally the areas from where

---

[41] Ahmed, F. (1998), *Ethnicity and politics in Pakistan*, Karachi; Oxford, Oxford University Press; Rahman, T. and T. Knight (1998) *Language and politics in Pakistan*, Karachi; Oxford, Oxford University Press.

the vast majority of Pakistani army personnel were recruited – were the only group in Pakistan who could be sons of the soil, as well as indisputably and trustworthily anti-Hindu; they were, in short, the best of all possible Pakistanis.[42]

Doxiadis's self-imposed conundrum of finding a *locally grounded* representation of a *national* identity could finally be resolved, courtesy of Ayub Khan's decision to create a new capital city in the north.[43] Having been removed from the Hinduized 'jungle' of the south, and now relocated to the most authentically Pakistani region of all, the capital of the future could be built using local and popular artistic styles. By virtue of its 'classical' inheritance, the folk architecture of the Himalayan foothills was more appropriate than any other for the national 'monument of the people' Doxiadis wanted to create.

He now had at his disposal a narrative and a set of arguments that helped to justify a notion of the Muslim city of the future that was radically different from what the Pakistani political class was accustomed to. The harking back to folk culture meant that there was now no more need for 'domes, arches and minarets', even if most contemporary observers found this hard to accept. The Greek element in this narrative opened up a space to marry the local to the international. Its association with the functional and its rejection of 'Hindu' ornamentalism meant that the cheapest available building techniques and mass-produced concrete modules could now be presented as culturally grounded – after all they, too, had 'clean' lines, just like the mud buildings of central Punjab or the beam constructions of the north. And having become absorbed into the 'classical', any notion of a specifically Muslim architecture was in itself opened up to Muslim architectures elsewhere, to what Doxiadis or his colleagues had seen in Syria, Egypt and Iraq. Finally, the association of city planning with 'development', and its targeting of a population rather than a state, meant that actual construction of this city of the future could reverse the normal order of priorities: Islamabad was to find its first visible expression not in any assemblage of buildings of state, any capitol complex, but in exemplary living spaces for 'ordinary' Pakistanis. The *polis* for Pakistan came into existence as an abstracted, stylized and mass-produced version of the Muslim village.

---

[42] This point was explicitly made to justify shifting the capital from Karachi to Islamabad. CDA Library, Islamabad: File DA PA 88(30 September 1960), Programme and Plan, p.86.

[43] Mahsud, A. Z. K. (2009), 'Extrovert synthesis in the design of Islamabad: Doxiadis's ambition for an evolutionary style of the new capital', *Ο Κωνσταντίνος Δοξιάδης και το Έργο του*, Athens, Τεχνικό Επιμελητήριο Ελλάδας, p.109.

A (dyna-)polis for Pakistan

The first 'proper' neighbourhood to emerge on the Islamabad site in 1962 was a cluster of mass housing units for the lowest ranks of civil servants. They are still more or less intact today, in the south-westerly corner – or section 1 – of the area demarcated on Doxiadis's master plan as sector G6.[44] (The same numbering system still applies today; in terms of landmarks the area in question includes the Aabpara Market and is close to the Red Mosque that became a symbol of violent extremism during the events of 2007.) As every visitor to the city knows – and as every piece of academic writing on Islamabad would need to point out – Doxiadis had made the 'sector', or in Ekistics speech a 'community class IV', the basic 'modulus' or building block of his urban design.[45] The entire prospective city area of Islamabad was divided up into sectors, most strictly rectangular in shape and separated from adjoining sectors of exactly the same size by high-speed roads and green spaces. The letter and number code referred to the grid coordinates calculated from a reference point high above the Sufi Shrine of Bari Imam at the north-easternmost point of the site. While the sequence of letters roughly denoting a north to south axis was limited – upon reaching the letter 'I', Islamabad would collide with the existing town of Rawalpindi and would not be able to grow any further in this direction – the numbers denoting distance from zero point on the east to west axis, in contrast, could expand indefinitely, epitomizing Doxiadis's trademark idea of a city with unlimited mono-directional growth potential, or 'dynapolis' (see more below). [See Figure 16]

The roughly 10,000 inhabitants of a sector were to have at their disposal all the facilities that were normally required in everyday life: places to shop, worship, be educated or simply hang around for social intercourse and recreation. Only for work or extraordinary purposes would the residents of a sector have to venture further afield into the city at large (a community class V). Although the sector was the most significant order of planning, it was not the smallest or most basic. Doxiadis's overall logic was to start with rows of individual housing units

---

[44] See CDA Library, Islamabad: File Dox-PA 97 (26 February 1961), Islamabad: Community Buildings for Sector G6, Volume 41; Dox-PA 96 (15 January 1961), Islamabad: Communities and houses for Sector G6, Volume 38.
[45] As elaborated theoretically in Doxiadis, C. A. (1968c), *Ekistics: an introduction to the science of human settlements*, London, Hutchinson, pp.354–380. On Islamabad see Doxiadis, C. A. (1965), 'Islamabad: the creation of a new capital', *The Town Planning Review* **36** (1): 1–28.

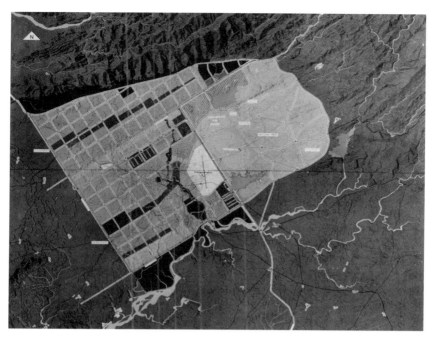

Figure 16 Model projection of the Islamabad Master Plan based on
Doxiadis's 'dynapolis' concept. Note the three distinct areas of the
proposed metropolitan area: the new capital 'proper', roughly
triangular in shape to the south of the Margalla Hills (with a central belt
of green areas running parallel to the hillside and Islamabad main
avenues), the Capital Park area to the north-east of the Rawalpindi–
Islamabad highway (demarcating the southern end of Islamabad proper
at zero point), and an expanding Rawalpindi (with its old town and
cantonment areas clearly visible) to the south-west. Although this was
never strictly implemented, Doxiadis conceived of Islamabad as a twin
conurbation in which Rawalpindi would also grow according to
dynapolis principles.
Source: CADA: Archive Files 17666.

(a community class I) which could then be clustered together to accommodate additional community facilities of an increasing order of importance. Several communities class I with a shared playground became a
community class II, for instance, while several 'communities class II'
were grouped together with some basic shops, a primary school, a
mosque and other facilities to form a 'community class III' or
subsector. Usually four of these subsectors then made up the sector,
which in addition to what was already provided at a lower order, also

Figure 17 Doxiadis's distinctive model of a hierarchy of communities.
Above a trademark sector (G6) consisting of four residential subsectors
(each with basic community facilities) and shared facilities of a higher
order (secondary schools, markets, etc.) at a central location along a
ravine.
Source: CADA: Model of a community class sector G6 (Archive
Files 17666).

offered a central shopping complex, and further schools and recreation
facilities like cinemas, hotels or restaurants. [See Figures 17 and 18]

The stated rationale for this modular structure was to keep much of
everyday life in as safe and intimate spaces as possible. While major road
traffic was banished to the outside of the sector, most facilities inside it
could be reached on foot, and as far as places most often frequented by

Figure 18 A residential street in one of the subsectors with some surviving low-cost housing designed by Doxiadis during the first phase of Islamabad's creation.
Source: author's own photograph, autumn 2007.

women, children or the elderly were concerned – playgrounds, primary schools, mosques or local shops – without having to cross any vehicular roads at all. Apart from protecting the 'human scale' against the dangerous intrusions of the motor car, which Doxiadis always highlighted as his trademark contribution to urbanism, this modular design was also ideally suited to achieving rapid visual results. Thanks to Doxiadis's planning, settlement could commence in Islamabad as soon as a community class III was complete. This required not much more than the provision of sewerage and water, some concrete shells for shops and some hundreds of simple mass-produced housing units which, as the Korangi project had already shown, could be assembled in a matter of months. Although life in such a new urban neighbourhood was still somewhat improvised, those with little money to spend could persist with community III facilities alone, and by the time a whole sector or community class IV was complete, even the more sophisticated needs of daily life were taken care of.

Islamabad could be declared 'open' while most of its proposed urban area was still virgin land, and before complex decisions about the design of more extraordinary buildings, for instance a new capitol for Pakistan, had been made.[46] This was an important consideration for a military regime that used urban projects of this kind to represent its developmental credentials to the wider world. To signal determination, government departments were shifted from Karachi into temporary accommodation in Rawalpindi next to the Islamabad site almost immediately after the decision to create a new capital was taken. This meant that government employees and bureaucrats could live in Islamabad even before they were able to work there. This was not a prospect many people cherished at the time, precisely because facilities were still poor and traffic connections only perfunctory. It is no coincidence that the settlement of Islamabad started with the poorest of its residents – who ironically were to influence the overall character of the city the least in the long term. They were quite simply the group easiest to force to relocate, as their entire life depended on the provision of government quarters. As far as a common moment of compulsion was concerned, and also by virtue of its first target demographic, Islamabad was not altogether different from Doxiadis's other major urban rehabilitation project, Korangi. It was little surprise that the first buildings also looked very similar. [See Figure 19]

The idea of a modular hierarchy of communities betrayed ideological choices that flowed directly from Doxiadis's developmental urbanism. Even though it was to be Pakistan's capital city, Islamabad was assembled not top-down but bottom-up. Political factors were of course behind the decision to build a new capital city, and also behind the selection of a suitable site (although one of Doxiadis's tasks as chief consultant was to couch the regime's decision into an ostensibly 'scientific' and politics-free jargon of climatic and geographic necessities). But Doxiadis's principles of urban design did not flow from questions of political and cultural representation as had been so clearly the case with the MRVP Plan for Karachi, with its vision of the giant central square as a battleground of ideological tensions.[47] Doxiadis's basic frame of reference was and remained 'population'. His entire theorizing rested on a categorization of human needs, starting off with the most basic – shelter, nutrition and procreation – which were accommodated in Doxiadis's basic unit of

[46] CDA Library, Islamabad: Dox-PA 74 (2 February 1960), Volume 24, First Notions of the development of the federal Capital area, p.34.
[47] Daechsel, M. (2014), 'Islam and development in urban space: planning "official" Karachi in the 1950s', *The city in South Asia*, C. Bates and M. Mio (eds.), London; New York, Routledge.

Figure 19 Doxiadis's design for the cheapest housing units in
Korangi. Note the distinctive rooftop windcatchers that were
omitted when a similar design was used in Islamabad.
(See Figure 18.)
Source: CADA: Photograph No. 30788.

analysis, the individual housing unit or 'shell'. Only in the second
instance would the analysis proceed from the biological to the social
and cultural and, if it ever got there at all, only in the third instance to
the political. Out of basic need grew a basic sense of sociability in the
neighbourhood, and out of the sector a sense that a fuller economic and
social life had been secured. The state was not needed as an overt
presence in this scheme even if had been the silent agency that prompted
the creation of a new city in the first place.

Doxiadis's emphases made Islamabad a subtly different kind of city
from its direct competitor across the Indian–Pakistan border: Chandigarh.
At the surface both projects had much in common. Pakistani policy maker
jealously admired Nehru's modernist achievement and often saw Islamabad as Pakistan's answer to Chandigarh.[48] There were conceptual

[48] Khwaja, Z. D. (1998), *Memoirs of an architect*, Lahore, distributed by Ferozsons
Publishers, p.84. Also CADA: Pakistan Volume 41, Diary PA 101, Pakistan Diary

similarities too. Like Islamabad, Chandigarh consisted of sectors
designed to keep fast-flowing motor traffic away from people's living
spaces, which Le Corbusier theorized as a hierarchy of roads (rather than
settlements) – the famous '7Vs'.[49] But in other respects the two projects
were strikingly different. Albert Mayer, author of Chandigarh's
first master plan before Le Corbusier's involvement, later admitted
that Chandigarh as a city was 'designed' rather than 'planned', in other
words, that physical planning took absolute precedence over social and
economic considerations, which the international team of experts largely
ignored.[50] For Doxiadis working in Islamabad, the reverse was true: he
was foremost a planner and only in the second instance a designer. It was
the very point about his Ekistics approach that physical planning must not
be separated from other aspects of planning.

The order of priority at Chandigarh was directly reflected in the hierarchy
of work: the most famous international architect, Le Corbusier himself
(also looking after some aspects of the overall plan), spent most of his
energy on iconic buildings of state, while the less glamorous tasks of
designing houses and public spaces fell to his less famous colleagues:
Maxwell Fry, Jane Drew and Pierre Jeanneret, Le Corbusier's cousin.[51]
As far as house design itself was concerned, the emphasis lay on expensive
high-quality homes for civil servants not mass housing. This, according to
Madhu Sarin, skewed the real estate market of the new city for decades to
come and was largely responsible for the proliferation of unplanned and
precarious living spaces for the poor.[52] Again, things were different in
Islamabad – even if the problem of unauthorized juggi (slum) settlements
did become a feature of Pakistan's capital in later decades.[53] The only
Doxiadis-designed structures to be built were, in fact, mass housing for
the poor, while the father of the city had little input into the design of iconic
buildings of state. This was not entirely intentional on Doxiadis's part (see
below). He did wish to design both Islamabad the capital and Islamabad's
capitol, but his professional trajectory and lifework left little doubt where his

from 24 to 31 October 1960; Pakistan Volume 239, File Dox-PAK A 265 5 April 1966,
Considerations on some questions related to the development of Islamabad.
[49] Sarin, M. (1977), 'c', The open hand: essays on Le Corbusier, R. Walden (ed.), Cambridge,
MA, MIT Press: 374–410, p.383.
[50] Evenson, N. (1966), Chandigarh, Berkeley, California University Press, p.10.
[51] See Fry, M. (1977), 'Le Corbusier at Chandigarh', The open hand: essays on Le Corbusier,
R. Walden (ed.), Cambridge, MA, MIT Press: 351–363; Jackson, I. and Bandyopadhya
(2009), 'Authorship and modernity in Chandigarh...', The Journal of Architecture 14(6).
[52] Sarin, M. (1982), Urban planning in the Third World: the Chandigarh experience, London,
Mansell.
[53] Hussain, D. (2014), 'Slum survey: over 80,000 people live in capital's katchi abadis says
report', The Express Tribune, Islamabad, 27 February.

emphasis lay. While Chandigarh was designed as a monumental city, Islamabad was first and foremost a functional space, and this formed part of a coherent vision of politics and governance. Chandigarh was testimony to the will and vision of the state as a sovereign agency; Islamabad – at least as it was originally envisioned by Doxiadis – stood for a social order to which the state was almost incidental.

Citizens without politics

Despite Doxiadis's admiration for the ancient *polis*, Islamabad was not a city of citizens, of political creatures (*zoon politikon*) as Aristotle famously envisioned the ideal urban dweller. While it shared the size of a *polis*, the sector had very different characteristics. Politics was of course not altogether excluded in Doxiadis's modular vision, but it was not a primary consideration, a *sine qua non* of human existence. In fact, what made the birth of 'democracy' possible in ancient Greece – the human scale of its urban communities – was now used to impede and quarantine the political. Politics was both conceptually and spatially removed from everyday life to communities of a higher order. Unlike access to basic developmental needs, access to political space involved crossing into the world outside the sector, into the world of fast motorized transport where mobility was linked to privilege and was easily policed by the state.

Islamabad was a city of developmental subjects whose progressive embedding in ever higher orders of community, from house to subsector and from sector finally to the city as a whole, was something like a stepladder from a state of deprivation and need towards a full sense of urbanity as it existed in the developed West. This was entirely consistent with Doxiadis's belief that the people of Pakistan were not yet city dwellers, their living spaces not yet cities, and that it was unwise to provide spaces or designs that in their characteristics were too urban for these people to handle. Islamabad as a whole may have been envisioned as a city of sorts, but its constituent units were not necessarily so. In a way, there was little difference between life in a community class III and life in a village, or between the definitive 'sector' (community class IV) and a small country town. Again this could not be more different from what the first Western urban planners had suggested back in the late 1940s when working on the old capital of Karachi. The men from MRVP had deliberately sought to create a city that was a place of experimentation, tension, '*joie de vivre*' and encounters with strangers.[54]

---

[54] Merz Rendel Vatten (1952), *Report on Greater Karachi Plan 1952*, Stockholm, A.B. kartografiska institutet, p.39.

Doxiadis planned a city to make it as safe, traditional and free of friction as possible. One could, was even encouraged to, live in Islamabad as if one had never left the countryside: that imaginary realm of stability, of contentment with paternalistic government and cultural authenticity.

Depoliticization of this sort was no peculiar response to ground realities in Pakistan, but stood at the very heart of Doxiadis's methodology. In a landmark speech at a meeting of Third World urbanists in Cairo in 1960 (sponsored by the CIA-funded Congress of Cultural Freedom), he gave a coherent and definitive answer to the conundrum of how to reconcile Islamic culture with modernity. Was there still an Arab metropolis in this day and age of international capitalism? he asked, before attesting to the sad reality that most of the buildings he observed around him 'have nothing Arabic about them at all, especially those which are air-conditioned and multistoreyed, those which no longer have a single element of Arab nature in them'.[55] In previous centuries everything had been clearly defined by local culture, now we had a confusing mix of the local and the 'international element'. This begged further questions: 'Shall we have a true Arab metropolis in the future? Or shall we simply have a metropolis in the Arab countries, which could, as a kind of courtesy title or because of its location only, be called the Arab Metropolis, but which will in fact be the same as any other metropolis all over the world?'[56]

For a less depressing and less politically unsettling future, modernity had to be somehow accommodated in the true Arab metropolis while still leaving a space for the authentically local. As Doxiadis always believed, some of the forces behind international homogenization were in fact inevitable and irresistible, such as global trade and technological progress, so it was clearly not an option to simply turn ones back on modernity and to go back to the models of the past. But even if this were so, 'There is no need to transfer the international forces to the microspaces of our living if we don't wish to', Doxiadis proposed. While it was wise to leave anything connected with the outside world to 'international modernity', ports, airports, business districts, fast road connections, the local could still remain Arab in '... the neighbourhood, the small community with internal cohesion and even administrative expression, with its local leader – an old Arab notion ... the human scale, the souk where people walk unimpeded by cars, which is an Arab tradition'.[57]

This was programmatic for what Doxiadis was trying to achieve both in the refugee resettlement of Korangi and in the capital Islamabad. While

---

[55] CADA: General Reports R-GA 211–248, 1961, 'The Arab Metropolis', p.2.
[56] Ibid. p.3.   [57] Ibid. p.29.

banishing the forces of modernity to the outside – in the first instance outside a community class III, and then outside the sector as a whole – it was at the level of the neighbourhood and the house where a preservation of local styles and cultural authenticity was attempted. After it had been confined to its appropriate domain, it was now possible not only to accommodate modernity, but to actively espouse it, even get ahead of developments elsewhere. The trademark aspect of Islamabad was the fact that it was the first purpose-designed 'dynapolis' anywhere in the world: a city where urban growth would not take place concentrically around an old centre, which could only lead to ever-expanding distances between suburb and centre and correspondingly to traffic gridlock, but where the centre grew in parallel with the expanding city itself.[58] [See Figure 20]

Cutting more or less horizontally through the Islamabad site from east to west, there was to be an avenue lined by shopping complexes, educational institutions and other typical city centre functions, soon to be referred to as 'Blue Area'. As new sectors emerged in the direction of expansion, new facilities could simply be added to this avenue. The distance between the sectors and the closest part of this city centre corridor would remain the same, avoiding the problems of concentric urbanization just outlined. If there was a city of the future par excellence this was it, a complete departure from what urban designers had believed for millennia.

Meeting Muslim needs

While the radical future orientation of dynapolis had little relevance while Islamabad's expansion remained limited to a few sectors, Doxiadis's other trademark vision was firmly situated in the present: the design of neighbourhoods in a manner that – in his eyes at least – preserved traditional modes of life. Korangi had already been a major test case for this vision, and as the speech about the *Arab* metropolis of the future already indicated, Doxiadis had attempted something similar when working in the Middle East. In fact, all of these precedents merged together when it came to the design of Islamabad's first neighbourhoods. Despite his earlier ruminations about the distinctive folk styles of Pakistan's north, Doxiadis had few hesitations about transplanting his Korangi designs to the new capital, give and take a few minor stylistic alterations like leaving out the rooftop windcatchers that he saw as typical for the region of Sind. To make things even less locally distinctive, the

[58] For one of many explanations of the concept see CADA: Pakistan Volume 16, Report Dox-PA 29, pp.6–8.

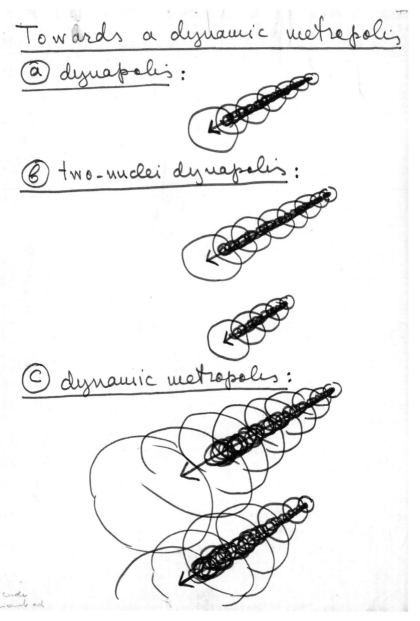

Figure 20 Doxiadis's sketch explaining the 'dynapolis' principle.
Instead of a single centre around which the city expands concentrically,
a 'dynapolis' consists of an open-ended ribbon of centres arranged on a
single axis. In consequence the distance between suburbs and centre(s)
does not increase as the city grows, making traffic problems much easier
to manage.
Source: CADA: 'Towards a dynamic metropolis' (Archive Files 17666).

Korangi designs had themselves been almost direct copies of designs used in rural resettlement schemes in Iraq.[59] The discourse of folk culture did not put any checks on such elisions of difference, since, when it came to actual urban designs, Muslims were not addressed in terms of aesthetic or artistic considerations, but in line with the logic of population as a sociological subject. There were specific Muslim 'needs', which an authentically Muslim neighbourhood would have to satisfy, even if the actual structures involved did not look particularly Muslim in their own right.

As always it was the task of the Ekistician to determine these cultural needs through research and mass observation. As Doxiadis proudly proclaimed in a different but related context: 'The social and private life of the muslim [sic] people of Pakistan, regulated by strict rules, so strongly affects the composition [of architecture designed for their use] that it is impossible for the architect to proceed in any sort of design work except through proper background knowledge.'[60] As the reference to 'strict rules' already indicates here, Doxiadis was highly aware of Islam as an orthopractic religion and took some care to familiarize himself with scriptural injunctions derived from the Qur'an and the Prophet's sayings (Hadith) in order to be aware of Muslim needs. Of crucial importance in this context was his long collaboration with the Egyptian architect Hassan Fathy, a proponent of a vernacular modernism and traditional building techniques, who had fallen out with Nasser's regime in the late 1950s and for some years entered into employment with DA. As Panigiota Pyla has pointed out, it was Fathy who became Doxiadis's chief consultant in Muslim affairs and who checked all of DA's proposals for the Muslim world for cultural appropriateness.[61] Although Fathy also commented on Pakistani affairs from time to time, his closest involvement was with planning in Iraq, where he was responsible for the design of community facilities for the Greater Musayib Resettlement Scheme and attempts to relocate nomadic peasants and scattered homesteads into central agricultural towns. Much of what he proposed for Greater Musayib was later adapted for Korangi, and later still made a reappearance in Islamabad's G6.[62]

[59] CADA: File Dox-QA 75, Greater Mussayib.
[60] CADA: Volume 17 Panjab University, May–October 1959, p.8.
[61] Pyla, P. (2007), 'Hassan Fathy revisited: postwar discourses on science, development, and vernacular architecture', *Journal of Architectural Education* 60(43): 28–39. For Fathy's architectural vision see Fathy, H. (1973), *Architecture for the poor: an experiment in rural Egypt*, University of Chicago Press.
[62] CADA: Pakistan Volume 71, Pakistan Correspondence, File C-PKH 1865.

This construction of a need-based Muslim identity enlisted what were presumed to be specific notions of gender separation, of privacy, or ways of shopping and cooking. Although such needs could be accommodated by highly functional and mass-produced concrete structures of little stylistic distinctiveness, certain forms of design had to be ruled out right from the start – for instance, any building more than one storey tall. Not only were high-rise flats unsuitable for the not-yet-quite-urban Muslim city dweller, they could also not be built without violating rules of purdah. The cheapest and, in Doxiadis's eyes, climatically most suitable way of accommodating life in the Middle East and Pakistan was to provide open but concealed spaces like verandahs and courtyards. In multistorey constructions these could be overlooked by strangers, thereby violating in Doxiadis's view a distinctly Muslim sense of privacy. Other needs had to be met in terms of interior design. Doxiadis's planners drew up blueprints for what they saw as distinctly Pakistani cooking arrangements, a 'choulah' (*chulha*) and 'kurrah' (*kura*) that were to be provided in every dwelling but always to be so positioned as to be invisible for outsiders,[63] [See Figure 21] and there was even talk of producing a standard issue prayer platform or 'takht posh'.[64]

When it came to mosques there was a good deal of debate about how many exactly were needed to satisfy 'normal' Muslim requirements, while much less care was spent on the actual design of these places of prayer. In the end it was neither design nor the calculation of provision that managed to satisfy the actual residents of Doxiadis's quarters, making mosque politics one of the focal points of popular resistance (see next chapter).

Yet other areas for which these Muslim neighbourhoods would have to have special provision made were markets and communal baths. Ever since his first travels in Pakistan, and reinforced by impressions he gained in Iraq, Doxiadis was firmly convinced that the concentration of shops in a covered pedestrian-only space – 'a bazzar [*sic*] or souk'[65] as he pointed out in his diaries – was a necessity for true cultural sensitivity. No survey of Doxiadis's community planning would be complete without his most beloved of all architectural creations, however, which sums up perfectly the strange melange of Middle Eastern and Eastern Mediterranean habits that he regarded as specifically 'Muslim': the tea house. It is not

---

[63] CADA: Volume 111, File C-PI 1722, 28 March 1961, also Dox-PA 16 March 1963, Lahore New Township, Volume 168.
[64] CADA: Fortnightly Progress Report, Islamabad No. 36, attached to File C-PI 4192, Volume 157.
[65] CDA Library, Islamabad: File Dox-PA 90, 30 September 1960, Islamabad Communities and Housing Volume 34, p.98.

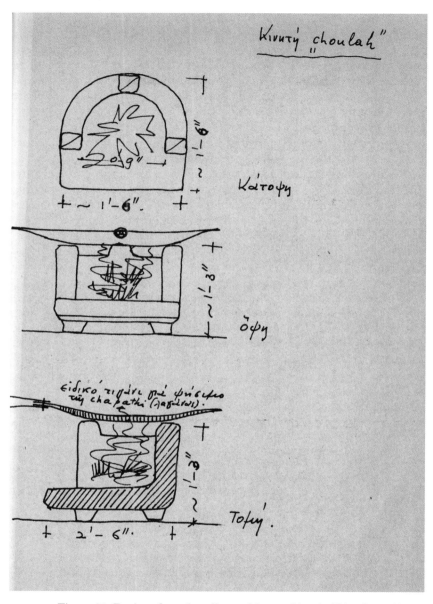

Figure 21 Designs for culturally sensitive cooking facilities for ordinary Pakistanis, as DA engineers saw them.
Source: CADA: 'Choulah' – attached to C-PI 1722, 28.3.1961, Pakistan vol.111, Archive Files 23645.

entirely clear why he attached so much importance to this institution, but photographs and comments as to the existence of such places of conversation and refreshment already occur in the first 1954 diary for Pakistan, and turn almost into an obsession in his later Iraq diaries, where countless tea houses in towns and markets and on the roadside, were catalogued.[66] Throughout his time in Pakistan, Doxiadis insisted on the presence of the tea house in his cities, even if there was not much demand for it locally, and defended his stance when he met incomprehension by some of his patrons. Brochures for both Korangi and Islamabad mention and depict tea house designs [See Figure 22] in prominent places.[67]

It is not easy to detect any particular strategic use here, beyond the assertion that Ekistics was a culturally sensitive approach to planning that would cater to all needs of its target population, but that point was already made with sufficient force in other contexts. Perhaps haunted by the ghosts of Athenian democracy, or drawn by the kaphenion culture of his native Greece, Doxiadis proposed an institution tailor-made for what Western sociologists have come to call 'a public sphere': a place where matters of politics or anything else of interest could be discussed in a state of relative tranquillity and comfort, but without any access restrictions or hierarchies of power. Such a connection was always more assumed than real, of course, as tea houses have not prevented the establishment of brutal dictatorships in the Middle East or, for that matter, in Pakistan itself. Maybe it was important to retain at least a moment of respite, an ideological fig leaf to alleviate the relentless sense of depoliticization that dominated Doxiadis's thought and practice in every other way.

Bureaucratic Islamism

The elite of the Ayub era never quite endorsed the relentless attempt to turn Pakistan's cities into the kind of emblematic representation of the nation's religious observance as demanded by the aforementioned letter writers Bakhteyar Husain and Raza Ali. But at least in the long run, they did seek a representation of Islam in urban space that differed significantly from Doxiadis's. The ambition to plan a city comprehensively for Muslim needs was noted with faint praise as far as Korangi was

---

[66] E.g. CADA: Iraq Volume 3, Iraq 3 Diary Dox-Q8, 1956, p.68; Iraq Volume 4, Iraq Reports 5 R-QA 1–53, p.7; Iraq Volume 8, Dox 12 May 1956, p.6.
[67] CADA: Archive Files 35839; CDA Library, Islamabad: File Dox-PA 90, 30 September 1960, Islamabad Communities and Housing Volume 34, p.98.

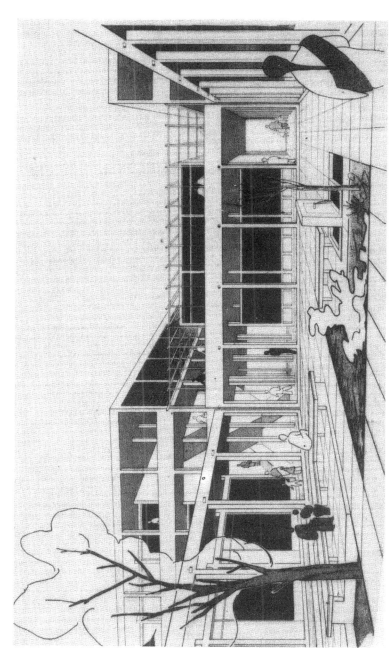

Figure 22 Sketch of Doxiadis's cherished tea house design for Korangi. A simplified version of this structure was actually built (see Figure 23) but never accepted by local residents.
Source: CADA: Archive Files 35839.

concerned[68] – in part because this was a city 'given' to the urban poor, and the paternalistic urge of providing for the perceived needs of 'the people' came naturally in this context. But in Islamabad things were different. It was after all a self-representation of the Pakistani state, which did not see itself merely as the dutiful provider of the cultural needs of its people, but as political agency for a better tomorrow, a resource of power that would ensure that Muslims would find their rightful place at the top table of world politics. For this reason Islam as the defining element of national identity had to be clearly visible in monumental architecture and not simply implicit in planning provisions. In fact, it was felt in some quarters that predicating urban functionality too much on religious tradition actually violated the other great concern of the time: a desire for being 'modern'.[69]

A good example of this difference in priorities was the fate of one of Doxiadis's most cherished of all Muslim community facilities: the tea house. When one of the first structures of this kind was completed – in Korangi [See Figure 23] – Doxiadis recounted the following conversation in one of his field diaries, presumably to signal to his financial backers in the United States just how culturally sensitive a planner he was:

We look at the tea house and I would like to remind to my [sic] colleagues of a discussion which was held lately with the Commissioner of Rawalpindi, Vice-Chairman of the Capital Development Authority [Ghiasuddin Ahmad]. He said that the word 'tea house' just does not sound well. It reminds of Japan or something else and he prefers much more the word 'Cafeteria' ... Mr. Tstitsis [chief of the DA Korangi field office] tells me that they also call them cafeterias in Korangi. It seems that common people use only the word 'hotel' for all these places and I wonder if the word cafeteria will appeal to them and if they will ever use it as it is much longer, and much more difficult to be written and pronounced ... Perhaps we must look back in to tradition if there is anything like 'Tsaihan'.[70]

This somewhat amusing anecdote highlighted that it was far from clear whether Muslim tradition actually required a tea house, or what if anything such a facility should provide. Ghiasuddin Ahmad did not seem to recognize even the existence of such a social institution in the Muslim world, associating it instead with the Far East. His suggestion of

---

[68] See Daechsel, M. (2011b), 'Sovereignty, governmentality and development in Ayub's Pakistan: the case of Korangi Township', *Modern Asian Studies* **45**(1): 131–157.

[69] For a longer discussion of how Doxiadis's notion of religion related to Pakistani middle-class norms and state policy, see Daechsel, M. (2014), 'Islam and development in urban space: planning "official" Karachi in the 1950s', *The city in South Asia*, C. Bates and M. Mio (eds.), London; New York, Routledge.

[70] CADA: Pakistan Volume 41, Pakistan Reports, Diary February–October 1960, p.154.

Figure 23 The Korangi tea house – note the empty upper storey where customers were expected to sit under matting or tarpaulin covers. Note also the communal water tap, which remained necessary as individual water connections could not be finished within the very tight schedule demanded by the Ayub regime, and the generally deserted look of Doxiadis's dedicated community centre. Residents carried out most commercial business in their own homes.
Source: CADA: Archive Files 17326.

'cafeteria' as the appropriate name betrayed a flair for westernized innovation, while also implying that this was a place where food would be served. The problem was that it was impossible to essentialize places of refreshment as part of a discourse of culture. Unable to accept this dispiriting conclusion, Doxiadis pressed on regardless, proposing that the solution to the problem of tea houses lay in a further indigenization of the name to 'Tsaihan' [after the Persian *chai khane*]. As it happened, the discussion of names was somewhat immaterial as the Korangi (or for that matter the Islamabad) 'tea houses' never took off. Rents were too high to attract tenants, and to Doxiadis's great consternation, cheap tea stalls soon proliferated in spaces earmarked for entirely different purposes in his plans.[71] He clearly had correctly anticipated the basic need of many

[71] Ibid. p.158.

Figure 24 Islamabad's 'covered market' awaiting final demolition after years of neglect.
Source: author's own photograph, October 2007.

Muslims to drink tea outside the house, but failed spectacularly in his attempt to translate this need into added cultural authority for the all-seeing, all-knowing planner. Community provisions designed by other architects on the Islamabad project at the same time and with a similar desire to appeal to local 'cultural' requirements did not fare much better. The covered markets designed by the Colombo Plan planner Gerard Brigden in the early 1960s never became the centrepieces of commercial life he had hoped for, with the last one demolished by the CDA after decades of neglect in 2007.[72] [See Figure 24]

All in all, there are surprisingly few exchanges *with Pakistani inter-locutors* about the correct Islamic character of Islamabad in Doxiadis's archive. While he himself was obviously obsessed with the question of Islam and identity, his partners found it far more pressing to speak about

---

[72] Gerard Brigden's work (along with housing designs by veteran Pakistani woman architect Yasmin Lari) was highly praised by Sten Nilsson when he visited Islamabad in the 1960s. Nilsson, S. (1973), *New capitals of India, Pakistan and Bangladesh*, Lund, Studentlitteratur, p.163–169.

more technical issues ranging from nuclear fallout shelters to urban heliports.[73] This did not mean that they found the matter of religion in urban planning unimportant, only that it was not something that the members of the FCC and later the CDA particularly wanted to discuss with him. This alone was evidence for Doxiadis's increasing marginalization. At least initially he had only himself to blame. Reporting an early conversation with Yahya Khan as chairman of the FCC, Doxiadis remembered being 'asked especially by the General what will be the characteristics of the city, as for example the pigeon-hole idea is of Chandigarh' or the 'reversed arch' in Brasilia. Ayub's regime wanted an Islamabad that was immediately recognizable as an iconic architectural ensemble: something that even ordinary observers unfamiliar with planning technology could immediately understand and appreciate. Unwilling to oblige what he saw as ill-advised attempts to 'impose on a city one characteristic element in all types of buildings from the poorest to the most expensive, from the most modest to the most monumental'[74], Doxiadis pushed himself onto the sidelines, although he did not immediately appreciate the degree of his exclusion. As recounted by Zaheer ud-Din Khwaja in his memoirs, 'Doxiadis with his extreme enthusiasm for the project was already preparing not only the master plan for which he had been duly commissioned but also the perspectives of major buildings including what he called the "Presidential Palace", the National Assembly Building and the Secretariat Building, for which he had assumed an implied assignment.'[75] As it happened, none of these speculative designs was particularly striking in architectural terms. They all conformed to an international modernist aesthetic with little space for distinctive markers of identity. In line with his thoughts about the 'Arab metropolis of the future', Doxiadis believed that the most public of buildings should also be most closely aligned with a style that reflected an increasingly globalized world.

The Pakistani establishment was unwilling to allow Doxiadis to be the grand master architect of Islamabad in the same way Le Corbusier had been the iconic 'creator' of Chandigarh. First, it was decided on the

[73] CADA: Pakistan Volume 41, Diary PA 100, Pakistan Diary from 7 to 16 February 1960, p.100; Pakistan Volume 157, Correspondence, File C-PI 3102, 26 February 1962. Doxiadis is alleged to have dabbled in science fiction himself when he waxed lyrically about hovercraft as the transport of the future. Khwaja, Z. D. (1998), *Memoirs of an architect*, Lahore, distributed by Ferozsons Publishers, p.115.
[74] CADA: Pakistan Volume 41, Diary PA 101, Pakistan Diary from 24 to 31 October 1960, p.47.
[75] Khwaja, Z. D. (1998), *Memoirs of an architect*, Lahore, distributed by Ferozsons Publishers, pp.94–95.

instructions of Ayub's Finance Minister, Mohammad Shoaib, to pair Doxiadis – now strictly confined to matters of planning only – with an international star architect who would look after all major building designs. Both Bauhaus founder Walter Gropius and the Japanese vernacular modernist Kenzo Tange were contacted, but neither was available at the time.[76] The idea to have a single lead architect was subsequently shelved and the number of consultants involved greatly expanded. After lobbying by several embassies, almost a dozen architects from several countries were each presented with assignments for individual buildings. As recounted by Orestes Yakas, Doxiadis was utterly surprised and depressed when he heard of his effective demotion – although like the irrepressible 'Zorba the Greek', he was reputedly seen dancing to the music of his native land in a Rawalpindi bar soon after.[77]

The first official building on the site – 'Pakistan House' – was commissioned to the Italian architect Gio Ponti – and duly savaged for its poor design by an increasingly disgruntled Doxiadis.[78] As it turned out, selection to the list of chosen architects for Islamabad could be a poisoned chalice. All of the men involved came from the rich North, and none of them was of Muslim background, reigniting the intractable controversy over how international modernism could be made commensurable with the nation's Islamic identity. The level of debate soon returned to where it had been in the days of Heinz and Muguruza with their ill-fated attempts to provide an Islamic–modernist synthesis to convince the Pakistani establishment. In 1964, the long-term champion of Punjabi commercial architecture and veteran of colonial modernism Moinuddin Chishti waded into the debate with a letter to the editor in the pro-regime *Pakistan Times*. After asserting once again the somewhat oxymoronic need for 'planning our public buildings after the traditional Muslim style without sacrificing the good points of modern architecture', he asserted: 'Obviously this kind of planning can best be done by Pakistani architects who understand their national requirements better than foreign architects [...] who in spite of their technical qualifications are strangers to our national aspirations.'[79] In other words, architecture was not simply a 'technical matter' where any architect was as good as the

---

[76] Ibid.

[77] Yakas, O. (2001), *Islamabad, the birth of a capital*, Karachi, Oxford University Press, p.144.

[78] Ibid. p.120.

[79] Attached to CADA: Pakistan Volume 202, Housing and Settlements Agency, 1964, R-PAK LU 12. On Chishti see Daechsel, M. (2014), 'Islam and development in urban space: planning "official" Karachi in the 1950s', *The City in South Asia*, C. Bates and M. Mio, London; New York, Routledge.

plans they proposed; it became a matter of the personal identity and cultural authenticity of the personalities involved. In Chishti's case – who lacked any formal qualifications – this was an ill-concealed attempt to capitalize on the single advantage he possessed over his foreign competitors: that he was a practicing Muslim and a native of Pakistan to boot.

Personality clashes and contests over who could regard himself as the proper arbiter of national taste soon engulfed matters of architectural design. Although Ayub Khan himself most probably had a soft spot for cutting-edge modernism, he invited a number of bureaucrats with Islamic predilections to have a major say on the Islamabad commissions. Zaheer ud-Din Khwaja mentioned several occasions in his memoirs when invited bureaucrats and academics without architectural training expounded on what an Islamic style was to be like. Professor M. M. Sharif of the Institute of Islamic Studies, for instance, drew up a list of eleven 'distinctive elements' – ranging from minarets to battlements, arabesques and arches to tile work – that had to be followed.[80] Others like Musarrat Hussain Zuberi and N. A. Faruqui were reportedly even more dogmatic in their views, basing their observations on superficial readings of generalist textbooks on Islamic culture. While both Khwaja himself and his modernist colleague Mehdi Ali Mirza were gradually removed from the decision-making process, these generalist bureaucrats entered into battle with the international greats of the architectural establishment and castigated their designs for not being Islamic enough or demanding the addition of Islamic stylistic elements that were entirely out of kilter with the original designs. Several contenders for the National Assembly Building bowed out because they were unwilling to heed such requests; for instance, the Danish architect Arne Jacobsen, a personal friend of Khwaja's. The American Louis Kahn, his successor in the competition, was flatly accused of not understanding the true spirit of Islam but then rewarded with the consolation prize of designing a Parliament Building for Dacca in East Pakistan, which he later turned into one of the most celebrated contemporary buildings in South Asia.[81] One of the more successful foreign architects in Pakistan, in contrast, was the American Edward Durell Stone, who was reportedly introduced to the CDA by Faruqui on the recommendation of the US Embassy in New Delhi.[82] Stone quickly learnt to make copious, if often merely

[80] Khwaja, Z. D. (1998), *Memoirs of an architect*, Lahore, distributed by Ferozsons Publishers, pp.126–127.
[81] Ibid. pp.108–109. For a critique of Kahn's work see Goldhagen, S. W. and L. I. Kahn (2001), *Louis Kahn's situated modernism*, New Haven, CT, Yale University Press.
[82] *Archi Times*, February 2006.

rhetorical, references to Islamic building norms in his sales pitch, while showing little sensitivity to such matters in actual architectural practice.[83]

Kamil Khan Mumtaz and other professional architects and critics have offered detailed accounts of how little changed in subsequent decades.[84] A single illustration may suffice for the purposes of this book: Kenzo Tange's Pakistan Supreme Court building, commissioned by General Zia ul-Haq's civilian frontman Muhammad Khan Junejo in the early 1980s and completed in 1990. Wanting to have somebody with Tange's prestige involved but unwilling to entrust outsiders with correct inter-pretations of religious matters, Zia's government insisted that Mughal-style arches were added and the original courtyard space scrapped to make it more 'Islamic', producing what is widely seen as a confusing and unsuccessful hotchpotch of styles.[85] What matters most in the context of this book is the historical continuity between such recent examples and the Ayub period. Concerns over an Islamic style were not introduced to Pakistan by the bogeyman of misguided religious policy Zia ul-Haq but can be traced back through Bhutto's 1970s and Ayub Khan's 1960s to the immediate post-independence period.

In the final analysis, Doxiadis's preferred representation of an Islamic identity in urban space was an almost perfect inversion of what his Pakistani clients had in mind. While he saw the architectural design of important buildings as the right place to seek an accommodation with international modernism, the latter wanted to create distinctiveness with the help of domes, arches or other elements of an 'Islamic' style; and where Doxiadis thought religion mattered the most – in the cultur-ally sensitive design of the most intimate living spaces of the city's inhabitants – the bureaucrats felt no particular need to signal adherence to an Islamic identity at all. If anything, the private and the purely functional were precisely where new technologies could be tried out to exemplify a modern lifestyle. To repeat the opinion of the Commissioner of Rawalpindi, Ghiasuddin Ahmad, Pakistan required 'cafeterias' not 'chai khane'. Underlying such contrasting notions of religious identity were contrasting notions of governance and the state. While Doxiadis clearly believed in the ability to shape and nurture the religious behaviour of citizens through the careful design of urban space, most Pakistani policy makers had no such ambitions. They were no doubt interested

---

[83] For a withering critique of Stone's modus operandi see Khwaja, Z. D. (1998), *Memoirs of an architect*, Lahore, distributed by Ferozsons Publishers, pp.115–118.

[84] Mumtaz, K. K. (1999), *Modernity and tradition: contemporary architecture in Pakistan*, Oxford; New York, Oxford University Press. Also Khwaja, Z. D. (1998), *Memoirs of an architect*, Lahore, distributed by Ferozsons Publishers, pp.125–134.

[85] Husain, H. (2005), 'Kenzo Tange – obituary', *Archi Times*, May, p.19.

in the political possibilities of urban development as a spectacle, and in the state's ability to make public statements through the design of public buildings; but there was no clear commitment to any kind of micro-managerial control. Doxiadis's marginalization from the Islamabad project over questions of religious identity constituted a highly significant moment in the wider encounter between development expert and the post-colonial state. It encapsulated in a unique fashion the central concern of this book: that development and post-colonial nationalism involved different modalities of power that were fundamentally incommensurable.

In Bari Imam's shadow

Doxiadis's vision was to integrate considerations of religious identity into the discursive framework of 'development'. This is to say, he approached Islam not as a living, changeable and highly politicized reference frame for belief and action, but as a set of objective behavioural patterns, to be accounted for by the planner in the same way as climate, demographic data or features of topography. In this sense, Islam was but one variety of a universal attachment to 'cultural needs' that all people across the poor South were believed to possess to a greater or lesser degree, and which had to be carefully accommodated to prevent them from becoming obstacles to development itself. But no matter how much Doxiadis sought to first ascertain and then satisfy the religious needs of 'normal' Pakistanis, he could never produce solutions that were universally accepted. This was not because he was Greek and an outsider to the debate, but because for most Pakistanis, Islam was not an objective need that could be satisfied in the same way as providing people with a minimum wage or a minimum nutritional package. As already pointed out by the petitioners demanding that the road layout of Islamabad be arranged in the direction of prayer, Islam was an aspiration to transform the world, not a reflection of what already existed. In this sense, there could never be enough Islam, nor any agreement over what constituted 'normal' or adequate Islamic behaviour.

A poignant illustration of how the worldview of 'development' collided with religious practice as a lived reality can be found in a touching note submitted to Doxiadis's office by one of the many low-ranking officials involved in the Islamabad project, a forest ranger by the name of Muhammad Sadiq Altaf. His task was to catalogue important landscape features on the Islamabad site, so a decision could be taken by the planners to either incorporate them into the design or have them cleared. He wrote (with reference to a prominent tree):

Height = 110 ft (approx)
Diameter = 10 ft.
Width of crown = 110 ft
Age = 100 years (Approx)
General: This old banyan tree has been the sitting place of
    Pir Bari Imam Zaman Shah (Motian wala) and Sakhi Shah
    Mahmood (father of Pir Bari Imam)
For favour of your information please.[86]

In the first instance, this was an attempt to reduce a tree to a scientifically measurable object, a botanical specimen, even if not all of the information supplied according to pro forma requirements was in fact entirely reliable as indicated by the qualification 'approximately'. But this act of classification is disturbed by that additional 'general' note, representing a very different mode of sense making: of the tree as a historically and religiously meaningful space. It had been a favourite spot of two famous Sufi saints, whose cult still formed a major part of religious observance among local people on the Islamabad site. Bari Imam's final resting place (dargah) is situated only a small distance away from the where the tree was located, and has long been the centre of worship for a whole range of people: Shiᶜa Muslims, prostitutes, women seeking help with childbirth, among many others.

Doxiadis had not asked for the additional information supplied by the forest ranger when he requested detailed landscape data for his plan, but the reply nevertheless unnerved DA local representatives enough to file the note and send it to Athens for consideration. Sadiq Altaf's remark was more than volunteering a piece of local trivia. It was an intrusion, a voice from outside development that demanded to be heard. The veneration of holy men was not a feature of religious life in Pakistan that Doxiadis had ever fully recognized in his attempt to construct the Muslim city of the future, despite his constant references to folk culture. This was a striking and important oversight. The veneration of saints has been a standard motif in descriptions of South Asian Islam since at least colonial times, and its presence is only too visible in the country's landscape. So how come that for Doxiadis Islam could be boiled down to only mosques, tea houses and living according to purdah? Part of the problem must have been the fact that shrines did not fit into his notion of 'developmental' Islam. They cannot be provided for in the same way as – let us say, mosques – because they derive their religious significance from their association with a holy man who may have lived and died centuries

---

[86] CADA: Pakistan Volume 158, File C-PI 3312, Horticulture, 12 April 1962.

ago. Shrines have to emerge; they cannot be planned. At the same time, shrine worship did not fit in with Doxiadis's notion of spatial secularization. Sufism may have been about the most private of religious sentiments and the most private of life's problems, but the cult was not necessarily located in the inner world of the neighbourhood or home; in fact, being centred on sites of pilgrimage, it was often by definition of the 'outside world' and highly public.

Finally, Doxiadis's neglect of Islamic saint worship may have reflected the preferences of his hosts and patrons. Although often powerfully connected to local and national politics, Sufism was not the kind of Islam that Ayub's developmental state wanted to be officially associated with.[87] This was not so much a case of religiously inspired hostility (as exists among certain sections of the ʿulama), but the result of a long-standing discourse that had portrayed Sufism as 'backward' and 'superstitious', a cult of miracles and questionable medical beliefs, as well as an emotionalism that offended middle-class sobriety. Doxiadis and Ayub agreed that Sufism had no place in a Muslim city of the future, if anything one could only hope that the worship of saints would cease as villagers became modernized as city dwellers.

Within this context, Sadiq Altaf's note was a political act, a demand for official recognition. By pointing out that two important seventeenth-century holy men had enjoyed the presence of a certain tree, he was also alerting the planners of Islamabad to the fact that their new city was not really built from scratch and on virgin territory, but that it intruded into the lives of historically grown communities. Judging by his name, Altaf was possibly a Shiʿa and very likely a follower of Bari Imam himself. He wanted his religious community and their traditions to be recognized as having a place in Ayub's Pakistan, not simply be written off as historical debris to be cleared away by the modernization process. At the same time 'development' actually gave him a chance to make this claim for recognition. The decision to build Islamabad put Ayub's regime on the spot. It had to make a choice about what kind of Islam should be recognized and represented in the capital, as the project itself invited all sorts of contradictory demands about what Islam should be like.

---

[87] This did not mean that the most fervent believers in technological modernism could not also be followers of Sufi saints. Ghulam Faruque Khan, stalwart of steel mills and hydroelectric power plants, was also a disciple of the Pir of Manki Sharif. Farooq, S., Ed. (2004), *Ghulam Faruque Khan: revolutionary builder of Pakistan*, Peshawar, Unique Books, p.19. For how different political regimes (including Ayub's) sought to control Sufism for political ends, see Ewing, K. (1983), 'The politics of Sufism: redefining the saints of Pakistan', *The Journal of Asian Studies* **42**(2): 251–268.

In the final analysis, planning for Islam was (and remains) an oxy-moron, a category mistake. Questions of religious identity became the Achilles heel of development discourse, as they offered an ideal access point for resistance. The more somebody like Doxiadis stressed that he had done everything he could to satisfy the presumed 'objective' religious needs of the people, the more these very people would seek to assert their own authority by concentrating on Islam as the field where they could contest the consultant's authority. Religious truth is not, and cannot be, of the same nature as the truth of medicine or psychiatry, or the truth of science, even if a long and distinguished list of religious 'reformist' thinkers going back to the mid nineteenth century have attempted to make it such.[88] This is not to say that religion is in any way less valid than science or medicine, but that it has remained to date far more resistant to closure. As long as there were contests over power and authority in the country, there would be contests over the right kind of Islam that no form of compromise and no amount of 'scientific' expertise could ever settle.

---

[88] There is a large literature on Islamic reformism in South Asia. For classic accounts see Smith, W. C. (1946), *Modern Islām in India, a social analysis*, London, V. Gollancz Ltd; Ahmed, A. (1967), *Islamic modernism in India and Pakistan, 1857–1964*, London, Oxford University Press; Metcalf, B. D. (1982), *Islamic revival in British India: Deoband, 1860–1900*, Princeton University Press.

6   The consultant under attack

Doxiadis's elaborate and resourceful, but ultimately unrealistic, attempt to bring together Islam and development was part of the larger problematic at the centre of this book: a fundamental incommensurability between the modalities of power involved in 'development' on one side and in the politics of post-colonial nationhood on the other. But this contradiction did not exist as a grand conceptual dichotomy: as if urban development was subject to an imaginary tribunal with the great planner and the post-colonial bureaucrat each making their respective cases before some kind of grand verdict was reached. The contradictions at the heart of this book were embedded in and played out through an ongoing *historical process* which constantly transformed both sides of the encounter as it unfolded. The negotiations and power struggles between the consultant and the Pakistani state did not cease when commissions had been awarded and master plans approved; they continued through the minutiae of project management, sometimes over a single blueprint, a single brick, a single beam of concrete. Unlike much of the story told so far, this was no longer only about Doxiadis interacting with generals or other high officials but a much larger confrontation, involving numerous planners, engineers and workmen. And while these men were still busy with their tools, Islamabad and Korangi became real settlements that provided a home to tens of thousands of Pakistanis who had their own formative influence on how these settlements turned out. As Madhu Sarin has noted in her classic study of Chandigarh, a city is never built by planners alone – no matter how grand they aspire to be – it is shaped by the ongoing interrelationship of the planned and the unplanned.[1]

   This concluding chapter combines a final journey into the most humdrum parts of the Doxiadis Archive – into a world of little notes and business letters, minutes of neighbourhood committee meetings and local petitions – with a final push towards conceptual synthesis. Following clues

---

[1] Sarin, M. (1982), *Urban planning in the Third World: the Chandigarh experience*, London, Mansell, p.3.

from Foucault's later work, old binaries are abandoned and a more dynamic interplay between managerial and sovereign modes of power is placed centre stage. What emerges at the end of Doxiadis's story in Pakistan is an outline of how the post-colonial state at large sought to establish control over its cities. In the shadow of a governmentality imported from outside, a local governmentality came into existence that in important respects was different from what would have existed if Doxiadis or other consultants had never set foot in the country. As writers like Ferguson and Escobar would have expected, plans did not simply 'fail': they failed productively, affecting the living world of real people as profoundly as any 'successful' plan would. However, none of the distinguishing features of 'development' identified in the literature was to any measurable extent reflected in Doxiadis's Pakistan: neither the ideal of the state as a service provider as dreamt up by development enthusiasts, nor the fear of development as an 'anti-politics machine' as attested by its critics. Instead, development produced a world that was both highly political and only to a marginal degree built on consent, a Pakistani variety of what Partha Chatterjee thinking about colonial and post-colonial India has called a 'political society'.[2]

At the Margalla Hills

By the time the first earth movements and concrete foundations appeared at the Islamabad site, Doxiadis's operations in Pakistan had been transformed from a one-man show to a substantial corporate presence. DA established field offices not only at the Margalla Hills but also in the major cities of Rawalpindi, Lahore, Karachi and Dacca, reflecting the wide portfolio of contracts they had managed to secure. More than a dozen planning experts and engineers were sent from head office in Athens to work full time and long term in Pakistan, aided by a small army of locally recruited planners, draughtsmen, peons, drivers and secretaries as well as by student volunteers and the occasional freelance consultant from Europe and America. As one would expect, working conditions varied significantly from place to place. Some of the Greek consultants enjoyed almost total freedom to do as they pleased, but at the price of no actual influence. The mission attached to the WPNHSA was the most glaring example. Operations in Islamabad, in contrast, were always kept on a much tighter leash. When actual building began on the capital site, Doxiadis's position in Pakistan was no longer as strong as it

---

[2] Chatterjee, P. (2004), *The politics of the governed: reflections on popular politics in most of the world*, New York, Columbia University Press, pp.38–41.

had been at his breakthrough moment in 1958. The regime had already decided by this point that he was a man on his way out, and that there was no longer any compelling political need for keeping him at the centre of the project.

The newly created CDA was a well-resourced executive agency, unlike the sometimes shambolic KDA that had come to rely so strongly on DA during the implementation of the Korangi project. CDA's first chairman, Gen. Yahya Khan, was not a bureaucrat with limited clout but a future Chief Martial Law Administrator and one of the junta's top military officers. The civilians who soon succeeded him in office did not feel they were on a scarcely lucrative punishment posting like the men in charge of the NHSA, but cherished the opportunity to extract maximum political credit from staying closely involved. This was after all a project of utmost national importance, closely observed both at home and abroad. As ever, they often indulged somewhat obscure pet concerns, being mostly unqualified to speak on more technical matters.[3] CDA Deputy Chairman (and later Chairman) W. A. Shaikh appears to have had a particular interest in the precise colour of tiles used on public buildings, for instance.[4] Or for another – and tellingly bizarre – example of wilful interference, consider a clipping from the British newspaper the *Daily Express*, which arrived at DA's field office in summer 1963. Its subject was an alleged initiative to abolish traffic lights in France, and there was a note attached that the planners of Islamabad should consider similar solutions in Pakistan. It had come from the General Headquarters of the Pakistan Army.[5]

The formal role of DA on the project was that of 'chief consultant'. This involved a characteristically wide-ranging brief that fitted in well with Doxiadis's ambitions as an omniscient Ekistician. According to an internal memorandum, 'the CDA expects from its Chief Consultant to advise on *all* ... items, following the general design of Islamabad and to propose methods, technics and standards'.[6] The questions that subsequently landed on the desks of the DA field engineers ranged from the appropriate number of doors in private houses to the right kind of water

---

[3] Zaheer ud-Din Khwaja recounts in his memoirs the amusing anecdote of Akhtar Mahmood, one of the civil servants, mentioning the nonsensical phrase 'cusecs/per hour' in an official report. Nobody among the higher bureaucracy ever picked up on the mistake. Khwaja, Z. D. (1998), *Memoirs of an architect*, Lahore, distributed by Ferozsons Publishers, p.94.

[4] CADA: Pakistan Volume 111, Files C-PI 1530, 4 February 1961, C-PI 1663, 13 March 1961; Volume 114, C-PI 2632, 31 October 1961.

[5] CADA: Pakistan Volume 193, File C-PI 5363.

[6] CADA: Pakistan Volume 111, File C-PI 1524, 3 February 1961.

treatment plant and from what kind of bushes to use when planting the capital's designated green belt to the colour scheme for future municipal buses ('Geranium G005 with stripes').[7] From the point of view of DA themselves, their role went substantially beyond 'advice', however. As is clear from virtually every page in the records, Doxiadis considered this to be his project, which he expected to be implemented in precisely the ways his plans prescribed. This was not simply an expression of the inability of the great planner to let go of his creation, but also central to Doxiadis's commercial strategy. He wanted to show Islamabad (and for that matter also Korangi) to the world as a sales model for possible contracts elsewhere. The site attracted numerous visitors from all over the world, including from the kind of people who were in a position to become new customers. As potential future partners, they were not interested in what the CDA or any other Pakistani party had contributed to the project, but what Doxiadis's own vision would look like.

The ambition to retain control of even minute details landed DA in battles on several fronts. Actual building work had to be inspected on the site to ensure that the overall plan was followed in all aspects. Non-compliance was common. When the first houses went up in sector G6, which in characteristic fashion had been planned down to the last detail by Doxiadis himself, it was found that the bricks made in local brick kilns were not of an even height and that prefabricated windows and doors would not fit;[8] when contractors began to pour concrete cantilevers, they showed 'basic discrepancies which may affect the safety of construction', so DA staff wanted to be forewarned of similar actions in the future so as to be able to be personally present to exercise oversight.[9] Coordination between different aspects of the project presented additional challenges. 'On various occasions, it has been unofficially brought to our attention that certain changes have taken and are taking place in the studies submitted by our office on lay-outs, roads, highways, facilities and house types', DA engineer Hadjopolous wrote with a sense of alarm to CDA Chief Engineer Zaheer ud-Din Khwaja in autumn 1962. Being unable to do much more than mention disquiet, however, he then went on to profusely thank Khwaja as well as the Director General of the Public Works Department and the Superintendent Engineer for better cooperation in the future,

[7] CADA: Pakistan Volume 193, File C-PI 5358, 29 June 1963.
[8] CADA: Pakistan Volume 114, File C-PI 2703.
[9] CADA: Pakistan Volume 194, File C-PI 5461 Letter to M. H. Hyderi, Deputy Director Works, CDA, 26 July 1963.

providing more than a hint of who the DA field officers suspected of being responsible for their sidelining.[10]

DA's extensive brief of responsibilities was not an accurate reflection of influence. Doxiadis's Islamabad project team started their work with the expectation of having the last say in all important planning matters and departed as little more than minions in the junta's international public relations machinery. Leaving aside larger disagreements over what planning and urban reconstructions were meant to achieve, seemingly trivial problems of daily life already imposed serious obstacles. Essential equipment to make DA an efficient executive agency was lacking throughout their stay in Pakistan. While maps at a scale of 1:1000 were urgently needed, for instance, even the supply of those with a less accurate scale of 1:4000 was forever lagging behind requirements, despite repeat admonitions to the Pakistanis to make this matter a top priority.[11] Blueprints could not be passed on to local public works departments for implementation as an adequate supply of the ammonia paper needed for their reproduction was unavailable;[12] and as their contractual term drew to a close, Doxiadis's men had to fight the CDA even over adequate office accommodation. Although more space and filing cabinets were continuously promised, the eighteen-member team found itself squeezed into '3 normal and 2 small rooms', which they had tried to sub-partition using hardboard panels. With peons and other menial staff 'constantly coming and going', this arrangement was 'hampering the smooth running of our everyday's work', as one letter of complaint pointed out, adding that 570 rupees in expenses had still not been paid.[13]

From development consultants – powerful and glamorous technicians of the future – Doxiadis's men were turned into consultants in a much more conventional and mundane sense. The extensive correspondence between the DA Islamabad office and their Pakistani partners demonstrates how DA was increasingly cut out of the loop of decision making and turned into something like a trouble-absorbent layer between the other parties involved in the project. With the regime setting a highly ambitious pace for development, conflicts arose at many points in the implementation process, for instance between individual contractors and the CDA, or among executive engineers from a range of subsidiary state

---

institutions like the Public Works Department or WAPDA. In this context, the 'chief consultant's' staff quickly emerged as the intermediaries that were not so much paid for their specialist knowledge as for their willingness to take decisions that nobody wanted to be seen to take, convey orders that others were loath to enforce or, more generally, for their (far from voluntary) availability as somebody to blame when things went wrong or when the timescale for completion began to slip.

While Doxiadis's name still counted to advertise the Islamabad project as yet another testimony to Ayub's developmental credentials to foreign dignitary and funding bodies, the CDA had in fact acquired enough expertise and self-belief not to require much technical assistance in the established sense. Although there was still a shortage of trained personnel at lower levels, Zaheer ud-Din Khwaja, their chief engineer, was internationally educated, widely networked with prominent architects around the world and, after stints on some of Pakistan's other development schemes, also highly experienced.[14] A man of his stature was inclined neither to give his foreign consultants a free hand, nor to remain in a subordinate position to them – which had been the common experience of Doxiadis in Pakistan before. In fact the CDA adopted a deliberate strategy of keeping the power of the chief consultant in check by involving a whole range of other consultants, financed by other sources such as the Colombo Plan. Often without any consultation with the DA mission, these experts would make their own recommendations. Even when not implemented, the flurry of proposals contributed to a sense of no consultant being in charge, and strengthened the position of the Pakistani coordinating agency. It was in this vein that Khwaja invited the services of Sir Robert Matthew, one of the most influential British architects of the post-war era, to advise on Islamabad in parallel to Doxiadis's plan. The CDA engineer made a great deal of Matthew's visit to Pakistan in his memoirs even if the latter only took up a loose coordinating role.[15] From Khwaja's point of view, Islamabad was never Doxiadis's project alone, but a collaborative effort of many international architects always working under the clear guidance of the Pakistani authorities themselves.

The balance of power and authority had shifted, particularly with reference to the young engineers who were actually on site to defend

---

[14] Khwaja in his long distinguished career had served on the Thal development project in West Pakistan as well as in East Pakistan and Karachi as a planner before he joined the Islamabad team; see Khwaja, Z. D. (1998), *Memoirs of an architect*, Lahore, distributed by Ferozsons Publishers, pp.35–80.

[15] He also involved other famous architects, for instance Marcel Breuer, Gerard Brigden and many more, ibid. pp.99, 109–111.

Figure 25 DA field engineer and Karachi Improvement Trust official in conversation with a local resident of Korangi – the Yunani Hakim (practitioner of Greco-Islamic medicine) A. R. B. Qudsi – running a *dawa khana* (dispensary) out of his own home. Note differences in dress. *Source:* CADA: Korangi – Diary PA-99, October 1959, p.67, Pakistan vol.13, p.207 (Archive Files 23564).

Doxiadis's interests. They had been flown in from Athens to serve in Pakistan with little or no prior knowledge of local conditions. Photographs taken at the time depict them as an immediately recognizable alien presence: dressed in shorts (which, in a professional context, would have looked somewhat odd even in their native Greece), they offered a striking contrast to local labourers in their *shalwar qamis*, or local functionaries in formal trousers and bush shirt. [See Figure 25]

One could spin this misfit into a somewhat amusing tale of the unfamiliar East; for instance when it was reported in Doxiadis publicity material that 'E. Djabiras [one of the site engineers in question] finds always difficulty with local people in spelling or pronouncing his name. In one of his last trips to Lahore, he found his name in the list of passengers written as Dj.B.Khan'.[16] Such suggestions of a Greek becoming an honorary Pakistani were funny precisely because men like Djabiras were never able to gain real access to Pakistan, either professionally or personally.

[16] CADA: Pakistan Volume 157, File C-PI 3008, Islamabad Newsletter.

One of the last surviving members of the Islamabad mission at the time of writing was Ioannis Frantzeskakis, a traffic engineer who later went on to found his own successful consultancy business in Athens and played a major role in organizing traffic solutions for the 2004 Olympics. When sharing his reminiscences[17] of what work was like in Ayub's Pakistan, a great sense of pride for what was achieved and an enduring admiration for Doxiadis's expertise and vision predominated. Perhaps unsurprisingly there was a great sense of adventure. Planning Islamabad was by no means a desk job, he pointed out, but physically demanding, as the actual site in its original state was difficult to access and required exhausting treks on foot. When asked about relations with their Pakistani partners in the CDA and elsewhere, Frantzeskakis's account remained upbeat, even when directly confronted with archival evidence of tensions. Whatever problems there may have been, he remembered, they were to be expected in a project like this, and when set into proper context should be considered as relatively minor. In comparison to working in Saudi Arabia, for instance, where political and personal interference were both constant and unpredictable, matters in Pakistan remained on the whole easy and well managed. Doxiadis himself had a very good rapport with General Yahya Khan, Frantzeskakis suggested, and his personal authority and charisma were usually sufficient to put any doubts on the Pakistani side to rest. The fact that the CDA kept relatively strong control was actually an advantage, as it provided DA with a clear point of communication while cutting out the need to deal with too many parties at the same time.

Frantzeskakis's words carry weight because as a professional planner and an eyewitness he was in a unique position to put archival evidence into context. However, it is significant that a less sanguine note appeared in his testimony when the interview went from his 'official' assessment of the project, so to speak, to describing living conditions and personal relationships with Pakistani colleagues. Many aspects of life in Pakistan presented considerable challenges: food was bad, entertainment limited and hygiene standards left a lot to be desired. (This said, medical facilities proved surprisingly good and in no way inferior to what one could have expected back in Greece, as the young engineer found out when his baby son was safely delivered in a Rawalpindi Hospital.) Like all junior members of Doxiadis's team, Frantzeskakis stayed with his young family at the Flashman's Hotel in the Rawalpindi Cantonment. Only Office Chief Orestes Yakas was accommodated in a rented house of his own.

---

[17] Interview Frantzeskakis (Maroussi, 30 June 2010).

The lack of a private space suitable to entertain families meant that social interaction with Pakistani colleagues remained formal, mostly taken up by lengthy games of bridge. With the exception of one Abdul Latif, none of the Pakistani engineers ever brought their families to social occasions, leaving Frantzeskakis's wife and children isolated. Although the engineer politely attributed this to cultural norms of purdah, this is unlikely to be the full reason. Among the colleagues who reportedly would never bring his wife to social meetings was Zaheer ud-Din Khwaja himself, the cosmopolitan chief engineer, who would have done so not for any cultural reasons but out of a deliberate choice to keep Doxiadis's men quite literally in their place, unable to establish contacts that could bypass formal hierarchies and channels of control.

In part to ward off challenges to their authority, every attempt was made by DA to keep Doxiadis's personal authority close to the forefront of operations. This was not only in line with the kind of public image Doxiadis had been cultivating for years, but was also designed to avoid his more junior representatives being too easily brushed aside by the newly confident Pakistani experts and bureaucrats. Not infrequently, local representatives sought to ward off criticism from the Pakistani side with assertions that 'Doxiadis himself' was now involved in a particular piece of design, or that what they proposed was based on Doxiadis's original plans.[18] But with the latter hardly ever present on site and preoccupied with new projects elsewhere, this strategy had its limits. All important decisions, as well as all maps and blueprints of more than draft quality, had to be referred back to the Athens headquarters. There the company's founder had converted a large part of an entire floor into a gigantic three-dimensional model of Islamabad, which he could survey from a mechanical platform suspended above it.

Communications between the Islamabad field office and headquarters relied almost entirely on a daily airmail pouch, frequently leading to delays and complications. Comments on complex proposals were often required faster than they could be sent to Athens and back.[19] An instructive note for DA's Karachi bureau, which acted as 'post office' for Islamabad operations because of its closeness to Pakistan's main international airport, exhorted staff not only to pass any communication to and from head office on immediately, but also to ensure that 'the mail delivered by you to the PIA definitely leave Karachi with the first available flight'.[20]

[18] CADA: Pakistan Volume 193, File C-PI 5176, Letter Hadjopolous to Ajaz Khan, 20 May 1963.
[19] CADA: Pakistan Volume 158, File C-PI 3340.
[20] CADA: Pakistan Volume 193, File C-PI 4698, 23 January 1963.

Akhtar Mahmood, a civil servant seconded from Cabinet duties to serve as Chief Secretary to the CDA, was distinctly unimpressed with Doxiadis's attempt to concentrate this much planning authority in his own person, while being unable or unwilling to really take charge after the project had moved from first designs to implementation. He wrote in an angry letter to DA's office:

> Dr. Doxiadis brings all the important reports in a bunch with him and this happens once in six or seven months. As his stay is generally very brief we do not find the time to have a fruitful discussion with him on these reports. Chief Consultant is requested once again to send his reports before his arrival ... Chief Consultant is further requested to persuade Dr. Doxiadis to visit Islamabad more often and for longer periods.[21]

Matters of detail

Whether his local patrons and collaborators liked it or not, Doxiadis would do everything in his power to ensure that Islamabad remained his 'show'. Doxiadis's antics suggest that his role was far more complex than a mere purveyor of discursive power, a mere 'expert' of development. His behaviour was never about *erasing* any clear location of power – which is what makes 'discourse' so powerful, as it deprives potential challengers of a suitable target to attack – but rather about *alerting* the world to his indispensable presence. In a way this was to be expected. There have always been certain aspects in the modus operandi of the consultant that did not fit in with the simple Foucauldian model of development as discourse: his need to make money, for instance, which has featured prominently in the Doxiadis story throughout this book; but also the emphasis on heroic failure, on masculinity, on the consultant's 'crazy' genius (Chapter 2). Doxiadis may have detested the cigar-smoking and development-sceptic 'feudal lord' he met on his journey through Punjab, but in important respects he did not act very differently himself. His authorized biography made constant references to his charisma, his 'sexy voice' and his natural sense of authority.[22] In fact, much of the distaste felt during the encounter with the 'feudal lord' seems to originate with Doxiadis actually half-recognizing himself in his opponent.

Not least for reasons of clarity, this book has often set up a binary distinction between 'discourse' and 'sovereignty', between 'development' and 'post-coloniality', between Doxiadis's proposals and what his

---

[21] CADA: Pakistan Volume 158, File C-PI 3347, Note Akhtar Mahmood 21 April 1962.
[22] Deane, P. (1965), *Constantinos Doxiadis, master builder for free men*, Dobbs Ferry, NY, Oceana Publications, pp.8, 15, 17.

Pakistani clients 'really' wanted. This intellectual crutch will now have to be abandoned. The clash between consultant and the Pakistani elite was not a clash between discursive power and sovereign power, but rather a clash between two different kinds of sovereign power. The relationship was not a simple distinction or opposition, but a far more complex one where each of the opposing sides was always already reflected and included in the other, rather like the famous Chinese emblem of yin and yang.

Development, one could argue, would begin to resonate with sovereignty when it encountered a place like Pakistan. Conflict itself had a transformative impact on the nature of power. A challenge could find its target only if it reconfigured, at least to a degree, the modality of power in which this target operated. Had he been a 'pure' expert, Doxiadis would have simply shaken his head about the 'feudal lord' that so annoyed him on his trip to southern Punjab,[23] and then moved on with his planning. To feel threatened in the way he did meant that somebody had to unsettle his persona as an expert, and to tease his 'inner sovereign' in order to bring it out into the open. A great deal of this process depended on manipulating interpersonal communication, on introducing notions of physicality and masculinity into the relationship.

But there was also a more structural logic of fundamental importance at work that transcended mere personal relationships. It revealed itself in a seemingly mundane problem that dominated the exchange between DA and their colleagues in the CDA. It was, quite literally, a matter of detail; not in the immediate sense of consultants quarrelling with their clients over minute issues (which was common enough too), but rather as a more general problem: *how much attention to detail* was actually required to make a success of a development project like Korangi or Islamabad? It was over this question, more than any other, that Doxiadis was prepared to fight, and it was over this question that his opponents began to build a case against him, leading to the eventual removal of DA from the Islamabad project.

The matter of detail had theoretical implications of fundamental importance. To an extent these implications were already recognized by Doxiadis himself, and as we shall see, they also fit perfectly into the kind of Foucauldian analysis attempted in this book. It needs no repetition that Doxiadis's case for development was predicated on his claim to have the right grasp of detail. He took pride in the fact that, unlike his opponents, he would base his planning on a close knowledge of the population in

---

[23] See Chapter 3, pp.145–146.

question: their economic make-up, cultural norms, history, social structure and so on. But at least in Doxiadis's best theoretical formulations, this was not omniscience pure and simple. Contrary to what James C. Scott argued in *Seeing like a state*,[24] the reason for knowing a good deal about a place and its people was more subtle than being able to control each and every one of their moves, let alone to comprehensively reconfigure their behaviour through the imposition of 'development' from above. The right grasp of detail was not necessarily knowing everything, but rather knowing what it was necessary to know. The ultimate power of detail lay in the fact that it could make power accurate, consensual, so light in touch that it would not even register resistance.

In a passage that anticipated Foucault's discovery of 'security' (and its relationship with controlling 'circulation') by over twenty years, Doxiadis insisted that planning was like hydraulic engineering: not an effort that could enforce solutions on 'actual life', as he called it, but one that took 'into consideration the *natural trends* [emphasis in the original] and serves them in the best possible way', one that 'regulates the flow of life' in a 'natural direction'.[25] 'As life is continuously changing, plans should be *flexible*', he insisted, only to point out that this was by and large the very opposite of what he saw across the global South. The difference is very important. Why would a planner in the South, as Doxiadis put it, stick to a plan 'as if it was the Kur'an', even if he understood perfectly well that this plan was too inadequate to capture reality? The reason was, once again, a lack of command over detail. When there were too few experts available, people would end up in a situation where they were 'interested only in rapid implementation'. Knowing too little meant an obsession with plans rather than their full mastery. In consequence, policy makers in the South would be desperate to have a plan at almost any price, even if they knew that the plan was bad, or had to be cobbled together by culling hopelessly inaccurate suggestions from 'handbooks and magazines'.[26] An excessive focus on getting things done on the flimsiest of foundations, as exhibited by General Azam Khan and other 'go-getters' in Pakistan, may have been great sovereign acts, but when seen from a 'security' perspective, they were in fact testimonies of impotence.

If the headlong plunge into implementation demonstrated the degeneration of 'developmentality' into a mere sovereignty game, there was a

---

[24] Scott, J. C. (1998), *Seeing like a state: how certain schemes to improve the human condition have failed*, New Haven, CT; London, Yale University Press, p.5.
[25] CADA: Pakistan Volume 3, Pakistan Ekistics, p.29.
[26] CADA: Pakistan Volume 2, Diary, p.16.

similar danger on the opposite side: that the planner became so deeply absorbed in knowing every detail of what a project involved that he would never be ready to implement anything to begin with. Orestes Yakas addressed this problem in characteristic fashion when he commented on Doxiadis's suggestion of involving a 'social scientist' in the planning of Islamabad. Yakas was of the opinion that 'specialist scientists are very hazardous workers in the Planning of settlements because they ... have a tendency in analysing the facts in a very detailed way, adding up an enormous amount of information, views and suggestions. To use a technical term they get themselves "out of scale"'.[27] To prevent such a falling 'out of scale' was precisely the purpose of Ekistics. It would provide a generalist knowledge that could be easily shared with experts from other disciplines, while also, to use the framework of an earlier discussion, possessing the right kind of 'resolution'; fine enough to be accurate for a plan to work, but not so fine as to prevent one from seeing the wood for the trees.

Doxiadis's own formulation goes right to the heart of a distinction that has not been made with sufficient clarity so far: that between development as 'discourse' and development as 'security'. Both are, of course, Foucauldian categories, and both can be easily juxtaposed to a sovereign modality of power. They both operate as far as possible in a centreless manner, through categories of knowledge rather than performative action, and in a deliberately hard-to-resist, non-political fashion. The main difference is that 'discourse' is a 'flat' and undynamic conception. In line with Foucault's trademark preoccupation with breaks and ruptures in intellectual history, it was conceived first and foremost as a marker of difference, not as a category that could account for processes of change. Discursive power and sovereign power together marked the two sides of the break that constituted the coming of modernity to Western Europe. In consequence, the power of development as described by Ferguson or Escobar in terms of 'discourse' simply 'is'; it is not seen in relationship with other modalities of power, and its effects are stable and resilient to challenges from the outside. 'Security' in contrast describes an equilibrial state that is inherently unstable, a state of interaction or 'triangulation' in which other modalities of power are not superseded but present and effective.

The matter of detail, of finding the right kind of 'resolution' for development work, highlights precisely this unstable, dynamic element. If the grasp of detail went either below or above what was right, 'security'

---

[27] CADA: Pakistan Volume 74, File C-PR 489, Yakas to DA, 'Socio-economic follow-up', 12 April 1960.

would lose its magic touch. Too rough, and development would degenerate into senseless implementation; too fine, and development would either not happen at all, or become so intrusive as to make life unbearable for those under its sway. Either error would make development an easy target of resistance. In fact, the two opposing alternatives led in the end to a similar place. As Foucault himself recognized in an important passage in his later work, the disciplinary power of discourse was not in fact as categorically removed from sovereign power as he had previously thought. The desire to see everything in order to control everything – his definition of the disciplinary power of the panopticon – was at its heart a sovereign desire par excellence.[28] Discourse could produce tyranny if it was really all-controlling, and in the cases where it did, it would no longer really be effective as discourse, i.e. as a centreless, dispersed power formation. For the miracle of depoliticization to take place, power had to operate within a modality of 'security', not simply disciplinary power; in short, it had to be *balanced*.

Undermining this balance by pushing 'development' interventions into either involving too much or too little detail became the means of contesting the power of development and its representatives. Conversely, defending the right degree of detail became the terrain where the power of the consultant itself had to be defended. One place where conflicts of this kind were immediately felt was in the relationship between the DA Islamabad office and the headquarters in Athens, connected, as they were, by their daily exchanges of airmailed documents. The team in Greece was often far more rigid in its understanding of Ekistics principles than the fast-moving situation in Pakistan allowed, and often refused to draw up plans for which necessary background data – the details in question – were lacking.[29] Planning without full knowledge of the society, history and culture of the target society was after all, in Doxiadis's view, the greatest crime a planner could commit. However, unable to obtain such data from their Pakistani partners – while also having to fend off demands to deliver according an ever-tightening schedule – left the DA field offices in an impossible situation. 'We will appreciate very much if for any additional required data (of minor importance) you could base your studies on your own assumptions ...',

---

[28] Foucault, M., M. Senellart, F. O. Ewald and A. Fontana (2007), *Security, territory, population: lectures at the Collège de France, 1977–78*, Basingstoke; New York, Palgrave Macmillan: République Française, p.66.

[29] For instance CADA: Pakistan Volume 193, File C-PI 4612; also Pakistan Volume 194, C-PI 5505, 10 August 1963.

begged an exasperated letter from Islamabad to Athens in the months leading up to the termination of the chief consultant's contract.[30]

Unsurprisingly, matters of detail nearly always cropped up when the engineers of DA came to blows with their Pakistani counterparts. It was the greatest fear on the Pakistani side to operate without at least a perfunctory reference to a plan – what Doxiadis had called the propensity to treat even the most inaccurate and hastily produced plan as if it was the 'Kur'an'. Any action taken without reference to the consultant's instructions by any one of the many executive agencies involved in the project – the CDA, the public works departments, WAPDA, etc. – risked turning into internecine warfare, as without ulterior discursive sanction it constituted a 'naked' expression of institutional sovereignty. Quarrelling over matters of detail became a perfect way of deflecting internal conflict into a conflict between the different executive agencies and the consultants. Whenever they came under pressure, Pakistani agencies would lambast Doxiadis's men for not having supplied sufficient detail to allow proper implementation, as demonstrated by the following letter by the Deputy Director of the Public Works Department, Masihullah Khan:

The plans attached with these papers [sent by DA] indicate the sizes of sewers which cannot be checked in the absence of the detailed report regarding the design and proposal of the main sewerage scheme which will be implemented ultimately. Complete data and design of the sanitary sewerage and storm water system including septic tank along with calculations is also required for necessary scrutiny.[31]

While Masihullah Khan wanted more detail in terms of sewerage design, DA, meanwhile, wrote to the Director General of the Public Works Department requesting the exact location of manhole covers all over the Islamabad site.[32] In this way Doxiadis's men could throw any challenge back at their Pakistani hosts. They were unable to provide plans on schedule, they would argue, precisely because somebody else involved on the project had failed to supply them with the necessary details. Whenever their expertise or ability to deliver was put into question, DA issued angry demands for more information, more maps, better data.

---

[30] CADA: Pakistan Volume 194, File C-PI 5505, Letter DA Islamabad to DA Athens, 10 August 1963.
[31] CADA: Pakistan Volume 114, File C-PI 2527, Letter Masihullah Khan to Yakas, 16 October 1961.
[32] CADA: Pakistan Volume 160, Files C-PI 4491, Letter to M. M. Hydri, PWD, C-PI 4466. See also Pakistan Volume 193, File C-PI 5505, DA Islamabad to DA Athens, 10 August 1963.

A race against time

If DA attempted to push the Pakistani side into a stark choice between having to wait for their directives and blind actionism, the latter hit back with their own preferred weapon: time pressure. They knew that Doxiadis's carefully crafted attention to detail could be upset by enforcing a relentless pace of implementation. When the first major disagreements appeared between the DA field office and the CDA, they were precisely over this problem. In an internal memo, the new CDA Chairman, W. A. Shaikh, contended that if Islamabad were to be a success, Doxiadis's men would have to abandon their penchant to plan bottom-up, to give as much attention to the height of windowsills or the culturally appropriate dimensions of toilets as they did to actionable overview plans. They would from now on have to work much faster – an order that was in itself marked 'for IMMEDIATE action'.[33] This line of attack could on occasion score some spectacular own goals. When the DA office was pressurized by the CDA to start building the ideologically important 'handicrafts sector' – it represented the importance of folk art as well as care for labour and low-paid residents – the DA engineers found that 'construction will not be possible in this section for a long time', because contractors working on a nearby road interchange had first excavated the ground for building materials and then, over-enthusiastically using their newly provided bulldozers, haphazardly filled it in again.[34] Now the ground was too unsettled to allow any building activity. Rushing one segment of the plan had actually made it impossible to proceed in another, once again demonstrating that only the right attention to detail adopted by the coordinating consultant's agency could keep a project like Islamabad on track.

Building Islamabad was always a race against time, and it was not only the confrontation between consultant and client that accelerated implementation out of control from the point of view of the planner. A simple, but easily overlooked, practical consideration was the fact that life had not come to a standstill on Pothowar plain while Islamabad was being constructed. The site was not, in effect, virgin territory, but a place where people still tilled the land and grazed their cattle. Their activities created their own ground realities in competition with the ongoing building work. Islamabad had to be constructed before new and wild settlements could spring up on building sites, before materials

[33] CADA: Pakistan Volume 112, File C-PI 2273, 16 August 1961.
[34] CADA: Pakistan Volume 193, File C-PI 4760, 4 February 1963.

could be stolen,[35] in short, before new facts could be created on the ground. There were pre-existing villages that had to be cleared to make space for Islamabad, and their inhabitants would not give up quietly but simply relocate to other areas on the site.[36] Doxiadis's attempts to pin these people down by making their permanent resettlement a priority did not always work, as files pertaining to the demolition of 'unauthorized quarters' built by 'oustees' demonstrate.[37] Incursions also came from other quarters. Rawalpindi rubbish collectors and 'night-soil' removal companies utilized the new road connections to the capital development area to use it as a dumping ground for waste.[38]

All considered, the Pakistani state's choice of time pressure to keep a check on foreign consultants had theoretical significance. One of the main characteristics of sovereign power was its peculiar relationship with time. Unlike the disciplinary power enshrined in discursive regimes, sovereign power did not operate continuously and alongside the flow of time, but in a punctuated fashion and across it, only at the moments when it was actually exercised. Being relentlessly driven from one such sovereign moment to the next to retain its efficiency became a hallmark of this kind of power, and the obsession with speed that was to be found in both the Korangi and Islamabad projects was testimony to just how sovereignty obsessed the Pakistani state was. As pointed out elsewhere, there was a deep theoretical link between the moment of decision as the central element of sovereignty – as suggested by Carl Schmitt – and the fact that the Korangi project was announced and offered to Doxiadis 'on the spot', with a demonstrative lack of prior planning and consultation. To decide to do something fast, without having considered the consequences and without first assessing whether it was really possible or not, was sovereignty in its purest form.[39] Similar considerations were also present at the Islamabad project. When Foreign Minister Zulfiqar Ali Bhutto was the first of Ayub's Cabinet to visit the site, along with Shaikh

---

[35] This did not only pertain to unauthorized buildings. The nullah (ravine) in sector G6 had become destabilized because of the unauthorized extraction of building materials by contractors. CADA: Pakistan Volume 193, File C-PI 5579, 2 September 1963.
[36] Hull, M. (2008), 'Ruled by records: the expropriation of land and the misappropriation of lists in Islamabad', *American Ethnologist* 35(4), pp.506–507.
[37] CADA: Pakistan Volume 112, File C-PI 2266, Demolition of quarters belonging to Muhammad Yusuf. Zaheer ud-Din Khwaja, when commenting on Doxiadis's suggestion to rehabilitate these 'oustees' within the Islamabad site, wanted to 'rule out' any such ideas on the bases of cost and of keeping land prices in residential sectors high. CADA: Pakistan Volume 111, File C-PI 1687, 21 March 1961.
[38] CADA: Pakistan Volume 113, File C-PI 2243, Garbage Disposal, 12 August 1961.
[39] Daechsel, M. (2011b), 'Sovereignty, governmentality and development in Ayub's Pakistan: the case of Korangi Township', *Modern Asian Studies* 45(1): 131–157, p.151.

and M. H. Sufi, he was 'pleased to hear that the progress achieved by the Capital Development Authority during the first two years of activities surpassed any previous record in the field of planning and developing new towns.'[40] It made a certain sense to emphasize speed in the case of refugee rehabilitation in Korangi – as one could always argue that the beneficiaries were people that required immediate redress of their problems. But in the case of a new capital city, one would have expected other considerations to be singled out for praise: that it was well planned, for instance, or that the houses that were beginning to appear were beautiful. Time would always retain some importance, of course – no capital city can take for ever to be built – but what difference did it make that this capital had been built *faster than those of other countries and nations*? The fact that speed mattered the most just demonstrated once more what the primary purpose of the project was: a theatrical staging of development activism to safeguard Ayub Khan's credentials as ultimate sovereign of Pakistan.

Time was the Achilles heel of development discourse. Ideally, it could keep 'development' in the kind of balance that made it work well in terms of Foucault's 'security', as a relatively light-touch intervention that would confine itself to knowing and planning only what it was really necessary to know and plan, precisely because there was always a need to get on with one's task. But more often, and this was clearly the case with Doxiadis in Pakistan, it could seriously unbalance this precarious arrangement and tip the development encounter into a naked game of competing sovereignties, with the 'go-getting' national state on one side pressing on the accelerator at the expense of all else, and the consultant on the other holding on ever more jealously and closely to his mastery of detail to defend his relevance. At its worst, development could become so 'unbalanced' that it was little more than a two-pronged sovereignty onslaught on its recipients: senseless implementation without consultation *combined* with a sense of know-it-all, control-it-all.

In a way, this propensity to become unbalanced under pressure was underpinned by the fact that development thought already included references to these extremes in its very fabric. It was, after all, an ideology that aimed at 'take-off' – to use Rosenstein-Rodan's famous formulation of the 1950s[41] – which must count as the most iconic celebration of speed

[40] CADA: Pakistan Volume 114, File C-PI 2769, Islamabad Newsletter.
[41] Meier, G. M. (1994a), 'From colonial economics to development economics', *From classical economics to development economics*, G. M. Meier (ed.), London, Macmillan: 173–196, p.179. Later appropriated by Rostow; see Singer, H. W. (1961), 'Trends in economic thought on underdevelopment', *Social Research* 28(4): 387–414, p.391.

in social theory of any time period. And simultaneously, as pointed out repeatedly throughout this book, development was a definitive project of knowledge, an attempt to make and explain the world through new categories. But it would be wrong to argue that development was some-how destined – by some kind of inner logic – to become a pure sovereignty game. An equilibrium of sorts was equally possible, as long as these two impulses could be triangulated in such a way as to produce a 'security' modality of power. When critics like Escobar and Scott describe the top-down imposition of a knowledge project as the *defining* element of development – and also as the key reason why it was inevitably bound to fail – they arrived at their conclusions through the atemporal study of only one element of development: its strictly 'discursive', sense-making aspect. It is only if we interpret development as a historical process, as a tussle quite literally over time – both in the sense that this confrontation happened in time and over a certain period, and in the sense that the bone of contention of the confrontation was itself time – that a fuller and more open-ended account of failure appears. In the final analysis, the problem was precisely *not* that development was a centreless 'discourse', but rather the very opposite: the fact that it was always embodied in somebody – Doxiadis, his men in Islamabad, Khwaja, the CDA, General Azam Khan, etc. – and hence could not operate easily as a dispersed grid of power. This embodiment was in itself a result of development's entanglement in time, its historical nature, but it was greatly enhanced by the fact that it took place in the context of a post-colonial nation state, whose sense of sovereignty exercised a powerful pull over how any kind of power would work under its sway. In a place like Pakistan it was never possible to forget *who* it was who carried out development, and, quite regardless of what development actually involved, whose sense of power was violated, enhanced or otherwise affected in the process. To truly account for development in a place like Pakistan, we will have to abandon the idea of 'discourse' and move on to something more dynamic and open ended.

The problem of circulation

Projects like Islamabad and Korangi revealed not so much a clash between two *modalities* of power – between 'development as discourse' on one side, and the Pakistani nation state exercising its 'sovereignty' on the other – but rather something more nuanced and complicated: the contradiction and interplay between two formations of power – two *'governmentalities'* – in which multiple modalities of power were combined in different ways. The difference between what Doxiadis proposed in the name of development and how the Pakistani state wanted to rule through development was never absolute. Sovereign power and disciplinary power, the will to act in time and the will to know, came together to produce some degree of managerial control on both sides of the encounter. But a significant difference remained with regard to their point and manner of 'balance'. There is no better field to investigate this difference than in the way each formation sought to deal with a key category of development subjects: labour. The latter featured prominently in all of Doxiadis's operations in Pakistan. Both Korangi and – to a significant extent – also Islamabad, in its very first stages, were not only built by labour, but also for labour.

Before getting into more detail, it is useful to sketch where the argument is coming from. When Foucault first introduced the term 'governmentality' (initially used synonymously with 'security'), he associated it with the act of managing risk, with the ability to know precisely when to intervene and how much, with a view to keeping intervention as light as possible so as to minimize potential resistance. Governmentality was – in a similar way to Doxiadis's metaphor of planning as channelling 'natural' flows – the careful management of pre-existing inclinations and desires, a technique dependent as much on letting go as on exerting pressure. In stark contrast to a disciplinary modality of power that sought to categorize people in order to pin them down – epitomized by problem categories like the criminal, the insane, the sexually deviant, the undeserving poor – the key object of intervention was the facilitation of 'circulation': of letting people, goods, capital, ideas, even pathogens move as much as possible through physical and social space.[42]

At first glance, this preference for circulation over fixity seems to offer an easy way to distinguish the power potentialities of Doxiadis's plans from the kind of control the Pakistani state sought to impose. It is striking that almost everything in the Islamabad and Korangi projects was designed to facilitate circulation. One of the key considerations of Doxiadis's planning methodology had always been the problem of traffic, a problem of circulation par excellence. The idea that there should be a clear separation of the 'human scale' of the sector and the surrounding 'space of the machine' and the very concept of *dynapolis*, which served as the guiding principle of Pakistan's new capital, were all about managing circulation. In a more extended sense, Doxiadis saw most aspects of life as flows of one kind or another, whether it was the supply and removal of

---

[42] Foucault, M., M. Senellart, F. O. Ewald and A. Fontana (2007), *Security, territory, population: lectures at the Collège de France, 1977–78*, Basingstoke; New York, Palgrave Macmillan: République Française.

water, the circulation of air through a room or, more generally, the flow of populations from the countryside to the city, the urbanization process itself. In contrast, what seemed to be upmost in the minds of Pakistani government officials was the restriction of movement. Both Korangi and Islamabad were located at sites that were deliberately remote from the main arteries of circulation in the country, and in both cases conspicuously little effort was made to connect them up. Korangi had to wait for a proper road and bus service far longer than its new residents could afford, and despite being the nation's capital, Islamabad was very deliberately never given railway access.[43] In fact, Islamabad's inaccessibility and disconnect from the main hubs of political and economic life were precisely its *raison d'être* in the eyes of the regime. As pointed out elsewhere, it was not meant to be a city but rather a latter-day equivalent of the old colonial hill station, a place where there was as little contact as possible between government and the governed, between civil servants and society.[44]

The difference between planning for circulation and governing according to keeping things fixed was already inscribed in the main social categories involved. Instead of the dynamic variables of development – the 'middle class' or the 'new city dweller' that Doxiadis constantly invoked in his plans – the regime saw Korangi and Islamabad as settlement solutions for two far more specific and *static* constituencies: 'refugee' slum-dwellers and bureaucrats. Contrary to its meaning in other contexts, the term 'refugee' was by no means a marker of mobility and fluidity in the context of 1950s Pakistan. Instead it had acquired ethnic undertones. Being increasingly defined as a group of Urdu speakers with a particular culture and political loyalties, the *muhajirs* (as refugees were known) were pinned down as just another colour in the mosaic of 'nationalities' and ethnic constituencies, alongside Bengalis, Baluch or Pathans. Bureaucrats, in turn, were by definition one the most fixed social categories of all, demarcated precisely by function, rank and salary. Both bureaucrats and refugees were singled out as development recipients precisely because they were perceived as unique problem categories; people that could not be allowed to circulate freely but who required continuous and thorough control, similar in this sense to Foucault's list of deviants and delinquents.[45]

---

[43] CADA: Pakistan Volume 41, Diary PA 100 Pakistan Diary from 7 to 16 February 1960, p.109.
[44] Daechsel, M. (2013), 'Misplaced Ekistics: Islamabad and the politics of urban development in Pakistan', *South Asian History and Culture* 4(1): 87–106, p.95.
[45] Ibid. pp.99–101.

264 The consultant under attack

The way the new townships were actually constructed emphasized their character as spaces of confinement, roughly similar in purpose to disciplinary institutions such as prisons, mental asylums or sanatoria that Foucault had used as his paradigmatic examples of disciplinary control. When Doxiadis, ever mindful of the requirements of circulation, insisted that both Islamabad and Korangi should be designed as integrated urban spaces, where rich and poor, refugee and non-refugee, bureaucrat and businessman, could easily mingle and connect to form a new and dynamic social order, his Pakistani patrons always demanded that they were kept as special category cities as far as possible. In Korangi little effort was ever made to attract the kind of more affluent residents that would turn it from a colony of the urban poor into a proper city, while in Islamabad official land allocations were handled in such a way as to discourage any significant presence of non-state dependent residents. Revealingly, one of the most hotly debated issues between Doxiadis and the Pakistani state was plot sizes. Doxiadis operated with European norms that sought to be (comparatively) economical with private space while reserving a substantial amount of space for public areas of different orders. The Pakistani bureaucrats in contrast insisted on very large plot sizes for the richest of their ranks – a need that reflected the colonial idea of putting as much open space as possible between the living spaces of white officers and the contaminants of native society. In addition, they felt that any difference in rank between civil servants should be rigorously reflected not only in the size of plots allocated, but also in terms of separating areas for the higher ranks as much as possible from those of lower ranks.[46] Islamabad was as much a city of confinement and isolation as Korangi.

But in a manner that has not been sufficiently recognized so far, including in my own published work on the subject, this distinction between a governmentality of development, on one side, and a disciplinary regime sponsored by the Pakistani state, on the other, does not exhaust the analysis. As rigorous as the Pakistani state was in defining problem categories and in doing nothing to facilitate their mobility, it never showed much consistency in actually policing these divisions when there was active opposition to them. In Korangi it was actually circulation-oriented Doxiadis who would constantly admonish the KDA to do more to enforce

---

[46] CDA Library, Islamabad: File Dox PA 64 (1 February 1960), Housing and Town Planning Committee No. VII, pp.14–15; File Dox PA 73 (February 1960) Volume 23, Problems of Size, pp.24–28. (This is the file in the library with the heaviest traces of use and with copious annotations by Pakistani civil servants!) File Dox PA 85 (16 June 1960), Islamabad Plot Sizes, Volume 32.

'his plan'. His careful division of space between residential quarters and what he saw as the key institutions of Muslim urban life – the market, the tea house, the mosque – was in fact usually ignored by Korangi's residents. They started to open up shops and small factories in their allocated houses, while dedicated commercial areas remained empty and underused. Green spaces were rapidly colonized to erect unauthorized places of worship. Doxiadis's much insisted-upon idea to offer new ownership structures to the residents by making them long-term lease-holders (rather than tenants) was misunderstood and, as time moved on, actively resisted. The point here is not that the Pakistani authorities were for the most part unable to prevent such contraventions of planning provisions, but that they did not even seem to have tried particularly hard.[47]

This attitude represented the wider 'imbalance' that characterized the state's policy mix. While sovereign power had been concentrated in single and spectacular acts of 'implementation', in such instances as shifting the government to a new capital or having 15,000 housing units built in six months, there was no ability to pursue less spectacular but more continuous control over time: hence the rush into actionism. In consequence, disciplinary power – the other ingredient – was reduced in its operation. Although the will to know, classify and contain was never given up – this was the whole point of having a new township for refugee slum-dwellers and for government bureaucrats – it remained to a large extent just that, a declaration of will rather than a sustained intervention. Doxiadis's point that there was this strange belief in the validity of a plan, even if this plan was not well worked out or did not make much sense, can once again be brought in as a perceptive observation of how disciplinary power became a mere emblem of sovereign power under these circumstances. But this is not all there is to the analysis. *Not* to police contraventions of the plan – even to abandon a project like Korangi rather than to insist on the collection of contributions from the residents – *was in itself a managerial choice*, the product of a calculation by Pakistani state officials that it was better in these cases to let the residents follow their own inclinations, rather than to intervene and enforce compliance. In short, this was some form of 'security' power in its own right, albeit a very different variety from what Doxiadis and other development experts proposed. The fact that parts of Korangi developed into (by local standards) perfectly well-organized townships, without much government

[47] Daechsel, M. (2011b), 'Sovereignty, governmentality and development in Ayub's Pakistan: the case of Korangi Township', *Modern Asian Studies* 45(1): 131–157, pp.154–155.

intervention and without any attempt to preserve Doxiadis's original plan, was in its own way a testimony to the potential success of such a 'security' policy.[48]

Governmentalities of labour

There were striking differences between how the development consultants and the generals approached the problem of circulation, and these differences were demonstrated with particular clarity in the field of labour management. Among the features of the Islamabad Plan most often singled out for praise by his own team was Doxiadis's insistence that the very first houses of Islamabad should be earmarked not for government servants, but for the actual workers constructing the city.[49] Such a consideration for labour had been notably absent at the Chandigarh and Brasilia projects, and was heralded as further evidence of Doxiadis's distinctiveness and superiority over his rivals. Doxiadis's personal enthusiasm in this regard contrasted sharply with indifference among his Pakistani partners who, for the most part, felt that the reproduction and welfare of labour was a matter for private contractors and not for any state agency.[50] The rationale behind the consultant's suggestion was far from philanthropic do-goodery, of course. Settling workers first was a hard-nosed strategy to secure a steady and reliable supply of personnel. In Doxiadis's estimation, the more than 3000 workers required for building a new capital could not be easily produced on site by wage

[48] This argument in large part contradicts Scott's interpretation of the failure of grand plans. He posits that grand plans fail despite allusions to omnipotence because even the best plan cannot capture everything, not even everything that it is meant to control, due to the irreducible complexity of the 'real world'. Scott, J. C. (1998), *Seeing like a state: how certain schemes to improve the human condition have failed*, New Haven, CT; London, Yale University Press, pp.4–6. My argument here is closer to the one proposed by Madhu Sarin in her study of Chandigarh. She insists that it would be wrong to see the growth of the 'unplanned' sectors of the city as a failure of the plan. 'Planned' and 'unplanned' are simply two sides of a single managerial choice by the planner. The 'unplanned' is no less controlled than the 'planned'; it is simply controlled in a different way, often so as to systematically downgrade and disadvantage certain groups of city dwellers. Sarin, M. (1982), *Urban planning in the Third World: the Chandigarh experience*, London, Mansell, p.4, Chapter 6.

[49] Interview Frantzeskakis, Yakas, O. (2001), *Islamabad, the birth of a capital*, Karachi, Oxford University Press, p.88.

[50] CADA: Pakistan Volume 112, File C-PI 1796, Comments by CDA Land Directorate on Industrial sectors I9 and I10, 14 April 1961. A similar attitude also pertained to other aspects of labour welfare, for instance health centres and dispensaries for workers, which again were placed squarely on the shoulders of 'Industrialists themselves' and therefore outside the remit of state planning. CADA: Pakistan Volume 157, File C-PI 2915, Medical Facilities, 6 January 1962.

incentives alone. The villages around Islamabad were too small to provide such vast numbers, and numerous other building projects in nearby Rawalpindi actually pulled labour away from Islamabad.[51] In consequence, workers had to be brought in from locations much further afield, which made them far less likely to stick around long enough to finish a major project like constructing a new city. DA operatives had experienced problems with long-distance recruitment first hand, and knew what the likely outcomes of such a policy would be. Some members of their own low-paid clerical staff came from as far away as Quetta, but despite such a willingness to travel were also notoriously unreliable in actually turning up for work; some even disappeared without notice while away on home leave.[52] Doxiadis's argument was that labour could be tied to the Islamabad project long term if housing – or at least free plots and materials – was provided by the CDA.

There were other benefits to such control through benevolence. Left for the most part to their own devices, contract workers had little choice but to erect squatter settlements close to the construction site, often in the very villages that were already earmarked for demolition to make way for the new city. In an ironic twist, Islamabad already produced its own slums even before the first authorized residents had moved in. 'It is obvious that this arrangement is absolutely against any public health regulations and it will, by no means, be satisfactory at the time when some of these workers will decide to bring their families', an internal memo pointed out at the time, while mentioning further that irregular 'shacks' on the new site 'will cause a lot of grumbling and complaints on the parts of the government servants ... This will give vent to feelings of jealousy and hostility amongst the workmen, who, after all, are and will be going to build Islamabad.'[53] In the long run, providing decent housing to construction labour was actually a cheaper and more time-efficient way to construct the city than to leave such matters to unaccountable outside agencies.

Doxiadis's proposal is a classic attempt to manage circulation through welfare, involving different modalities of power combined in a distinctive

[51] CADA: Pakistan Volume 130, File Dox PI Islamabad – Plots and Houses for Labour Force, 28, 25 June 1962. There was in fact a labour shortage on the site at various points. CADA: Pakistan Volume 157, File C-PI 2933, Highways.
[52] One such case was a draughtsman called Sharif Ahmad Shahab, of 'Popular Leather and General Store, Suraj Gang Bazaar, Quetta', who was urged telegraphically to report back for work after failing to return from home leave. CADA: Pakistan Volume 193, File C-PI 5273. Another was one Rashid Ahmad Khan, of Slim&Co, Queen's Road, Lahore, whose contract was terminated and tools demanded back after being absent without authorization for a week. Pakistan Volume 193, File C-PI 5638, 19 September 1963.
[53] CADA: Pakistan Volume 130, File Dox PI 28, 25 June 1962.

governmentality; he does employ elements of disciplinary power, for instance by insisting that irregular settlements be cleared and that workers be accommodated in spaces directly designed for them. In fact, the whole purpose of his intervention was some curtailment and control of movement, but an element of letting people act according to their own volition was also involved. As soon as good housing was available, labour would not have to be forced to stay in Islamabad or, for that matter, forced out of existing slum settlements; they would do so simply as a result of their own best interests. Note here the difference to Pakistani attitudes to the same problem: most local civil servants and planners did resolutely not see it within the remit of a state agency to provide housing to non-salaried staff. Government quarters were an important perk of government service, and the distinction between 'ordinary' or private sector labour and even the lowest rungs of the bureaucracy could not be undermined at any cost. While Doxiadis wanted to avoid creating jealousies between construction workers and poor state employees over housing, the Pakistani state would have found such sentiments useful, to maintain the distinction of categories so crucial to control through favouritism. In the eyes of the Pakistani state, members of the bureaucracy were the subjects of harsh disciplinary power, while no restrictions at all were imposed on the circulation of 'private' labour. Outside forces, such as the work of contractors and other non-state social structures, were expected to provide as much control as was necessary. The same logic was also visible in Korangi, even if an industrial area was in fact planned at a convenient distance from the new township. Labour stability was never the reason why people were relocated to the new township – it was entirely justified with a discourse of refugee rehabilitation – and nor was the potential advantage of binding a new working class to their jobs through housing provisions utilized with any conviction. As in Islamabad, the expectation was that individual employers would provide workers' housing, if and when they felt it necessary to do so.[54]

Both Doxiadis and the Pakistani state assumed that labour possessed certain features that made it amenable to controlled 'circulation'. In Doxiadis's case, the key consideration was economic self-interest; everybody, according to his calculation, would understand the obvious advantage of having a purpose-built and permanent house over living in a shanty town. Workers shared with all human beings the basic need to

---

[54] One of the first aspects of the Korangi project to be dropped by the KDA was the provision of dedicated housing for the Lyari industrial zone, with the justification that such matters should be taken up by private industrialists themselves. CADA: Pakistan Volume 71, File C-PKH 2201, Meeting reaction KDA, 14 December 1960.

have shelter, and this need was sharply increased by the process of modernization, by the necessity to find work in new and typically urban locations. These people would settle in Islamabad if good housing was provided, no matter whether they were Sunni Muslim or Shi^{c}a Muslim, Punjabis or Baluch, even peasants or urban labourers, prior to being hired for a construction job. 'Labour' in this sense was a typical category of development discourse, a universalized, individualistic and depoliticized construction that would have held equal validity in Doxiadis's native Greece as it did in Iraq, Ghana or Pakistan. For Pakistani policy makers, circulation was managed in a strikingly different manner: not by a universal and individual category like 'the average worker', but by specific group identities; not by development, but by methods of control that had been inherited and fine-tuned from colonial methodologies of governance.

Let us illustrate this approach with some further material. An extensive file in DA's Korangi records[55] concerned the allocation of plots to a particular group of petitioners: the 'Benarsi silk weavers'. It is not entirely clear whether they were actually from the city of Benares itself, where a certain type of highly elaborate and luxurious saree is famous, or whether they were from other localities producing the kind of product associated with the city's name. At any rate, they had come to Karachi from North India, and hence were 'refugees' according to the official nomenclature and potential recipients of government patronage. Their case was further enhanced by the fact that theirs was a spectacular and highly skilled occupation with resonances of Mughal glory and, at least as it had been traditionally perceived, a distinctively 'Muslim' one.

In the summer of 1960, their case was passed on to DA from the office of the administrator of Karachi, the highest executive authority in the city, and recommended by both Colonel Humayune, the part-time head of the NHSA (when it was still confined to the Korangi project), and M. Rahimtoola, the KDA chief engineer. The original weavers' request to have plots allocated to them had been formulated by other state functionaries lower down the line: by a 'social worker' A. Y. Malik working with a military officer at the rehabilitation department, one Major Rasheed, and with the Registrar of Cooperative Societies, K. A. Rehman, who had toured and surveyed weaver communities throughout Karachi. They had listed a total of 358 families scattered over a number of irregular settlements in small clusters ranging from 4 to 20 families – only the Jahangirabad slum accounted for one large block

---

[55] CADA: Pakistan Volume 96, File R-PKH 122.

of 200 families. They argued that since all belonged to a single 'community' of Benarsi weavers, they should all be settled in a single location to facilitate the government's 'great effort to patronize and preserve an important industry'.[56] The survey was accompanied by a series of written petitions from one Habibullah, the secretary of the Pakistan Sanati Cooperative Anjuman Ltd, who similarly demanded an allocation of plots in Korangi in the interest of the proper economic development of his community.[57]

Further details scattered throughout the documentation quickly reveal that the settlement of the Benarsi weavers was a complex example of controlling and subordinating labour. Once the 'core' of the community had been identified, other surveyors were quick to discover an ever-increasing number of peripheral members, in the range of 1000 to 1500 families. While most of the weavers lived in temporary mud huts in irregular settlements and were under constant danger of having their equipment damaged by floods, there were actually significant differences between them. Some of them owned as many as twenty-five looms each and earned as much as 400 rupees per year, and even those with a handful of looms were considered 'rich' who 'except for emergencies are able to feed their families quite respectably'.[58] Many others, meanwhile, did not own any looms at all and were acting as hired labourers for the better off. The establishment of a cooperative society (which was also a limited company) under Habibullah's leadership was an attempt to streamline production processes and to increase the hold of loom owners over non-loom owners, all with the help of the state and Doxiadis's building regulations. What Habibullah demanded from the representatives of the KDA – with much invocation of God, 'your honour' and 'the abject calamity' of the people he claimed to represent[59] – was in effect that the state provide subsidized housing to the poorest weavers so that they could be settled in direct proximity to the loom owners, who as he assured the KDA would be able to pay the normal Korangi lease instalments with ease. Being cleared from their various locations of residence across the city and concentrated in Korangi would make the poorest weavers entirely dependent on the 'Cooperative Society', not only for raw materials and marketing, but also for shelter and housing. Any prospect of them using their expertise to become small

[56] Ibid., Memo A. Y. Malik [social worker].
[57] Ibid., Letters Habibullah, Secretary Benarsi Co-Operative Anjuman, Bahadur Shah Market, Mohan Town to KDA, 10 June 1960, to National Housing and Settlements Agency, 13 July 1960, 11 August 1960.
[58] Ibid., Memo Vassiliadis, 18 February 1961.   [59] See Footnote 56.

entrepreneurs in their own right, and hence creating competition with existing loom-owning families, would be eliminated.[60] After getting permanent settlement in Korangi quarters, no one would be allowed to fix up handlooms separately. 'Those who will do against the rules of the Society, a strict action is to be taken by the society', was one resolution minuted at the Anjuman's meetings.[61] Doxiadis's insistence on keeping places of work separate from living spaces was instrumental here: in line with the official bye-laws for Korangi residents, the Anjuman promised to force the weavers not to work in their private houses – which had always been a popular fall-back option, not least because it allowed smaller producers to hold on to their trade 'secrets' and resist collectivization. After settling in Korangi, these people would have to agree to work in centrally controlled workshops, according to the Society's specifications.

This state-backed attempt to in effect break the autonomy of a cottage industry, and to turn it into a proper 'industry' with a much sharper division of labour and capital, was couched in a language of community initiative, refugee rehabilitation and protecting traditional arts and crafts. Habibullah's right to make petitions rested on the assumption – happily indulged by the agents of the Pakistani state – that all producers of Benarsi fabrics were in fact part of a single 'community', a pre-existing, non-economic formation of kinship, a distinctive subcategory of refugees of special merit. But the way his case was justified actually belied the very premises it was based on. Not only were the supposedly united members of this community in fact scattered over several Karachi locations, but also a memo by the social worker concerned even stated explicitly that it was the whole purpose of collective settlement to 'facilitate community feeling'.[62] In other words, only the act of settlement and economic consolidation would really produce the 'community' of Benarsi weavers that everyone pretended was somehow already in existence, and had been making official demands for their representation and betterment. As stated explicitly by Habibullah, anybody who worked with a member of his Anjuman was by definition also a 'Benarsi weaver', as 'it was not the habit of any of his community to do any business with outsiders'.[63] Once established through such circuitous lines of reasoning, being labelled a 'Benarsi weaver' became itself an instrument of control. Unlike Doxiadis's Islamabad workers, who were to be individually enticed to move to Islamabad with the promise of settlement, the Pakistani state

---

[60] Ibid., Memo A. Y. Malik, 22 June 1960.
[61] Ibid., Copy of the Minutes of Meeting dated 24 July 1960.   [62] See Footnote 56.
[63] See Footnote 56.

could deal with the Benarsi weavers as a single unit represented by a single community leader like Habibullah. Even if the process by which this 'community' was actually constituted involved a complex interplay of tactics of exploitation, real existing traditions and histories, and experiences of settlement, there was no way that once classed as a Benarsi weaver anybody could actually resist slum clearance and resettlement. Once the government agreed to heed Habibullah's request to resettle 'the community', they would all have to move, as they were all considered to be Habibullah's people.

What actually happened to them in the end is less well documented in the Doxiadis Archive. Their case is mentioned again, by S. S. Hasan of the NHSA a year later, when he reminded Doxiadis that sectors 36B and 32B of the Korangi scheme were meant to accommodate 400 Benarsi weavers.[64] By 1962, things looked decidedly different, however. Some of the weavers must have settled in Korangi without official authorization, as their dwellings were now referred to as 'juggi' and earmarked for demolition, ironically to make space for the 'low-cost housing units' they had always asked for.[65] By the time close state management of the Korangi scheme ceased in 1963, their dwellings are mentioned again as still awaiting clearance. Their ability to realize at least some aspects of their demand for a space in Korangi, after all, made them a prime example of effective labour management through doing nothing – closely resembling the policies followed by the authorities in Chandigarh, who declared unplanned labour colonies as 'authorized' without providing any services or legal security whatsoever to their inhabitants.[66]

The settling (or not) of the Benarsi weavers was not a case of development welfare as it had been proposed by Doxiadis. It did not rest on the rationale that there were newcomers to the city whose presence needed to be regularized and stabilized by providing them with a home and a place of work. The Pakistani state acted in the name of preserving a social order that was believed to be pre-existent, not in the name of managing fluidity and change. It related to its beneficiaries not as individual workers, but as groups preformatted according to essential identities modelled on typically Indian categories of 'locality', 'caste' and 'biradari'.[67] This way of organizing labour was by no means new, but had been at the heart

---

[64] CADA: Pakistan Volume 109, File C-PKH 3554, Attached Letter Hasan to Doxiadis, 18 August 1961.

[65] CADA: Pakistan Volume 154, File C-PKH 4404, 11 April 1962.

[66] CADA: Pakistan Volume 187, File C-PKH 6077, 27 August 1963. Sarin, M. (1982), *Urban planning in the Third World: the Chandigarh experience*, London, Mansell, p.112.

[67] For the colonial policy of using caste in this way, see Dirks, N. B. (2001), *Castes of mind: colonialism and the making of modern India*, Princeton University Press. On the more flexible

of colonial policies that similarly relied on community elders, 'jobbers' or similar figures to mobilize and manage labour (even if important questions can be raised as to whether at least sections of the labour force managed to face capitalists and the state as workers pure and simple).[68] Unsurprisingly, the Benarsi weavers were not the only group of workers considered for getting houses allocated in Korangi on those terms. In Doxiadis's files we find mention of the potter caste ('Kumhars'), another category of the 'traditional' village economy as depicted by colonial anthropology, and to the community of 'paper manufacturers', in effect pulp recyclers who produced cheap-quality blotting paper for the Pakistani bureaucracy. They demanded to be housed with the argument that their traditional methods of work demanded 'pucca' (brick-made) walls on which they could stick their output to dry.[69]

Wherever such neat assignations of communal professional identities failed, there were numerous other ways in which traditional identities could be invoked and justified. A good example was the letters of petition sent to the KDA and DA by the residents of another make-shift refugee settlement, Baldia Colony (now Baldia Town).[70] The colony had been

and less easily state-managed term 'biradari', see Gilmartin, D. (2012), 'Environmental history, biradari, and the making of Pakistani Punjab', *Punjab reconsidered: history, culture and practice*, A. Malhotra and F. Mir (eds.), Delhi, Oxford University Press: 289–319. Also his classic, Gilmartin, D. (1988), *Empire and Islam: Punjab and the making of Pakistan*, Berkeley, University of California Press.

[68] The extent to which such a deployment of imagined traditional identities actually exhausted labour control and labour mobilization has been the subject of much discussion in social histories of India. While 'orthodox' Marxist authors such as Subho Basu maintain that, despite colonial attempts to privilege such identities, the Indian working class managed to develop a more properly 'class'-based identity along Marxist lines, Dipesh Chakrabarty and Raj Chandavarkar (from different perspectives) have insisted that such a class-identity position is inapplicable to South Asia. Nandini Gooptu occupies a middle ground in pointing out both the limits and possibilities of a separate cultural consciousness of informal sector workers in the towns of late colonial UP. Basu, S. (2004), *Does class matter? Colonial capital and workers' resistance in Bengal, 1890–1937*, New Delhi; New York, Oxford University Press; Chakrabarty, D. (1989), *Rethinking working-class history: Bengal, 1890–1940*, Princeton University Press; Chandavarkar, R. (1994), *The origins of industrial capitalism in India: business strategies and the working classes in Bombay, 1900–1940*, Cambridge; New York, Cambridge University Press; Gooptu, N. (2001), *The politics of the urban poor in early twentieth-century India*, Cambridge; New York, Cambridge University Press.

[69] Their story resembles that of the Benarsi silk weavers. First an allocation was promised to the potters. CADA: Pakistan Volume 110, File C-PKH 4011. Then years later, they were still waiting. Letter Mohammad Husain, Lyari Pottery Producers Co-Operative Society to NHSA, Attached to CADA: Pakistan Volume 154, Correspondence April to June 1962, File C-PKH 4541. M. Husain insisted that he was promised a slot for his society in the presence of DA! For papermakers see ibid., Letter by Ahmad Bukhsh of Sanganer Hand Made Co-op Paper Industries, attached to File C-PKH 4603.

[70] CADA: Pakistan Volume 108, File C-PKH 2807, 12 April 1961.

initiated five years earlier (in 1955) by the KDA (hence the name after the Urdu/Arabic word for 'municipality'), even though it appears from official descriptions of the neighbourhood that it was far from planned. The first residents had been shifted from Mirza Adam Road, another refugee cluster in Karachi, with vague promises of permanent allotments and were later joined – sometimes with and more often without government promptings – by newcomers from other locations, creating a precarious cluster of temporary buildings that some bureaucrats suspected would not survive the next monsoon. The local residents were fearful of being moved again, even if their living conditions were precarious. The chairman of a deputation of refugees, S. Y. Kermani, pleaded that, despite the hardship involved, 'we live here in an organised way' and that the 'benign revolutionary regime' may desist from yet another haphazard slum clearance measure and instead provide secure plots for the residents nearby.[71] The KDA bureaucrats, in contrast, pushed for rapid removal, and Doxiadis's men used the case to justify the construction of the never-to-be-built 'Third Township' (alongside their ongoing projects at Korangi and 'North Karachi').[72]

What is of interest here is how the residents of Baldia Colony were described by the Pakistani state and how they described themselves. Kermani's petition described his neighbourhood as one made up of 'Mill hands, labour class and low paid servants', but aside from establishing that this made the colony deserving of official benevolence on account of poverty, such designations did not play any great role in how he later described the history of the colony or its population make-up. Instead of class categories, he used geographic references to earlier slum settlements from where certain groups of people had come – Kumbharwada, Delhi Mohallah, Delhi Santras, Anjam Colony – but also to 'various other *Jamats* living in the city'. The term 'jama^cat' is based on the Arabic term for 'community', 'society', even 'political party', and here seems to denote any group of people with some sense of pre-existing identity and affinity to each other. In the kaleidoscope of jama^cats in Baldia Colony, there was a 'Turk Jama^cat', for instance, not one but six 'sipahi jama^cats', and a Kumhar jama^cat, in addition to refugees unspecified. 'Turk' and 'sipahi' denoted groups of Muslims from the Western Indian region of Gujarat, who had fortified their sense of difference from other *muhajirs* with the help of a solidification of historic 'caste' identities, based on a shared memory of ancestral service in the Mughal armies.[73]

---

[71] Ibid., Letter to Chairman, KDA, 22 November 1960.
[72] Ibid., Memo, 12 April 1961.
[73] Ibid., Statement prepared by S. Y. Kermani, n.d. [November 1960].

Such identities differed sharply from Doxiadis's invocations of 'the worker' in that they could not be easily reduced to measurable 'needs'. The need for shelter and nutrition was more or less the same whether somebody was a 'Sipahi' or a 'Turk', or for that matter a 'Benarsi weaver' or a 'Kumhar'. What mattered was not any substantial content of difference but difference itself: the fact that each of these groups was duly recognized as 'special' by the Pakistani authorities, even if the resources then allocated on this basis were not special at all. Housing for the Turk was in essence the same as housing for weavers. Relating to these groups in the context of development remained first and foremost a political relationship, a relationship between people that was defined by their competition over power; moreover, it was a play of relationships that could never be resolved or made safe, as showing special recognition to one group made it necessary to overlook others, or the very sense of being recognized would have lost its meaning. In short, behind different governmentalities of labour stood different governmentalities at large.

Basic Democracies

A unique glimpse of the officially sanctioned politics in a place like Korangi – and its relationship with 'development' – has been preserved in the minutes of its so-called 'Basic Democracies'. Like many other official records of the Pakistani state, they were sent for information (and sometimes action) to the DA Karachi office and then passed on to be duly filed at Athens headquarters. Basic Democracies were local councils of sorts that existed across the land in both rural and urban areas. They consisted partly of elected and partly of appointed community leaders, and formed the bottom tier of General Ayub Khan's post-1960 constitutional set-up, whose main purpose was the affirmation of General Ayub Khan's role as president.[74] The idea was to allow a limited amount of electoral politics at the local level, without parties and without the participation of politicians. Already indicating where the real power lay in Korangi, the minutes were not drawn up by one of the 'basic democrats' themselves, but by a bureaucrat of the KDA, 'Deputy Chief Administrative Officer' Maghrub Ahmed. Not anywhere is there a record of any difference of opinion among the assembled delegates; in fact, other than in the attendance register, none of them is ever referred to by name. Instead, the very first line of the April 1960 minutes (the earliest on

---

[74] Mellema, R. L. (1961), 'The Basic Democracies system in Pakistan', *Asian Survey* **1**(6): 10–15; Sayeed, K. B. (1961), 'Pakistan's Basic Democracy', *Middle East Journal* **15**(3): 249–263.

record in the archive) made it very clear that this was not an exercise in local self-government, but an encounter between 'the state' and its 'people': '*I* [Maghrub Ahmed] *addressed* a meeting of the members of the Basic Democracies ... and *the following grievances were put forth* by various members for the benefit of the residents of the township.'[75]

The issues covered by the Basic Democracies of Korangi are highly indicative of what the development encounter meant for local residents. First up on the list, for instance, was the question of whether one Shamsuddin, who had 'adopted an attitude which amounted to defying Government instructions',[76] should be allowed back into his allocated house with his family. As becomes apparent from the documentation that follows, he had not paid his monthly lease instalments, a widespread problem that eventually put a question mark behind the financial viability of the township as a whole. In 1960, the state still attempted to clamp down on offenders like Shamsuddin, threatening eviction; in later years it would concede defeat and withdraw from mass housing development altogether.[77] The fact that this particular case remained on the books for some time already indicated that, even in 1960, non-payment had already found a certain amount of backing among the residents and could not simply be punished without some measure of public debate and accommodation. Shamsuddin, whose case 'has been hanging fire', was to be given a chance to 'give assurance for behaving properly' in the future.

Non-payment was in the first instance the consequence of poverty, but there were also differences in attitudes towards state power involved. A fundamental provision in Doxiadis's plan demanded that payments had to be made in order to give the residents a sense of participation, even if alternative sources of funding were available to the state. Crucially, he also stipulated that, by virtue of making such payments, residents were not tenants but owners, with full title deeds to be granted in due course. The Greek planner wanted to avoid any suggestion that mass housing was simply 'welfare', and believed that the prospect of property would turn the erstwhile slum-dwellers into stakeholder citizens; in Foucault's terms, into self-interested building blocks of a 'population' that no longer needed to be dragooned into what the state wanted them do, but who responded out of their own volition to gentle

---

[75] Minutes of the Meeting of Korangi Basic Democrats, 10 April 1960, p.1; attached to CADA: Pakistan Volume 69, File C-PKH 1434, 'Meeting Basic Democracies', 18 June 1960.

[76] Ibid.

[77] CADA: Pakistan Volume 188, File C-PKH 6109, Commerce and Works Department, Minutes meeting with Abdul Aziz, Sunday, 25 August 1963.

management. This was an essential part of the 'developmental' function of a project like Korangi. It was to take Pakistan towards an urban modernity, where housing clusters without urban culture could finally become cities in the full sense. The people affected, meanwhile, understood these payments as something entirely different. They regarded them as 'rent' which the state had no right to impose.[78] In their own view, the residents had been shifted to Korangi as part of a coercive slum clearance measure in which the state had acted as unaccountable sovereign.[79] It was only logical to expect this sovereign now also to 'provide' for them, and to allocate quarters free of charge – just as the colonial state, and before it the principalities of South Asia, had awarded land and housing to their subjects in order to make them part of a political order that had been created without their consent and through acts of force. As it happened, the residents' understanding of their status and relationship with authority was perhaps closer to ground realities than Doxiadis's pious hopes of proprietor-citizens. In a clear demonstration of how little credence Ayub's state officials gave to any notion of empowering local people, it was in the end not up to the 'democrats' to decide the fate of somebody like Shamsuddin; all they could do was to recommend that his case be 'examined by the Administrative officer'.

The overbearing and bureaucratic nature of the encounter between the local state and the people remained apparent in nearly every other sentence of the minutes. To complaints about inadequacies in 'night-soil' collection, to pick one example, Maghrub Ahmed reacted with a characteristic mixture of didacticism and blaming the claimants themselves, all formulated in the passive tense[80] so as to underline the impersonal and unquestionable power of his office: '*It was explained to* the members of Basic Democracies that the night-soil drums *were provided* in the township with proper covers and that it was the responsibility of the members of the Basic Democracies along with some smaller teams of

---

[78] CADA: Pakistan Volume 96, File R-PKH 157, p.144. For a detailed study of attitudes (with eviction figures) see Anwar Jafri, A study of the factors contributing to the problem of overdue instalments in the Drigh Village Township, (Masters Dissertation, Athens School of Ekistics, August 1964).
[79] Ibid. p.4. CADA: Pakistan Volume 188, Petition by Aziz Ahmad Bukhar, along with other allottess through attorney Mr. Salamat Ali Siddiq, translated into English by Mashooq Ali Siddiq, attached to File C-PKH 6271, 30 October 1963, 15 October 1963.
[80] Also noted in Hull, M. (2003), 'The file: agency, authority, and autography in an Islamabad bureaucracy', *Language and Communication* 23: 287–314, p.88. For a wider theoretical discussion of the nature and construction of government files from an anthropological perspective, see Hull, M. (2012a), 'Documents and bureaucracy', *Annual Review of Anthropology* 41: 251–267.

each sector to ensure that the *Government property* which was for the *betterment of the people* could not be stolen in the future.' The 'unanimous request' to have additional openings in the lavatory walls, from where the drums could be taken away without sweepers having to come into the houses themselves, was recorded with the following comment: 'I told the members that apparently there was no objection to this but as the matters involves alteration and addition the advice of Engineering staff will have to be sought. I remember that earlier also this matter was dealt with in a file and if I correctly remember this should be made a part of that file and a letter addressed to the Dy. Chief Engineer (Housing).'[81]

Closely resembling the bureaucratic behaviour of contemporary Islamabad CDA officers, as described in Matthew Hull's path-breaking ethnography,[82] Maghrub Ahmed was placing his concern for files over the concerns of the people. This was a transparent attempt to protect the majesty of the state and its due procedures even in the face of criticism. This stalling manoeuvre was hardly successful in silencing local self-assertion, however. At least some of the Korangi residents were articulate enough to appeal to the DA field office directly, bypassing Pakistani representatives of the state. There is a letter of complaint by one Zahiruddin, 'son of Allah Baksh', for instance – the name itself is testimony to his modest social standing and possibly illiteracy – once again raising the matter of sweepers intruding into a family's living quarters, which was received only a few months after the matter had been kicked into the long grass at the Basic Democracies meeting.[83]

Zahiruddin's request was not to find a much more favourable response from the chief consultant's staff than it had done with the KDA bureaucrats, however. In actual practice, Doxiadis's own vision of the responsible and self-motivated owner-occupier as the goal of urban development was as much of an ideological mystification as the 'democratic' element in Basic Democracies. This was made very clear in how he and his company responded to requests to alter prescribed designs in order to make them more suitable for local needs, for instance to construct additional roof top windcatchers in one room accommodations that residents found 'devoid of air', to put metal bars on 'jali' openings, to raise the height of tin sheet roofing, or to build additional rooms. They all reflected precisely the kind of spirit of responsible residency and a will

---

[81] Minutes of the Meeting of Korangi Basic Democrats, 10 April 1960, p.1; attached to CADA: Pakistan Volume 69, File C-PKH 1434, 'Meeting Basic Democracies', 18 June 1960, p.2.

[82] Hull, M. S. (2012b), *Government of paper: the materiality of bureaucracy in urban Pakistan.* Berkeley, University of California Press.

[83] CADA: Pakistan Volume 71, File C-PKH 1848, 11 October 1960.

for self-improvement that Doxiadis had always wanted to nurture. But they rarely got anywhere. Several residents had saved the necessary funds for substantial home improvements, but could not obtain building materials due to shortages. The KDA kept substantial stock at the site but felt unable to help before 'sanctions' could be obtained 'from the ICA [the US development agency] and the Ministry of Finance', which judging by the previous track record of these institutions could take longer than anybody would be prepared to wait.[84] Moreover, Maghrub Ahmed made any approval conditional on statements of 'no objection' by officers of higher authority, passing the matter up via several Pakistani bureaucrats of increasing seniority to the DA field office, and ultimately to Doxiadis himself. Contrary to his professed emphasis on listening to the people and to encouraging self-help and initiative, the latter maintained an almost obsessive interest in even the slightest deviations from his plans, and would seek to protect his authorship and brand value over any expression of local agency.[85]

The following statement by a local DA official neatly summed up the somewhat schizophrenic nature of Doxiadis's position:

While talking to the people of two roomed quarters they expressed a desire that they want to carry out certain additions and alterations in the existing houses and in fact one of these people have actually filled in the usual form prescribed by the engineering staff posted at Korangi. I do not think that the engineering staff would be able to accord permission for additions and alterations unless regular plans are approved by the Consultants. It is therefore desirable that we may take action in this direction for the preparation of various plans for additions and alterations befitting the necessity of various people so that this can facilitate additions and alterations according to the wishes of the people and according to our requirements.[86]

Talking to people to find out about their wishes remained a worthy ambition that was thwarted by the overriding concern of frontline staff not to violate the overriding power of their superiors. Just as the local state's majesty resided in the keeping of appropriate files, the consultant's majesty resided in its plan, even when – as is apparent here – the men on the spot could quite clearly see what needed to be done. At times, the

---

[84] Minutes of the Meeting of Korangi Basic Democrats, 10 April 1960, p.1; attached to CADA: Pakistan Volume 69, File C-PKH 1434, 'Meeting Basic Democracies', 18 June 1960. Comments I. M. Rahimtoola, Chief Engineer, p.8. See also memo A. S. Najm, Attachment to CADA: Pakistan Volume 109, File C-PKH 3313/4, 4 July 1961, where S. S. Hasan gives a very similar reply with regard to some minor alterations of wall heights.

[85] E.g. in Korangi, CADA: Pakistan Volume 188, File C-PKH 6109.

[86] Letter attached to CADA: Pakistan Volume 109, File C-PKH 3313/4, 4 July 1961.

intransigence of the consultant could create real hardship on the ground. Z. A. Nizami, another executive engineer on the Korangi project, implored DA to reach a quick decision on the design of windcatchers for shops to stop wares stored in the premises from going bad in the heat. Making allowances in advance for Doxiadis's all too well-known concern for maintaining his signature design, he promised that '... we think they should be allowed on condition that they be of a unitary type and that they be placed at specified places on the roof'.[87]

In addition to sanitation, 'rents' and alterations, the Basic Democracies also dealt with other typical points of friction between developers and the developed. Most were the direct consequence of allocating housing well before the necessary infrastructure had been completed. There were complaints about exorbitant bus fares to the city of Karachi, for instance, where most Korangi residents had to travel to work as the local industrial site was still unoccupied when the first residents moved in. As it happens, these grievances were simply dismissed by senior bureaucrats on the grounds that bus fares in London and Bombay were even higher.[88] Then there was the problem of an intermittent water supply, again immediately countered by suggestions that things were no better elsewhere.

Islam, development and the governed

There were special circumstances that made the parrying of such demands more difficult. When a serious water outage occurred on ceid day, for instance – as virtually the entire male population of the township went to wash for the most important prayer service of the year – senior officers adopted a much more cautious and accommodating attitude than normally. This was no longer just a case of asking residents to shut up and put up, but a dangerous public failure of the Pakistani state to protect the *raison d'être* of its national existence.[89] Religion in the widest sense emerged as the space where some notion of politics could enter the development encounter. The matter that came to dominate this terrain was the demolition and construction of mosques. There was ample historical precedent for this. Conflicts over mosques had already occupied an established place in popular politics in colonial times. The

---

[87] CADA: Pakistan Volume 109, File C-PKH 3337, 7 July 1961.
[88] Minutes of the Meeting of Korangi Basic Democrats, 10 April 1960, p.1; attached to CADA: Pakistan Volume 69, File C-PKH 1434, 'Meeting Basic Democracies', 18 June 1960. Comments I. M. Rahimtoola, Chief Engineer, p.9.
[89] Ibid., Notes by A. A. Jafri, 21 April 1960, p.7.

closure and desecration of Delhi's Jama^c Masjid had been one of the punishments meted out to the city's Muslim 'community' for their support of the great rebellion in 1857, for instance, and it was a dispute over the boundary walls of a mosque building in Kanpur that heralded the onset of a new era of Muslim mass agitations against the colonial state in the early twentieth century. It was followed by countless incidents of 'communal' disturbances over 'music before mosques', or over whether a particular building was in fact a mosque, a temple or a gurudwara.[90] Similar disputes still occupy a central place in Pakistan's popular religious politics today, whether it is in the 'takeover' (*qabza*) of mosques by radical Islamic groups, or fights to save illegally constructed mosques against the planning machinery of the CDA.[91]

This did not mean that back in Ayub's time the state conceded ground easily, even on religious matters. When the subject of mosques first appeared at Basic Democracies meetings in April 1960, Administrative Officer Maghrub Ahmed once again tried to limit any sense that there could be a legitimate grievance against the Pakistani state while effortlessly assuming the role of chief interpreter of religious doctrine for himself:

> The question of mosques also came up for discussion and the members of the Basic Democracies pointed out that the existing number was very inadequate. I told them that from Islamic point of view [*sic*] also it was of no use enhancing the number of mosques if they were not properly used and they looked deserted. The members of Basic Democracies were also informed that whatever sites were demarcated so far should be fully utilised and let the subject be open for further examination if some more mosque-sites were essential.[92]

This directive was at first largely confirmed by the more senior bureaucrats who left their comments in the file. While Maghrub's immediate line manager, 'Chief Administrative Officer KDA' A. A. Jafri, remained non-committal and wanted the matter 'to be thoroughly examined', the Deputy Chief Engineer, I. M. Rahimtoola, and the Director General of the NHSA, Colonel Humayune, both affirmed that requests for more mosque building should be kept in check until all sites proposed

---

[90] See Freitag, S. B. (1989), *Collective action and community: public arenas and the emergence of communalism in north India*, Berkeley, University of California Press; Gilmartin, D. (1988), *Empire and Islam: Punjab and the making of Pakistan*, Berkeley, University of California Press, pp.73–107.

[91] Khan, N. (2010), 'Mosque construction or the violence of the ordinary', *Beyond crisis: re-evaluating Pakistan*, N. Khan (ed.), London; New York, Routledge: 482–519; Hull, M. (2010), 'Uncivil politics and the appropriation of planning in Islamabad, *Beyond crisis: re-evaluating Pakistan*, N. Khan (ed.), London; New York, Routledge: 452–481.

[92] Minutes of the Meeting of Korangi Basic Democrats, 10 April 1960, p.1; attached to CADA: Pakistan Volume 69, File C-PKH 1434, 'Meeting Basic Democracies', p.3.

in Doxiadis's plan had been duly developed. Rahimtoola even speculated that the sudden explosion in demand for more mosques may be more than an outbreak of piety: '... I would like to avoid any chance of speculation in the land by the Mullas'.[93] Strict control was subsequently imposed on impromptu prayer meetings in open spaces, so as to prevent them from becoming focal points for illegal construction.[94]

By 1961 Ayub's officials become increasingly nervous, however. One reason appears to be the appearance of sectarian overtones in the debate. Many of the unauthorized structures that were now subject to removal orders had been built by Shi[c]a residents in Korangi, who did not feel that they had a place in the official mosques envisioned in Doxiadis's plans, which were invariably taken over by the Sunni majority community. A local body representing the denomination – the Anjuman-e Husainiya – sent a petition to the NHSA and DA, demanding not only to have the illegally constructed imambara (a particularly Shi[c]a place of worship associated with the commemoration of Imam Husain's martyr-dom at Karbala) and musafir khana recognized as legal, but also to be granted land to enlarge them. Faced with a decision of whether to demolish or not, the Pakistani Director General of the NHSA decided not to 'disturb ... people and institutions unless it is absolutely essential to do so'. The structures were tolerated.[95] A month later, a larger directive was issued to DA stating that the provision of mosques on Doxiadis's master plan [See Figure 26] was considered inadequate by the Pakistani bureaucracy, and that mosques should be allowed to be built on designated green spaces as required.[96]

Toleration of Shi[c]a places of worship soon led to a backlash from aggrieved Sunni communities, who saw their own space encroached upon. A letter signed by 'the residents' of a locality where an imambara had recently been constructed questioned that Shi[c]as had any right to build anything at all, as 'they have got only three houses', whereas Sunnis were in the majority. 'These people tried to build this Imambara in other localities as well, but due to resistance from the people of those localities they did not succeed', the letter continued, before threatening darkly that 'the peace of this locality can be endangered at any time'.[97] On a later

[93] Note Rahimtoola, Minutes of the Meeting of Korangi Basic Democrats, 10 April 1960, p.1; attached to CADA: Pakistan Volume 69, File C-PKH 1434, 'Meeting Basic Democracies', p.8.
[94] CADA: Pakistan Volume 186, File C-PKH 5597, 16 April 1963, To NHSA.
[95] CADA: Pakistan Volume 108, File C-PKH 2833.
[96] CADA: Pakistan Volume 108, File C-PKH 2983.
[97] Letter Residents of 2-A, Area, Landhi Colony to Chairman of KDA, 10 November 1961, attached to CADA: Pakistan Volume 110, File C-PKH 3940.

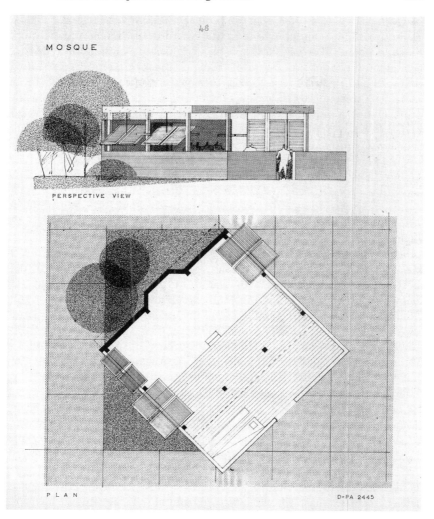

Figure 26 Doxiadis's design for a Korangi neighbourhood mosque based on scientific principles. Note the complete absence of any culturally significant stylistic elements such as domes, minarets or arches. Instead the main consideration was optimal climatic conditioning for South Asian summers and winters with movable blinds.
Source: CADA: Archive Files 17329.

occasion it was one of Korangi's official market overseers, one Qaisar Raza (possibly a Shi^c a) who demanded from the KDA that a Sunni mosque of the 'Kurrisian' [Qureishi?] community be demolished, triggering another round of petitions from the mosque committee claiming that they had already spent 2000 rupees on the construction.[98] By March 1962, DA were forced to accept that several dozen of proposed housing units in two Korangi sectors would never be built, because the space earmarked for them had been taken up by illegally constructed mosques that the government by this point was no longer in any position to clear. Even government-sponsored bodies like neighbourhood Social Welfare Committees had by now rallied behind the demand of building more mosques, on one occasion directly attacking the KDA and DA's negligence in catering to a population that 'by the grace of God is 100 per cent Muslim'.[99]

Similar demands became common place over the next few years, not only in Karachi, but also in North Karachi, the second township under construction.[100] Outside sponsors and philanthropists moved in to support local mosque-building activities, from the fundamentalist Jama^c at-i Islami to the Seth Isma^c il Dossa Benevolent Trust, set up by a rich Khoja merchant from Bombay, and the Agha Khan's Isma^c ili Council.[101] The local authorities sought to get on top of the situation not only by retrospectively legalizing existing structures, but also by revising the master plan to provide additional spaces for prayer in the future. In 1963, a directive was issued that Doxiadis would have to go back to the drawing board and plan for the provision of Shi^c a as well as Sunni mosques for all neighbourhoods. The Greek planner complied but not without registering his incomprehension. He had, after all, done some careful research with his Egyptian collaborator, Hassan Fathy, to establish exactly and in advance how many mosques were needed to satisfy an area's 'objective' need for prayer space. It was all about functionality in his eyes. A madrasa in Korangi 'looked ridiculous' with its three small domes over a tiny internal space, as it was entirely unsuited to local climatic needs.[102]

What Doxiadis singularly failed to understand was that mosque building was only in the second instance a question of having a communal

---

[98] CADA: Pakistan Volume 153, File C-PKH 4427, Letter Mashooq Ali.

[99] Social Welfare Committee Y area, Letter to DA 26 March 1962, attached to CADA: Pakistan Volume 153, File C-PKH 4448.

[100] CADA: Pakistan Volume 186, File C-PKH 4559, Letter Syed Wajid Ali, Anjuman-e Karwan-e Haideri to NHSA, attached to ibid., File C-PKH 5319.

[101] CADA: Volume 186, File C-PKH 5234, Letter Azam Farooqi to Commissioner of Karachi, 28 February 1963; Pakistan Volume 187, File C-PKH 5735.

[102] CADA: Pakistan Volume 41, Diary PA 102, October 1960, p.160.

space to pray; it was first and foremost to establish a visible representation of a community's presence, solidarity and power in a neighbourhood.[103] For this very reason, what was now arguably an over-provision of mosques did not put a stop to ongoing agitation. Demands soon shifted from the correct number of mosques to their actual location. Some were considered to be inconvenient, and others too close to worldly places such as cinemas to be usable for prayer.[104] Once again the recognition by the state authorities of the collective will of certain communities was at stake, not any objective sociological need. The Pakistani authorities understood this logic and usually gave in to demands as far as possible.

Mosque politics in Korangi and North Karachi was a highly significant reflection of the wider interaction of the Pakistani state, the consultants and local people in what could finally be called a specific 'governmentality of development'. To appreciate fully what was involved, it is useful to consider official attitudes towards mosques in a wider context. One of the striking aspects of the Islamabad project was the low priority that was given to the construction of a central mosque of state. Ayub had, as already mentioned, demarcated a plot for the purpose on his very first visit to the site, but then nothing much happened. Other mosques of lesser importance were soon constructed, often sponsored by businessmen and other philanthropists,[105] but an official place of prayer did not materialize for almost another decade and a half. When Faisal Masjid, Islamabad's well-loved central mosque, was finally built in the mid 1970s, it was under far from straightforward circumstances. Strangely for what is meant to be Pakistan's 'official' mosque, it was funded by an outside donor – the King of Saudi Arabia – and based on a design by another non-Pakistani – the Turkish Kemalist Vedat Dalokay, who was not allowed to realize it in his native Turkey, because it was deemed insufficiently 'traditional'.[106] It seems that the Pakistani state had neither the intellectual nor the financial capacity or determination to take care of such an important project itself, which contrasts strangely with historical precedent. The last Muslim rulers of India, the Mughals, had been assiduous sponsors of mosques of state that could have easily served as a reference point.

Ayub's lack of ambition to have a great central mosque built in his cherished new capital must not be mistaken for religious indifference.

[103] Daechsel, M. (2011a), 'Seeing like an expert, failing like a state? Interpreting the fate of a satellite town in early post-colonial Pakistan', *Colonial and post-colonial governance of Islam: continuities and ruptures*, M. Maussen, V. Bader and A. Moor (eds.), Amsterdam University Press: 155–174, p.164.
[104] CADA: Pakistan Volume 188, File C-PKH 6237, 17 October 1963.
[105] CADA: Pakistan Volume 193, File C-PI 5306, 19 June 1963.
[106] Interview Kamil Khan Mumtaz (Lahore, November 2007).

As we have seen in the context of architectural competitions for other Islamabad buildings, Pakistani officialdom could hold robust views on Islamic identity and heritage; and the Korangi experience demonstrated that the state was only too happy to indulge demands made in a religious language. The point about mosques – and this is what makes them so important for an analysis of a developmental governmentality – is that they were not considered to be within the normal remit of governance, or at least not to begin with. Mosque building was considered not as an act of state but as an expression of public agency, be it of poor self-help communities of workers and refugees, or of rich philanthropists or politicians. The state would look with favour on their initiatives, but it would not 'provide' mosques of its own accord. Revealingly, a directive sent by the KDA to Doxiadis when the Korangi mosque agitations were in full swing urged him to desist from providing more than concrete foundations and, at the most, some suggestive outline plans for such buildings. It was important, the officials argued, to let the people construct and design their own mosques themselves.[107]

One of the earliest mosques in Islamabad clearly demonstrates this logic even in the most 'official' of contexts. It was attached to the very first building of state, Ponti's National Assembly hostel. The request to have it built was made in 1962, by the veteran Muslim Leaguer from East Pakistan and newly 'elected' speaker of the National Assembly, Maulvi Tamizuddin Khan, who also demanded that the hostel be renamed 'Pakistan House'.[108] The occasion provided Tamizuddin with an opportunity to act as the spokesman of popular religious observance that Ayub found necessary to appeal to in the wake of his promulgation of a new constitution. The Maulvi had only been allowed to return to politics briefly, after years of open hostility to the bureaucratic-military establishment. Revealingly, the generals did not of their own accord commission Ponti (or any other architect) to provide a mosque to the parliamentarians so as to appear in harmony with the new public sentiment; rather they allowed a hand-picked regime outsider to voice such demands first, before graciously acceding to them.

Mosques came after rather than before politics. This was what Doxiadis always got wrong, but also what made him particularly useful for the regime. His developmental vision allowed Ayub's officials to play a three-step game: a particular design for mosques would be put forward by the consultant and his plan. This was an open invitation to 'the public' to react outraged and demand changes to the number or location of the

---

[107] CADA: Pakistan Volume 109, File C-PKH 3405.
[108] CADA: Pakistan Volume 159, File C-PI 3914, 4 August 1962.

mosques, or to their design. Any such proposal – no matter how well designed – would always attract a considerable amount of criticism, as any self-designated representative of religious rectitude was now under an obligation to increase their own sense of authority through launching a challenge. The state – usually personified by a senior official not closely involved with the consultant – would then step in and decide in favour of public demand. A new alignment had been created between the sovereign power of the state – epitomized by its act of *decision* – and the will of the people. Had the state started proposing mosques of its own accord, it would have become the subject of contestation between itself and 'the people'. Doxiadis's presence was crucial because it allowed the state to split into two opposing personae at the crucial point in the game. While it was of course the power behind Doxiadis when the latter made his proposals, it could easily transform into the power that kept Doxiadis in check. Once again, Doxiadis's designation 'consultant' has to be understood in its full contemporary meaning, rather than in terms of the self-assigned hero-ism of the age of development; consultants were not bringers of wisdom to facilitate a nation's quest to secure a better future (or for that matter, diabolical figures leading a nation into the deadly embrace of Western capitalist modernity), but people paid handsomely for their willingness to act as trouble-absorbent layers in situations of conflict.

Leaving aside its considerable ideological value for maintaining good relations with the West, this is where the structural utility of 'develop-ment' lay for Ayub's regime: it was an opener in a game of interchanges between the state and the people, a way of either inviting the people to engage with the state or, where necessary, forcing them to do so. It did not really matter in this context whether 'development' worked or not, only that through the development process a relationship was established that constituted the people as 'governed', as coming under the remit of state agency. When the urban poor of inner-city Karachi slums were forcibly and without consultation moved to Korangi, they may not have been 'rehabilitated' according to the grand plans that somebody like Doxiadis had made for them, but they were no longer left to their own devices.[109] Becoming 'governed' did not involve any provision of services or welfare, it rested entirely on the fact that the state had in some way made an intrusion into their lives, and that it was the state that they now had to struggle against. Even the worst of antagonisms was a form of

[109] Even if they had never been entirely outside the state's embrace before – their slums often had a history of evictions, and at the very least they would have to deal with daily intrusions of the police and market regulators – the act of resettlement certainly strengthened this relationship.

recognition. Being governed did not mean a positive acceptance of the state, let alone any sense of loyalty to it. Petitions had to be sent, rent strikes organized, Basic Democracies meetings and mosque committees utilized to make demands. Meanwhile, new opportunities arose to use the relationship with the state to advance sectional interests – like those of the loom-owning Benarsi weavers at the expense of their poorer neighbours, or of Shi^{c}a groups at the expense of Sunnis.

In the process of reacting to the state's sovereign agency, the 'governed' had to reconstitute themselves into easily legible subgroups and units: the communities or jama^{c}at already discussed in the context of labour management. It did not really matter whether such structures were already in place for historical reasons, or whether they were created simply out of the need of geographically defined groups of residents to react to a particular intrusion, or for that matter whether they were based on religion, family, profession or any other identity trait. Sovereign action would immediately produce such structures; much like a powerful jolt to a test tube containing a supersaturated solution can trigger the sudden crystallization of its contents. Once again, it is the *act* of development itself that brought about this change, not the kind of new 'discursive' categories that Doxiadis and other development consultants were seeking to establish. Urban populations became accessible to Pakistani modalities of 'security' simply through the fact that they were no longer one amorphous mass, but that they formed discrete units that could be manipulated through intermediaries or other personalized strategies of control. There was no need to produce 'individuals' or managerial categories of 'needs' as demanded by typical Western readings of 'security'. Development did not produce a new epistemic order in Pakistan; it added further fuel and solidification to the old play of caste, tribe and biradari.

It is beside the point to argue that development 'failed' because its categories of sense making could not account for the complexity of 'real life'. No such penetrating sense of control was ever intended. And it is no closer to the point to suggest that development led to a wholesale depoliticization of governance, to a new managerialism. Development was never depoliticized in a place like Pakistan and never even meant to be depoliticized. It was designed precisely to create a new arena for the political, by opening up a whole range of policy fields where the state could launch the kinds of sovereign jolts that would crystallize or recrystallize populations to keep them legible. Doxiadis's dream of a new - Mohenjo Daro, of creating a city for a state without a sovereign, never materialized, but his presence nevertheless enhanced the power potential that a sovereignty-obsessed military regime could bring to bear on its people.

Conclusion

Constantinos Doxiadis was closely involved with urban planning in Pakistan for over a decade. He (and his collaborators) designed the new capital city of Islamabad, rehoused hundreds of thousands of poor refugee families in purpose-built satellite towns around Karachi, and created an extensive new university campus in Lahore and colleges from Dacca in the East to Sargodha and Rawalpindi in the West. Other projects were drawn up but not implemented. An ambitious national school building programme never got off the ground, and regional planning at an unprecedented scale and level of integration ran into the quicksand of political intrigue. In the eyes of some contemporaries, this track record earned Doxiadis a reputation as one of the twentieth century's greatest urbanists. But the Greek architect himself remained frustrated by the unrealized potential of his work – to the extent that he deemed his Pakistan decade an overall failure. 'What we have achieved is not enough!' he lamented in a confidential letter to a collaborator as his involvement with the country was gradually wound down.[1]

This disappointment stemmed in part from the sheer amount of energy Doxiadis had put into Pakistan between 1954 and the middle of the 1960s, and which he felt delivered only a fraction of the financial returns he had hoped for. Despite his busy global schedule, he had made time to visit the country on numerous occasions and for extended periods. He had travelled thousands of miles by air, road, train and boat in both the Eastern and Western wings. By all accounts, he took to the intellectual challenge of understanding this vast and unfamiliar terrain with genuine curiosity and dedication. As a theoretician of urbanism, he condensed his impressions into distinctive ideas about historical agency and change, popular culture and vernacular knowledge, and above all into a new methodology of development. Based on the right kind of holistic approach, Pakistan could not only be transformed into an urban

---

[1] See Chapter 4, Footnote 86.

civilization fit for the future, he promised; this transition could also be managed in such a way as not to upset the conservative sensibilities of a Muslim population and their way of life. Even if development involved a colossal effort by the planner himself, it would not appear to its recipients as a burdensome imposition but rather as the natural extension of their own sense of agency.

As an entrepreneur, Doxiadis tirelessly sought to build personal relationships with Pakistani town planners, architects and bureaucrats, military generals, ministers and prime ministers. His game was to match up the political impulses coming from major donor countries like the United States with those arising in Pakistan itself: a formidable task that required vigilance, flexibility and above all a feel for what made these very different political environments tick. Incurring losses was part of the game. Sometimes the goodwill of patrons had to be reinforced with all-expenses-paid information holidays to Greece. On other occasions – most notably in the run-up to the Islamabad commission – Doxiadis presented beautifully produced plans and reports free of cost to entice his clients. But success was never guaranteed. Major contracts were awarded to commercial rivals at the last minute, simply because a key person somewhere within the byzantine machinery of international development administration had been replaced by somebody with different political loyalties.

In the final analysis, Doxiadis's success – where it did materialize – came down to neither entrepreneurship nor intellectual ability. He was simply the right man at the right place at the right time. What earned him the breakthrough project of Korangi, for instance, was his availability as a neutral outsider to reboot American development policy in Pakistan at a time of crisis, and his (desperate or reckless) willingness to shoulder the risk of an uncertain and overambitious project on behalf of the new military dictatorship. Whenever Doxiadis actually sought to expand his activities in line with his stated expertise and trademark development discourse, he was rebuffed. His proposal for a grand national housing and settlements plan as derived from his science of Ekistics was never pursued by the Pakistani state, and even the new capital Islamabad was not allowed to become the great monument to Doxiadian developmentalism he had originally hoped for.

This book has presented the story of Doxiadis's self-ascribed 'failure' in Pakistan in order to understand a larger process: the coming of development to a recently decolonized country of the global South. Within this wider context an evaluation in terms of 'failure' and 'success' no longer makes sense. It is undeniable that important changes did take place in Pakistan, even when individual projects all too often did not go according to plan. (It is important to remember here that Doxiadis's disappointment was far from unique: most American project aid in 1950s Pakistan failed, and even ostensible 'successes' like the Harvard Advisory Mission were far from unequivocal.) But the activities of international experts, the dispensation of aid, and more generally an ideological readjustment of government policy according to new Cold War requirements all created a distinctive new historical environment. 'Cardiac embarrassment' – that endemic feeling of listlessness among Pakistani government servants that senior bureaucrats wanted to be recognized as a medical condition by the World Health Organization – may have defined the immediate post-independence period, but was out of place in the new age of Islamabad. The sheer ability to move hundreds of thousands of people to new urban spaces was not the only sign of how different the Ayub Khan period was from the preceding decade. While the authorities of 1954 had struggled to produce even the rudimentary documentation demanded by the Colombo Plan, Pakistan in 1960 had a Five Year Plan that was internationally admired. If development aid could be measured in tens of millions of dollars at the time of Doxiadis's arrival, it reached billions at the time of his departure.

The traces of the old had not disappeared from the picture altogether, of course. There were still times when bureaucrats favoured no action over action, and could be extremely condescending to those whom they administered – as the assembled residents of Korangi would experience at first hand when they sought redress for some of the most blatant development failures in their new township. The old staple of colonial administrative wisdom – that the safest way to govern was to relate to the governed not as individuals but as members of pre-political 'communities' based on caste or religion – was not weakened by the coming of development to Pakistan but actually reinforced. But what matters equally is that there now was a township like Korangi, a National Housing and Settlements Agency, a system of 'Basic Democracies' and the very need to talk with the representatives of the state about issues like water supply, traffic connections or mosque building. The penetrative reach of the Pakistani state was incomparably greater in 1965 than in 1954, and it was the coming of development to the country that had made all the difference.

The strange combination of failure at the personal or project level with a sense of great change in the bigger picture cannot be resolved either way. Both aspects were equally 'real' and remain crucial for any historical interpretation of development. In fact, it was precisely the combination of agency and failure that produced the enduring miracle of 'development': of how a vague ideology born out of transparent geostrategic interests could become a world-making discourse, whose truth value appears so secure that most people take it as self-evident. Doxiadis's story in Pakistan confirmed a mechanism already well known from other parts of the world such as Lesotho or Colombia: after constructing the country 'objectively' as a landscape of problems and deficiencies through his travel diaries, photographs and planning documents, the question of why development was necessary became obsolete. When reality itself was configured as a deficiency or absence, the need for remedial action became as natural and self-evidently true as reality itself. In the eyes of Doxiadis and his colleagues, the very fact that their projects failed in one way or another only proved just how 'underdeveloped' a country Pakistan really was and, therefore, how much more development was needed to set it right. In short, development became all conquering and all colonizing not despite but *because* it had failed on so many occasions.

The analysis offered in this book went beyond this well-established reading of development as 'discourse', however. The use of a new body of sources from a private company archive was instrumental in pushing the argument further. When the static textual landscapes of development discourse are set alongside the dramatic turns of fortune experienced by individual consultants like Doxiadis, it becomes inescapable that the latter have to be understood as more than mere minions of an all-powerful formation of power/knowledge. Men like Doxiadis were ultimately defined by qualities that had little to do with their technical expertise and all with their personal character. They needed to be tough and resilient to survive in hostile climates and terrains, full of empathy and curiosity when dealing with alien cultures, patient but resolute in the face of political opposition. In fact if they followed only their scientific knowledge, they would end up not as heroes of development at all, but as their much maligned opposite: as the 'one-size-fits-all', 'out-of-touch' technocrats that were as reviled in Doxiadis's own time as they are now in the days of globalization. The truly great and visionary planner was not simply the engineer who stuck to his expertise, important as this remained, he was somebody who also dared to transcend scientific truth in order to endorse something impossible or 'crazy' – as Doxiadis himself argued in a memorable passage in his Pakistan diaries.

Doxiadis's emphasis on the personal heroism of the consultant brought into view what could be called the 'subject' of development: a sense of a clearly identifiable location of agency, of a 'who' that wills development to take place. Although the involvement of a self-styled visionary architect undoubtedly added to its prominence, this 'subject' element was also present in mainstream development discourse as it was written for a wide range of technical experts by early theorists like Pieter Roest or Claire Holt. The 'subject' of development emerged, somewhat obliquely and between the lines, at the point where the optimism of sharing one's expertise with 'Mr. Underdeveloped Region' – as a 1950s pamphlet so memorably idealized development's recipients – flipped over into an unsettling experience of irredeemable cultural difference. When the chips were down, development was a project not for engineers, who could master whatever technical challenge was thrown at them, but for tragic heroes, who would soldier on despite their own realization that the task at hand was ultimately destined to fail. At the end of the day, development could only be willed but not entirely explained or justified. This is why it was unthinkable without men like Doxiadis or, for that matter, 'go-getting' generals like Azam Khan or Ayub Khan who provided their necessary counterfoils.

It is within this context that some sense of 'failure' would again prove productive. An experience of hardship was integral to what made Doxiadis the 'Lawrence of Development' that he aspired to become, in imitation of T. E. Lawrence's exploits in the wilds of Arabia. This is why he so carefully constructed a sense of tragic heroism out of his encounter with Pakistan. After all, it is from his own narrative that we know how much he struggled with scheming or cruel Pakistani politicians, how his best intentions were brought to nought by 'colossal' difficulties, and of how he remained forever locked away from the only people that he felt truly understood him: the common folk in the villages and towns of Pakistan to whom he dedicated his most ambitious plans. There was an overwhelming sense of romance, a tragic love story, at the heart of the venture of development. It was as important for its historical power as the world-making conceptual toolkit of the development sciences. Romance insured development against failure. Those of its agents that struggled a little in their work were ennobled as consultants of true dedication and experience, and those who failed comprehensively became martyrs for a greater good, bequeathing an even stronger obligation onto their successors to continue the fight for a better world. In neither case would failure lead to a fundamental rethink about the validity of development as a world-changing venture itself.

The consultant 'subject' was the nail that held development discourse together, even where it was deliberately concealed from the discursive surface. It is striking that such a decisively heroic consultant like Doxiadis could also be the author of some of the *least* top-down visions of development planning available at the time. The latter did not just lend themselves to Foucault's notions of centreless managerial power, they were fully fledged anticipations of it; for instance, in Doxiadis's insistence that the good planner did not aim to see all or understand all, but only as much as was needed to ensure good implementation – which precisely maps on to Foucault's ideas about risk, statistics and population. The ideal of controlling circulation (rather than confinement), meanwhile, was central to Doxiadis's notion that the good planner was like a minimalist hydraulic engineer: somebody who intervened only sparingly and otherwise sought to let the waters run according to their own natural inclination. Then there was the Greek architect's much confessed love for people's agency and vernacular knowledge and, of course, for mythical Mohenjo Daro as a perfect representation of what modern government should do.

The 'tyranny of experts', which so many development-critical writers from James Scott to William Easterly have routinely invoked in their accounts,[2] could be far more complex in nature than the customary invocation of development's tendency to 'see like a state' or to offer 'one-size-fits-all' solutions. Doxiadis's entire thinking was driven by a painful awareness of the dangers of such an assumed omnipotence, and his trademark methodology was designed explicitly to avoid any misguided desires to know all, see all or change all. But this did not make Doxiadis's visions any less powerful or imposing. Counterintuitively, Doxiadis represented development at its most fortified, its hardest to resist, because his theoretical work was careful to anticipate and preempt any potential criticism before it could even be articulated. Who would even want to oppose a planner who merely followed the people's own natural inclinations? Here Doxiadis was strikingly different from somebody like Le Corbusier – often chosen as the perfect example of developmental tyranny gone berserk.[3] While it was true that Le Corbusier combined a firm belief in the rectitude of his own vision with an overwhelming entitlement to change the world, he was actually always vulnerable to resistance. Precisely because he made no apologies for being a tyrant, Le Corbusier would immediately divide opinion between acolytes and opponents. His grandiosity and arrogance was an open justification to stand up to him. The same was not true for somebody like Doxiadis, who in so many ways came across as a development tyrant but whose theoretical musings seemed to offer no legitimate access point to counter-attack.

---

[2] Scott, J. C. (1998), *Seeing like a state: how certain schemes to improve the human condition have failed*, New Haven, CT; London, Yale University Press; Easterly, W. (2013), *The tyranny of experts: economists, dictators, and the forgotten rights of the poor*, New York, Basic Books, a member of the Perseus Book Group.
[3] Scott, J. C. (1998), *Seeing like a state: how certain schemes to improve the human condition have failed*, pp.103–114.

As it happened, Doxiadis was seen by many in Pakistan as no less tyrannical than Le Corbusier himself.[4] If the fundamental difference between the two architects was all but annulled in the cut and thrust of development politics, it was precisely because development was not only about discourse but also about heroic personalities. What looked from one perspective as yet another ideological immunisation of development – romantic heroism as a way of explaining why the great venture to make a better world remained a worthwhile task, even when the people of the poor South proved themselves to be un-developable – would turn out as development's Achilles heel. Even if development was (nearly) unchallengeable as discourse, its protagonists remained eminently challengeable as *men*. In fact, there was an inverse relationship at play: the less one could challenge development as discourse, the more one would be compelled to challenge its men; and since Doxiadis proposed a discourse that was even harder to disable intellectually than most, he would get to feel the resistance and subversion directed at him personally more keenly than most.

It is easier to grasp this connection instinctively than to explain it theoretically: here is Doxiadis – self-assured, if not overbearing – who brings expertise to Pakistan that he has designed to be impenetrable to criticism. The Pakistani elite need to engage with him to safeguard their geopolitical interests, and they have no choice but to order their own experts and bureaucrats to play along with Doxiadis's proposals. Power is felt but it cannot be countered directly, as one cannot really explain what's wrong about it. One can criticize Doxiadis on matters of detail, but this does not get him off his pedestal as he can quickly incorporate such criticism into a revised version of his wisdom. Yet, nobody is fooled about what is at stake: this is expertise that furthers the ambitions of its creator more than anything else; and like most expertise with unquestionable truth value at the time, it comes from the outside world and hence inevitably shows up local inadequacy. Both sides of the development encounter understand only too well that development is not simply a neutral tool that one can adopt without asking questions about its origins. It is yet another proof that true world historical agency rests with the rich North, another slap in the face for a people intent on finding self-determination. How to react? If one cannot win by arguing because the other side always has the better arguments, one has no choice but to go for other measures: for instance, when Doxiadis is subjected to the deliberately humiliating swagger of local bureaucrats and 'feudal' big men

---

[4] Ahmed, S. (1976), *The Muslim concept of town planning*, Karachi, The Pakistan Institute of Arts and Design, pp.19, 82, 88.

who felt threatened by his presence; or when the military regime – without engaging much with the actual nature and scope of his proposals – flip-flops between making Doxiadis wait for instructions and demanding an impossible speed of implementation.

Development politics was all about manoeuvres of outflanking, of changing the way in which power operated. In order to grasp this process theoretically, this book had to move beyond notions of 'discourse', and to operate with the more complex triad of powers that Foucault proposed in his later work: sovereign, disciplinary and managerial (or as he called it 'security') power. Although each of the three operated at a different level and according to a different logic, they were nevertheless connected through transition points: moments when the character of the game could be tipped from one modality to another. This insight accounts precisely for the tactical shifts that plagued somebody like Doxiadis: development could be defended or contested as discourse, as managerial 'security' or as a particular kind of heroic subjectivity. Which one of these alternatives became operational at any given moment in time depended on the context and the opportunities for tactical outflanking available to the contestants.

If development was incontestable as a managerial governmentality (or for that matter as 'discourse'), it could be quite effectively contested through the deployment of deliberate unpredictability. Argument is helpless in the face of somebody who does things without recourse to argument, and higher truth does not bite when power is happy to operate independently from truth. Tactical unpredictability can be theoretically grasped as the appropriation of the moment of *decision*: the moment when the willing subject that stood at the heart of any sense of agency constituted itself without any reference to anything but itself. This was of course the very moment when sovereign power as conceived by theorists of agonism following in the wake of Carl Schmitt comes into being,[5] and it was used in a similar and related sense by Foucault himself. This power stood centre stage not only in contestations between the international consultant and the men who represented the Pakistani state, but also at all other levels of politics where development assumed an important role, for instance between different branches of the Pakistani state or between a hierarchy of bureaucrats and its subject citizens. The fate of Korangi was perhaps the most iconic example of how unpredictability generated sovereign power. In a striking case of decisionism, the urban poor of Karachi were cleared from slums with unprecedented enthusiasm and

---

[5] Mouffe, C. (1993), *The return of the political*, London; New York, Verso, pp.117–134.

attention to detail by Ayub's men in 1959, only to be entirely abandoned to their own devices by the same administrative machinery the year after. Sovereignty contestations of this kind were highly productive. They brought into being the whole range of 'sovereign bodies' that became the dramatis personae of the development encounter: the heroic consultant, the benevolent dictator, the 'go-getting' general, the 'feudal' landlord, the Islamic custodian of morals, the community leader and the recalcitrant resident refusing to pay his rent.

Islam proved a particularly tenacious obstacle to the smooth operations of managerial power. The Muslim world constituted a major component in Doxiadis's area of operations, and he was always especially proud to conduct urban planning with a full awareness of the customs and cultural requirements of Muslims, from his provisions for purdah to his beloved designs for tea houses and bazaars. His archive was full of research papers on what made a city Muslim, with copious input by local informants, from famous Middle Eastern architects like the Egyptian Hassan Fathy to the countless students from the Athens School of Ekistics who returned to their home countries to conduct extensive social surveys. And yet, there was no other policy area affecting Doxiadis in Pakistan that proved so resolutely *political*, so strikingly beyond the grasp of development and so inescapably entangled in irreducible contestation and power play. Whether it was the provision of mosques to the inhabitants of Korangi, the role of Sufism in Islamabad, or finding the right design formula to express Pakistan's identity aspirations, it proved impossible to impose a politics of truth on matters of religion, no matter how sophisticated the discursive apparatus designed to make it manageable. The representatives of the Pakistani state knew this only too well, and they used their advantage to turn Doxiadis's plans into a springboard for their own sovereign ambitions.

Another typical case of power 'tipping over' from one modality into another has been examined at some length in the context of the seemingly mundane question of exactly how much target data was required to make the process of development planning 'work'. If the planner and the implementing authority got the level of detail carefully balanced – not too rough, but also not too precise – development could work as the magical managerial control that Doxiadis always dreamt of: so light in touch and already so mindful of people's own sense of agency that it could not be easily resisted by those who came under its sway. If the balance was upset by involving either too much or too little detail, managerialism would be tipped into tyranny or impotence. The story of Islamabad was full of such instances. In a country like Pakistan, Doxiadis observed with great astuteness, there was often only an alternative between no plan at all or a very bad plan that was nevertheless adhered to as if it were holy scripture. In either case, the magic power of the expert manager disappeared in the face of head-on confrontations. It was either him who had to be a tyrant or the members of the local bureaucracy who employed him.

To arrive at a final conclusion about how to interpret the development encounter theoretically, it is of absolute importance not to lose sight of the interconnectedness of the different modalities of power involved. They were what Ernesto Laclau called the 'constitutive outside'[6] for each other; in other words, they gained their respective meaning only by being juxtaposed to each other. Without managerial power there would have been no sovereign power and vice versa. That the distinction between them was also at times undecidable – precisely at those tipping points exploited by the proponents of development politics – was in the final instance a function of the undecidability of language itself.[7] These are not merely theoretical concerns but matters that closely inform how we should judge the development encounter historically. In the final analysis, the story of Doxiadis was not a case of some well-meaning but alien vision of managerial power imported into Pakistan, only to be smashed to smithereens on the harsh cliffs of the sovereignty-obsessed political culture of a post-colonial nation. It was also not a case of development 'failing' in Pakistan, of leaving the country at best only superficially affected. Without needing a plan in the first place, Pakistani bureaucrats would not have had to make the stark and uncomfortable choice between admitting impotence and implementing a badly conceived plan with tyrannical vigour, to quote Doxiadis's exemplary insight once more. There would have been other ways to govern, other governmentalities involving complex practices of thought and deed, inaction and action that lie beyond the conceptual toolkit deployed in this book. Sovereignty obsession was not a pre-existing part of Pakistan's timeless and essential nature, it was in itself the product of the country's encounter with development as it unfolded over the 1950s and 1960s. The discursive nature of development was precisely the problem: had it been a mere ideology that was simply hiding the West's geostrategic designs, one could have argued with it, critiqued it, even owned it. But since it came as an absolute truth, it left the people of the global South with little choice but to cultivate a political culture in which truth had no place.

---

[6] Laclau, E. (1990), *New reflections on the revolution of our time*, London; New York, Verso, pp.17–18.
[7] An idea derived from Jacques Derrida; see Bauman, Z. (1991), *Modernity and ambivalence*, Ithaca, NY, Cornell University Press, Introduction.

Development did not depoliticize; it created an exuberance of politicization that turns Foucault's original insights on their head. While the people of the rich North had to be told by a maverick philosopher that power and knowledge constituted each other, and that scientific truths needed to be interrogated for their political effects in order to bring the tyranny of the experts out into the open, the people of Pakistan have not been under any such illusion. As practical Foucauldians by habit, they have long come to understand that truth was ever only a manifestation of power. Theirs was, and is, the opposite problem: that they have to live in a world without truth. Conventional analysis has often addressed this problem: it is commonplace to say about Pakistan that there is too much religious sectarianism and not enough education, too many competing versions of what constitutes the nation and too little agreement on how to find a binding truth for all through civil society deliberations.[8] The most invoked remedy to such problems is none else than development. It is the contention of this book that this is a serious misunderstanding. It is only in a world where development no longer holds sway that new forms of truth and new governmentalities better suited for the people of Pakistan can emerge.

---

[8] E.g. Shaikh, F. (2009), *Making sense of Pakistan*, New York, Columbia University Press, pp.2–13.

Bibliography

Archives

Capital Development Authority Library, Islamabad: reports.
Constantinos A. Doxiadis Archive, Athens (CADA): country volumes Pakistan, India, Iraq; subject files; Doxiadis's personal papers.
Historisches Archiv Krupp, Essen: files relating to Pakistan steel mill project.
National Archive of Bangladesh, Dhaka (NAB): Commerce and Industry (B) proceedings, Public Health (B) proceedings.
National Documentation Centre, Islamabad (NDC): Pakistan Cabinet records.
National Archives and Records Administration, Washington D.C. and College Park, Maryland (NARA): Record Group 469 Foreign Assistance Agencies, State Department Central Files, Pakistan 1945–49, Record Group 233.

Oral history accounts

Ioannis Frantzeskakis, C. A. Doxiadis's associate and town planner, Maroussi (Athens) 30 June 2010.
Parvaiz Chishti, architect, Chishti Brothers, Lahore 2 November 2007.
Shaikh Abdul Rashid, urban planner working in the 1960s, Lahore 31 October 2007.
Syed Babar Ali, Chairman of Packages Ltd, Doxiadis's business partner and industrialist, Lahore 10 November 2007.
Tariq Rahim, son of late S. A. Rahim, town planner Lahore in the 1950s and 1960s, acquaintance of C. A. Doxiadis, Lahore 10 November 2007.

Literature consulted

(1952). 'The Ford Foundation.' *Social Service Review* **26**(1): 90–92.
Commonwealth Consultative Committee on South and South-East Asia (1950). *New horizons in the East: the Colombo Plan for Co-operative Economic Development in South and South-East Asia*. London, HMSO.
Pakistan, Planning Board (1958). *The First Five Year Plan, 1955–60*. Karachi, Manager of Publications.
USAID *Greenbook*. Data. https://eads.usaid.gov/gbk/data/country_report.cfm [accessed 10/10/2011].

Adamson, M. R. (2006). '"The most important single aspect of our foreign policy": the Eisenhower administration, foreign aid and the Third World.' *The Eisenhower administration, the Third World and the globalization of the Cold War*. K. C. Statler and A. L. Johns (eds.), Lanham, MD, Rowman & Littlefield.

Adey, P. (2010). *Aerial life: spaces, mobilities, affects*. Chichester; Malden, MA, Wiley-Blackwell.

Ahmad, N. (1958). *An economic geography of East Pakistan*. London, Oxford University Press.

Ahmed, A. (1967). *Islamic modernism in India and Pakistan, 1857–1964*. London, Oxford University Press.

Ahmed, F. (1998). *Ethnicity and politics in Pakistan*. Karachi; Oxford, Oxford University Press.

Ahmed, S. (1976). *The Muslim concept of town planning*. Karachi, The Pakistan Institute of Arts and Design.

Ahsan, A. (1996). *The Indus saga and the making of Pakistan*. Karachi, Oxford University Press.

Ali, A. (2011) 'History of PIA.' www.historyofpia.com/history.htm [accessed 21/03/11].

Ali, T. (1983). *Can Pakistan survive? The death of a state*. Harmondsworth, Penguin.

Altaf, S. W. (2011). *So much aid, so little development: stories from Pakistan*. Baltimore, Johns Hopkins University Press.

Althusser, L. (1984). 'Ideology and ideological state apparatuses.' *Essays on ideology*. London, Verso: 1–60.

Amrith, S. S. (2006). *Decolonizing international health: India and Southeast Asia, 1930–65*. Basingstoke; New York, Palgrave Macmillan.

Anderson, C. (2004). *Legible bodies: race, criminality, and colonialism in South Asia*. Oxford; New York, Berg.

Ansari, S. (2005). *Life after Partition: migration, community and strife in Sindh 1947–1962*. Karachi, Oxford University Press.

Apthorpe, R. J. and D. Gasper (1996). *Arguing development policy: frames and discourses*. London; Portland, OR, Frank Cass in association with the European Association of Development Research and Training Institutes (EADI), Geneva.

Arnau, F. (1960). *Brasilia: Phantasie und Wirklichkeit*. Munich, Prestel-Verlag.

Arndt, H. W. (1987). *Economic development: the history of an idea*. University of Chicago Press.

Arnold, D. (1993). *Colonizing the body: state medicine and epidemic disease in nineteenth-century India*. Berkeley, University of California Press.

Ayub Khan, M. (1967). *Friends not masters: a political autobiography*. London; New York, etc., Oxford University Press.

Aziz, K. K. (1993). *The murder of history: a critique of history textbooks used in Pakistan*. Lahore, Vanguard.

Azoulay, A. (2008). *The civil contract of photography*. New York, Zone Books.

Barrett, R. C. (2010). *The greater Middle East and the Cold War: US foreign policy under Eisenhower and Kennedy*. London, I.B. Tauris.

Basu, S. (2004). *Does class matter? Colonial capital and workers' resistance in Bengal, 1890–1937*. New Delhi; New York, Oxford University Press.

Bauman, Z. (1991). *Modernity and ambivalence*. Ithaca, NY, Cornell University Press.

Bayly, C. A. (2011). *History, historians and development policy: a necessary dialogue*. Manchester; New York, Manchester University Press: distributed exclusively in the USA by Palgrave Macmillan.

Behrman, D. (UNESCO) (1952). *They can't afford to wait. (A story of UNESCO technical assistance in South-East Asia.) [With plates.]*, Paris.

Bell, P. D. (1971). 'The Ford Foundation as a transnational actor.' *International Organization* **25**(3): 465–478.

Bhuiyan, A. H. A., A. H. Faraizi and J. McAllister (2005). 'Developmentalism as a disciplinary strategy in Bangladesh.' *Modern Asian Studies* **39**(2): 349–368.

Blackton, C. S. (1951). 'The Colombo Plan.' *Far Eastern Survey* **20**(3): 27–31.

Boyer, C. (2003). 'Aviation and the aerial view: Le Corbusier's spatial transformations in the 1930s and 1940s.' *Diacritics* **33**(3/4): 93–116.

   (2006). 'The archive of Ekistics.' *Space and progress: Ekistics and the global context of post World War II urbanization and architecture*. Athens, unpublished conference paper.

Bridson, D. G. (Great Britain, Treasury, Information Division) (1953). *Progress in Asia: the Colombo Plan in action*. [With plates.] London.

Bromley, R. (2003). 'Towards global human settlements: Constantinos Doxiadis as entrepreneur, coalition-builder and visionary.' *Urbanism: imported or exported?* J. Nasr and M. Volait (eds.). New York, Wiley: 316–340.

   (2006). 'From global urban futures to America's urban crisis: Doxiadis in the United States.' *Space and progress: Ekistics and the global context of post World War II urbanization and architecture*. Athens, unpublished conference paper.

Burki, S. J. (1980). *Pakistan under Bhutto, 1971–1977*. London, Macmillan.

   (1986). *Pakistan: a nation in the making*. Boulder, CO, Westview Press; Pakistan, Oxford University Press.

Chauhdrī, Z. h. and H. a. J. Zaidī (1989). *Pākistān kī siyāsī tārīkh*. Lāhaur, Idārah-yi Muṭāla'ah-yi Tārīkh.

Chakrabarty, D. (1989). *Rethinking working-class history: Bengal, 1890–1940*. Princeton University Press.

   (2008). '"In the name of politics": sovereignty, democracy and the multitude in India'. *Varieties of world making*. N. Karagiannis and P. Wagner (eds.). Liverpool University Press: 115–124.

Chandavarkar, R. (1994). *The origins of industrial capitalism in India: business strategies and the working classes in Bombay, 1900–1940*. Cambridge; New York, Cambridge University Press.

Chatterjee, P. (1997). 'Development planning and the Indian state.' *State and politics in India*. P. Chatterjee (ed.). Delhi; New York, Oxford University Press: x, 576.

(2004). *The politics of the governed: reflections on popular politics in most of the world*. New York, Columbia University Press.

Cohen, J. B. (1951). 'The Colombo Plan for Cooperative Economic Development.' *Middle East Journal* 5(1): 94–100.

Cohen, S. P. (2004). *The idea of Pakistan*. Washington, D.C., Brookings Institution; [Bristol: University Presses Marketing, distributor].

Cohn, B. S. (1996). *Colonialism and its forms of knowledge: the British in India*. Princeton University Press.

Collingham, E. M. (2001). *Imperial bodies: the physical experience of the Raj, c. 1800–1947*. Cambridge, Polity Press.

Conklin, A. L. (1998). 'Colonialism and human rights, a contradiction in terms? The case of France and West Africa, 1895–1914.' *The American Historical Review* 103(2): 419–442.

Cooper, F. (1997). 'Modernizing bureaucrats, backward Africans, and the development concept.' *International development and the social sciences.* F. Cooper and R. M. Packard (eds.). Berkeley, University of California Press: 64–92.

(2005). *Colonialism in question: theory, knowledge, history.* Berkeley, University of California Press.

Cooper, F. and R. M. Packard (eds.) (1997). *International development and the social sciences: essays on the history and politics of knowledge.* Berkeley, University of California Press.

Corn, J. J. (1983). *The winged gospel: America's romance with aviation, 1900–1950.* New York, Oxford University Press.

Curtin, P. W. E. (1954). 'The effect of the Colombo Plan.' *Pakistan Horizon* 7(2): 76–79.

Daechsel, M. (1997). 'Military Islamisation in Pakistan and the spectre of colonial perceptions.' *Contemporary South Asia* 6(2): 141–160.

(2006). *The politics of self-expression: the Urdu middle-class milieu in mid-twentieth century India and Pakistan.* London; New York, Routledge.

(2009) 'An elite clings on to power: the idea that Pakistan is being "Talibanised" helps stifle dissent and protect privilege.' *The Guardian – comment is free.* www.theguardian.com/commentisfree/belief/2009/mar/11/pakistan-islam-zardari [accessed 10/10/2013].

(2011a). 'Seeing like an expert, failing like a state? Interpreting the fate of a satellite town in early post-colonial Pakistan.' *Colonial and post-colonial governance of Islam: continuities and ruptures.* M. Maussen, V. Bader and A. Moor (eds.). Amsterdam University Press: 155–174.

(2011b). 'Sovereignty, governmentality and development in Ayub's Pakistan: the case of Korangi Township.' *Modern Asian Studies* 45(1): 131–157.

(2013). 'Misplaced Ekistics: Islamabad and the politics of urban development in Pakistan.' *South Asian History and Culture* 4(1): 87–106.

(2015). 'Islam and development in urban space: planning "official" Karachi in the 1950s.' *Cities in South Asia.* C. Bates and M. Mio (eds.). London; New York, Routledge.

Darling, M. (1930). *Rusticus loquitur; or, The old light and the new in the Punjab village*. London; New York, Oxford University Press.
(1977). *The Punjab peasant in prosperity and debt*. New Delhi, Manohar Book Service.
Deane, P. (1965). *Constantinos Doxiadis, master builder for free men*. Dobbs Ferry, NY, Oceana Publications.
Dewey, C. (1993). *Anglo-Indian attitudes: the mind of the Indian Civil Service*. London; Rio Grande, Hambledon Press.
Dirks, N. B. (2001). *Castes of mind: colonialism and the making of modern India*. Princeton University Press.
Doxiadis, C. A. (1959). 'The rising tide of the planners.' *Ekistics* 7(39): 5–10.
(1965). 'Islamabad: the creation of a new capital.' *The Town Planning Review* **36**(1): 1–28.
(1968a). *Between dystopia and utopia*. London, Faber.
(1968b). 'A city for human development.' *Ekistics* **25**(151): 374–394.
(1968c). *Ekistics: an introduction to the science of human settlements*. London, Hutchinson.
(1970). 'Man's movement and his settlements. *Ekistics* **29**(174): 296–321.
(1971). 'Confessions of a criminal.' *Ekistics* **32**(191): 249–254.
(1972). *Architectural space in ancient Greece*. Translation of the author's thesis, prepared at the Berlin Charlottenburg Technische Hochschule and published in 1937 under title *Raumordnung im griechischen Städtebau*.
Doxiadis, C. A. and J. G. Papaioannou (1974). *Ecumenopolis: the inevitable city of the future*. New York, Norton.
Dreyfus, H. L. and P. Rabinow (1982). *Michel Foucault, beyond structuralism and hermeneutics*. University of Chicago Press.
Dutt, R. C. (1916). *The economic history of India under early British rule, from the rise of the British power in 1757 to the accession of Queen Victoria in 1837*. London, K. Paul, Trench.
Eagleton, T. (1994). *Ideology*. London; New York, Longman.
Easterly, W. (2006). *The white man's burden: why the West's efforts to aid the rest have done so much ill and so little good*. Oxford University Press.
(2013). *The tyranny of experts: economists, dictators, and the forgotten rights of the poor*. New York, Basic Books, a member of the Perseus Book Group.
Escobar, A. (1988). 'Power and visibility: development and the invention and management of the Third World.' *Cultural Anthropology* **3**(4): 428–443.
(1995). *Encountering development: the making and unmaking of the Third World*. Princeton University Press.
Evenson, N. (1966). *Chandigarh*. Berkeley, University of California Press.
Ewing, K. (1983). 'The politics of Sufism: redefining the saints of Pakistan.' *The Journal of Asian Studies* **42**(2): 251–268.
Farooq, S. (ed.) (2004). *Ghulam Faruque Khan: revolutionary builder of Pakistan*. Peshawar, Unique Books.
Fathy, H. (1973). *Architecture for the poor: an experiment in rural Egypt*. University of Chicago Press.

Ferguson, J. (1990). *The anti-politics machine: 'development,' depoliticization, and bureaucratic power in Lesotho*. Cambridge University Press.

Foucault, M. (1970). *The order of things: an archaeology of the human sciences.* London, Tavistock Publications.

(1977). *Discipline and punish: the birth of the prison.* New York, Pantheon Books.

Foucault, M. and J. Lagrange (2006). *Psychiatric power: lectures at the Collège de France, 1973–74.* Basingstoke; New York, Palgrave Macmillan.

Foucault, M., M. Senellart and Collège de France (2008). *The birth of biopolitics: lectures at the Collège de France, 1978–79.* Basingstoke; New York, Palgrave Macmillan.

Foucault, M., M. Senellart, F. o. Ewald and A. Fontana (2007). *Security, territory, population: lectures at the Collège de France, 1977–78.* Basingstoke; New York, Palgrave Macmillan: République Française.

Frampton, K. (2001). *Le Corbusier.* New York, Thames & Hudson.

Frankel, F. R. (1978). *India's political economy, 1947–1977: the gradual revolution.* Princeton University Press.

Freitag, S. B. (1989). *Collective action and community: public arenas and the emergence of communalism in north India.* Berkeley, University of California Press.

Fry, M. (1977). 'Le Corbusier at Chandigarh.' *The open hand: essays on Le Corbusier.* R. Walden (ed.). Cambridge, MA, MIT Press: 351–363.

Gant, G. F. (1959). 'The Ford Foundation Program in Pakistan.' *Annals of the American Academy of Political and Social Science* 323: 150–159.

Gauhar, A. (1996). *Ayub Khan, Pakistan's first military ruler.* Oxford; New York, Oxford University Press.

Gautherot, M., K. Frampton, S. Burgi and S. Titan (2010). *Building Brasilia.* London, Thames & Hudson.

Geddes, P. and J. Tyrwhitt (1947). *Patrick Geddes in India.* London, L. Humphries.

Gilman, N. (2003). *Mandarins of the future: modernization theory in Cold War America.* Baltimore, Johns Hopkins University Press.

Gilmartin, D. (1988). *Empire and Islam: Punjab and the making of Pakistan.* Berkeley, University of California Press.

(2012). 'Environmental history, biradari, and the making of Pakistani Punjab.' *Punjab reconsidered: history, culture and practice.* A. Malhotra and F. Mir (eds.). Delhi, Oxford University Press: 289–319.

Goldhagen, S. W. and L. I. Kahn (2001). *Louis Kahn's situated modernism.* New Haven, CT, Yale University Press.

Gooptu, N. (2001). *The politics of the urban poor in early twentieth-century India.* Cambridge; New York, Cambridge University Press.

Gordon, D. L. A. (2006). *Planning twentieth century capital cities.* London, Routledge.

Grillo, R. D. and R. L. Stirrat (1997). *Discourses of development: anthropological perspectives.* Oxford; New York, Berg.

Haines, T. D. (2013). *Building the empire, building the nation: development, legitimacy, and hydro-politics in Sind, 1919–1969.* Karachi, Oxford University Press Pakistan.

Hall, P. (1988). *Cities of tomorrow: an intellectual history of urban planning and design in the twentieth century*. Oxford; New York, Blackwell.

Hansen, T. B. (2002). *Wages of violence: naming and identity in postcolonial Bombay*. Princeton, NJ; Chichester, Princeton University Press.

Hansen, T. B. and F. Stepputat (2005). *Sovereign bodies: citizens, migrants, and states in the postcolonial world*. Princeton University Press.

Haq, M. u. (1966). *The strategy of economic planning: a case study of Pakistan*. Karachi.

Harper, T. N. (1998). *The end of empire and the making of Malaya*. New York, Cambridge University Press.

Harper, T. N. and S. S. Amrith (2014). *Histories of health in Southeast Asia: perspectives on the long twentieth century*. Bloomington, Indiana University Press.

Hartung, J.-P. (2014). *A system of life: Mawdūdī and the ideologisation of Islam*. New York, Oxford University Press.

Hasan, A. (1997). 'The growth of a metropolis.' *Karachi: megacity of our times*. H. Khuhro and A. Mooraj (eds.). Karachi, Oxford University Press: 171–196.

(2006). *The scale and causes of urban change in Pakistan*. Karachi, Ushba Publishing International.

(2010). *Participatory development: the story of the Orangi Pilot Project Research and Training Institute and the Urban Resource Centre, Karachi, Pakistan*. Karachi, Oxford University Press.

Hasan, A. and Shehersaaz (2009). *Planning and development options for Karachi*. Islamabad, Shehersaaz.

Hashmi, T. u.-I. (1992). *Pakistan as a peasant utopia: the communalization of class politics in East Bengal, 1920–1947*. Boulder, CO, Westview Press.

Hettne, B. R. (1995). *Development theory and the three worlds: towards an international political economy of development*. Harlow; New York, Longman.

(2009). *Thinking about development*. London; New York, Zed Books.

Hodges, S. (2008). *Contraception, colonialism and commerce: birth control in South India, 1920–1940*. Aldershot; Burlington, VT, Ashgate.

Holston, J. (1989). *The modernist city: an anthropological critique of Brasilia*. University of Chicago Press.

Hull, M. (2003). 'The file: agency, authority, and autography in an Islamabad bureaucracy.' *Language and Communication* 23: 287–314.

(2008). 'Ruled by records: the expropriation of land and the misappropriation of lists in Islamabad.' *American Ethnologist* 35(4).

(2010). 'Uncivil politics and the appropriation of planning in Islamabad.' *Beyond crisis: re-evaluating Pakistan*. N. Khan (ed.). London; New York, Routledge: 452–481.

(2012a). 'Documents and bureaucracy.' *Annual Review of Anthropology* 41: 251–267.

(2012b). *Government of paper: the materiality of bureaucracy in urban Pakistan*. Berkeley, University of California Press.

Huntington, S. P. (1968). *Political order in changing societies*. New Haven, CT, Yale University Press.

Husain, H. (2005). 'Kenzo Tange – obituary.' *Archi Times*. May: 19.

Hussain, D. (2014). 'Slum survey: over 80,000 people live in capital's katchi abadis says report.' *The Express Tribune*. Islamabad. 27 February.

Illich, I. (1978). *Toward a history of needs*. New York, Pantheon Books.

Inden, R. B. (1990). *Imagining India*. Oxford; Cambridge, MA, Basil Blackwell.

Jackson, I. and Bandyopadhya (2009). 'Authorship and modernity in Chandigarh: the Ghandi [sic!] Bhavan and the Kiran Cinema designed by Pierre Jeanneret and Edwin Maxwell Fry' *The Journal of Architecture* 14(6).

Jalal, A. (1985). *The sole spokesman: Jinnah, the Muslim League and the demand for Pakistan*. Cambridge University Press.

(1990). *The state of martial rule: the origins of Pakistan's political economy of defence*. Cambridge; New York, Cambridge University Press.

(1995). 'Conjuring Pakistan: history as official imagining.' *International Journal of Middle East Studies* 27: 73–89.

Johnston, D. S. (1991). 'Constructing the periphery in modern global politics.' *The new international political economy*. C. N. Murphy and R. Tooze (eds.). Boulder, CO, Lynne Rienner: 149–170.

Kalia, R. (1999). *Chandigarh: the making of an Indian city*. New Delhi; Oxford, Oxford University Press.

Kapila, S. (2005). 'Masculinity and madness: princely personhood and colonial sciences of the mind in Western India.' *Past and Present* 187(1): 121–156.

(2007). 'Race matters: orientalism and religion, India and beyond c. 1770–1880.' *Modern Asian Studies* 41(3): 471–513.

Kaufman, B. I. (1982). *Trade and aid: Eisenhower's foreign economic policy, 1953–1961*. Baltimore, Johns Hopkins University Press.

Kazimi, M. R. (2003). *Liaquat Ali Khan: his life and work*. Karachi, Oxford University Press.

Khan, L. A. (1950). *Pakistan, the heart of Asia: speeches in the United States and Canada, May and June 1950*. Cambridge, MA, Harvard University Press.

Khan, M. A. (1996). *Pakistan, the first twelve years: the Pakistan Times editorials of Mazhar Ali Khan*. Karachi; New York, Oxford University Press.

Khan, N. (2010). 'Mosque construction or the violence of the ordinary.' *Beyond crisis: re-evaluating Pakistan*. N. Khan (ed.). London; New York, Routledge: 482–519.

Khan, Y. (2007). *The great Partition: the making of India and Pakistan*. New Haven, CT; London, Yale University Press.

Khilnani, S. (1998). *The idea of India*. New York, Farrar Straus Giroux.

Khwaja, Z. D. (1998). *Memoirs of an architect*. Lahore, distributed by Ferozsons Publishers.

Kim, J. (2006). 'C. A. Doxiadis and the funding of the ecumenopolis.' *Space and progress: Ekistics and the global context of post–World War II urbanization and architecture*. Athens, unpublished conference paper.

(2009). 'C. A. Doxiadis and the Ford Foundation.' *Hunch* (13): 78–91.

King, A. D. (1976). *Colonial urban development: culture, social power, and environment*. London; Boston, Routledge & Paul.

Kothari, U. (2005). *A radical history of development studies: individuals, institutions and ideologies*. London; New York, Zed Books.

Krasner, S. D. and C. Pascual (2005). 'Addressing state failure.' *Foreign Affairs* **84**(4): 153–163.

Kux, D. (2001). *The United States and Pakistan, 1947–2000: disenchanted allies.* Washington, D.C., Woodrow Wilson Center Press.

Kyrtsis, A.-A. (2006). *Constantinos A. Doxiadis: texts, design drawings, settlements.* Athens, Ikaros.

La Porte, R. (1976). *Power and privilege: influence and decision-making in Pakistan.* Berkeley; London, University of California Press.

Laclau, E. (1990). *New reflections on the revolution of our time.* London; New York, Verso.

Latouche, S. (1993). *In the wake of the affluent society: an exploration of post-development.* London; New York, Zed Books.

(1996). *The westernization of the world: the significance, scope and limits of the drive towards global uniformity.* Cambridge, Polity.

Le Corbusier, C. E. (2007). *Journey to the East.* Cambridge, MA, MIT Press.

Legg, S. (2007). *Spaces of colonialism: Delhi's urban governmentalities.* Oxford, Blackwell.

Lévi-Strauss, C. (1961). *[Tristes tropiques.] A world on the wane. Translated . . . by John Russell. [With plates.].* London, Hutchinson.

Leys, C. (1996). *Rise and fall of development theory.* Oxford, James Currey.

Louis, W. R. and R. Robinson (2006). 'The imperialism of decolonization.' *Ends of British imperialism: the scramble for empire, Suez and decolonization.* London, I.B. Tauris: 451–502.

Ludden, D. (1992). 'India's development regime.' *Colonialism and culture.* N. Dirks (ed.). Ann Arbor, Michigan University Press: 247–287.

Lyons, J. (1951). *The Colombo Plan.* London, Bureau of Current Affairs.

Mahsud, A. Z. K. (2008). *Constantinos A. Doxiadis's plan for Islamabad: the making of a city of the future, 1959–1963.* PhD, Katholieke Universiteit Leuven.

(2009). 'Extrovert synthesis in the design of Islamabad: Doxiadis's ambition for an evolutionary style of the new capital.' *Ο Κωνστντίνος Δοξιάδης και το Έργο του.* Athens, Τεχνικό Επιμελητήριο Ελλάδας.

Mallaby, S. (2002). 'The reluctant imperialist: terrorism, failed states, and the case for American empire.' *Foreign Affairs* **81**(2): 2–7.

Mannheim, K. (1929). *Ideologie und Utopie.* Bonn, F. Cohen.

Marshall, J. H. S. (1921). *A guide to Taxila.* Calcutta, Superintendent Government Printing.

Mayer, A. (1958). *Pilot project, India: the story of rural development at Etawah, Uttar Pradesh, by Albert Mayer and associates, in collaboration with McKim Marriott and Richard L. Park. With a foreword by Govind Ballabh Pant.* Berkeley, University of California Press.

(1967). *The urgent future: people, housing, city, region.* [With illustrations.] New York, McGraw-Hill Book Co.

McGarr, P. M. (2013). *The Cold War in South Asia: Britain, the United States and the Indian subcontinent, 1945–1965.* Cambridge University Press.

Meier, G. M. (1994a). 'From colonial economics to development economics.' *From classical economics to development economics.* G. M. Meier (ed.). London, Macmillan: 173–196.

(ed.) (1994b). *From classical economics to development economics*. London, Macmillan.

Mellema, R. L. (1961). 'The Basic Democracies system in Pakistan.' *Asian Survey* **1**(6): 10–15.

Merz Rendel Vatten Pakistan. (1952). *Report on Greater Karachi Plan 1952*. Stockholm, A.B. kartografiska institutet.

Metcalf, B. D. (1982). *Islamic revival in British India: Deoband, 1860–1900*. Princeton University Press.

Metcalf, T. R. (1989). *An imperial vision*. Berkeley, University of California Press.

Miescher, S. (2012). 'Building the city of the future: visions and experiences of modernity in Ghana's Akosombo Township.' *Journal of African History* **53**(3): 367–390.

Mikhail, B. (2008). 'Ich hatte Angst dass Schlangen meine Söhne anknabbern.' *Spiegel* online, Eines Tages. http://einestages.spiegel.de/static/ topicalbumbackground/13741/1/_ich_hatte_angst_dass_schlangen_ meine_soehne_anknabbern.html [accessed 31 October 2011].

Mitchell, T. (1988). *Colonising Egypt*. Cambridge; New York, Cambridge University Press.

(2002). *Rule of experts: Egypt, techno-politics, modernity*. Berkeley, University of California Press.

Moreau, R. (2007). 'Pakistan: the most dangerous?' *Newsweek*. 20 October.

Mouffe, C. (1993). *The return of the political*. London; New York, Verso.

Mumtaz, K. K. (1999). *Modernity and tradition: contemporary architecture in Pakistan*. Oxford; New York, Oxford University Press.

Munir, M. (1980). *From Jinnah to Zia*. Lahore, Vanguard Books.

Nederveen Pieterse, J. (2010). *Development theory: deconstructions/reconstructions*. London, SAGE.

Niaz, I. (2010). *The culture of power and governance of Pakistan, 1947–2008*. Karachi, Oxford University Press.

Nilsson, S. (1973). *New capitals of India, Pakistan and Bangladesh*. Lund, Studentlitteratur.

Noman, O. (1988). *The political economy of Pakistan 1947–85*. London, KPI. (1990). *Pakistan: a political and economic history since 1947*. London, Kegan Paul International.

Noon, F. K. (1993). *From memory*. Islamabad, National Book Foundation.

Packenham, R. A. (1973). *Liberal America and the Third World: political development ideas in foreign aid and social science*. Princeton University Press.

Papanek, G. F. (1967). *Pakistan's development: social goals and private incentives*. [S.l.], Cambridge, MA, Harvard University Press.

Pearce, K. C. (2001). *Rostow, Kennedy, and the rhetoric of foreign aid*. East Lansing, Michigan State University Press.

Pinney, C. (1997). *Camera Indica: the social life of Indian photographs*. University of Chicago Press.

Prakash, G. (1999). *Another reason: science and the imagination of modern India*. Princeton University Press.

Prakash, V. (1997). *Theatres of decolonization: architecture, agency, urbanism.* Seattle, University of Washington Press.

(2002). *Chandigarh's Le Corbusier: the struggle for modernity in postcolonial India.* Seattle, University of Washington Press.

Preston, P. W. (1996). *Development theory.* Oxford; Cambridge, MA, Blackwell Publishers.

Pyla, P. (2007). 'Hassan Fathy revisited: postwar discourses on science, development, and vernacular architecture.' *Journal of Architectural Education* **60**(3): 28–39.

Qadeer, M. A. (1983). *Lahore: urban development in the Third World.* Lahore, Vanguard.

Qasmi, A. U. (2014). *The Ahmadis and the politics of religious exclusion in Pakistan.* New York, Anthem Press.

Rahman, F. (1980). 'A survey of modernization of Muslim family law.' *International Journal of Middle East Studies* **11**(4): 451–465.

Rahman, T. and T. Knight (1998). *Language and politics in Pakistan.* Karachi; Oxford, Oxford University Press.

Rahnema, M. and V. Bawtree (1997). *The post-development reader.* London, Zed Books.

Rand, C. (1963). 'The Ekistics world.' *The New Yorker.* 11 May.

Rashid, A. (2008). *Descent into chaos: the US and the failure of nation building in Pakistan, Afghanistan, and Central Asia.* New York, Viking.

Rashid, H. E. (1965). *East Pakistan: a systematic regional geography & its development planning aspects.* Lahore, Sh. Ghulam Ali & Sons.

Rist, G. (1990). 'Development as part of the modern myth: the Western socio-economic dimension of "development".' *European Journal of Development Alternatives* **2**(1): 10–21.

(1997). *The history of development: from Western origins to global faith.* London; New York, Zed Books.

Rizvi, S. A. A. (1972). *Fatehpur Sikri.* New Delhi, Director General, Archaeological Survey of India.

Robinson, F. (2001). *The 'ulama of Farangi Mahall and Islamic culture in South Asia.* New Delhi; Bangalore, Permanent Black.

Roest, P. K. (1927). *Glimpses of anthropology: abstracts of lectures delivered at the Brahmavidya Ashrama, Adyar, 1926–27.* Adyar, Brahmavidya Ashrama.

Rosen, G. (1985). *Western economists and Eastern societies: agents of change in South Asia, 1950–1970.* Baltimore, Johns Hopkins University Press.

Rosenstein-Rodan, P. N. (1943). 'Problems of industrialisation of Eastern and South-Eastern Europe.' *The Economic Journal* **53**(210/211): 202–211.

Rostow, W. W. (1985). *Eisenhower, Kennedy, and foreign aid.* Austin, University of Texas Press.

Rotter, A. J. (2000). *Comrades at odds: the United States and India, 1947–1964.* Ithaca, NY, Cornell University Press.

Sachdev, V. and G. H. R. Tillotson (2002). *Building Jaipur: the making of an Indian city.* London, Reaktion.

Sachs, W. (1992). *The development dictionary: a guide to knowledge as power.* London; Atlantic Highlands, NJ, Zed Books.

Sarin, M. (1977). 'Chandigarh as a place to live in.' *The open hand: essays on Le Corbusier*. R. Walden (ed.). Cambridge, MA, MIT Press: 374–410.
    (1982). *Urban planning in the Third World: the Chandigarh experience*. London, Mansell.
Sarkar, A. (2007). 'Nandigram and the deformations of the Indian left.' *International Socialism*. www.isj.org.uk/index.php4?id=333&issue=115 [accessed 15/10/2008].
Sarkis, H. (2005). 'Dances with Margaret Mead: planning Beirut since 1958.' *Projecting Beirut: episodes in the construction and reconstruction of a modern city*. H. Sarkis and P. G. Rowe (eds.). Munich; New York, Prestel: 187–202.
Sarmad, K. (1984). *A review of Pakistan's development experience (1945–50 to 1979–80)*. Islamabad, Pakistan Institute of Development Economics (PIDE).
Sayeed, K. B. (1961). 'Pakistan's Basic Democracy.' *Middle East Journal* 15(3): 249–263.
    (1968). *Pakistan, the formative phase, 1857–1948*. London, New York, etc., Oxford University Press.
    (1980). *Politics in Pakistan: the nature and direction of change*. New York, Praeger.
Schmitt, C. (2005). *Political theology: four chapters on the concept of sovereignty*. University of Chicago Press.
Scott, J. C. (1998). *Seeing like a state: how certain schemes to improve the human condition have failed*. New Haven, CT; London, Yale University Press.
Sen, S. (2000). *Disciplining punishment: colonialism and convict society in the Andaman Islands*. New Delhi; Oxford; New York, Oxford University Press.
    (2005). *Colonial childhoods: the juvenile periphery of India, 1850–1945*. London, Anthem Press.
    (2012). *Disciplined natives: race, freedom, and confinement in colonial India*. Delhi, Primus Books.
Shaikh, F. (2009). *Making sense of Pakistan*. New York, Columbia University Press.
Sherman, T. C., W. Gould and S. Ansari (2011). *From subjects to citizens: society and the everyday state in India and Pakistan, 1947–1970*, Cambridge, Cambridge University Press.
Singer, H. W. (1961). 'Trends in economic thought on underdevelopment.' *Social Research* 28(4): 387–414.
Sinha, M. (1995). *Colonial masculinity: the 'manly Englishman' and the 'effeminate Bengali' in the late nineteenth century*. Manchester, Manchester University Press.
Sloterdijk, P. (1983). *Kritik der zynischen Vernunft*. Frankfurt am Main, Suhrkamp.
Smith, W. C. (1946). *Modern Islām in India, a social analysis*. London, V. Gollancz Ltd.
Statler, K. C. and A. L. Johns (eds.) (2006). *The Eisenhower administration, the Third World, and the globalization of the Cold War*. Lanham, MD, Rowman & Littlefield.
Stoler, A. L. (1995). *Race and the education of desire: Foucault's history of sexuality and the colonial order of things*. Durham, NC, Duke University Press.

(2002). *Carnal knowledge and imperial power: race and the intimate in colonial rule.* Berkeley, University of California Press.

Sutton, F. X. (1987). 'The Ford Foundation: the early years.' *Daedalus* **116**(1): 41–91.

(2001). 'The Ford Foundation's transatlantic role and purposes, 1951–81.' *Review (Fernand Braudel Center)* **24**(1): 77–104.

Swaminathan, V. S. (1950). 'Pakistan problems and prospects.' *Middle East Journal* **4**(4): 447–466.

Talbot, I. (1994). 'Planning for Pakistan: the Planning Committee of the All-India Muslim League.' *Modern Asian Studies* **28**(4): 875–889.

(2012). *Pakistan: a modern history.* London, C. Hurst & Co. Publishers Ltd.

Talha, N. (2000). *Economic factors in the making of Pakistan (1921–1947).* Oxford; New York, Oxford University Press.

Tucker, V. (1999). 'The myth of development: a critique of a Eurocentric discourse.' *Critical development theory: contributions to a new paradigm.* R. Munck and D. O'Hearn (eds.), London; New York, Zed Books.

van Moos, S. (1977). 'The politics of the open hand: notes on Le Corbusier and Nehru at Chandigarh.' *The open hand: essays on Le Corbusier.* R. Walden (ed.). Cambridge, MA, MIT Press: 413–457.

Verkaaik, O. (2004). *Migrants and militants: fun and urban violence in Pakistan.* Princeton, NJ; Oxford, Princeton University Press.

Wagner, K. (2013). 'Treading upon fires: the mutiny motif and colonial anxieties in British India.' *Past and Present* **218**(1): 159–197.

Wasti, S. A. T. (1979). *Islamabad . . . the city of peace.* Islamabad, Directorate of Public Relations, Capital Development Authority.

Wilber, D. N. (1956). *Afghanistan.* New Haven, CT, Human Relations Area Files.

Williams, J. (1979). *Japan's political revolution under MacArthur: a participant's account.* Athens, GA, University of Georgia Press.

Wint, G. (1952). *What is the Colombo Plan?* London, Batchworth Press.

Wohl, R. (2005). *The spectacle of flight: aviation and the Western imagination, 1920–1950.* New Haven, CT, Yale University Press.

Wurgaft, L. D. (1983). *The imperial imagination: magic and myth in Kipling's India.* Middletown, CT, Wesleyan University Press.

Yakas, O. (2001). *Islamabad, the birth of a capital.* Karachi, Oxford University Press.

Young, R. (1990). *White mythologies: writing history and the West.* London, New York, Routledge.

Zachariah, B. (2005). *Developing India: an intellectual and social history, c. 1930–50.* New Delhi, Oxford University Press.

Zachariah, B. and S. Bhattacharya (1999). '"A great destiny": the British colonial state and the advertisement of post-war reconstruction in India, 1942–45.' *South Asia Research* **19**(1): 71–100.

Index